LIBRARY LIT. 20– The Best of 1989

edited by

JANE ANNE HANNIGAN

The Scarecrow Press, Inc.
Metuchen, N.J., & London
1990

ISBN 0-8108-2374-8
Library of Congress Catalog Card No. 78-154842

Copyright © 1990 by The Scarecrow Press, Inc.
Manufactured in the United States of America

Printed on acid-free paper

TABLE OF CONTENTS

Introduction vii
The Best of Library Literature Jury for 1989 xi
Notes on Contributors xiii

PART I: ACADEMIC LIBRARY ISSUES

The Model Research Library: Planning for the Future.
 Anne Woodsworth, Nancy Allen, Irene Hoadley,
 June Lester, Pat Molholt, Danuta Nitecki and
 Lou Wetherbee 3
The Unintended Revolution in Academic Libraries:
 1939 to 1989 and Beyond.   Barbara B. Moran 21
Stagnant Budgets: Their Effects on Academic
 Libraries.   Murray S. Martin 50
The Growth of the Profession.   Leigh Estabrook 68

PART II: PUBLIC LIBRARY ISSUES

The Grail of Goodness: The Effective Public Library.
 Thomas Childers & Nancy A. Van House 87
Can We Save the Public's Library?   Charles Robinson .. 101
Serving Young Adults: Why We Do What We Do.
 Dorothy M. Broderick 115
The Public Library & The Latchkey Problem:
 A Survey.   Frances Smardo Dowd 126
Mitch Snyder on the Homeless in America.
 Mitch Snyder 139

PART III: POLITICAL ISSUES

There Are No Neutrals in Politics.   John Berry III 157

Toward a National Information Policy: What Should
    We Expect From a Second White House
    Conference?   Patricia W. Berger 159

Librarianship & Political Values: Neutrality or
    Commitment?   Henry T. Blanke 176

Whittle's Ed-Tech Trojan Horse.   Lillian N. Gerhardt 187

Information Drought: Next Crisis for the
    American Farmer?   Nancy C. Kranich 190

PART IV: PROFESSIONAL ISSUES

Information Malpractice: Some Thoughts on the
    Potential Liability of Information Professionals.
    Martha Dragich 207

Recruiting, Retaining, and Rewarding Research
    Faculty: Art or Atmosphere?   Richard W. Budd 221

Women's Work Within Librarianship: Time to Expand
    the Feminist Agenda.   Suzanne Hildenbrand 229

Research and the Use of Statistics for Library
    Decision Making.   Peter Hernon 234

Networks and School Library Media Centers.
    Phyllis Van Orden and Adeline W. Wilkes 245

PART V: REFERENCE AND COLLECTION
DEVELOPMENT ISSUES

Reference Services: A Model of Question Handling.
    Barbara M. Robinson 263

Literary Style in Reference Books.   David Isaacson 286

Library Jargon: Student Comprehension of Technical
    Language Used by Librarians.   Rachael Naismith
    and Joan Stein 305

A Survey of American Zoo and Aquarium Archives.
    Linda Rohr................................... 322

Learning About CD-ROM Technology: An Educator's Perspective on Sources, Issues, Criteria, Breakthroughs, and Research. Richard S. Halsey . . . 332

PART VI: CHILDREN'S LITERATURE

Merging Dreams and Consummate Realities: The Collaborative Ventures of Dick Roughsey and Percy Trezise. Karen Patricia Smith 345

The Ghost of Nancy Drew. Geoffrey S. Lapin 356

From Labyrinth to Celestial City: Setting and the Portrayal of the Female Adolescent in Science Fiction. Hilary Crew 371

PART VII: READING AND LITERACY

Toward a History of Reading. Robert Darnton 381

Striking a Balance: Print vs. Nonprint in the Library. Bill Katz 402

Saying it Louder. Dorothy Butler 408

Latching on to Literature: Reading Initiatives Take Hold. Bernice E. Cullinan 420

Reinventing the Medical Librarian. Rachael K. Anderson 431

The "Quiet Revolution": A Profession at the Crossroads. Herbert S. White 449

INTRODUCTION

The past year was, as always, one in which many issues in library and information science were discussed in the literature. The range of interests and concerns considered by the profession is reflected in the articles contained in this volume. These articles, representative of the Best of 1989, help to remind us of who we are as librarians and information specialists at this time in our history and identify some of the major areas of concern as our profession enters the last decade of the 20th century.

Part I, "Academic Library Issues," includes four articles of prime importance to leaders in this field. Woodsworth and her collaborators identify, using a conceptual model, the need for collaboration, flexibility, and fluidity as key attributes of the research library of the future. They emphasize the current responsibility of all research libraries to plan the transitional steps necessary to assure institutional relevance on the campus. Moran traces the emergence of significant trends and influences in academic librarianship from 1939 to 1989 and extrapolates a series of useful generalizations. Her stress on the role of technology and the potential issues arising in handling the long-distance user who is an unknown entity to the staff are worthy of discussion as we move through this last decade of the century. An insightful presentation of "stagnant" or "steady-state" budgets is presented in Murray's article. He delineates causes of and responses to budget changes and highlights cost containment, substitution, choice and priorities as essential to the new fiscal management approach. Estabrook examines the dynamics of growth of the profession of college and research librarianship within the framework of contemporary sociological research on professions.

Part II, "Public Library Issues" includes five very different articles each addressing an aspect of increasing importance in public librarianship. Childers and Van House report the findings of their national study on what comprises an effective public library. Using earlier research from Cameron as a theoretical base, they explore a series of 61 indicators of effectiveness with varying populations. Critical in their study are the challenges it presents for more research that will validate, rank and develop multiple measures that will lead to effectiveness. Robinson makes a strident attack on the perception of public libraries as academic-like institutions, stating that it is essential for the public library to see its mission clearly and to respond to the needs of its clientele realistically. Broderick defines a sharper role for those working with young adults while linking this work to both the life of the adolescent and the literature written for that young person. Dowd reports the findings of her study of the public library and latchkey children and offers five recommendations, including identified goals for libraries. The late Mitch Snyder discusses with emotional clarity the urgency of recognizing and realizing the humanity of people who are homeless and the need to act in response to help save these members of society.

Some of the diverse concerns of our profession are addressed in the five articles included in Part III, "Political Issues." Berry alerts us to the continuing battle between partisan groups who seek to move us away from political and social stands through our professional associations and those who seek to have us support a partisan position. Berger details some major issues to be considered in the next White House Conference and argues that we must face the major issues of national information policy, fostering of scientific and technological productivity while simultaneously protecting national security interests. Blanke contends that our reluctance to define our values in political terms and to cultivate a sense of social responsibility allows us to become bedfellows with the dominant political and economic powers. He warns of the sacrifice of public service to service to the technocratic elite. Gerhardt raises the serious question of business invading the minds of children in schools using the Whittle Communications case as an example. Her comparison with *Nineteen Eighty-Four* challenges us not to relax our guard. Kranich continues to express her concern about public access to information, in this instance, the American farmer. She provides empirical evidence of the effects of technology on the government's provision of information in her study of a specific government database, Electronic Dissemination of Information (EDI) of the U.S. Department of Agriculture.

Part IV, "Professional Issues," includes five vastly different articles, but each is focused on an issue of professionalism that concerns us today. Dragich concentrates on providing an objective view of potential library malpractice in the provision of information. Budd offers a clear and strong set of views about library education and its environment for the nurturing of young faculty and the continuing support of established faculty. Hildenbrand asks if there are other fronts in the ceaseless battle for equity that need to be defended. Hernon addresses the question of how much research and statistical competence library managers and decision makers should have. Van Orden and Wilkes report the findings in their exploratory study of the networking experiences of school districts in order to identify the services and implications of that networking for the collections and technical services of school library media centers.

Part V, "Reference and Collection Development Issues," contains five articles that address some fundamental questions in those areas of our profession. Barbara Robinson provides a planning and decision making tool in her question handling model, which offers a snapshot of the series of decisions which librarians make in answering client questions and matches level of resources to levels of service. Isaacson examines the assumption that reference books ought to be written in an objective style and argues that personal opinion is sometimes evident in reference tools. Naismith and Stein report findings from their examination of the use of jargon in librarianship, including terminology in handouts and in conversations with users, which may lead to a lessening of communication. Rohr reports findings on her survey of zoos and aquariums to identify the presence and condition of archival materials, showing the precarious condition of such resources. Halsey provides a reasoned analysis of CD-ROM technology and suggests the use of two techniques, interrogation and confrontation.

Part VI, the section on "Children's Literature," includes three articles which reflect very different approaches to this field of study. Smith discusses the unusually strong friendship and collaboration between Roughsey and Trezise whose visual and verbal interpretations of a number of aboriginal legends preserve them for children. Authorship of the Nancy Drew stories is explored in detail by Lapin who traces the role of Mildred Wirt Benson in the Stratemeyer production. Crew explores science-fiction novels for adolescent readers and argues the significance of setting as a metaphor in the portrayals of young female protagonists.

Part VII, "Reading and Literacy," begins with a scholarly history of reading by Darnton who identifies various means used to identify not only what people read over time but why and how they read. In a delightful view of new media and technologies, Katz makes a plea for the role of books in our lives. Butler, in a clarion call, warns us that the power of the book is increasingly unrecognized and that we have an important role in bringing books and children together. Cullinan reports her findings from a national survey of literature-based reading programs and indicates six of the problems arising in this movement.

Part VIII, "Special Library Issues," includes two articles. Anderson offers an analysis of what the medical librarian should be and a discussion of the context and evolution of critical attributes of this professional. White strongly suggests that special librarianship faces a crossroad, either it accepts and adjusts to information as a commodity or it joins the ranks of trivial clerical task production.

No book is completed without the support and help of a number of people. I would like to thank the professional community who share their ideas, research and expertise in our journals and all those who nominate articles for the jury's consideration. The 1989 Jury's diligence in reading the recommended articles and their lively, sometimes argumentative, discussions before closure are greatly appreciated. I owe a special debt of gratitude to Betty Jean Parks whose patience was matched only by her care in typesetting this book and in preparing it for printing. Finally, I thank all of those contributors whose articles were selected for inclusion in this twentieth volume of *The Best of Library Literature*.

> Jane Anne Hannigan
> Editor and Professor Emerita
> Columbia University
> New York, New York

Note:
All those who wish to nominate articles for consideration by the Jury should send them to the editor at 24 Starview Drive, Neshanic, New Jersey 08853.

THE BEST OF LIBRARY LITERATURE JURY FOR 1989

John Berry, III
Vice President and Editor-in-Chief
Library Journal
New York, New York

Arthur Curley
Director
Boston Public Library
Boston, Massachusetts
Editor of *Collection Building*

Jane Anne Hannigan
Professor Emerita
Columbia University
New York, New York
Chair of 1989 Jury

Norman Horrocks
Vice President, Editorial
Scarecrow Press
Metuchen, New Jersey

Bill Katz
Professor
School of Information Science and Policy
State University of New York, Albany
Albany, New York
Editor of *The Reference Librarian*

Patricia Glass Schuman
President
Neal-Schuman Publishers, Inc.
New York, New York

NOTES OF CONTRIBUTORS

RACHAEL K. ANDERSON, Director, Health Sciences Library, Columbia University, New York, New York.

PATRICIA W. BERGER, 1989–1990 President of the American Library Association and Director, Information Resources and Services, National Institute of Standards and Technology, Gaithersburg, MD.

JOHN N. BERRY, III, is Editor-in-Chief of *Library Journal*.

HENRY T. BLANKE, Reference Librarian, Shanahan Library, Marymount Manhattan College, New York, New York.

DR. DOROTHY BRODERICK, Editor, *Voice of Youth Advocates*.

RICHARD W. BUDD, Dean and Distinguished Professor, School of Communication, Information and Library Studies, Rutgers University, New Brunswick, NJ.

DOROTHY BUTLER, New Zealand author, editor and lecturer. Author of *Cushla & Her Books, Babies Need Books, Reading Begins at Home (with Marie Clay) Five to Eight*, and other titles.

DR. THOMAS CHILDERS, Professor, College of Information Studies, Drexel University, Philadelphia, PA.

HILARY S. CREW, Ph.D. Candidate and Teaching Assistant, School of Communication, Information and Library Studies, Rutgers University, New Brunswick, NJ.

DR. BERNICE E. CULLINAN, Professor of Early Childhood & Elementary Education, School of Education, New York University, New York, NY.

DR. ROBERT DARNTON, Distinguished Davis Professor of European History, Princeton University, Princeton, NJ.

DR. FRANCES SMARDO DOWD, Assistant Professor, School of Library and Information Studies, Texas Woman's University, Denton, TX.

DR. MARTHA J. DRAGICH, Special Projects/Administrative Librarian, Jacob Burns Law Library, George Washington University, Washington, DC.

DR. LEIGH ESTABROOK, Dean and Professor, Graduate School of Library and Information Science, University of Illinois at Urbana-Champaign, IL.

LILLIAN N. GERHARDT, Editor-in-Chief of *School Library Journal*.

DR. RICHARD S. HALSEY, Dean, School of Information Science and Policy, Nelson A. Rockefeller College of Public Affairs and Policy, University at Albany, State University of New York, Albany, NY.

DR. PETER HERNON, Professor, Graduate School of Library and Information Science, Simmons College, Boston, MA.

DR. SUZANNE HILDENBRAND, Associate Professor, School of Information and Library Studies, University at Buffalo, State University of New York at Buffalo, Buffalo, NY.

DAVID ISAACSON, Assistant Head of Reference and Humanities Librarian, Waldo Library, Western Michigan University, Kalamazoo, MI.

DR. WILLIAM KATZ, Professor, School of Information Science and Policy, Nelson A. Rockefeller College of Public Affairs and Policy, University at Albany, State University of New York, Albany, NY.

NANCY C. KRANICH, Director of Public Services at New York University Library and Chair of the Coalition on Government Information, New York, NY.

GEOFFREY S. LAPIN, 'Cellist with the Indianapolis Symphony Orchestra and Adjunct Professor of 'Cello at Purdue University.

He is a featured critic on the Indianapolis affiliate of National Public Radio, reviewing new classical music recodings. As a free-lance writer, he has had orchestra program notes published, as well as articles on theater history and children's literature. His collection of children's series books is considered to be one of the world's largest, consisting of more than six thousand volumes.

MURRAY S. MARTIN, Library Consultant, Martin Associates and Aaron Cohen Associates and Executive Director, Association of College and University Libraries.

DR. BARBARA B. MORAN, Dean and Associate Professor, School of Information and Library Science, University of North Carolina at Chapel Hill, Chapel, NC.

RACHAEL NAISMITH, Reference Librarian and Library Instruction Coordinator, Carnegie Mellon University Libraries, Pittsburgh, PA.

JOAN STEIN, Head, Resource Sharing and Collection Maintenance, Carnegie Mellon University Libraries, Pittsburgh, PA.

BARBARA M. ROBINSON, Management Consultant specializing in strategic planning and cost analysis for non-profit, public sector organizations, and small businesses.

CHARLES W. ROBINSON, Director, Baltimore County Public Library, Baltimore, MD.

LINDA ROHR, Librarian for the Boston MetroParks Zoos, Franklin Park, Boston, MA.

DR. KAREN PATRICIA SMITH, Assistant Professor, Graduate School of Library and Information Studies, Queens College, The City University of New York, New York, NY.

MITCH SNYDER, deceased. He was a Member of the Community for Non-Violence, Washington, DC.

DR. NANCY VAN HOUSE, Associate Professor, School of Library and Information Studies, University of California, Berkeley, CA.

DR. PHYLLIS J. VAN ORDEN, Professor and Associate Dean for Instruction, School of Library and Information Studies, Florida State University, Tallahassee, FL.

HERBERT WHITE, Professor, School of Library and Information Science, Indiana University, Bloomington, IN.

DR. ADELINE W. WILKES, Assistant Professor, School of Library and Information Studies, Texas Woman's University, Denton, TX.

DR. ANNE WOODSWORTH, Associate Professor, School of Library and Information Science, University of Pittsburgh, Pittsburgh, PA.

PART I:
ACADEMIC
LIBRARY ISSUES

THE MODEL RESEARCH LIBRARY: PLANNING FOR THE FUTURE

Anne Woodsworth, Nancy Allen, Irene Hoadley, June Lester, Pat Molholt, Danuta Nitecki, and Lou Wetherbee

The future mission of the research library will be

to ensure that a ready and free flow of information-based services, collections, and library services are integrated into the research, teaching, and administrative functions of the university. To pursue this mission the library must assume a central and integral role in formulating policy, and in fostering collaborative activities within the university and with other actors in the scholarly communication process.[1]

To describe the future is speculative and risky. To articulate what the future *should* hold, however, is another matter—and requires more insight than foresight. To influence the shape of libraries in the future, not only is it desirable to describe what the future should be—to outline a vision or an ideal—but doing so is a first step in ensuring that the vision becomes reality.

The above mission statement differs from most others because it asserts a more integral and primary role for research libraries in educational and research processes than they currently have. It assumes that libraries will become more active participants in the scholarly communication process as information technologies and information resources converge and become inseparable parts of all functions within the university. The mission statement and the resultant model of the future research library presented here were developed by participants at a 1988 conference "Options for the Future," sponsored by the Council on Library Resources.[2]

"The Model Research Library: Planning for the Future," by Anne Wordsworth Nancy Allen, Irene Hoadley, June Lester, pat Molholt, Danuta Nitecki and Lou Wetherbee in *The Journal of Academic Librarianship* Vol. 15, no. 3 (July 1989), pp. 132–138; reprinted with permission of *The Journal of Academic Librarianship*.

The conceptual model shows how the research library of the future will operate, and is followed by the transitional steps needed to build a sound foundation for it. As the model and transition steps are outlined in the following pages, it should become apparent that flexibility, collaboration, diversity, and fluidity will become key attributes of all those involved in the future of North American research libraries.

The Conceptual Model

The components and categories of information activities in the research library of the year 2020 are best depicted as a tripartite and interconnected system (see Figure 1). Each of the three components of the system has a set of characteristics that distinguishes one from the others. The elements of this set, displayed in Figure 1, consists of

- focus for its activities,
- functions,
- a set of primary resources with which it deals,
- appropriate groups with which it communicates,
- staffing patterns and expertise, and
- distinctive results for which it is accountable.

The arrows in Figure 1 show communication among the three components to be multi-directional within the system. Externally, all components have two-way interaction with users and others engaged in the scholarly communication process. Although all three components communicate externally, each component has a different set of primary external connections. For example, component 1, which handles information in various formats, will deal with the external information environment from which the information products and services are acquired. At the same time, the information access system designers (component 2) will be communicating with individuals and groups on campus, at other institutions, and in industry who are working to improve or design access systems and networks. Component 3, the group that delivers and evaluates programs and services, will deal most often with the users of information such as faculty, researchers, and students. However, the third component will not be the exclusive point of contact for users since the staff who are expert in organizing, acquiring, and packaging information will also be working directly

**FIGURE 1.
Information Activities of the Research Library of the Future**

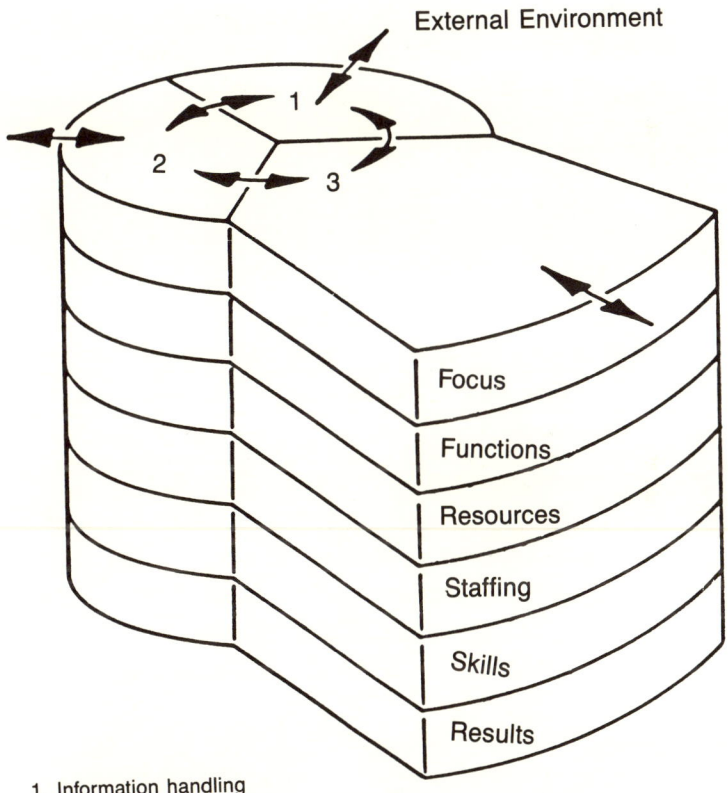

1. Information handling
2. Designing access systems
3. Evaluating user needs and delivering services and programs

with users—e.g., advising them how to structure personal information files.

As shown in Table 1, each component has a distinctive character that stems from its primary responsibility or focus.

Component 1 handles information in various formats; it will deal with greatly diversified collections and other physical expressions of information. Although most of its activities will focus on traditional printed materials, it will handle information available online, on microfiche, on CD-ROM, and in other formats as well. Component 2 designs access systems; it will be concerned with files related to the information carriers, including the structure of electronic information files, and with establishing electronic connections among objects and files.

The functional component that evaluates needs and delivers programs and services, component 3, will have the most user interaction on a day-to-day basis and will have information users as its primary focus. This com-

TABLE 1
Information Activities of the Research Library of the Future

Elements	Component 1	Component 2	Component 3
Focus	Handle information in various formats	Design access systems	Recognize and provide for user needs
Function	Acquisition Organization Preservation	Design and maintain access systems	Evaluate user needs Deliver user programs and services
Resources	Objects Collections	Objects Files	People
Staffing	Centralized High-level support staff	Centralized Information professionals	Dispersed Library professionals
Knowledge/Skills	Preservation techniques Collection organization and development	Artificial intelligence uses Information structures User support systems	Subject orientation and knowledge Interpersonal skills Technological and information literacy
Results	Objects are organized and presented	Access systems are user-sensitive	User needs are met

ponent, for example, will develop the user profiles that are integrated into information retrieval systems and will provide the data and analyses needed to develop AI applications for libraries. Most of the library's professional staff will be deployed in this area of the operation.

Generally, staff who are involved in handling information in various formats and in designing access systems will be centralized, while those involved in delivering and evaluating programs and services will be dispersed, functioning in "service clusters" close to their main user groups. The results of this more user-sensitive information "system" will be products and services that are more readily measurable and highly visible since they will be targeted at specific groups of users.

The following sections expand on the nature of the programmatic and service changes in the research library and illustrate in more detail the functions of the three primary components. To facilitate understanding and to link the components to current concepts, they are grouped under terms that are in common use at present.

> **User services.** Future user services will be characterized by
> - proactive identification or anticipation of user needs,
> - provision of access to almost all information at the level of the user's workstation,
> - collaboration with faculty in developing new and customized services, and
> - delivery of faster, more convenient access to bibliographic information and physical forms of information, irrespective of location.

In the main, the library's human resources will focus on service to users and will have a high level of interaction with other information providers on campus. The library will be a more integral part of the teaching, learning, and research processes in the university and, as a result, will lose some of its current insularity.

In this environment, the library staff will carry out functions that are presently only ideas or, at best, in nascent or experimental form. They will

- create databases and other information products for both individuals and groups of users;

- work with others in the institution to make these databases commercially available beyond the university;
- deliver documents in many formats;
- transform information from one format to another;
- evaluate the validity and relevance of information;
- package information to suit the user, including conversion of format or "container" when needed; and
- provide instruction to ensure information literacy.

The library's staff will work as partners in the research process with discipline-based scholars; serve as consultants on the design of databases and the management of information files and resources; and identify and adapt external information services to meet local needs. Staff from all three components of the system will be needed to provide these kinds of responsive services.

Collections. The value of a library will not be measured by the size, depth, or breadth of the collections owned but rather by its ability to provide access to information in all formats. Bibliographic access systems and digitization will continue to improve, expanded by whole-text retrieval and in-depth access to materials not in machine-readable form. This improved access will permit more on-demand acquisitions, dispersed access to primary and secondary sources in different formats, and, last but not least, widespread realization of coordinated collections and preservation efforts among institutions. Organization and preservation functions will rely heavily on shared expertise, networked systems, and cooperative efforts. Acquisitons, except in the largest research libraries, will be demand driven.

Facilities. Although materials will continue to be produced in print and paper format, new functions for library and information services will dictate changes in the use of existing facilities. With the exception of a small number of research libraries that will continue to maintain large collections of record, most capital expenditures will go toward the construction of storage and preservation facilities that are separate from "use" facilities. Each campus will resolve the offsite-onsite and local-regional debates relating to storage, but materials will not necessarily be housed permanently in the facilities used to deliver service.

Existing library and campus facilities will be adapted to function as service nodes, close to user groups. These service points will have less staff work space and more user space; will be secure and easily accessible; and will have warm, friendly interiors conducive to research and scholarship. Somewhere on campus, perhaps in the library, facilities will exist that can transform information from one format to another, according to user need, and can arrange for delivery to the user or the user's service cluster. The amount and configuration of library space will be determined to a large extent by institutional values and the degree of emphasis on ownership of materials versus access to information.

Staffing. Staffing configurations for the three components will vary due to the different functions and concerns of each (see Table 1). The capabilities and skills possessed by the composite research library staff will include, along with an understanding of libraries and librarianship,

- knowledge of cognitive and disciplinary research processes and of psychology,
- technological sophistication,
- well-developed interpersonal skills,
- knowledge of information policy development and analysis,
- political acumen, and
- planning skills.

In addition, librarians will be assertive risk-takers and synthesizers and have the ability to function in an atmosphere of ambiguity and change.

On the whole, future research library staff will be better educated; also, a greater percentage will have degrees in disciplines other than librarianship. All library personnel will perform a higher level of work and have more responsibility than they do in current staffing configurations. Staff skills will be supplemented by "knowbots"—expert systems that help define needs, facilitate information access, and tailor the information packages to suit individuals or groups of people.[3] There will be a need for discipline-based subject expertise, specific to the character of the institution, that will permit a more successful integration of the library into the research and scholarly processes on campus. Many routine operations will be handled by external contractors. Decisions to contract out will be made by careful examination of make-or-buy benefits/drawbacks as determined by the character of the institution and needs of the users.

Administration. The relationship of service clusters to each other and to the administration of the library will be fluid and complex. The shape and composition of service clusters will vary over time and among institutions, depending on the needs of users and on the characteristics of information generation, production, and use within the discipline and/or group being served. Groups will be formed to work together across the three categories as needed; their group affiliations will range from very short term to semi-permanent. To pool more narrow expertise, some support will be centralized, with personnel perhaps flowing in and out of the clusters as required in a manner similar to the formation of mission-based research groups.

Due to dispersal of staff into user-oriented clusters, the administration of the library will become more complex than it has been to date. In order to maintain their user-driven service orientation, administrators will be increasingly accountable and sensitive to market needs. Library administrators will also participate to a greater extent in the development of information policy on campus. Similarly, more time and effort will be spent on interinstitutional cooperation, consortia, and nationally coordinated efforts, as well as on external development of information policies at regional, national, and international levels.

Internally, the role of the administration in this model will be to facilitate, coordinate, and orchestrate the work of each component. The functions of the library administration will vary with the mission of the institution and will change in response to changing environmental conditions. This organization concept is radically different from today's hierarchical library structures, but it is common in organizations operating under matrix management principles. The construct is also consistent with a trend observed in highly automated corporate environments, where one of the impacts of technology has been the flattening of organizational structures through the elimination of middle management. In order to respond quickly to changing user needs, budget control, decision making, and accountability will reside at the level of the service cluster.

Boundary Conditions

The above model of the future research library did not develop quixotically. It was derived after consideration of future boundary conditions and premises about the university, the information industry, technological developments, and governmental priorities. Premises and assumptions that form the boundary conditions for research libraries in the future range from local, university-based factors to broad societal trends.

The university. The university will not change significantly over the next 20 or 30 years in mission, character, or organizational structure. It will remain essentially a medieval institution. However, some of the inner workings that will change include the following.

Instructional delivery will be more geographically decentralized. The student body will be more diverse in age and ethnicity, will be multilingual and multinational, and will come to the university with more divergent technical and academic preparations. While the role of faculty governance will remain the same, the nature of the faculty will undergo changes.

- Both greater interdisciplinary alliances and greater divergence in research patterns and information needs of scientists and humanists will take shape.
- Because of a continuing brain drain to the private commercial sector, the overall quality of the faculty may be less consistent.
- More funding will come from the private sector, with one result being more effort directed to applied research.
- More researchers will be trained outside the university, in corporate or private educational settings.
- The gap between research and instructional missions of the university will have widened.
- The faculty in most disciplines will measure excellence of the library and the university in new ways, focusing on excellence in technological support services (computing and electronic information access) rather than on the size of the library's book collection.

The administration of the university will assume a corporate decision-making approach or attitude, expecting more accountability from divisions and units in the institution. Competing forces within universities will seek control of information policies and funds.

The library. While the character of the library's services and operations will change, not all future research libraries will be identical in scope, structure, and service emphasis. Some will be funded to retain their national resource mission, and remain relatively unchanged in continuing to focus on the acquisition of comprehensive collections. At the opposite end of the spectrum, some will dedicate most of their efforts and funds to providing electronic access to information resources. Common characteristics will include the following.

- Collections will include data files and resources in electronic form.
- Libraries will be packaging information and services with the convenience of users in mind.
- Librarians will take an increasingly proactive role in advising individuals and departments on information processing for both research purposes and the operation of the university.
- Library staff will include subject specialists, technicians, and professionals from other information fields—e.g., programmer/analysts, network designers and managers, marketing specialists, and experts in artificial intelligence and the cognitive sciences.
- Fund reallocation decisions within each library will become key factors in engendering diversity among academic libraries.

- Because of increasingly diverse student bodies, librarians will support and participate in general education programs to create a base of information skills. One of their primary roles will be teaching, including serving in an advisory capacity for faculty and graduate students.
- The number of routine, clerical tasks will decrease in libraries and be performed elsewhere or by computers (e.g., as in present technical services), enabling more of the library's human resources to engage in direct user services.
- Training and recruitment for the library of the future will be critical.

The government. It is assumed that governments at all levels will have increasing influence on higher education, be it through priorities for research and development, information policies such as privatization, or financial support. Several assumptions about the future have influenced the formation of our conceptual model of tomorrow's research library.

- Universities and libraries will face more accountability from sources of funding for services and programs.
- More restrictions will be placed on the flow of information; this will mean that libraries will have to deal with classified materials.
- Although no single government agency is now responsible for information policy, a new over-arching policy agency may be put in place to coordinate policies and to reemphasize the international position of the U.S.
- Because information has unusual properties as a commodity (e.g., is procurable, shareable, transportable), libraries will need to take a vigorous role in developing new intellectual property policies, particularly since they will be producing and/or marketing information as well as acquiring it for dissemination to users.

Information industry. Underlying all of the assumptions made about information products and technology is a tacit acceptance that the publishing industry will change more slowly from print to electronic publication outputs than has been previously envisioned. Nevertheless, the following factors are some that will influence research libraries.

- Standardization of information products and technology will occur of necessity, and libraries must put forth effort to influence the development of standards for both products and services.
- Because of competition with and within the private-sector portion of the information market place, the "bestseller" (commercially successful) products and technologies will end up as the property of the private sector. Because libraries will control esoteric, unusual, or rare information, they may lose power and influence in the commercial market place, but might gain them in the scholarly communication process since they will have control of specialized files and resources.
- The general availability and value of information as a commodity will influence libraries to sell information systems and access, and will lead them to package information for the academic market, and possibly for the general public.

- There will be more offshore ownership of information by multinational corporations with holdings portfolios of a very broad nature. Hence, the content and accessibility of information products and services may be shaped by vendors with economic, social, and cultural values that differ from those held in an open democratic society.
- The information industry will work more closely with the information producers such as scholarly societies and libraries. For example, faculty working with libraries will be producing specialized, marketable databases and coordinating access and distribution of them with information vendors.

Fiscal factors. While sources of funding and choices in the reallocation of expenditures have already been mentioned, it is recognized that decisions about capital versus operational investment and related priority questions will usually be made on an institution-by-institution basis. Nevertheless, there will be some basic fiscal issues that will face all universities in the information age with respect to research libraries.

For instance, marketing of information products and services is a potential source of revenue. The university's role could be one of developing databases that could either be sold directly or contracted out to the private sector for marketing or sale. Also, libraries will, of necessity, move toward a commercial, private-sector attitude about their collections—that is, they will act on the premise that collections are not only assets to be guarded but also properties to be exploited in order to support the mission of the library.

The philosophy of keeping library services and collections as free goods may be at risk, and this tenet must be examined. The current fee-or-free duality that plagues the issue of information access must be recognized, and decisions must be made about the extent to which a revenue-producing approach will be carried into the new information environment.

To illustrate, the following questions must be answered by each academic community: Should traditional library services and collections continue to be funded as university overhead? Should new services, including new information technologies, and especially customized/tailored services, be funded by users/departments and developed as self-supporting services?

New definitions of the base-line information services that will be made available free of charge will have to be developed, with greater clarification of funding and support for value-added information services. The changed needs inherent in a swing from ownership to access can be funded in part from the sales of information from locally produced databases. This source of revenue, however, will not fully support either the continuation of traditional and existing library services or the newer, access-oriented library services.

Information technology. Information technology, which is continuing to develop at an exponential rate, will provide universities and libraries with unforeseeable opportunities for the creation, storage, and transmission of information. With respect to information handling in and for research libraries in the future, the following assumptions are made.

- Technology will be transparent to the user and therefore will be of less concern than the content of the information access systems.
- Telecommunications and standards will provide the backbone for connectivity sufficient to support campus information needs and for interinstitutional coordination of library/information services.
- Appropriate hardware and software will permit shared use of systems and resources, exchange of information in various formats, access to remote and distributed databases, and shared development of systems that provide information access and delivery, both among libraries and directly to users.
- Satisfactory models for local, regional, and state consortia and networks will have developed for multitype and multipurpose cooperation among libraries and information agencies.

Turning the Model into Reality

Some library leaders have already started to make the changes that will enable research libraries to incorporate the concepts presented in this paper. Over the next 20 to 30 years, many steps will have to be taken to enable the research library of the future to serve increasingly divergent needs of faculty and students; to establish the appropriately flexible, fluid, and responsive organizations; and to foster a climate of cooperation with and among librarians, scholars, researchers, publishers, others in the information industry, and key government agencies. What follows is a selection of some of the transitional steps that must be pursued in order to successfully position research libraries in the coming decades of societal, economic, and technological changes.

Facilities. Some building blocks are relatively easy to identify and put into place. For example, to ensure that physical facilities are planned and built to meet (not impede) future needs, several steps can be taken in the near future. At the local level, each campus can articulate a strategic direction for its library and information services and then build and renovate physical facilities in the coming decades based on its long-range plan. Nationally, agencies such as the Council on Library Resources and the Association of Research Libraries can conduct space inventories and, as they have done with preservation, assist with the design and implementation of national and international strategies to deal with a shortage of space for research library collections.

On campus. There are other, broader transitions that are more difficult to implement, since they call for modification (at best) or total transformation (at worst) of attitudes and skills. Consider for example, the changes needed to achieve the following states.

- Diversity in the services, programs, and collections of research libraries is recognized and appreciated.
- Differing measures of effectiveness, specific to the nature of the individual research library, are the norm.
- The role of librarians is broadly seen as that of a partner with faculty and researchers in the generation, production, and management of information.
- Units and specialists within the library function in a highly collaborative mode in order to meet users needs.
- The campus community perceives the library as the facilitator of access to information, rather than as a repository of information containers and artifacts.
- Administration of the library is highly complex as a result of (1) the centralization of university-wide information technology decisions and related policies, and (2) the increased significance of interinsti-

tutional systems and relationships in the provision of access to information.
- Librarians are accepted as having key local, national, and international roles in determining information policy at all levels.

In these areas, as in all the transitional steps mentioned, librarians must first and foremost prepare themselves to change—to begin making moves toward realizing their vision of the research library 30 years hence. Outside the library, other key players need to shift their perceptions and attitudes. Students, faculty, and researchers, who form the primary groups of information users; campus administrators, who control the planning mechanisms, academic programs, and other intersecting interests; those running bibliographic utilities and other components of the information industry; those involved in scholarly associations and foundations; and government officials at various levels—all will have to recognize and support the new role for the research library of the future.

At first glance the task seems awesome. On college and university campuses alone, however, some initial steps may be taken.

- Articulate and promote on campus a concept or vision of the library that better defines its unique role as an information provider.
- Experiment with new or enhanced services to special target groups in order to gain experience in evaluating user needs and to build credibility in functioning as part of the team that generates/produces/manages information.
- Foster more information contacts for librarians with faculty and administrators.
- Establish mechanisms and funding sources for research, development, and implementation of new services as the information technologies evolve. In so doing, ensure that the experience is widely shared and that these new concepts are incorporated into on-going decision making and planning.
- Begin offering new services on campus by identifying campus data files and data resources that could be campus-wide resources. Promote access to these faculty/research files through the campus online public access catalog.
- Develop and implement services tailored to student needs.

- Incorporate information literacy into the curriculum by (1) establishing informal and formal contacts with academic program decision makers, and (2) educating faculty about the importance of information literacy.
- Focus the planning activities of the university on information needs and information management.
- Establish campus policies that will govern access to and control of information services. Begin to develop cost and funding structures that will endure and build a foundation for the future research library.
- Ensure that librarians are involved in information technology decisions on campus.
- Change the mandate and scope of the library advisory committee to encompass management of and access to information resources throughout the university.

Inside the library. Inside the library, transitional steps will have to lead toward acceptance of more proactive and diverse roles for staff and more frequent and diverse organizational changes. As pointed out, the skills and attitudes of library staff will need to shift dramatically. Some ways to foster these needed changes follow.

- Articulate and broadcast a vision of the future within the library itself.
- Educate existing staff, both attitudinally and technologically, to work in a more collaborative manner with users and to promote the use of information technologies. Accomplishing such change will require that staff throughout the organization, at all working levels, be given greater responsibility and decision-making power. It also will demand that educational opportunites be provided for staff to develop subject expertise, interpersonal skills, technological competency, and leadership ability.
- Use performance expectations and reward systems to reinforce and encourage changes that mesh with the future vision of the library.
- Experiment; take risks with organizational structures.
- Recruit library staff from a broader base of education and experience, e.g., from nonresearch libraries and other professions.
- Adopt an attitude of partnership with library schools in responsibility for the preparation of librarians through (1) the redesign of library

education or creation of alternatives, (2) the provision of more in-house training and education, and (3) increased practitioner interaction with library educators.
- Actively recruit "the brightest and the best" into the library and information science professions.

Beyond the library. Beyond the library there are many steps that must be taken for the concepts outlined in this paper to materialize. Outside of a single institutional boundary, there are several that are seen as key to a successful transition.

- Librarians must become active partners in the scholarly process and in discussions pertaining to the generation, production, and access of information, including those on archival and preservation needs in the electronic environment.
- Librarians must be increasingly involved with those responsible for the development of information technology for the university and the information industry.
- Librarians must influence information policy as it affects information use and technology by collaborating with other stakeholders, especially in the political arena, at various governmental levels, and in scholarly associations.

In all of these efforts, librarians must take responsibility for positioning themselves in the appropriate groups and situations; they must not sit and wait to be noticed. Key actors with whom research librarians should establish ongoing contact include faculty involved in information research, computing center staff, publishers, information producers and vendors, those involved in telecommunications networks, and state and government librarians.

Finally and more broadly, there must be discussion and reconceptualization of the research library in light of forthcoming technological, societal, and economic changes. The model presented here is not intended to be ideal or definitive. Since there will be more, not less, diversity among research libraries in the future, the spectrum along which research libraries will develop will require elaboration of more transitional steps and continual reviews of boundary conditions.

However, no matter how a given research library defines its future, collaboration, flexibility, and fluidity will be the key attributes that characterize its operations and services. No research library can afford to drift toward the turn of the century without a vision for the future. Strategic directions need to be articulated *now* so that resources and efforts in the intervening years are most effectively deployed. Only with a clear vision of its future mission and a strategy for navigating the transition can a research library retain and improve both relevance and support on campus.

References

1. From the mission statement produced by conference participants at "Options for the Future," UCLA, August 20-23, 1988.
2. Participating in the conference were representatives from the Council on Library Resources and its Research Library Committee; the Dean and Assistant Dean of UCLA's Graduate School of Library and Information Science; and librarians who had participated in UCLA's Senior Fellows Program (a leadership development program also sponsored by CLR) between 1982 and 1987. For the three days of the conference, 36 Senior Fellow participants were divided into four groups, each charged with the following goals: describe the ideal research library; clarify the assumptions, including the predicted environmental conditions, upon which the ideal is based; and identify the transition steps needed to achieve the ideal. One of the groups developed the vision that is presented in this paper. While not all members of the group accepted all of the details, or even agreed to all of the underlying premises, there was enough unanimity about the model to generate a sense of urgency and excitement about sharing it beyond the conference and its participants. The group that developed the concepts in this paper from August 20-23, 1988, included Nancy Allen (Colorado State), Irene Hoadley (Texas A&M), June Lester (ALA), Pat Molholt (Rensselaer), Danuta Nitecki (Maryland), Richard Talbot (Massachusetts), Louella Wetherbee (AMIGOS), and Anne Woodsworth (Pittsburgh).
3. The "Knowbot" concept was developed by Robert Kahn of the Corporation for Research Initiatives. A similar concept, the "Knowledge Navigator," was presented by John Scully at EDUCOM in 1987.

THE UNINTENDED REVOLUTION IN ACADEMIC LIBRARIES: 1939 TO 1989 AND BEYOND

Barbara B. Moran

In 1989, the Association of College and Research Libraries (ACRL) celebrates its fiftieth anniversary. The years since its founding have been a period of great change and progress in academic librarianship. Academic libraries have evolved from relatively small, self-sufficient institutions to large, multifaceted organizations electronically interconnected and linked in ways not yet envisioned fifty years ago. The librarians who work in these institutions, although sharing many of the same attitudes and values of their predecessors, are called upon to have knowledge of processes and to provide services unforeseen in 1939. Academic librarianship in the United States has changed more rapidly and radically during the past fifty years than it had during its prior 300-year history.

This paper will examine some of these changes and attempt to chart the course of academic librarianship from 1939 to the present. To do justice to this history, far more space would be needed than is provided here. What follows is a much compressed and highly selective look at the topic, but it is hoped that the account will be comprehensive enough to permit the identification of the most important trends and influences and to isolate some useful generalizations.

Tracing the development of academic librarianship results in two seemingly contradictory impressions. On one hand there are fundamental changes: Libraries have begun to make the transition from manual to electronic systems, and many central components, including collections, organ-

---

"The Unintended Revolution in Academic Libraries: 1939 to 1989 and Beyond," by Barbara B. Moran in *College and Research Libraries* Vol. 50, no. 1 (January 1989), pp. 25–41; reprinted with permission from the American Library Association, copyright © 1989 by ALA.

ization, personnel, and services, have been modified. The libraries of today are very different institutions from those of fifty years ago. On the other hand there are great similarities, so that an old adage seems to be applicable: the more things change the more they stay the same. Many contemporary issues and concerns were articulated and shared by academic librarians working in the field fifty years ago. More discouragingly, many of the problems that seemed intractable in the late 1930s have indeed proven to be unyielding and are yet to be resolved. The first issues of *C&RL* contained articles on topics such as the appropriateness of the Ph.D. and the advisability of faculty status for academic librarians, the necessity for research by academic librarians, the problem of low salaries for librarians in relation to faculty, the percentage of the institutional budget that should be devoted to libraries, and the advantages and disadvantages of library centralization. These topics are still on the agenda.

The following account focuses largely on the changes in librarianship but also examines some of the similarities that indicate, perhaps better than anything else, both the strengths of academic libraries and the weaknesses where improvement and progress still need to be made. In closing, this paper turns briefly from the past to the future: What lies ahead for the academic librarian in the next half century, and what should librarians be doing now to prepare for that future?

The Academic Library in 1939

Many present-day librarians can only dimly imagine an academic library of the late 1930s. In what type of library were the founders of ACRL likely to have worked? According to one librarian who worked in such a library,

> The year 1938 was back in the era of typewriters and adding machines (both non-electric), of duplicate hand-written or typed book cards (one filed under call number and one under borrower's name), of typing short-form original cataloging if LC cards were not available, when bill in duplicate for book orders was sufficient. Bibliographical resources of this period were also limited. Of the great national library catalogs in book form only that of the Bibliotheque Nationale, completed to the letter "R", offered much assistance in searching. The new edition of the British Museum *General Catalogue of Printed Books* had progressed only into

the "B's", and there was no general record of Library of Congress's vast holdings except the depository catalogs or proof sheets found only in large libraries.[1]

Although there were exceptions, the typical academic library in the years before World War II had a small collection and a small staff. The usual educational preparation for librarians was a fifth-year bachelor's degree (B.L.S.) from a library science program, and librarians carried out many tasks that were essentially clerical in nature. The pay was low. There was rarely faculty status for any academic librarian below the administrative level. Some reference service was probably provided, but little effort was put into teaching students about the use of the collections, especially on a formal basis. Book selection was commonly done by interested faculty, not librarians. The acquisition budget was small, and most major collections were shaped by gifts and by development techniques that emphasized curricular needs and serious, scholarly material. The collection was composed almost entirely of books and journals; only a few libraries held any type of audiovisual materials or microfilm. Librarians had little input into decisions made by administrators, and the head librarian might be a recruit from the teaching faculty. Only a few cooperative ventures were in existence, and most librarians, operating in relative isolation, had no formal relationships with other libraries or with librarians outside of their own institutions.

Academic libraries of the late 1930s were not only very different from contemporary libraries but also from the libraries that had preceded them. If it is accepted that the fundamental purpose of the academic library is to support the educational mission of its parent institution, then, as institutions of higher education change, so will the libraries associated with them. There had been significant changes in U.S. higher education since the founding of Harvard University in 1636. The most important of these had resulted from the impact of the German research university and the land grant acts in the latter part of the nineteenth century. For the most part, the modifications to higher education had been incremental, and both academic institutions and libraries had had sufficient time to alter and adapt in response to them. In 1939, however, the academic library, along with its parent institution, was standing at the brink of the greatest period of change ever encountered, and the changes would occur so swiftly and unrelentingly that all of higher education would have to struggle to keep abreast of them.

The Revolution in Higher Education

Thomas Bonner, in a recent article in *Change* magazine, describes the "unintended" revolution in American higher education since 1940—a revolution resulting in a contemporary system of higher education that he argues is as different from that of 1940 as our present-day colleges and universities are from those in the developing nations of Asia and Africa.[2] And, as Bonner points out, "The changes that crumbled the ivory tower of 1940 were not only unforeseen and unplanned but were largely unintended and unwanted."[3] In his view, higher education did not control the developments that resulted in these changes but instead was carried along by swift social and demographic currents. Bonner lists the demands of World War II, impact of the returning veterans, economic growth, international crises, the baby boom, political strife, Vietnam, campus revolts, economic decline, and changing public support as the most important developments that have changed higher education during the past five decades. To this list must be added the growth of electronic technology, which has produced broad-based changes within institutions of higher education, especially in the last ten years.

If only one word could be chosen to describe the changes in both higher education and libraries, it would have to be *growth*. In academic libraries the growth—in size of collections and staff, in number of services provided and patrons served—mirrors the growth that took place in American higher education during the same time period.

Only about half of today's colleges and universities existed in 1940, and they served a student population of fewer than 1.5 million. These students were predominantly male and white, drawn almost exclusively from upper- and middle-class families. The federal government played an insignificant role in funding; the support of higher education just prior to World War II came almost entirely from a combination of student tuition and state government expenditures. The total national expenditure for higher education amounted to only 700 million dollars in 1940 compared to the 956 billion dollars spent in 1985.[4]

Spurred by the GI bill, the expansion in American higher education began after World War II, but grew most rapidly in the sixties and seventies. During this period new universities were established, state colleges became universities, normal schools and teachers' colleges expanded into state colleges or universities, and hundreds of community and technical colleges were opened. By 1950 there were 2,300,000 students enrolled in American colleges and universities; by 1960, 3,600,000; by 1970, 8,650,000; and by 1980, 12,100,000.[5] Despite the much-discussed "baby bust," enrollments have not dropped as feared; standing today at approximately 12,400,000; the enrollment figure is kept up primarily by the expanded number of nontraditional students.[6]

The new students who flocked to higher education were the impetus for new courses, programs, schools, and degrees. The liberal arts, the major of choice for almost all students fifty years ago, is now selected by only a third of them. In the 1980s nearly 60 percent of all college students are pursuing degrees in a wide range of professional and occupational studies. Students of today are a much more heterogeneous group than those enrolled in 1939. There are now more female than male students in institutions of higher learning. Blacks and most other minorities, although still underrepresented in relationship to their numbers in the population as a whole, have made tremendous strides since 1939, when many institutions of higher education were still closed to them. Despite cuts in federal aid for students during the last decade, there has been a broadening of opportunities to earn a degree—no longer is a college education the prerogative of children from upper- and middle-class families only. Although higher education in the U.S. still does not provide universal access, it serves a higher percentage of the college-age population than does any other country.

Higher education is no longer the exclusive preserve of the eighteen- to twenty-two-year-old. Perhaps the most striking indication of this change is the fact that, among more than twelve million college students, only about two million are full-time, living on campus, and aged eighteen to twenty-two.[7] Older students, many attending college on a part-time basis, now constitute an important segment of the enrollment on most campuses.

The growth and expansion of U.S. higher education over the past half century has made a dramatic impact upon academic libraries. Although today's libraries are larger according to almost any variable that might be measured, growth alone is not an adequate explanation of the changes that have occurred since 1939. Two other factors have been driving forces behind the changes, especially those of the past twenty years: the greater acceptance by librarians of interinstitutional cooperation and the adoption of new technologies.

Over the past fifty years, academic libraries have come to realize that interinstitutional cooperation is essential to meeting the needs of their users. The move to a more cooperative stance has been necessitated by economic circumstances and has been facilitated by the development of online data that can more easily be shared among institutions. Today's libraries are relying on networking and resource sharing as an integral part of their activities.

During the past twenty years, the changes brought about by technology have been so extensive that it is difficult to assess their total impact. Librarians adopted technology with great enthusiasm and, despite the fact that they have sometimes been viewed as a conservative group, were pioneers in the use of computer technology. The library was usually the first academic unit on campus to computerize. The match between automation and libraries was a natural one because librarians usually spend much more time processing data about their collections than they do working with the collection itself. Growth in the size of the collection and demand for services were added incentives for librarians to explore the ways in which automation could assist in performing routine library operations. Today, even the smallest academic libraries have been affected by the technological changes that have swept through librarianship.

The causes of the transformation in academic librarianship are many and varied. The following section focuses primarily on the three factors discussed above—growth, cooperation, and technology—and examines their impact on the critical components of collections, budgets, organization, buildings, staff, and services.

Library Collections

In 1939 the median size of the book collections in U.S. universities was 329,706; in small colleges, 62,285; and in teachers' colleges, 25,341.[8]

Today the average collection in all types of libraries has increased dramatically. For just one example, the median for ARL university libraries is now more than two million volumes.[9] During the post-World War II era, many distinguished collections were amassed. Collection building and growth were among the major concerns of academic librarians; libraries were ranked by collection size, and bigger was always better.

Growing both in numbers and diversity, academic library collections now routinely consist not only of books and journals but of microforms, audiovisual materials in many formats, and increasing numbers of machine-readable databases, online texts, and software programs. The broad spectrum of courses being offered in today's institutions of higher education has led to the collecting of library materials in areas that would have been unheard of previously.

No account of the past fifty years would be complete without a mention of the information "explosion" and its impact upon academic libraries. Beginning after World War II, the amount of published material skyrocketed as fields of study grew and subdivided, resulting in the production of more and more new and specialized journals. The numbers of monographs being published both here and abroad also ballooned, increasing 14 percent a year during the sixties and 2.8 percent a year during the seventies.[10]

As acquisitions librarians know all too well, the cost of publications escalated along with the amount of material being published. The largest cost increases began to occur in the 1970s, at a time when libraries' materials budgets were beginning to stagnate; the increases resulted in a severe erosion of purchasing power. Librarians reluctantly acknowledged that their previous levels of collection building could no longer be maintained and that the days of the comprehensive, self-contained collection were over. Perhaps one of the greatest changes of the past fifty years is the realization that, because of the rising level of scholarly output, no library, however large, can be self-sufficient but instead must be part of a system in which users are linked to needed resources in other collections.

The resource sharing that is such a clear hallmark of the academic library in the 1980s was spurred by the hard realities of increased publication and decreased budgets but is not a new development. Although there were some examples prior to 1939, the most notable cooperative efforts have been attempted throughout the past fifty years. Many geographically close libraries began cooperative acquisition plans during the 1930s. The New England Deposit Library opened in 1942, the Universal Serial and Book Exchange and the Farmington Plan began in 1948, and the Midwest Interlibrary Center (later to become the Center for Research Libraries) was established in 1949.[11] Interlibrary loan existed before 1939; but with new tools that permit both efficient verification and ordering of items, ILL has become an integral part of library cooperation in the past few decades.

Libraries have gradually moved away from collection building and growth to a new emphasis on providing access to information from many sources. Academic librarians of the future must remember, however, that access depends on ownership by at least one party. On the whole, today's libraries can provide access to material because they own the material collectively. Since self-sufficiency is no longer possible, greater attention will need to be paid to coordinated, cooperative collection development such as that being attempted by the Research Libraries Group's *Conspectus*.[12]

During the past fifty years, academic librarians have also begun to face up to the physical deterioration of large parts of the collections. Prior to this time, preservation was a neglected activity, and today's collections reflect that neglect.[13] The problem of brittle books has been compounded by the preservation problems associated with some of the newer media such as film, videotape, and magnetic tape, which are just as fragile and apt to deteriorate as pulp paper. Despite advances in preservation techniques, academic librarians are far from having a cure for this malady, and the preservation problem is one that must wait for solution in the years ahead.

Although some new preservation techniques and storage devices such as optical disks hold promise, funding, as usual, provides the major obstacle. At a time when libraries need to find funding sources in order to invest in technology, they are faced with the concurrent need to invest in preservation to save their collections. Because of the size of the problem and the overwhelming cost required to solve it, cooperative action will be needed. A coalition of librarians, scholars, academic administrators, publishers, and all who use the records of civilization is needed to forge an alliance and seek a common solution to this problem if tomorrow's scholars are to have access to the collections built with great care and cost in the past.

Library Budgets

The actual increases in academic libraries' budgets are less dramatic if they are adjusted to reflect the inflation of the dollar that has occurred. In 1938 institutions of higher education spent $17,588,000 on libraries;[14] in 1985, the last year for which figures are available, they spent $2,361,000,000.[15] The 1960s were a period of especially great affluence for academic libraries, but this prosperity was followed by the stringent budgets of the seventies and eighties. And, even with an increased library budget, there was no way to keep up with the growth in publications.

One of the reasons that technology was embraced so eagerly was the hope that the use of automation would reduce the day-to-day costs of operation. Many library directors justified the heavy capital expenditures necessary for computer-based systems by promising lower operating costs in the future. These trade-offs—capital investments for lower operating costs—almost never succeeded. As Richard De Gennaro wrote,

> When we first started to use computers in libraries 15 years ago, we thought we would save money, but we soon learned there would be no net savings from automation. Then we thought that automation would at least "reduce the rate of rise of library costs," but even this is proving to be illusory as we demand and receive an ever increasing variety of new and expensive services from our network and local systems.[16]

By automating, the library multiplied its capabilities and raised the expectation level of library staff and user alike. Thus, as library services became more efficient and useful, demand for them increased. While the unit cost of any given service might decline, the total cost of satisfying the increased demand would go up.

One of the constants in academic librarianship over the past fifty years has been the portion of the parent institution's budget that has been devoted to libraries. Before the 1960s, academic libraries received, on the average, about 3.1 percent of the total institutional budget. During the late sixties and early seventies, the figure rose to about 4 percent but, after 1976, drifted down again.[17] The percentage varies from institution to institution, with large universities devoting a smaller percent of their budgets to libraries than small colleges. The true significance of the pattern is what it reveals about institutional budgeting for libraries. It seems clear that library funding is not based on the library's need because, if it were, the percentage would fluctuate from year to year. Academic library costs have not been determined by need but by available revenue. Libraries have not been successful in providing a rationale for the funds they need and seeing those needs met by their parent institutions. This invariant pattern does not augur well for the future when libraries, more than ever, will require increased budgets to meet the demands of their expanding role in the use of technology.

If the percentage of the institutional budget has been constant, one of the most inconstant elements in library funding over the past fifty years has been federal funding. Although federal aid to libraries was almost nonexistent in 1939, it began to increase after World War II, reached a high point during the late 1960s, and then began a slow decline. One of the greatest factors supporting the growth of librarianship during 1945–70 was federal funding. The Higher Education Act of 1965 provided three library programs: Title IIA, funds for acquisition of books, periodicals, and other materials; Title IIB, library training and research demonstration programs; and Title IIC, a centralized cataloging and acquisition program under the direction of the Library of Congress. The Library Services and Construction Act and the Academic Facilities Act were also important pieces of legislation for academic libraries.[18]

Budgeting for technology has been one of the major difficulties since the 1960s. Traditionally, 60 percent of the library budget had been used for salaries, 30 percent for materials, and 10 percent for other expenses. The percentage used for "other" needed to be increased during the past few decades because this is the section of the budget used to finance automation. As a result, libraries had to cut back on the percentages for personnel and materials. Within the materials budget, they are now facing the problem of balancing the cost of new electronic sources against the cost of traditional library acquisitions. It would be reassuring to think that universities will increase the budgets of libraries sometime soon, but this does not appear to be likely in the near future. Too many competing claims exist.

As the new information technologies become more widespread, they will make students and faculty more productive, and there will be a need to shift funding from faculty to infrastructure. Both libraries and computing centers would benefit from this move,[19] but it will likely be resisted by many units on campus. In addition, librarians themselves will need to find ways to limit the need to provide services through both print and electronic means. The decisions to be made in these areas will not be easy ones.

Organizational Patterns

The growth in the size of libraries has led to the adoption of different organizational patterns. In 1939, almost all college and university libraries, regardless of size, were organized along departmental lines with all department heads reporting directly to the chief librarian. As libraries grew in size, the number of departments grew also so that the span of management became too broad to be workable, and this highly centralized organizational pattern needed to be modified. Various experiments at reorganization were attempted, but, by the early 1950s, the bifurcated organizational pattern with its division of functions into public and technical services had been widely accepted by most large academic libraries.[20] Since then, some libraries have produced modifications to this structure; for instance, in 1973 the library at Columbia University organized its activities into a services group, a resources group, and a technical support group. Nonetheless, the bifurcated structure is still the most common in large libraries while most smaller libraries continue to be organized departmentally. Although much has been written about the merger of technical service and public service departments in academic libraries, this type of reorganization is still more conjecture than reality.

As libraries grew in size and complexity, the number of middle managers proliferated. In addition to the traditional line managers, most large libraries now include a team of individuals who provide specialized managerial expertise in areas such as personnel, budgeting, planning, and automation.

The past fifty years has been a period when libraries have continued to grapple with the thorny issue of centralized versus decentralized services. Fifty years ago, Robert A. Miller argued the pros and cons of centralized and decentralized collections in areas such as accessibility, efficiency, interrelationship of subject field, and cost.[21] Today's library directors are still trying to arrive at a balance between the efficiency of centralized services and the greater convenience of decentralized services. At most institutions, the present trend has been to continue to centralize services as much as possible.

In a similar vein, academic librarianship has seen the waxing and now the waning of interest in undergraduate libraries. Harvard's Lamont Library was built in 1949, but the real proliferation of this type of library came in the 1960s and the early 1970s when the number of undergraduates on campus was expanding most rapidly. The interest in establishing new undergraduate libraries has dwindled in the past fifteen years because of cuts in library budgets, stable enrollments, and the assumption of many that separate libraries for undergraduates are unnecessary now that bibliographic instruction programs are available to make the main library more comprehensible to undergraduate users.

The future place of both undergraduate and branch libraries is not clear. Still to be factored in is the impact of the new technologies and the advent of new methods of document storage and retrieval. Many of the arguments in favor of centralization will disappear when materials can be shared electronically among libraries. Some writers predict that the library of the future will consist of small, decentralized units which will provide users with the convenient, individualized services they have always preferred.[22] The new technology will likely be a driving force in determining the organizational structure of the library of the future, but the shape of that library is still to be determined.

Library Buildings

Indicative of the growth of higher education is the spurt in library building that went on during the middle of the period under consideration. With the infusion of federal money in the sixties and seventies, a large number of academic libraries were built. Between 1967 and 1975, 647 academic library projects were completed in the U.S. at a cost of $1,900,000,000. Many of the projects were partially funded with federal money authorized under the Higher Education Facilities Act.[23] Many of the old main libraries that were replaced were refurbished and used for other purposes such as undergraduate libraries or classroom buildings.

Not only have library buildings grown in sheer numbers and in size, but the change in architectural design over the past fifty years has seen a shift from the "monumental" library building, still the most common type in the 1930s, to a more functional style of library architecture. Edna Ruth Hanley's *College and University Library Buildings*, published in 1939, provides a good introduction to the style of architecture popular in academic libraries at that time.[24] The book presents photographs and floor plans of 42 college and university libraries that had been erected between 1922 and 1938, the most expensive of these libraries costing $1,200,000. The columns, cupolas, and towers associated with "old fashioned" library buildings are all well represented.

The architecture of the buildings built since 1939 has been very different from that of the earlier era. The older, fixed form buildings were replaced by buildings with functional flexibility which provided facilities for group discussion rooms, conference rooms, individual study carrels, and comfortable reading areas. The new buildings had good lighting and ventilation, air conditioning, open stack design, comfortable furniture, and adequate acoustical properties.[25]

During the past few years, the "flexibility" of some of these new buildings has been strained as librarians have attempted to accommodate the computer hardware, especially the terminals, being added in libraries. The need for space is critical as libraries are going through a transition period between online and manual systems. Libraries with online catalogs still need space for traditional card catalogs and reference departments are attempting to find room for CD-ROM terminals among the reference stacks. The clatter of the printer in public use areas is a new sound in most libraries, and librarians are struggling to find a way to accommodate harmoniously the old and new technologies of librarianship.

Staff

The size of the library staff has increased commensurately with the growth of the rest of the library. When *C&RL* published its first annual statistics in 1941–42, the median number of full-time personnel in the largest academic libraries was thirty-seven.[26] Today, each of those same libraries would have a full-time staff that numbers in the hundreds.[27] But to describe the changes in the personnel aspects of academic libraries as growth alone would obscure the truly significant advances made in this area.

In the past five decades, the tasks professional librarians perform have become more clearly differentiated from those performed by nonprofessionals, and, in many instances, tasks that had been done by professionals have been transferred to members of the support staff. As Allen Veaner has written, this displacement provides an illustration of technological imperative in that once technology is used to accomplish complex, routine mental work, that work is driven downward in the work hierarchy away from professional to support staff. The professional's work then expands to include new and more challenging tasks, and, as a result, librarians have acquired a more clearly defined professional responsibility.[28]

In terms of professional-level staff, the academic libraries of today are "leaner and meaner" organizations. As recently as 1950, the staff of most college and university libraries was composed of fifty to ninety percent professional librarians. In most contemporary libraries, the ratio is now one professional librarian to two support staff members, and in some large libraries, the proportion of professional librarians is still lower.

Professional librarians of today, taken as a group, are better educated than those of fifty years ago. Almost all of them have at least a master's degree, and a large number have, in addition, a second master's degree or a Ph.D. They are graduates of professional schools whose curricula are less practice-oriented and more research- and problem-oriented than they were fifty years ago.

Librarians not only enter the profession with a better education, but they strive to continue that advantage not only by recognizing the value of continuing education and staff development but also seeking out opportunities to avail themselves of further education. Without this willingness to continue to learn, librarians would have found their knowledge and skills had become outdated in the rapidly changing academic library field.

The past fifty years also have seen librarians assume tasks that were not considered totally within their sphere of competence in the late 1930s. Individuals trained as librarians, not bookloving faculty members, are found as directors, almost without exception. Librarians, not teaching faculty, now do the bulk of the book selection (although often with the advice of interested faculty), and collection development is considered to be the right of the library staff. Librarians now routinely engage in teaching, both within the library and without, by means of bibliographic instruction programs.

These changes have led to a greater professional maturity among academic librarians. Most of today's academic librarians have a clear view of their place and purpose within academe and recognize that they play a role of central importance in the instructional and scholarly life of the university. This greater professional maturity has been reflected in the growth of the number of professional journals, in the increase in research and publications, in interest in professional organizations, and in the establishment of policies and standards.

Academic librarians have also made tremendous strides in their quest for participation in library governance. In 1939 almost all libraries were organized in a traditional hierarchical structure, and the most common management style was authoritarian with the director making all decisions relating to the library. Although there are still a few authoritarian directors remaining, non-administrative librarians are now involved to some degree in decision making in almost every academic library. The committee system has been found to be an effective method of providing librarians' input. Although a few small libraries have adopted the faculty model of collegial governance, the sheer size of most academic libraries makes that model an inappropriate one. A few libraries have also experimented with matrix or project management organization patterns in an attempt to provide greater staff input and involvement, but on the whole, the academic library of today is still organized in a traditional, pyramidal fashion. The difference is that librarians have been successful in finding ways of providing opportunity for staff participation in decision making within the confines of the bureaucratic structure.

The now generally accepted premise that academic librarians should have input into decision making provides an interesting contrast to the still unresolved issue of what is the appropriate status for academic librarians. This is an issue that was being discussed fifty years ago (and before) and is still far from being resolved today. Miriam Maloy wrote in a 1939 *ALA Bulletin* article:

> [W]riters have pointed out the important function of the librarian as a teacher and his obligation to pursue higher studies and broaden his outlook by travel, just as regular faculty members are expected to do. These are good arguments for the inclusion of librarians in the academic ranks rather than the administrative ranks. . . . However, some groups of librarians have felt that more immediate advantage could be gained in their particular institutions by stressing and developing their unique status as librarians, raising their own standards, developing their own potentialities, and bringing to the attention of college authorities the educational and cultural requirements of the library profession.[29]

Maloy's words describe the situation in 1989 as well as they did fifty years previously. The quest for faculty status for academic librarians began well over 100 years ago,[30] but it began to become a central concern for librarians starting in the fifties and sixties. The concern about the most appropriate status for librarians has extended up to the present and is reflected in the fact that perhaps more has been written about this particular aspect of academic librarianship than about any other during the last 25 years.

The move toward faculty status was advanced by the decision of the American Association of University Professors (AAUP) to admit librarians as members in 1956. At the 1969 ALA Conference, ACRL approved a motion establishing as one of its chief goals, full faculty status for all academic librarians. ACRL, the Association of American Colleges, and AAUP drafted a joint statement on faculty status of college and university librarians urging the granting of faculty status to librarians as well as the same rights, privileges, and responsibilities of faculty members.[31] Although recent surveys have shown that nearly 80 percent of librarians report having faculty status,[32] it is clear that few librarians have full faculty status "with the same rights, privileges, and responsibilities."

In the past decade, a large number of academic librarians have begun to reconsider the issue, and some now feel that perhaps the quest for faculty status was misguided. It is their judgment that academic librarians have assumed the dual responsibilities of teaching faculty members and librarians to their own detriment. Despite the fact that faculty status still has its strong proponents, a growing number of individuals now advocate having librarians organize as a separate academic group to seek recognition and status as librarians. Under this status, it would be necessary for librarians to set strict standards for performance, education, and professional competence if they wished to earn the respect of their faculty colleagues, but at least librarians would be judged by criteria appropriate not to another profession but to their own.

The debate about the appropriate status which has consumed so much energy and effort during the past fifty years has yet to be resolved. Perhaps, the ultimate resolution will be the realization that there is no one "ideal" status for academic librarians and that the appropriate status can best be worked out on an institution-specific basis. In those institutions which have granted full faculty status to librarians including the released time and the institutional support needed for doing research, faculty status may indeed be a realistic option. In those other, more numerous institutions where faculty status has been granted in name only, librarians might do well to seek to be judged on criteria directly related to what they do in their own profession.

Here again, the impact of technology will be a significant factor. If libraries of the future are the decentralized units foreseen by some, where a "holistic" librarian with an advanced subject degree and knowledge of the research process works in close relationship with faculty and students in a specific discipline or field of study, the faculty status model might fit very well.

Some of the changes in the personnel patterns in academic libraries have been the result of the changes in personnel patterns within academe as a whole. The push of collective bargaining units into institutions of higher education beginning in the 1970s has resulted in the unionization of a large number of librarians, especially those in large public systems. Interest in better working conditions has led to increased attention being paid to the quality of the working life within libraries. Most libraries now have instituted formal grievance policies which can be used to redress employee complaints.

Academic libraries have also mirrored the improving conditions for women and minorities within the society as a whole. Interestingly, women had an easier time securing positions in library administration in the late 1930s than they did in the sixties and seventies. In 1930, only 9 percent of all librarians were male; by 1940, the percentage of males in libraries had increased to only 10 percent.[33] Males were encouraged to enter the field of academic librarianship after World War II. The percentage of males increased until now it is estimated that approximately 20 percent of all librarians are males, with a higher percentage of males working in academic libraries than in any other type of library. The most recent statistics show that approximately 35 percent of all academic librarians are male.[34] As males entered academic librarianship, females were displaced from administrative positions, especially in the large, research university libraries, where their representation in administration had always been low. In 1930, in the 74 institutions of higher education with enrollments of more than 2,000, there were fifty-five men and nineteen women serving as chief librarians. As women retired, men were hired to take their places. By 1967, 70 of these libraries were headed by men and only 4 by women—not one of the fifty largest academic libraries was directed by a woman. In the late 1960s, even the women's colleges that had traditionally employed female head librarians were employing males.[35] In the 1970s, federal Equal Employment Opportunity legislation was made applicable to institutions of higher education, and conditions for women improved. Today, 28 of the 103 ARL university libraries have female directors, and there is a higher percentage of females at the middle management level than ever before. Academic libraries, like other institutions in our society, still need to make progress in the area of equal opportunity for women, but they have left behind, forever it is hoped, a time when an advertisement like the following could appear: "Stymied in your present job? Want to broaden your experience? Like to work in brand-new building under ideal conditions? Insist on liberal fringe benefits? Want faculty status? If so, and you are male, you may be interested."[36]

In terms of equal opportunity for racial minorities, academic libraries have also made progress. In 1939, an article in the *ALA Bulletin* reported the problems associated with library education for blacks.[37] At that time Hampton Institute, the only library school for blacks, was on the verge of closing. The article urged the establishment of another library school to prepare black librarians. The problem today lies not in availability of education but in how to get more minority students to enroll. Despite the efforts of many academic libraries to increase the number of minorities on their staffs, the profession has not been successful in attracting minorities to the field. Librarianship has to compete with other more lucrative professions, and is, too often, coming in second. The latest statistics show that almost 90 percent of all academic librarians are white; 4.5 percent, Asian/Pacific Islander; 4.1 percent black; 1.5 percent, Hispanic; and .02 percent, Native America.[38] It seems obvious that libraries will not be able to compete on the basis of pay but must look for other ways to attract minority entrants. Some academic libraries and some library schools have instituted innovative scholarship and internship programs to attract minorities to the field. More efforts in this area need to be made if librarianship is committed to increasing the number of minorities in the profession in the future.

Services

Not surprisingly, library services have changed along with the rest of librarianship. Technology has had an enormous impact on technical services. Automation was first used to make the work of librarians easier, especially the "recordkeeping" work of librarianship including acquisitions and cataloging. Librarians developed their own local systems or bought turnkey systems to help with acquisitions and serial control. The growth of the bibliographic utilities, especially OCLC, during the seventies and eighties revolutionized cataloging and led to a restructuring of the catalog department in almost every academic library.

Because technology was first used in technical services and thus was invisible to the library user, many users were unaware of its heavy use in libraries during the sixties and seventies, even though much of the growth in collections and services during that period was made possible by its implementation. Today, especially in large libraries, things are very different. Patrons themselves have become eager users of technology such as CD-ROM discs and online public access catalogs.

Public services in libraries have increased both in number and in comprehensiveness over the past fifty years. Circulation was the first service provided in academic libraries, and, by the late 1800s, some academic libraries were providing reference service. As Samuel Rothstein has shown, however, this service was provided on a minimal basis until the 1940s.[39] Throughout the last fifty years, academic librarians have increased the amount of specialized and in-depth assistance in the use of collections, not only in answering users' questions, but in preparing bibliographies and in providing telephone information services. Many libraries have employed subject specialists to provide reference service in specific areas.

In addition, two new services have been developed: bibliographic instruction, which has become an integral part of academic librarianship over the past twenty years, and online searching of bibliographic or natural-language databases.

The librarians of 1989, like those of 1939, have a strong commitment to service to users. This commitment to service may be needed even more in the near future as library users have greater opportunities to interact directly with library technology and need to be trained in its use. As C. Lee Jones has pointed out, "This era of technical innovation in libraries has become for patrons an age of discontinuity of library services as library practices they have grown accustomed to are rapidly replaced by new ones."[40] It will be the librarians of the present and the future who will need to refamiliarize patrons with the library.

As long as technology stayed in the backroom, librarians were not faced with this problem. Even when online searching became common, in most cases trained librarians performed the searching. It was not until the availability of online catalogs and CD-ROM discs that librarians found they had to spend an increasing amount of their time in the teaching of the new technologies. Reference librarians in departments which have just recently acquired CD-ROM discs frequently mention the way their time is being redistributed away from traditional reference service to the instruction of patrons in the use of the CD-ROM. These demands for new instruction and new services will only increase as librarians make more computerized information technology available to patrons. It is likely that in the near future librarians will be called on to help in new ways, for instance, assisting patrons with downloading information and constructing their own tailored databases. The possibilities in this area are limitless and will be constrained only by the amount of time librarians have available to be divided among competing demands.

Quo Vadis?

If growth, acceptance of cooperation, and the adoption of technology were the driving forces behind the changes in academic libraries over the past fifty years, what will be their impact in the future? It seems likely that the relative importance of these factors will not remain the same.

Growth, which was perhaps the strongest force for change over the past fifty years, will likely be the weakest in the future. This is because the great expansion in higher education that served as an impetus for the growth of libraries has plateaued and is likely entering a period of decline. Although it is impossible to predict exactly the number of students who will be going to college in the future, the best available estimates are that between now and 1996, enrollments may decline from 12.4 to 11 million students.[41] This decline will not affect all institutions equally; some types of institutions and some parts of the country will be more hard hit than others. Nonetheless, on the whole, most institutions of higher education are expecting a smaller number of students to enroll between now and 1996, and that decrease will affect libraries in many ways from budget freezes and cuts to the need for fewer seats in the reference room.

The increase in publication rate that led to the spurt in the size of library collections has leveled off, but straitened budgets and increasing costs, especially for foreign serials, mean that librarians will still not be able to acquire a larger proportion of this output. With a shrinking enrollment and no increases seen in federal spending, there may be fewer new libraries built in the future. Librarians will need to continue to experiment with remote storage facilities and steady-state collections.

The cooperative efforts of libraries will likely increase and strengthen in the future. The move away from acquisitions to access will continue and be made even more necessary as costs for technology compete with funds for collection development. Many library users who would prefer to see their libraries continue to purchase the bulk of the scholarly material they need will likely resist this new emphasis on access. Nevertheless, it is inevitable that the collection development policies of even the largest academic libraries will respond to the economic realities. Librarians will accelerate "the trend away from each library being a self-contained unit, toward a system in which the library will be a service center, capable of linking users to national bibliographic files and distant collections," which was advocated by the National Enquiry into Scholarly Communication in 1979.[42] Advances in technology will make both the interinstitutional and the intrainstitutional sharing of resources less burdensome.

Technology will play the greatest role in transforming the library of the future. It is clear that the process of technological innovation in libraries (and in higher education) is an ongoing one. The library of today is in a process of transformation that has already produced great changes but which promises to produce a great many more in the future. It is important to remember that as much as technology has already changed libraries, the changes it has made are likely to be just the beginning. This is because technology is usually adopted in three stages and libraries are not even halfway through the process yet. This three-stage model of technological adoption was first described by O'Connell in 1969. In the first stage, technology is used to do the same things but to do those things more quickly. In the second stage, technology is used for new applications and to do new things. In stage three, technology is used in ways that create fundamental changes within organizations and societies.[43]

It is clear that at this point, most of the use of technology in libraries is still at stage one. Librarians have used computers to speed up cataloging, circulation, and acquisitions. Libraries began to enter stage two with technological advances such as online catalogs which have greater search capacities than traditional card catalogs and with database searching which permits searchers to search materials electronically in ways that were never possible using print sources.[44]

Stage three, the one that will lead to fundamental changes within a society and its institutions, has not yet made its appearance, but when it does, the academic library, like the rest of higher education, will undergo dramatic changes. At this time, the changes this stage will bring can only be dimly and imperfectly glimpsed. It is this new use of technology that will most strongly affect the shape of the library of the future.

The Library of the Future

Much has already been prophesied about the library of the future, but these seers share no common vision. Some see the library of the future as relatively similar to today's but with new technological "bells and whistles" to make it work more efficiently and effectively. On the other hand, there are those who have predicted the virtual demise of the library as users' information needs are satisfied entirely by electronic information available in homes or offices.

Foretelling the future is both difficult and risky. A perusal of library literature of the thirties and forties dealing with the future of academic libraries reveals that librarians of that time were not particularly prescient.[45] Although many authors foresaw the growth of libraries, none of them had an inkling of the impact of computer technology upon today's libraries. This is not surprising. Although the first computer was built just before World War II, general purpose computers were not common before 1960. But there is no reason to think that today's librarians are going to be any more accurate in their visions.

Prophets are usually led astray by linear projection—they take today's trends and interpolate them into the future. The problem lies in the fact that the future is often not linear or deterministic. As John Naisbitt has written, "The gee-whiz futurists are always wrong because they believe technological innovation travels in a straight line. It doesn't. It weaves and bobs and lurches and sputters."[46]

What weaves, bobs, lurches, and sputters lie ahead for academic libraries in the next fifty years? It seems that the answer to this question depends on the larger question of what lies ahead for higher education in that same time period. Remember Bonner's description of the changes of the past fifty years as "not only unforeseen and unplanned, but . . . largely unintended and unwanted."[47] Will the changes of the next fifty years be planned and foreseen any better? It seems unlikely.

Higher education has learned the lesson about demographic planning. The students who will be entering the college classroom in the first decade of the twenty-first century have already been born. Both birth and enrollment rates are being closely watched by institutions of higher education. But demographic planning, despite its uncertainties, is the easiest part of planning for the future.

The biggest unanswered question related to the future of higher education is what impact the electronic information technologies will have on this nation's colleges and universities. It is impossible to know now what the ultimate result will be. Computer technology has the potential to produce as much change in our society as the invention of the printing press. As a society, we are still in the early stages of the adoption of technology and may not even realize it has begun to change our life-styles and reshape our institutions until it is too late either to control the effects or shape the future.

It is possible that higher learning might be completely deinstitutionalized as information technology and computer networks are improved and become common on all campuses. Higher education may no longer be identified with institutions as defined by bricks, faculty, and libraries, but with a content of knowledge that could be learned wherever and whenever it best suited the student. Our institutions of higher education, as presently constituted, would be anachronistic in such a learning environment. As one writer put it,

> Some wealthy institutions may seek to perpetuate their present form. But the unique structure of the American research university, in which professors do research aided by assistants who support themselves in part by teaching undergraduates what they should have learned in secondary schools may come undone.[48]

Perhaps this is one possible future for higher education. In that case, there would be no need to worry about the future of academic libraries—they would disappear along with their parent institutions. There are, however, many counterarguments that could be put forth against such a future. It could be asserted that the personal interaction between teacher and student will never be replaced by a machine. Naisbitt has written about the need for "high touch" in a high-tech world.[49] The humanistic elements of education would still be important to most individuals. One might also contend that institutions of higher education play an important role in socializing students which could not be duplicated in an environment where a learner studies in isolation connected to others only by means of telecommunication channels.

But, regardless of how alien the above vision seems, higher education is likely to be transformed at some point in the future as the result of technology. It is impossible now to do more than conjecture about what shape this transformation will take and when it will occur. It seems highly unlikely that this transformation will take place within the next fifty years, since it has been shown that forecasters tend to overestimate what is likely to occur in the short run and underestimate or fail to anticipate at all what will happen in the long run.[50] So dramatic change will not come quickly to higher education but it will come eventually. To avoid the fate of the carriage makers of the nineteenth century who had no idea they would be replaced by the automakers of the twentieth, all individuals involved in higher education, including librarians, need to think about the future direction of the field. While this will not stop the flow of change, at least the changes may not be as "unplanned and unintended" as they might be. Of course, the task is complicated by the fact that the participants have a stake in the existing structure but that is all the more reason for them to want to exert as much influence as possible in shaping the future of higher education.

If the long-term future of both higher education and academic libraries is unclear, the short-term future is much easier to describe. The academic library of the early part of the twenty-first century will still be a strong and vibrant institution. As today, there will be a great diversity in these libraries. Some of the smallest ones may still have made only modest investments in technology although the proliferation of microcomputers will have made technology more affordable for all. Many libraries, especially those in large and wealthy institutions, will have transformed themselves into "electronic" libraries. They will be active participants in an environment where the library serves as the connecting agency or gateway between users and information in all formats. Their services will be available in a much more decentralized fashion, and users will not have to come to a physical entity, the *library*, to use its resources. There will be a much closer relationship (or possibly, a merger) between the library and the computer center, as each discovers that the scholarly information needs of individual institutions can be met only by cooperative effort.

Librarians in this setting will have to learn to handle long-distance users—library patrons whom they have never seen. There will be opportunities for librarians with their specialized knowledge of both information skills and technologies to play more active roles in instruction. The development of electronic libraries will impose still greater demands on academic libraries because the less visible the medium the greater the need for the intermediary.[51]

But despite the heavier use of technology in all types of academic libraries, book collections will continue to be heavily used. Books and computer output will coexist. Libraries will continue to add new technologies but these new technologies will not completely replace the existing ones.

What should librarians be doing now to make the transition to this short-term future easier? First of all, they should be taking an active part in their institution's planning for electronic technologies. Academic librarians need to be at the forefront in discussions about electronic technologies on campuses. They should be working collaboratively with other units on campus such as the computer center and the telecommunications center to explore new ways to exploit the powers of the new technology. They should be discussing how to secure the funding, both for capital costs and ongoing expenditures, that will be necessary to finance the new technologies and services that libraries may provide and how to balance these new costs against the costs for traditional library materials and services that will still be needed. They should be investigating the type of education (and reeducation) necessary for staff to function effectively. Librarians also should be working on difficult issues such as how to handle copyright and ownership of materials in machine readable files and how to provide maintenance for electronic databases that are in a constant state of change. Finally, and most important, academic libraries should be attempting now to define the roles they want libraries and librarians to play, because if they do not, others will define those roles for them. Librarians should seize the initiative to take advantage of opportunities the new technologies are presenting them to make the restructured library a major force in the university's new information environment.

Despite the uncertainties of the future, the opportunities for libraries are bright. Libraries have existed as institutions for nearly 3,000 years because they have had a vital role to play in society. That role will continue. Fifty years from now academic libraries will still be in existence. They will have changed, no doubt as much or more than the libraries of today have changed from those of 1939. Yet, in 2039, when ACRL celebrates its 100th anniversary, there will be an opportunity for someone else to write an article for *C&RL* about the changes in academic libraries in the last fifty years. It is likely that author too will discuss the unforeseen changes that occurred in libraries since 1989 and how unprepared in some respects libraries were for the changes that befell them. Perhaps, he or she will marvel that the librarians of the twenty-first century are still wrestling with some of the same problems as their predecessors. Will the most appropriate status for academic librarians still be a matter of concern? But there is every reason to believe that the underlying theme of that article as of this one will be that libraries have come through another period of challenge and change and are stronger entities than ever before in institutions of higher education.

References

1. Jean M. Ray, "The Future Role of the Academic Librarian as Viewed through the Perspective of Forty Years," *New Horizons for Academic Libraries*, ed. R. D. Stueart and R. D. Johnson (New York: Saur, 1979), p. 405.
2. Thomas N. Bonner, "The Unintended Revolution in American Colleges since 1940," *Change* 18:44–51 (Sept./Oct. 1986).
3. Ibid., p. 44.
4. Ibid., p. 45.
5. V. R. Cardozier, *American Higher Education* (Aldershot, England: Avebury, 1987), p. 11.
6. U. S. Department of Commerce, Bureau of the Census, *Statistical Abstracts of the United States, 1988* (Washington, D.C.: Govt. Print. Off., 1987), p. 140.
7. Harold L. Hodgkinson, "The Changing Face of Tomorrow's Student," *Change* 17:38 (May/June 1985).
8. Willis H. Kerr, "Summary of 123 Reports from College and University Libraries," *ALA Bulletin* 33:98 (Feb. 1939).
9. *ARL Statistics, 1986–87*, comp. Nicola Daval and Margaret McConnell (Washington, D.C.: Assn. of Research Libraries, 1988), p. 25.
10. John F. Harvey and Peter Spyers-Duran, "The Effect of Inflation on Academic Libraries," in *Austerity Management in Academic Libraries*, ed. J. F. Harvey and P. Spyers-Duran (Metuchen, N.J.: Scarecrow, 1984).
11. George Bobinski, "The Golden Age of American Librarianship," *Wilson Library Bulletin* 58:342–43 (Jan. 1984).
12. Peter Briscoe and others, "Ashurbanipal's Enduring Archetype: Thoughts on the Library's Role in the Future," *College & Research Libraries*, 47:123–24 (Mar. 1986).
13. Pamela W. Darling and Sherelyn Ogden, "From Problems Perceived to Programs in Practice: The Preservation of Library Resources in the U.S.A., 1956–1980." *Library Resources & Technical Services* 25:9–29 (Jan./Mar. 1981).
14. U.S. Department of Commerce, Bureau of the Census, *Statistical Abstracts of the United States, 1950* (Washington, D.C.: Govt. Print. Off., 1949), p. 124.
15. U.S. Department of Commerce, Bureau of the Census, *Statistical Abstracts of the United States, 1988* (Washington, D.C.: Govt. Print. Off., 1987), p. 146.
16. Richard De Gennaro, "Libraries and Networks in Transition: Problems and Prospects for the 1980's," *Library Journal* 106:1048 (May 15, 1981).

17. Richard J. Talbot, "College and University Libraries" in Julia Ehresmann, ed., *The Bowker Annual of Library and Book Trade Information*, 29th ed. (New York: Bowker, 1984), p. 76.
18. Bobinski, p. 340-41.
19. David W. Lewis, "Inventing the Electronic University," *College & Research Libraries* 49: 301 (July 1988).
20. Arthur M. McAnally, "Organization of College and University Libraries," *Library Trends* 1:22-23 (July 1952).
21. Robert A. Miller, "Centralization versus Decentralization," *ALA Bulletin* 33:75-79, 134-35 (Feb. 1939).
22. See, for example, Hugh C. Atkinson, "The Impact of New Technology on Library Organization," in Julia Ehresmann, ed., *The Bowker Annual of Library and Book Trade Information*, 29th ed. (New York: Bowker, 1984); and Charles R. Martell, Jr., *The Client Centered Academic Library: An Organizational Model* (Westport, Conn.: Greenwood, 1983).
23. Jerrold Orne and Jean O. Gosling, "Academic Library Buildings in 1976," *Library Journal* 101:2435 (Dec. 1, 1976).
24. Edna Ruth Hanley, *College and University Library Buildings* (Chicago: American Library Assn., 1939).
25. Ralph E. Ellsworth, *Planning Manual for Academic Library Buildings* (Metuchen, N.J.: Scarecrow, 1973), p. 17-18.
26. "College and University Library Statistics," *College & Research Libraries* 4:158 (Mar. 1943).
27. Edward G. Holley, "Organization and Administration of Urban University Libraries," *College & Research Libraries* 33:176 (May 1972).
28. Allen B. Veaner, "Librarians: The Next Generation," *Library Journal* 109:623-24 (Apr. 1984).
29. Miriam C. Maloy, "Faculty Status of College Librarians," *ALA Bulletin* 33:302 (Apr. 1939).
30. H. A. Sawtelle, "College Librarianship," *Library Journal* 3:162 (June 1978).
31. Association of College and Research Libraries, *Faculty Status for Academic Librarians: A History and Policy Statements* (Chicago: American Library Assn., 1975). The ACRL approved the joint statement in 1972 and the AAUP in 1973. The document initially had the backing of the Association of American Colleges, but the AAC declined to endorse the joint statement after having participated in its drafting.
32. John N. DePew, "The ACRL Standards for Faculty Status: Panacea or Placebo," *College & Research Libraries* 44:407-13 (Nov. 1983).
33. Anita R. Schiller, *Characteristics of Professional Personnel in College and University Libraries* (Urbana: Univ. of Illinois, Library Research Center, 1968), p. 12.
34. American Library Association, Office for Library Personnel Resources, *Academic and Public Librarians: Data by Race, Ethnicity, and Sex* (Chicago: American Library Assn., 1986), p. 3.
35. Schiller, p. 45-46.
36. "Classified Advertising," *Library Journal* 84:2098 (June 15, 1959).
37. Anita M. Hostetter, "A Library School for Negroes," *ALA Bulletin* 33:246 (Apr. 1939).

38. American Library Association, Office for Library Personnel Resources, *Academic and Public Librarians*, p. 3.
39. Samuel Rothstein, *The Development of Reference Services through Academic Traditions, Public Library Practice and Special Librarianship*, ACRL Monograph no. 14, (Chicago: Assn. of College and Reference Librarians, June 1955).
40. C. Lee Jones, "Library Patrons in an Age of Discontinuity: Artifacts of Technology," *Journal of Academic Librarianship* 10:152 (July 1984).
41. Michael O'Keefe, "What Ever Happened to the Crash of '80, '81, '82, '83, '84, '85?" *Change* 17:40-41 (May/June 1985).
42. National Enquiry into Scholarly Communication, *Scholarly Communication: The Report of the National Enquiry* (Baltimore: Johns Hopkins Univ. Pr., 1979), p. 159.
43. J. D. O'Connell and others, "Electronically Expanding the Citizen's World," *IEEE Spectrum* 6:30-39 (July 1969).
44. C. Lee Jones, "Academic Libraries and Computing: A Time for Change," *EDUCOM Bulletin* 20:9-12 (Spring 1985).
45. See, for example, Emily Miller Danton, ed., *The Library of Tomorrow: A Symposium* (Chicago: American Library Assn., 1939); Carter Davidson, "The Future of the College Library," *College & Research Libraries* 4:115-19 (Mar. 1943); Fremont Rider, "The Future of the Research Library", *College & Research Libraries* 5:301-8 (Sept. 1944).
46. John Naisbitt, *Megatrends: Ten New Directions Transforming Our Lives* (New York: Warner Bks., 1983), p. 41.
47. Bonner, p. 44.
48. Francis Dummer Fisher, "Higher Education Circa 2005: More Higher Learning but Less College," *Change* 19:45 (Jan./Feb. 1987).
49. Naisbitt, p. 39.
50. Manfred Kochen, "Technology and Communication in the Future," *Journal of the American Society for Information Science* 32:148 (Mar. 1981).
51. Allen B. Veaner, "1985 to 1995: The Next Decade in Academic Librarianship, Part I," *College & Research Libraries* 46:228 (May 1985).

STAGNANT BUDGETS: THEIR EFFECTS ON ACADEMIC LIBRARIES

Murray S. Martin

For many years, academic librarians worked in a fiscal environment of rapidly increasing budgets. Management of growth was the major problem. Today, though, most academic librarians face "steady-state"—or stagnant—budgets. This situation, more pronounced in recent years, has been with us for more than a decade, a fact most librarians and university administrators have been slow to recognize.[1] These budgets require new fiscal management techniques whose key words are cost containment, substitution, choice, and priorities.

While librarians are adjusting to these new realities, they must also face substantial changes in the information environment. They must not simply plan to buy fewer books and journals—an approach which, though fraught with problems, does not change the library's basic mission and its support structure. They must also cope with the introduction and maintenance of new technologies which expand and change both mission and structure.

Before considering these changes, we must explore the meaning of a steady-state budget. The phrase usually implies a budget with increases sufficient to cover the effects of inflation. It assumes that most parent institutions will provide enough money to cover increases in salary and the costs of supplies, books, and other materials. The result is a larger dollar amount, but unchanged purchasing power. Unfortunately, the institutional definition of inflation does not always match the reality.[2] The result is more likely to be a decline in purchasing power.

"Stagnant Budgets: Their Effects on Academic Libraries," by Murray S. Martin in *Bottom Line* Vol. 3, no. 3 (1989), pp. 10–16; reprinted with permission from Neal-Schuman Publishers, Inc.

Several variations in this type of budget can have an even more severe impact. The first is an actual budget freeze. This may or may not be accompanied by frozen salaries. If not, the budget will appear to increase, concealing an increasing divergence in the buying power of various segments of the budget.

The second is a selective freeze, usually the product of program budgeting. Portions of the budget hold steady, while others expand or contract. If this process is carried out in consultation with library management, the effects can be controlled. If not, the library has to implement changes after the fact, often disrupting programs.

Finally, the effect of any budget decision is determined by the size of the library budget, its distribution, its position within the spectrum of automation—beginning, partway along, or fully implemented—and its relation to the goals of the library and the parent institution.

In summary, steady-state includes a wide range of budgetary strategies —from one that allows for inflation to one that freezes a budget at the existing level. For this reason, I prefer the term *stagnant*, since there is no visible direction of flow from one state to another and stirring the pool seems simply to raise the detritus of the past to the surface.

Causes of Budget Problems

The present budget crisis in libraries arises from three basic causes. The first, about which libraries can do little, is the budget problems of higher education in general. A declining enrollment pool, rapidly increasing costs, and loss of revenue (either from state sources or from static tuition fees) combine to force institutional parsimony. As a major budget item, the library has to bear its share of the cutbacks—and sometimes more than its share, since the institution must maintain its academic programs to attract students.[3]

Price Increases
The other two causes relate directly to the library and its programs. First, 24%–33% of a library's budget goes for materials. Historically, the annual cost increase for materials has exceeded inflation, frequently by a very wide margin. Beginning in 1986, and accentuated by the decline in the value of the dollar, the prices for foreign and sci-tech periodicals have risen

rapidly—by an average of 15 percent a year. No university, no library budget has proved adaptable enough to meet such increases.[4]

Technological Changes

Second, changes in the nature of information exchange have increasingly forced libraries to turn to automation. But while automation has undoubtedly increased productivity and improved services, it has not proved the source of operating economies so confidently predicted by its early proponents.[5] Another external effect of automation is represented by CD-ROM or the database terminal. These new data retrieval mechanisms offer great benefits, but their costs have had to be borne by budgets constructed before their coming. Are they a type of library material? Are they automation? Are they equipment? Where do their costs come from? Should the user pay? All such questions are asked of budgets which did not include the existence of such services.[6]

Convergence of Forces for Change

Any one of these changes could be handled, but all three together have tilted the delicately balanced library mechanism. The results are as varied as the players. Some institutions, frightened by the prospect of massive subscription cancellations, have found emergency funds to enable them to hold on for another year. Some have accepted them as a fait accompli. Others have enforced alternate cuts or slow-downs. Few, however, have sought to address the underlying need—a clear definition of the institution's expectation of its library.[7] Without such a definition, mutually set and agreed upon, all other courses of action are palliative.

In order to reach such a definition, more knowledge of the interaction between budgets and programs is essential. While many libraries have begun such an investigation, the process is, inevitably, slow. *The Economics of Academic Libraries*[8] sets out some basic facts, which have not changed greatly since 1973. The Fifth International Conference on Academic and Research Libraries[9] discussed many of these concerns in detail, and several of the papers subsequently published presented a first groping towards solutions.

Studies of costs abound, particularly in discrete areas such as interlibrary loan,[10] but general studies of budgetary theory are lacking. ACRL has sponsored a research project to develop performance measures, building on the work of Paul Kantor and others. In time, these efforts will help both institution and library to develop realistic goals and the budgetary strategies to support them. In the meantime, though, the need is to handle wisely a very different budget problem—how to make do with less.

Library Materials

What is the current situation? The first and most obvious problem is the massive realignment of expenditures on library materials. Whereas libraries have, for years, aimed at a distribution that would hold periodical subscriptions at about 50%–60% of the total, the increases of the past few years have driven that total well over 60 percent. When standing orders and binding are taken into account, the committed portion of the library materials budget for most academic libraries now exceeds 70 percent. The result has been a severe reduction in book purchases.[11]

To mitigate the effects of budget shifts, many libraries have undertaken cancellation projects. Though essential for fiscal survival, these projects have had little effect. The underlying reasons are simple: there is generally little fat to remove. And there is likely to be even less fat to cut in smaller libraries, whose already low level of funding makes them even more vulnerable to price increases. Moreover, essential subscriptions are those most likely to be subject to high price increases. The publishers' argument that both the quality and quantity of the contents have been improved does nothing to reduce the cost.

Inspection of any list of titles by discipline quickly reveals that a major cut (say, ten percent or more) would entail cancelling either all the less expensive titles or the key titles. Neither option accords with the library's goal of providing information to its users.

Cooperation

At this point the possible solution of cooperative or coordinated projects is usually raised. Such projects have never been truly fruitful in the past. The present crisis may improve their probability of success, but any major effort is likely to take years. Each library must first serve its own constituency and, in rare instances only, cooperative access may provide a major portion of that service. The real problems relate to the cost of *basic* periodicals. Not only are these often the most expensive, but their importance to scholars would prevent libraries from relying on interlibrary loan to provide them, even if there were no legal problems with copyright in doing so.[12] If cooperative projects can relate only to marginal or little-used titles, the resulting savings will also be marginal.

Cooperation of this kind also bears a cost: first, the cost of agreeing to maintain jointly-owned titles; second, the added staff cost of providing interlibrary loan or telefacsimile transmission. In a controlled setting, though, cooperative ventures can be useful.[13]

A more promising avenue is the coordinating of subject specialities. The earlier Farmington Plan addressed this topic, as does the current RLG collection development project. Such large-scale ventures have great governance problems, and their pay-off is delayed.[14] Less far-reaching goals, as with local consortia, may prove more beneficial, since contact is close and users are more likely to be able to go to the resources. These projects still carry with them the cost of meeting external user needs, which may involve special procedures or modified hours of opening.

The Library Materials Budget

The most serious repercussion of the serial price increases of the past few years is not the realignment of the library materials budget (which could, with adequate funding, be corrected over the next few years) but its effects on already-reduced book budgets. In the same way that population distribution diagrams can show the effects of wars and plagues, the purchasing records of libraries will show a severe thinning over the period. In the absence of increased, dedicated funding, the late 1980s are likely to be severely underrepresented in library collections. One-time shots in the arm cannot overcome such problems. Their effects will be felt not only by present but future scholars who attempt to retrieve the works of that period.

Electronic Information Resources

Proponents of the new automated technologies feel that they have an answer. They suggest that libraries rely on access through terminal or CD-ROM. The presentation closely parallels earlier claims for cost and space savings from using microform, which never met expectations. Even though the new media will eventually have a place in the range of library materials, that place remains unclear.[15] Dictionaries, encyclopedias, and other similar types of publications may find their home in CD-ROM. It will be easier to judge the future when the CD-ROM escapes from the prison format of one station, one terminal, one user, (i.e. an automated book).

There are two budgetary effects related to CD-ROM that must be taken into account: the initial capital expenditure and the ongoing maintenance costs. Setting up CD-ROM stations is not cheap, and the donors who earlier funded such experiments now tend to regard them not as innovative, but routine. More outside funding is likely to link them to Local Area Networks or to automated bibliographic systems.

Most installations are leased rather than purchased, which, in effect, simply adds the cost to existing subscriptions. Any lease or purchase must be funded from somewhere and so is largely in competition with other library materials—a situation it was intended to relieve—or with the purchase of other essential equipment. Once installed, the stations require maintenance (part of the lease agreement) and supplies of paper, along with staff time to supervise use, to provide catalog access, and to call the vendor or effect repairs.[16] The staff time required is considerable and competes with time needed for other services, a situation not unlike that caused by microforms.

While database searching and online delivery of materials do offer extensions of library capacity, they also require staff support, frequently one-on-one with the user. That kind of time is very expensive and stretches the reference staff across yet another mode of service.[17] If—as also appears likely, given the problem with the maintenance of existing subscriptions—these services tend to replace subscriptions, they pose further ethical dilemmas. There are costs involved with each search. Are they to be passed on to the user? If not, can the library budget absorb them? What if they also include royalty payments that would not be incurred by using interlibrary loan?

If, maintaining that these are alternative information costs caused by library policy, the library elects to pay them, the expenditure must be balanced by a decrease elsewhere in the budget. If not, the library ventures into a business style by charging for services. While some libraries are already doing this, there is no general model for such a transformation and it is in conflict with the institutional model. Typically, a student expects, in return for tuition, to take courses, use the library, etc., without paying extra fees.

Access technology is expected to expand and to become more attractive. The rapid growth of faculty and student work stations has decentralized activity to the level that individual initiative has replaced institutional strategy. Few institutions, if any, can determine what is being spent, and by whom, on these technologies. Nor can they, except in defiance of general educational goals, seek to limit their use. Libraries find themselves in a situation where any response is likely to cause budget or program problems, none of which is understood by the parent institution. These innovations thus become yet one more decision point, where libraries must choose between economic goods because the budget cannot sustain both.

These issues require a reconsideration both of the information-based world within which the library operates and of the library's institutional role. Different institutional solutions are likely, ranging from aligning all information services under the library to branching off yet one more element. None of these solutions will solve the cost and service problems involved; they will simply be transferred to another locus. For libraries, any competition for or division of funds will affect their ability to sustain traditional programs and, especially, to innovate.

Automation

The third major factor contributing to library budget problems is automation itself. Most academic libraries either use bibliographic utilities or have fully installed operating systems. The first adds to the operating budget an item whose cost structure is externally determined, a good example of the loss of internal control. The second bears not only operating costs, but substantial capital costs. Most of the capital cost has come from a combination of grants, redirected internal savings, institutional reserves, or loans.[18] As systems become more common, donors tend to move on to other fields, which means that libraries still looking to install systems will find funding more difficult to obtain. The extent of expenditure will, therefore, be determined by the institution's ability to raise money. In short, the library must compete with other institutional agencies for risk capital.

Operating costs, however, rest squarely within the institution. Early claims that automation would result in sufficient internal savings to make up for the added costs proved to be overstated. Libraries have had to seek budget increases, raise funds, or cut other services.

One cost element in particular has wide implications. Systems require new skills to operate and, while these may be found among existing staff, they require nurturing. Automation causes shifts in priorities and may well result in shifts of staff if no new personnel are available. This adds costs—first the cost of training (including time lost from regular tasks) and then the cost of rewarding new skills and duties.

New hardware and software entail maintenance costs and, eventually, capital costs for replacement. Universities have never practiced depreciation funding on an adequate scale, making deferred maintenance a major problem. Tinkering with automated systems is the equivalent of minor building repairs when total renovation is required. Libraries now face five- to seven-year cycles of system replacement. These considerations add yet another budget cycle to libraries that already operate in several budget worlds.

Costs and Benefits

While system costs are only too visible, system benefits are diffused and often intangible. We have not yet found a way to measure the benefits of better catalogs or quicker circulation. Demand for library services is elastic in some respects. For example, in the early days of automation, circulation is likely to increase due to the enhanced access and ease of use it offers. Similarly, the use of the catalog from distant stations may well increase.

As the novelty wears off, though, users tend to revert to earlier patterns. A good example is the reserve book system. While automation may make access and use easier, students are already reading as much as they are likely to read for their courses. Total time available has not changed; there are still only 24 hours in the day and many other things to do. If more books are borrowed, more time is needed to read them. Although distant use of the catalog reduces travel time, other demands have not slackened, and not all students will opt to spend the time gained in library-related pursuits. The statistics will not increase. Observers will then claim that library service is dropping off and that automation was a failure. The staff may know that the use made of the library is more efficient, but costly surveys are needed to validate such a claim.

Staff

In all these discussions, the needs of and for library staff have been key, but they are seldom drawn together into a coherent, budget-directed statement. The old 60:30:10 division (60 percent staff, 30 percent books, 10 percent other) has been changed by automation and warped by differential cost increases. It did testify that libraries are labor-intensive,[19] and it serves to remind budget officers that changes in the proportions will do violence to the programs offered. More work on the direct and indirect relationships between acquisition rates and staff (including shelving and circulation), on the best ratios of reference staff to user numbers, and on the effects of multiple service points will help to clarify budgets.

Some institutions have attempted to impose program budgets without allowing for their crossover effect on other areas of service. Nor do they take into account that library programs do not correspond with library organizations. There has also been little research on library budget theory. It is not surprising that administrators are unsympathetic to requests for staff, yet libraries face staff needs to meet continually changing needs and expanding services.[20]

Responses

While the problems are obvious, their solutions are not. The first and most important step towards a resolution is to engage the academic institution in the process. Frequently, it has, after all, been a part of the problem, taking the library for granted, paying little attention to the shifts that have changed the nature of the library. Librarians, for their part, have too often wanted to be left alone. This lack of common understanding on goals and needs has led to budget stand-offs and, worse, scapegoating. The dialogue must include not only those who provide the financing, but those who use it—faculty and students—and the librarians.

One-time relief in the shape of year-end subsidies—the most common institutional response—only aggravates the longer-term problem. The second most common response has been to cut the budget across the board, leaving the details to the library administration. Both are an abdication of the institution's responsibility. But, in order to effect longer-term solutions which may take years to apply fully, it is vital to plan carefully and articulate needs and goals clearly. It is also critical that there be full institutional involvement in library development.

Limits to Growth

Clearly, the era of unchecked library growth is over. There was a time when, to meet increasing demands for resources and services, libraries incurred enormous capital and operating costs (e.g. new buildings). A key influence in changing this picture has been new technology. And the library of the future is likely to emerge as very different from today's. For one thing, the primacy of the stacks, with their thousands of unused books, is being challenged. Programs for the acquisition and retention of materials can no longer be seen as self-justifying. Instead, they must be linked much more clearly to academic objectives. And, importantly, institutions must recognize that shifts in academic programs have far-reaching library effects. They must also realize that changing direction is a slow and difficult process for a library.

Electronic Alternatives

In the future, alternative information sources will become more important and need to be seen as part of the collection management budget, along with the associated personnel and equipment costs.[21] In fact, together these items may account for as much as 70% of the library budget. This calls for administrative understanding as expenditures are realigned to reflect the provision of basic resources and services rather than the older line-item approach to budgeting, or even the more recent programmatic approach. The process involves the making of choices not only by the library but also by the parent institution. The latter must set academic priorities—a difficult process, but one that is essential to help the library apply its resources properly.

Cooperation

Cooperative collection development, which has received lip service for decades, must now be taken seriously. Such a path no longer means parcelling out library responsibilities by area or by title, but broader understanding about specializations, about access to resources and about sharing expertise. Like everything else, cooperation costs money and must be treated as a budget category. Not only are there membership fees, but transaction costs and the costs of maintaining group resources. There are also operating issues, since no library is able to cope with a widely extended clientele without added resources.

Interwoven with these concerns is the strand of automation, which can, over time, contribute to their resolution. We have all seen how the bibliographic utilities facilitated, and therefore increased, interlibrary loan. In doing so, they imposed a lateral, or horizontal, pattern over a previously hierarchical, or vertical, one. Some larger libraries imposed fees to control traffic, while some smaller libraries assumed a greater share of the load. All of this resulted in changes in workload and, therefore, in staffing patterns.

With the many new networks and interconnected systems, the game is being played out again, at a lower level, through the use of shared circulation systems. In many such cases libraries are grappling seriously with the equalization of the burden, whether by carefully structured fees or systems of reimbursement for net lenders. The negotiations tend to be easier because the partners are closer and more similar to one another. Nevertheless, there will be long, sometimes acrimonious discussions before the new structures of fees and reimbursements are operating smoothly. There are also likely to be many more instances where libraries are paying other libraries for such services as the management of automated systems or specialized cataloging.

Administrators must be aware, however, that shared services cannot replace basic service at home, and that these costs, which may amount to 5%–10% of the total budget, are additional costs, not merely substitutes for old ones.

Offsite Storage

The same is true of offsite storage for less-used materials. The cost of housing library materials on campus has passed the limit of institutional budget support. Offsite locations are needed but must either be owned or rented; they will also result in added retrieval costs. In the long term they are justified by lower building maintenance costs on campus. In the short term they require capital investment. Now is the time to consider truly cooperative storage. The cost of having each library store separately much of the same material is prohibitive, yet the obsession with numbers, quite apart from legal limits on the disposition of materials, has prevented even existing cooperatives from considering the consolidation of collections. The time has come to reexamine this issue. Equally, libraries must face the fact that material that can be stored offsite indefinitely, without being needed, may well be a candidate for disposal.

New Budget Elements

The library budget itself is undergoing massive change. The proportion spent for operations is growing rapidly and will continue to grow.[22] Its present treatment as "Other" is entirely inadequate. The increases relate directly to program but in a diffuse manner. For example, libraries in the age of automation need more money for maintenance, telecommunications, and new supplies such as bar-code labels. Smaller savings in the acquisition of catalog cards or from discontinuing existing paper records help in maintaining budget stability but cannot offset all new costs. Basic library needs cannot be arbitrarily contained, any more than reference staff costs can be reduced by imposing limits on the number of questions asked.

Most library budgets barely cover essentials. There is an urgent need to communicate to budget officers and other administrators that the millions of dollars they believe can cover all eventualities are in fact predicated. Ninety-five percent of all operating costs are committed from the beginning of each year. Nearly 75% of the book budget will go for subscriptions, standing orders, and binding. And the only way to reduce the expenditure on staff is to reduce staff numbers. This is the setting that turned a 15% increase in serial prices into a disaster.

Personnel

Despite the many studies on staff needs, activities, and workloads, there is little agreement on the fundamental personnel structure needed by libraries. The statistical reports from ARL and ACRL show clearly how diverse staffing patterns are, even in libraries that are very similar in size and purpose. The more detailed staff allocations available from medical libraries show no greater similarities.

The better definition of professional, semiprofessional, and clerical tasks shows promise for understanding staffing patterns. To date, this has proved easier in the more readily definable areas of technical services. In public service areas, where tasks are less easily segregated, there is a much greater need for individual expertise. The application of technical models often backfires, as in the clericalization of interlibrary loan, where too much reliance has been placed on automated systems and too little allowance made for the complexities of bibliographic research.

Although libraries have begun to understand the complex shifts of skill required to exploit fully automated systems, human resources departments have been slow to respond by opening up classifications or evaluating new skills. These new needs require a complete reexamination of personnel structures, a slow process when the replacement or attributions of staff, rather than its addition, is the general rule. Libraries must reevaluate each position as it becomes vacant, seek to import new skills and to move positions to the areas of greatest need. Again, this can only be done in the context of a fully thought-out mission.

Goal Definition

Goals must be redefined if major changes are to be made. Despite librarians' all-too-frequent reluctance to reexamine existing programs, this can be a good starting point. If reducing costs is a primary goal, consolidation of service points offers one solution, but this must be supported by the user. Another is to reduce hours of service, but students and administrators generally resist this. The cost of keeping the library open is much greater than usually recognized. Reducing that cost may require the redesign of some library areas to control access, and will certainly inhibit continued use of multiple-access points. Redistributing staff hours at some service points may allow better use of existing staff, but is unlikely to contribute much to savings.

In the long run, the only way to achieve substantial savings is to reduce spending or to restrict services, activities that can only be done successfully with the help of the institution. Lowering sights is a painful process, and some things of value are likely to be lost. Lessons can be learned from past experiences—for example, the study carried out at Lehigh University, demonstrated that selling off a special collection could be counterproductive.[23]

Other lessons can also be learned. Libraries have too long been regarded as expensive overheads, divorced from the academic programs they serve. Recognition of the added value they produce is slow to come, largely because the direct relationship between library and learning is very difficult to demonstrate in budgetary terms.

Librarians will have to learn ways to demonstrate this fact, whether through use measures or by reference to actual use by professors and students. They will also need to show the value of the educational programs they conduct.[24] These are being recognized by accrediting teams and others concerned with institutional outcomes, notably in seeking answers to questions about how well students are being prepared for their post-educational experience.[25] Libraries will have to rely on program evaluation using objective measures, not on subjective experiences.

Income

Most libraries have some small income. The most common sources are fines, book replacement costs, fees for searching or interlibrary loan photocopy. Although the library community has been debating "fee or free" for many years, a coherent philosophy has been slow to emerge. While it seems reasonable that the user should pay for any services beyond the general level, such a stand has serious educational implications. If the goal is simply to provide money to carry out services which the general budget cannot support, then those services—essential though they may be—will be limited to those who can pay.

The more profitable line to pursue seems to be the concept of charging for substitutional services, i.e. those already available in some other format. A good example would be payment for a list of acquisitions, since the information is already available in the catalog. This rationale has enabled libraries to develop fee schedules for database searching, usually with differential fees for outside users. Other services can be investigated similarly to determine when or whether charges can be levied.

Always, however, libraries must be wary of simply seeking income. If, for example, serial subscriptions are discontinued, charges for database searches, interlibrary loan, or purchase on demand are a kind of double tax on the user. Nor should charges simply be nuisance fees. If the service is offered on a business basis, then the full cost should be recovered. Half solutions contain the seeds of their own failure.

As a corollary, institutions must be willing to recognize the costs that go into producing the income. In many instances, the institution simply asks for a calculation of the likely income and then allows for it in setting up the budget. While the procedure may be justified from an accounting point of view, programmatically it makes no sense. It is impossible to balance income and expense unless the items in question are separately budgeted. For all such activities the library should maintain separate accounts and be prepared to defend them on a business basis.

Libraries should, however, be wary of venturing into real business endeavors. Unless there is a sufficient expert or resource base for the service offered, it will not be profitable. Marketing is also necessary, but seldom adequately supported. The total cost of offering fee-based services to the community is high and cannot be subsidized from the regular budget.

Fund-raising

Libraries are now much more active fund-raisers than in the past,[26] not simply for annual gifts or for special purchases of materials, but for projects, buildings, operating expenses, and endowments. This trend can be expected to intensify, but firm commitment is needed from the institution. Too often the institution simply seeks money for building and books, neglecting the essential infrastructure of people and operating costs. New fund-raising campaigns will have to tie these library needs into other approaches to donors. Institutions will also have to forego the practice of reducing the regular budget by the amount of money raised if such endeavors are to attain their stated purpose: the improvement of the library.

Again, there are costs—especially in staff time—associated with raising funds. Few libraries are in a position to allow much time for such endeavors. One way to gain more time is to recognize fund-raising as a legitimate library activity and incorporate it within the budget by allowing for mailing, functions, etc. How this is done will vary with the institutional setting. What is essential is that the library have real power in determining fund-raising directions. Libraries should also set regular goals for smaller grants and gifts. For example, a simple first step would be to aim for gifts and grants equivalent to 1% of the library budget. With experience, that goal could be increased. As is done in some academic departments, the number of faculty can even be determined by the level of success in fund-raising.

One of the goals frequently overlooked by libraries is that of replacement funds. A few thousand dollars for a small project that pays part of a salary, while it will not increase the staff time available, frees up some funds for other uses, perhaps even a student scholarship, which can, in turn, lead to other funding support. This snowball effect is very important.

Stagnant budgets, far from simply preserving the status quo, have caused major turmoil. They are non-answers to the problem of providing information. The provision of adequate library service in a time of inadequate budgetary resources and poorly defined goals requires a complete reexamination of the library/university relationship. This process is inhibited by lack of knowledge, both of the real needs of libraries and of the real needs of scholarship. Until these issues are attacked directly, libraries will be asked to do more with less, even though more is already expected of them.

References

1. Richard De Gennaro, "Austerity, Technology, and Resource Sharing: Research Libraries Face the Future," *Library Journal* 100 (1975): 917–23.
2. John F. Harvey and Peter Spyers-Duran, "The Effect of Inflation on Academic Libraries," *Austerity Management in Academic Libraries*, John F. Harvey and Peter Spyers-Duran, Editors (Metuchen, N.J.: Scarecrow Press 1984): 1–42.
3. F. G. Stanbrook, "Changing Climate of Opinion about University Libraries," *Canadian Library Journal* 40:5 (1983): 273–76 and Daniel Sullivan, "Libraries and Liberal Arts Colleges: Tough Times in the Eighties," *College and Research Libraries* 43:2 (1982): 119–23.
4. Richard M. Dougherty, "Are Libraries Hostage to Rising Serial Prices?" *Bottom Line* 2:4 (1988): 25–7.
5. Herman H. Fussler, *Research Libraries and Technology* (Chicago: University of Chicago Press, 1973): 1. Also Michael Gorman, "On Doing Away with Technical Services Departments," *American Libraries* 10 (1979): 436–437.
6. Ann Bristow Beltran, "Funding Computer-Assisted Reference in Academic Research Libraries," *Journal of Academic Librarianship* 13:1 (1987): 4–7, poses these questions in response to earlier articles advocating and opposing funding such services from the materials budget. The discussion has scarcely begun, and so far no consensus has been reached.
7. Dennis P. Carrigan, "The Political Economy of the Academic Library," *College and Research Libraries* 49:(4) (1988): 325–31. See also the numerous references in the revised University Library Standards approved by ACRL in 1989.
8. William J. Baumol and Matityahu Marcus. *Economics of Academic Libraries* (Washington, D.C.: American Council on Education, 1973). In fact, these patterns have been in existence for much longer, and may be seen as persisting. An earlier study commissioned by the National Advisory Commission on Libraries. *Libraries at Large*, Douglas M. Knight

and E. Sheply Nourse, Editors (New York: R. R. Bowker, 1969) especially Chapter 5, sets out the same concerns.
9. The theme of the Conference, held at Boulder, Colo., February 28—March 1, 1984, was "Contemporary issues in Academic and Research Libraries." The papers were published under the title *Financing Information Services*, Peter Spyers-Duran and Thomas W. Mann Jr., Editors (Westport, Conn.: Greenwood, 1985).
10. J. E. Herstand, "Interlibrary Loan Cost Study and Comparison," *RQ* 20 (Spring 1981): 249-56.
11. Robert L. Houbeck, Jr., "If Present Trends Continue: Responding to Journal Price Increases" *Journal of Academic Librarianship* 13:4 (1987): 214-20, and "Paying the Piper: ARL Libraries Respond to Skyrocketing Subscription Prices" *Journal of Academic Librarianship* 14:1 (1988): 4-9.
12. Noelene P. Martin, "Interlibrary Loan and Resource Sharing: New Approaches" *Financial Planning for Libraries*. Murray S. Martin, Editor (New York: Haworth Press, 1983): 99-108.
13. Eva Martin Sartori, "Regional Collection Development of Serials" *Collection Management* 11:1/2 (1989): 69-76.
14. David Henige, "Epistemological Dead End and Ergonomic Disaster? The North American Collections Inventory Project" *Journal of Academic Librarianship* 14:4 (1987): 209-13.
15. Michael K. Buckland, "Library Materials: Paper, Microform, Databases" *College and Research Libraries* 49:2 (1988): 117-22.
16. Brian Aveny, "Electronic Publishing and Library Technical Services" *Library Resources and Technical Services* 28:1 (1984): 68-75; Brownrigg, Edwin and others, "Technical Services in the Age of Electronic Publishing" *Library Resources and Technical Services* 28:1: 59-67; Meredith Butler, "Electronic Publishing and its Impact on Libraries: A Literature Review" *Library Resources and Technical Services* 28:1: 41-58; Gordon B. Neavil, "Electronic Publishing, Libraries and the Survival of Information" 28:1 (1984): 76-89.
17. Jane P. Kleiner, "The Configuration of References in an Electronic Environment" *College and Research Libraries* 48(4): 302-13, 1987.
18. Murray S. Martin, "Financing Library Automation" *Bottom Line* (Charter Issue 1986): 11-16.
19. William J. Baumol and S. A. Blackman, "Electronics, the Cost Disease, and the Operation of Libraries" *Journal of the American Society for Information Science* 34 (1983): 181-191. In this paper the authors stress that libraries are not only labor-intensive, but also labor inflexible, that is they have only limited ways of redirecting employee activities because they are dependent on human abilities which cannot be replaced by machines.
20. Barbara B. Moran, *Academic Libraries: The Changing Knowledge Centers of Colleges and Universities* (Washington, D.C.: Association for the Study of Higher Education, 1984). Also Paul Metz, "The Role of the Academic Library Director" *Journal of Academic Librarianship* 5 (1978): 148-52; "College and University Libraries" *The Bowker Annual of Library and Book Trade Information*, 29th ed. Julia Ehresmann, Editor (New York: R. R. Bowker, 1984): 80-81.
21. Murray S. Martin, "Financial Planning: New Needs, New Sources, New Styles" *Financing Information Services*: 91-108.
22. Moran, *op. cit.*, and Hugh F. Cline and Loraine T. Sinnott, *The Electronic Library* (Lexington, Mass.: Lexington Books, 1983): 172.

23. Rebecca R. Martin, "Special Collections: Strategies for Support in an Era of Limited Resources" *College and Research Libraries* 48:3 (1987): 241–46.
24. For example: Jan Horner and David Thornwall, "Online Searching and the University Researcher" *Journal of Academic Librarianship* 14:4 (1988): 225–30, and Sonia Bodi, "Critical Thinking and Bibliographic Instruction: The Relationship," *Journal of Academic Librarianship* (1988): 150–53.
25. Correspondence from the North Central Association of Colleges and Schools and the Middle States Association of Colleges and Schools to Kent Hendrickson, Chair of the ACRL University Library Standards Revision Committee underlined this point, laying stress on outcomes rather than inputs.
26. Barbara F. Fischler, "Library Fund-Raising in the United States: A Preliminary Report" *Library Administration and Management* 1:1 (1987): 31–4.

THE GROWTH OF THE PROFESSION

Leigh Estabrook

This article offers an account of the processes shaping the professionalization of college and research librarianship. It does not address the question of whether academic librarianship is or will become a profession. Nor does it offer a history of college and research librarianship. Instead, it examines the arenas in which academic librarians struggle—the academic community and the wider information society—and the ways in which librarians strive to shape that environment to achieve professional growth. The article presents an interpretation of the dynamics of growth of the profession of college and research librarianship within the framework of contemporary sociological research on professions.

Occupational groups do not become professions simply by deciding and asserting that they are so, nor by some naturally occurring set of events. Those occupations that are regarded as professions achieve that recognition as a result of ongoing struggles to achieve control over their work, to control the external markets in which their services are delivered, and to achieve social and political status. The medical profession provides painful illustrations of ways in which professional authority is fought for and maintained. Recent examples include lobbying and legislation regarding the rights of nurse-midwives and physicians' arguments with health maintenance organizations over autonomy in ordering medical procedures. The struggle for power is ongoing because the environment in which professionals practice changes constantly: new professional groups emerge, new technologies are invented, and the political environment shifts.

Similarly, the growth of college and research librarianship as a profes-

---

"The Growth of the Profession," by Leigh Estabrook in *College & Research Libraries* Vol. 50, no. 3 (May 1989), pp. 287–296; reprinted with permission from the American Library Association, copyright © 1989 by ALA.

sion has involved a complex process of actions taken by librarians, shifts in roles and relations of librarians to others in their academic communities, and actions and demands by external bodies. When librarians speak of growth, they are concerned less with the question of how many librarians practice than with the question of "to what effect." Growth is understood to encompass increased status, increased autonomy, and increased control within the workplace and within society. In other words, growth includes recognition by others of the value of the profession and the opportunity to practice in ways that professionals believe to be most appropriate.

THE SOCIOLOGICAL FRAMEWORK

Several recent sociological studies suggest ways of approaching the growth of professions and their struggle for control. Although these monographs give greatest attention to the medical and legal professions, their theoretical analysis provide important insights for the analysis of academic librarianship.

In his thoughtful study *Professions and Power*,[1] Terrence Johnson demonstrates the limits of those theories of professionalization that treat all occupational groups similarly and rank them according to the number of "professional traits" that they can claim or that they are in the process of obtaining. Johnson argues that professions vary widely according to the arenas in which they operate. He suggests that variations in power groupings within the profession, professional-client relationships, and the "levels of professionalization" of different occupational groups can only be explained by accounting "for variations in the institutional framework of professional practice."[2]

Eliot Freidson, who previously studied the ways in which physicians achieve autonomy and dominance, has recently turned to the examination of the relationship between knowledge and professional power. In his book, *Professional Powers: A Study of the Institutionalization of Formal Knowledge*, he distinguishes between a profession's formal body of knowledge, which is developed through basic research and taught within academic institutions, and the "working knowledge" that is employed by practitioners.[3] When professionals work in institutions, professional knowledge is transformed by the exigencies of the work environment. Professionals are influenced by administrative rules, the power of some clients, limited resources, and the like. Freidson says,

> My basic thesis is that the actual substance of the knowledge that is ultimately involved in influencing human activities is different from the formal knowledge that is asserted by academics and other authorities whose words are preserved in the documents that are so frequently relied on.[4]

Magali Larson's 1977 work, *The Rise of Professionalism*, has a significantly different thesis: "professionalism [is] . . . an attempt to translate one order of scarce resources—special knowledge and skills—into another—social and economic rewards."[5] The characteristics of professions, such as formal training, credentialing, professional association, codes of ethics, and work autonomy, are significant because they contribute to and legitimate an occupation's claim to higher social status, and thereby to its ability to gain control over markets for its services.

Building on these theories but consciously diverging from them, Andrew Abbott in *The System of Professions*[6] addresses the limits of the concept of "professionalization" as presented by Freidson and Larson. He argues that it is useless to look at any one occupational group in isolation: professional groups develop interdependently. Furthermore, one must examine the connection between a profession and its work ("jurisdiction" in Abbott's terms)—and not merely the structure of the profession—if one wishes to reach an understanding of the growth of a profession. In a series of case studies, including one on the information professions, Abbott offers an alternative theory:

> Each profession is bound to a set of tasks by ties of jurisdiction, the strengths and weaknesses of these ties being established in the process of actual professional work. Since none of these links is absolute or permanent, the professions make up an interacting system, an ecology. Professions compete within this system, and a profession's success reflects as much the situations of its competitors and the system structure as it does the profession's own efforts.[7]

In summary, these authors suggest that an understanding of the growth of college and research librarianship may be aided by examining (1) the external environment within which librarians practice; (2) working knowledge employed in practice; (3) strategies used to increase professional status; and (4) the jurisdictions within which college and research libraries operate.

THE EXTERNAL ENVIRONMENT

The pages of fifty years of *College & Research Libraries* provide a constant reflection of academic librarians' awareness of the environment within which they work. One could easily track the changing concerns of higher education by noting themes within the journal, e.g., the library's contribution to the war effort, the library's contribution to undergraduate education, and the library's contribution to the research community. Those issues of concern for the library range from changes within the higher education community to political and economic changes in society at large. The growth of the profession is not immune to any of these forces.

Arthur McAnally and Robert Downs called attention to many of the issues still critical to the internal academic community: information explosion, curricular demands generated by increasing interdisciplinary work, reductions in budget, and technological change.[8] These forces continue to challenge the profession; but they are now combined with rapid structural changes within the university driven by dramatic increases in capital and operating expenditures needed to support information technologies, research equipment, and personnel, and equally significant transformations in scholarly communication and information transfer facilitated by new technologies. Issues raised by McAnally and Downs remain for the profession but are compounded by these economic and technological forces.

Administrative Changes

The changing economic structure has led to closer administrative scrutiny of those facilities and services funded as unassessed overhead, e.g., the university library. In many institutions, units such as the publications office, the office of telecommunications, and even the development office now provide services only to those departments that can afford to purchase them. Departments that once provided free services to other units as a public good now charge for those services. At the same time, most academic institutions are increasingly aggressive in examining ways to reallocate resources, as well as in seeking external sources of revenue from such sources as alumni or corporate partners.

Libraries have experienced fully these economic and technological changes as they have coped with increasing costs of materials and technology. Capital investments displace personnel lines; cataloging networks displace much on-site original cataloging and the type of staff performing it. The impact on professional staff appears to be profound. Ruth Hafter's study of cataloging professionals, library assistants, and administrators led her to conclude that "increased reliance in networks creates a trend toward the deprofessionalization of cataloging. Control over the organization and scheduling of work is shown to be shifting from cataloging departments to administrators."[9] She also found that work is being restructured to allow a lower level of personnel to perform tasks previously assigned to professionals. A current study of this author supports these findings and suggests that similar patterns are evident in public services.[10]

The profession is changing not only in its internal structure, but also in its relationships to its institutional base and its clients. Within the university, deans and directors of libraries are subject to the same shift in role that is being experienced by other academic administrators. In addition to being scholars, they are expected to have external visibility; entrepreneurial skills; and the ability to deal effectively with constituents and to raise funds from grants, contracts, and gifts. Although these political skills are possessed by a number of professional librarians, other academic administrators do not always associate these talents with the library profession. Search committees for academic librarians point to the success and visibility of people like Vartan Gregorian and James Billington and more readily look to individuals outside librarianship to fill currently open dean- and directorships. Whether it is because individuals outside the profession are thought to appear more sophisticated when dealing with the rich and famous or whether librarians are not credited with being aggressive enough for the current academic arena, a battle about the importance of professional education for professional positions, thought to have been won several decades ago, has reemerged as the nature of the work has changed.

Shifting Client Relationships

The changing political and economic climate of higher education has obvious implications for librarian/client relations and consequently for the growth of the profession. So, too, does the changing technological environment in which universities carry out their work.

As libraries seek solutions to the problem of how to fund expensive information systems, new power relationships with external clients have developed. The capital investment in an online catalog and the labor costs incurred in adapting a library's records result in significant dependence on the performance of vendors. Poor systems cannot be junked with the ease with which one might have discarded poorly constructed wood catalog drawers. Moreover, computer systems adopted by libraries may need to be integrated with systems from other libraries, with a university accounting system, with the computing center's operations, or with other institutional or external technologies. When this occurs, the library's operations become increasingly bound up with the operations of campus and/or state systems. At the same time, professional staff develop a new form of dependency on vendors and the institution. Choices must be made that satisfy these external bodies. When differences of opinion occur, factors beyond professional judgment affect decisions.

The new information technologies employed by libraries are also changing professional relationships with users. Online public access catalogs and remote access to bibliographic and textual information distance the particular library from its local clientele. If the OPAC provides data for many libraries, the limitations of the local library's collection become less critical. When users gain access to information resources through remote systems, their relationships with library professionals and with the physical collection begin to change. These developments may enhance clients' regard for academic librarians if (1) users recognize the complexities of retrieving information from these new systems and (2) librarians' professional expertise is employed in systems development. It is equally likely that developments to increase the quality of end-user searching may reduce use (and therefore the perceived value) of the professional intermediary.

Freidson notes the importance of client control to the growth and status of a profession. Professionals who can determine the course of treatment, or even whether one should be treated at all, wield immense power. That power is consciously given over by the client; and as that is done, the client effectively recognizes the authority of the professional. It could be easily argued that new information technologies have given librarians more opportunity for control of their clients because new systems require greater expertise in design and implementation, but it is not necessarily evident to a user of such systems the extent to which librarians' expertise and control is affecting their use.

The Extra-University Environment

Academic libraries have always been affected by changes in the publishing industry, in the copyright law, and in the policies of the suppliers of such goods as library furniture. In recent years the economic and legal systems have assumed even greater importance in library operations due to the shifts in ways in which information is stored and retrieved. Government decisions about copyright, about telecommunications regulation and tariff rates, and about ways in which data will be collected and disseminated are having a significant impact on user services. Such decisions affect more than the cost of and means of access to certain materials. They are influencing the form of publication and even what government information is disseminated in a nonproprietary fashion. The professional voice in these decisions is muffled by the government's concern for profit over access. The level of professional control and influence over significant policy matters has been diminished.

Professionals also struggle in their relationship to the private sector, particularly with vendors from whom they purchase equipment. The mutual dependence of librarians and suppliers of books, materials, and supplies is long-standing; but the capital required for an automated system (and the ongoing expense of maintaining it) significantly changes the relationship between buyer and seller. First, the professional expertise of library staff only partially determines a final decision. University decisions about technology, demands from consortia with which the library cooperates, and the amount of money available for purchasing the system are among the factors that limit the professional decision. Second, when a vendor sells a system to a library, the relationship does not end. Installation, maintenance, system support, and development of enhancements are expected from the vendor. Third, one sale to one institution can represent several months' profit for a small systems developer. Alternatively, some library purchases that may represent a significant investment for the library may be trivial for the vendor.

In the current environment, the relationship between librarians and vendors is complex—sometimes hostile and sometimes collaborative.[11] The ability of professionals to articulate their needs and to exert professional control will be more a function of the money the library is able to spend than of the strength of the argument. Library professionals are weakened in their individual roles but achieve strength in community. As Susan Baerg Epstein notes, "The library community is unique in the degree of communication among its members. One library tells another library—everything. A vendor cannot work in this field without acknowledging and respecting this professional interaction."[12]

LEGITIMACY: WORKING KNOWLEDGE VS. PROFESSIONAL KNOWLEDGE

Within this institutional framework, academic librarians are challenged to maintain their intellectual claim for legitimacy as professionals. A recent book by Michael Winter[13] seeks to identify the characteristics of librarianship as a profession. Beginning with the assertion that "professionalization . . . is rooted in the much larger development of the growth of occupational expertise and the use of human service,"[14] the author defines that expertise by saying it is "the maintenance of culture through maintenance of access to knowledge records . . . that legitimates that authority of librarianship as an occupation."[15] Few would argue about the validity of this assertion. An understanding of collection, preservation, organization, and dissemination of information in the service of maintaining access to knowledge records [information] provides the knowledge base of the library profession. But the changes occurring from without the profession—and even on its behalf—raise questions about how professional expertise is employed.

Demands on the director for entrepreneurial skills place that individual in the service of the profession; but the expertise that she or he employs is rarely the expertise of the professional librarian. Freidson notes this phenomenon in all professions:

> Some administrative and managerial positions are mandated to members of professions and must be classified as professions. They are a function of professions' efforts to preserve their control by using their own members to mediate between practitioners and the surrounding social environment.[16]

Those librarians who do hold responsibility to employ professional knowledge in such positions as collection managers or original catalogers also are limited in how they use that knowledge. They are limited in their authority to allocate resources, and they are limited by the use of professional expertise from outside the library. Freidson makes a critical distinction about the nature of professional autonomy:

> Professional employees possess technical autonomy or the right to use discretion and judgment in the performance of their work. . . . Furthermore, within certain limits, they must be able to select the work they do and decide how to do it. The limits, however, are set by management's resource allocation decisions. In the former sense they are autonomous, possessing a distinctive measure of freedom and independence on the job that conventional workers lack. . . . In the latter sense, however, they are helpless and dependent because they have no control over the "economy" of the organization that employs them.[17]

To the extent that responsibility for obtaining resources and for allocating them is removed from those making professional decisions, the professional role is limited.

Within individual libraries the professional role is increasingly limited by what might be called the migration of expertise. Changes in cataloging practice provide the best example of this. The increasing proportion of cataloging done by professionals from other libraries may increase the level of expertise required by a few catalogers in any one library, but the important relationship to users has shifted. When cataloging was done in-house, there was the possibility of a strong connection between the professional and the user. Understanding of the needs of the user and the library's unique collection was part of professional expertise. Not only are there fewer of those professional experts in any one library now, but there is also the loss of that expert connection between user, collection, and professional knowledge about bibliographic control. The level of expertise required by any one cataloger may now be greater, but it is employed in a different context and there are recent suggestions that this migration is leading to a lowering of professional standards.[18]

Legitimacy of a profession is also dependent on the relationship between the academic institutions that educate professionals and the professionals who practice (and who may also conduct research). The academic knowledge system provides legitimation, research, and instruction as well as new treatments, diagnoses, and inferences for practitioners. In doing so it helps shape professional work and the territory in which the profession operates.

The critical issue for the growth, and even survival, of a profession is to maintain a strong connection between academic knowledge and knowledge in practice. When the academic work in which a profession is based becomes too distanced from the practitioners, it no longer serves the important legitimating function. (Some suggest that this is happening in the law.) When professionals in practice make decisions too far removed from the research base, their claim to professional status based on specialized knowledge can be challenged. (Some see evidence of this in contemporary psychotherapy.) As the conduct of academic library work is changed by environmental conditions and new technologies, so, too, is the work within schools of library and information science. The ability of the academic library research community and practitioners to maintain strong links with one another will affect the legitimacy of the profession in the future.

STATUS: STRATEGIES AND ENVIRONMENT

The relative status of librarianship has been an ongoing concern of its members. Status—that intangible measure of respect accorded by society to an individual or group—is valued not only for reasons of self-esteem. Many librarians recognize that higher status in our capitalist, status-conscious society is a reflection of and can be used to enhance economic and political power. However much one might wish to dismiss existing rankings of occupational status because of disagreement with the values inherent in them, it is impossible to disentangle the issue of status from the issue of the growth of the profession.

In our society the status of a profession is linked to the tasks it performs, the status of the institutions with which it is connected, and the status of the clients it serves. The tasks of college and research librarianship have become increasingly valued since World War II with the discovery of the value of information and the growth of research institutions.[19] More recently, recognition by major corporations of the value of managing information has helped raise the status of all those who can connect their work with information management. At the same time, academic librarians have not always been the beneficiaries of this new perspective. The unresolved debate about faculty status for librarians, driven in part by the persistent belief of many teaching/research faculty that librarians are not full faculty, remains.[20] As vendors push end-user searching and universities deliver information services through individual departments and the computer center, the relationship between the library and information delivery may be even less clear to library users. It is not sufficient for the tasks to be more valued; the tasks must also be associated with the particular profession. It is not surprising, therefore, that a major issue for academic librarians recently has been to assert the importance of the information intermediary and bibliographic instruction and more particularly, on some campuses, to work to be linked to the position of information "czar."

Within the profession at large, the differentiation of librarians by the type of institution in which they work has benefited college and research librarians due to the higher status accorded by society to academic institutions and faculty. Measures of perception of the relative status of types of library repeatedly rank academic librarianship above school and public librarianship. Service to higher-status clients is associated with higher professional status.

Academic librarians themselves have contributed to this process in various ways, such as (1) differentiating the higher-status institutions from others through development of the Association for Research Libraries; (2) differentiating college and research librarianship from other library professionals by holding separate ACRL meetings; and (3) seeking higher-status benefactors for the library through corporate partnerships, individual giving, and friends groups. While it would be inaccurate to say that the process of differentiation between types of librarians and types of libraries has been carried out for reasons of professional growth, it is nonetheless true that that process benefits certain segments of the college and research library profession.

While increased status may help librarians gain added resources for their institutions, the factors that relate to that increased status may work against the profession in other ways. For example, higher professional status is related to greater control over clients, but higher-status clients may be less likely to give over authority to professional experts. A librarian working at Harvard may have high status within the library profession but have relatively limited scope for professional work within an institution in which the users think they are the experts in information seeking. And just as librarians work to increase their status by relating their work to the information age, so too do other workers within the academic environment.

THE PROFESSION'S JURISDICTION

The growth of the profession must be related to the scope of its work and to the territory in which that work is carried out; yet this is not easily done. The structure and scope of work are changing and shifting among different professions. The territorial boundaries are becoming blurred, leading to increasing possibilities of border dispute. Questions about jurisdictions are raised within the profession itself, between units within the college or university in which librarians work, and even between the library and outside organizations.

Some of the changes in professional work have already been noted in the previous section on professional knowledge, but there are other aspects to these changes. Academic librarians readily admit that tasks previously performed by paraprofessionals are now being carried out by student workers. Professional jobs are being done by paraprofessionals and the nature of professional work is changing. Such changes raise questions about not only the knowledge base anchoring the profession but also the jurisdiction of professional workers.

Abbott notes that there is always overlay in tasks performed between categories of workers. Nurses may determine appropriate medication. Executives may type their own letters. Paralegals may do most of the research on a case. But to say that the phenomenon of overlapping job performance is common to all professions does not dismiss it as an issue for the growth of college and research librarianship. Prior to installation of computerized systems in libraries, there was relative clarity about what was and was not professional work. Cataloging and reference were, for example, clearly the domain of professionals. That is no longer true *for the profession as a whole*. My current research, for example, reveals significantly different institutional patterns about the work of professionals. In some academic libraries, reference is reserved solely for professionals. In others a decision has been made to staff reference with paraprofessionals.

Increasingly, libraries need to hire professional workers who are not librarians. These include systems analysts, development officers, and human resource managers: people with professional expertise vital to the library's growth but not necessarily related to the knowledge base of the profession. This situation raises different questions about professional domain.

Questions about jurisdiction within the wider educational community can be illustrated by asking questions such as, "Where will 1990 census materials reside and who will be the intermediary for users?" When academic librarians are asked this question, a variety of answers are offered. In some institutions the sociology department or statistical services unit will provide access to the data and assistance in interpretation. In some the computer services office will house the data, but other units, including the library, will be responsible for user assistance.

The variety of answers suggests several things. First, libraries do not have a well-recognized claim to providing access to all types of information regardless of form. And second, the ways in which new formats of information are handled are partially determined by institutional history and the relative strength of different campus units.

The academic library's role in providing access to new forms of information is also a function of power and politics. Those same economic forces within higher education that are changing the professional role of library director lead to competition among individual campus units for money, prestige, and visibility. When IBM promoted access to DIALOG to the University of Illinois' division of administrative computing, the computer services office, and the library, each unit demonstrated interest.

While libraries seek to provide coherent access to information regardless of form, computer centers seek new territory to compensate for the demise of mainframe computing and shifting patterns of use. The mergers of library and computing centers are seen as a logical way to address the problem of boundaries. Few organizations, however, have successfully carried out a merger. In fact, mergers raise new issues about the professional role of the librarian.[21]

Finally, intrauniversity questions about jurisdiction are compounded by the encroachment of information services from organizations outside the academic community. Faculty and students who subscribe directly to BRS or DIALOG or who are able to gain access to other academic libraries through an online catalog no longer have the same professional relationship to their home institution. It is not simply that library users seek out alternative suppliers. The publishers of *Chemical Abstracts* and other similar organizations aggressively seek out new markets and intentionally compete with professionals within the academic setting.

At present both competition and conflict characterize relationships between academic librarians and others who wish to deliver information services to members of the academic community. As new forms of information technology create openings for academic librarians, there are opportunities for significant professional growth. At the same time professionals in other academic units are exploiting ways in which information technologies can be used to enhance their own growth. Differences in the resolutions to these territorial disputes among institutions of higher education will depend on how they decide to structure relationships between potentially competing units.

Implications

This discussion suggests that growth of college and research librarianship is not entirely within the control of its members. Moreover, because adequate resources are critical for the delivery of high-quality library services and because the political and economic models that shape resource allocation within our society and within our institutions are capitalist models, the library profession is in a profoundly difficult position. To continue to grow as a profession necessitates continued, and probably increased, involvement in competition for status and territory. If librarians do not compete, other groups will look for ways they can increase their own status and territory through involvement in library and information services. Not to compete, or not consciously to seek growth, may lead to a profound loss of even basic library services.

The cost of growth may be high because it may mean casting off certain services, certain types of clients, certain standards of practice, and even certain of our colleagues. There are pressures to violate the ethical principles of equality of service that underlie the profession. If librarians become dependent on individuals and organizations with money to support services, there are incentives to skew services to those with greater resources. As noted above, the cost of increasing status may be separation from lower-status groups, even within the profession. The cost of increasing the academic library's market share may entail entering directly into competition with alternative providers.

Although these are possible consequences, it is important to recognize that the profession need not violate its fundamental principles as it strives for growth. Strategies of integrity adopted in the past continue to help the profession grow. These include the work of the Association of College and Research Libraries, the growth of other organizations such as ARL, and the formation of various user groups.

One of *College & Research Libraries* original goals was to promote professional growth. In the first editorial it was asserted that *C&RL* was established to provide a *professional* voice, which would "help to develop the ACRL into a strong and mature organization."[22] The journal provides, among other things, a means for consolidating the opinions of academic librarians, for building a knowledge base for the field, and for informing those outside of the scope and status of the profession.

College and research librarians also exert professional control through their involvement in the legislative process, although they have been criticized for not being as active as they should. Harold Shills notes that:

> Impressive though the overall growth in Legislative Day involvement may be, academic librarians still comprise only 7 percent of the total number of persons participating in 1987. Given ACRL's status as the largest division of ALA, the large number of national issues affecting academic libraries, and the high stakes involved in those issues, the level of Legislative Day participation by academic librarians has been undesirably low.[23]

The type of education provided professionals continues to be critical to professional growth. In 1958 Paul Wasserman espoused the value and importance of teaching library administration.[24] Today it could be argued that there is equal value in teaching administration of higher education, with an emphasis on such factors as environmental scanning, strategic planning, and marketing of services. The educational system also provides a critical gateway as it admits individuals to professional programs and socializes them into the expectations of the profession.

Abbott concludes his discussion of the information professions by asking about the current structure of professionalism for information workers, a category he construes broadly. He suggests,

> All the professions in the information area will follow the prior example of statistics, market research, and computing itself. They will end up as small, elite professions with intellectual jurisdictions over large areas. In these areas they will oversee commodified professional knowledge executed by paraprofessionals, serving the elite clients directly themselves.[25]

Such a conclusion seems premature. The growth of the profession depends on many factors beyond the control of its members, but that is true for all professions, not just college and research librarianship. The changes in the economic structure of colleges and universities and the revolution in information technologies clearly drive many broader changes that affect this profession, but the future is not scripted. The growth of the profession will also be shaped by members themselves, both individuals acting alone within their local institutions and, more importantly, individuals acting in concert as a profession to achieve the goal of providing effective access to information for all users.

References and Notes

1. Terrence Johnson, *Professions and Power* (London: Macmillan, 1972).
2. Ibid., p. 90.
3. Eliot Freidson, *Professional Powers: A Study of the Institutionalization of Formal Knowledge* (Chicago: Univ. of Chicago Pr., 1986).
4. Ibid., p. xi.
5. Magali Sarfatti Larson, *The Rise of Professionalism: A Sociological Analysis* (Berkeley, Calif.: Univ. of California Pr., 1977) p. xvii.
6. Andrew Abbott, *The System of Professions* (Chicago: Univ. of Chicago Pr., 1988).

7. Ibid., p. 33.
8. Arthur M. McAnally and Robert B. Downs, "The Changing Role of Directors of University Libraries," *College & Research Libraries*, 34, no. 2:103-25 (March 1973).
9. Ruth Hafter, *Academic Librarians and Cataloging Networks: Visibility, Quality Control, and Professional Status* (New York: Greenwood, 1986), p. 125.
10. Leigh Estabrook. "The Effect of Technology on the Library Labor Force" (forthcoming).
11. Ellen Hoffmann, "Library-Vendor Relations: An Era of New Challenges," *Canadian Library Journal* 44:89-92 (April 1987).
12. Susan Baerg Epstein, in "Automating Libraries: The Major Mistakes Vendors Are Likely to Make," *Library Hi Tech* 3, no. 2:107-13 (1985).
13. Michael F. Winter, *The Culture and Control of Expertise* (New York: Greenwood, 1988).
14. Ibid., p. 32-33.
15. Ibid., p. 77.
16. Freidson, p. 49.
17. Ibid., p. 155.
18. For evidence of this see Hafter and Estabrook.
19. Barbara E. Markuson, "Bibliographic Systems, 1945-76," in "American Library History: 1876-1976," *Library Trends* 25:1 (1976).
20. Patricia Knapp, "The College Librarian: Sociology of a Professional Specialization," *College & Research Libraries*, 16, no. 1:66-72 (Jan. 1955). It is striking how relevant Knapp's 1955 article remains today.
21. ACRL Task Force on Libraries and Computer Centers, "Libraries and Computer Centers" *College & Research Libraries News* 48, no. 8:443-47 (Sept. 1987).
22. "Introducing 'College & Research Libraries,'" *College & Research Libraries*, 1, no. 1:9 (Dec. 1939).
23. Harold B. Shill, "Influencing the Information Environment," *College & Research Libraries News*, 49, no. 1:19-21 (Jan. 1988).
24. Paul Wasserman, "Development of Administration in Library Service: Current Status and Future Prospects," *College & Research Libraries* 19, no. 4:283-94 (July 1958).
25. Abbott, p. 246.

PART II:
PUBLIC
LIBRARY ISSUES

THE GRAIL OF GOODNESS: THE EFFECTIVE PUBLIC LIBRARY

Thomas Childers & Nancy A. Van House

The "Goodness" question has been asked about all kinds of organizations, probably forever. Regarding organizations, the goodness question is implied in attempts to describe the benefits derived from organizations, to explain their impact, to restructure them, to count their accomplishments, and, on rare occasion, to disband them. Organizations are supposed to be good; libraries are supposed to be good.

Under the name of Organizational Effectiveness, "goodness" has been studied for decades. In the last 20 years or so, the studies have proliferated, especially in the nonprofit sector, fueled by a mix of social, economic, and political factors. Among those are a more competitive environment for service organizations; a scarcity of financial and other resources; the rise of strategic marketing and public relations in the nonprofit sector; and the increasing demand for accountability.

The Library's Quest

The library profession has joined the crusade. The pursuit of the Grail of Library Goodness[1] has resulted in thousands of publications and unpublished in-house reports, including studies of use and users, cost-benefit and cost-effectiveness analyses, reports of standard library statistics, works on measurable objectives and output measures, and myriad other writings, all aimed at describing the goodness of the library.

In the library realm, the most substantial effort addressing effectiveness has been in the area of public libraries. Within a 15-year period, the Public

Library Association officially abandoned nationwide standards for public libraries; produced two planning manuals oriented toward establishing local objectives (especially service objectives);[2] produced two editions of a manual for output measurement;[3] and seemed to achieve widespread acceptance of the two manuals.

In its concentration on *output* measures and *service* objectives, PLA seems to have assumed that the appropriate directions for public libraries and measures of its achievement (i.e., effectiveness) are related to organizational *outputs* (i.e., service capacity or consumption of services). While the manuals offer choice, that choice is confined to outputs. Moreover, the development of the output measures was done without an empirical base; there was no systematically laid foundation for choosing which measures to adopt. Nor is there a systematically laid foundation for selecting output measures over other kinds of measures to describe library effectiveness.

The emphasis on outputs has been beneficial. It has advanced public libraries in probably the toughest area of self-definition (setting service objectives) and measurement (attaching numbers to the service objectives). However, the search does not end there. Librarians need a firm basis for deciding how to measure their organizations' effectiveness and thus how to represent themselves to the world. Like the manager of any other organization, the librarian needs a better idea of what an effective organization (public library) is before deciding how to measure it.

What Defines Effectiveness?

The management field has broken new ground in the area of effectiveness in the past ten years. Riding largely on the work of Cameron,[4] the management literature now displays a more mature understanding of organizational effectiveness. First, the definition of effectiveness is accepted as *multidimensional*; that is, to describe an organization's effectiveness, one probably must do so in several ways, using several different aspects of the organization.

Second, there seems to be *no single all-purpose definition* of effectiveness that can be applied to all organizations: not all nonprofit organizations, not all libraries, not even all public libraries. Rather, each type of organization needs its own definition. Third, no single definition of or approach to organizational effectiveness is inherently *most valid*. Fourth, at least *four broad approaches* to (models of) effectiveness can be identified in recent management literature. Whereas the literature in the field seems to assume that a library's service outputs are the sole valid measure of effectiveness, that approach is only one of several possible.

- The *goal* model views effectiveness in terms of the organization's achievement of specific ends. It stresses outputs and productivity, such as consumption of services and proportion of usership. This is reflected in both *Output Measures for Public Libraries* and *Planning and Role Setting for Public Libraries*.
- The *process* model says that organizations do not exist solely to attain their goals. They are also social groups, seeking to survive and maintain their equilibrium. Thus, effectiveness is measured by internal processes and organizational health (for instance, internal communication and degree of turnover) as well as by goal attainment.
- The *open systems* model emphasizes the organization's need to secure resources from its environment. Relationships with external resources and their controllers—such as those with power in the budgetary process or the ability to pass a tax referendum—thus become the basis for judging effectiveness.
- The *multiple constituencies* model is concerned with the organization's constituent groups. It defines effectiveness as the degree to which the needs and expectations of strategic constituencies, such as certain user groups or leaders in the community, are met. It differs from the open systems model in that constituencies to be satisfied are not necessarily the power elite.

The models emphasize different aspects of the organization's effectiveness. They should be seen as overlapping rather than contradictory. Different approaches may be appropriate under different organizational circumstances. Different constituent groups of the same organization, and even different members of a constituent group, may adopt different approaches to evaluating an organization's effectiveness. For instance, a small stockholder may view Widgetcorp's effectiveness in terms of payment of short-term dividends, while a large stockholder may see it in terms of long-term market share.

The Public Library Effectiveness Study

In 1988-1989 the authors performed a national study to discover what comprises an effective public library.[5] The study was intended not to *assess* the effectiveness of libraries or to identify libraries that were effective, but to help *define* effectiveness for public libraries. The study was intended as a prototype for other types of libraries. From the management literature the study assumed that 1) there were multiple ways of viewing effectiveness, and 2) different people or "constituents" of an organization might see effectiveness in different ways.

On a long list of items—potential *indicators* of organizational effectiveness—people were asked to express how useful they considered each indicator to be in describing a public library to another person. The question was tantamount to asking them to identify the facets of the public library that are salient for them. The responses could be seen as tapping their views of the public library—that is, what criteria they use to judge a library's effectiveness. What about the public library is more important to them and what less?

The study was designed not only to identify what particular indicators are important to people, but also to disclose the *broad* views people are inclined to take of the public library.

Constituent Groups

Seven key constituent groups of public libraries were chosen in order to test the hypothesis that different groups would view the effectiveness of public libraries in different ways. The groups chosen were considered by the researchers and their advisors to be influential, directly or indirectly, in organization-level decisions.

1. *Library managers* at the highest level of the library
2. *Library service staff* who serve the public directly, in a professional capacity with or without formal professional status
3. *Trustees* of the library, elected or appointed
4. *Users* chosen as they come through the library's doors
5. *Friends* of the Library group members, or equivalent, currently active

6. *Local officials* from the library jurisdiction, with an official role related to the library, elected or appointed
7. *Community leaders* who have some influence, direct or indirect, on library decisions

Methodology

First, published and unpublished library literature was scoured for items that might indicate effectiveness. Then interviews were held with library staff, city officials, trustees, and users on the East and West coasts. Thus we identified 257 indicators related to the effectiveness of public libraries —such specific things as bookmobile service, speed of acquisitions, number of periodical titles, percentage of holdings intended for juveniles compared to juvenile percentage of population, interlibrary loan fill rate, reserve service, and capital expenditures. The 257 specific indicators were collapsed into 61 broader indicators, such as "Number of materials (items) owned by the library"; "Amount of total expenditures"; "Flexibility of the library, or ability to change" (see chart).

A random sample of public libraries was drawn, with proportional representation in all quadrants of the continental United States and in all size categories of libraries above 25,000 service population. Eighty-four libraries participated. Directors of those libraries were then asked to name individuals in the seven constituent categories.

The questionnaire was mailed to the 2,689 people named, asking:

> Imagine that you want to describe a public library's effectiveness to another [member of the same constituent group, such as trustee, library manager, etc.]. How important would it be for you to know each of the following about that library?

Each indicator was then rated independently on a scale of one to five, unimportant to important; and open-ended questions at the end asked them to add any that were not covered in the 61 listed. Confidence in the findings was bolstered by the response rate: 89.8 percent overall. Even the local officials and community leaders—constituents whom we were sure would be the most reluctant—replied at a better than 80 percent rate.

Indicators in Rank Order, by Constituent Group, Annotated

	COMMUNITY LEADERS	LOCAL OFFICIALS	FRIENDS	TRUSTEES
1.	Convenience of Hours*	Convenience of Hours*	Convenience of Hours*	Convenience of Hours*
2.	Range of Materials*	Range of Materials*	Range of Materials*	Staff Helpfulness*
3.	Range of Services*	Services Suited to Community*	Staff Helpfulness*	Services Suited to Community*
4.	Staff Helpfulness*	Range of Services*	Range of Services*	Range of Materials*
5.	Services Suited to Community*	Staff Helpfulness*	Services Suited to Community*	Range of Services*
6.	Materials Quality*	Materials Availability	Convenience of Location	Public Opinion
7.	Materials Availability	Convenience of Location	Materials Quality*	Managerial Competence
8.	Awareness of Service	Materials Quality*	Contribution to Community Well-being	Staff Morale
9.	Convenience of Location	Awareness of Services	Awareness of Services	Materials Quality*
10.	Free-ness of Services	Users' Evaluation	Materials Availability	Staff Quality
11.	Contribution to Community Well-being	Contribution to Community Well-being	Free-ness of Services	Users' Evaluation
12.	Users' Evaluation	Public Opinion	Staff Quality	Awareness of Services
13.	Speed of Service	Number of Visits	Building Easy to Identify	Contribution to Community Well-being
14.	Staff Quality	Managerial Competence	Public Opinion	Number of Visits
15.	Public Opinion	Speed of Services	Special Group Services	Convenience of Location
16.	Handicapped Access	Handicapped Access	Staff Morale	Circulation
17.	Parking	Free-ness of Services	Managerial Competence	Goal Achievement
18.	Managerial Competence	Staff Quality	Handicapped Access	Flexibility of Library
19.	Newness of Materials	Circulation	Support of Intellectual Freedom	Users per Capita
20.	Flexibility of Library	Special Group Services	Speed of Services	Materials Availability
21.	Number of Visits	Building Easy To Identify	Newness of Materials	Special Group Services
22.	Building Suitability	Parking	Flexibility of Library	Speed of Services
23.	Staff Suited to Community	Flexibility of Library	Parking	Support of Intellectual Freedom
24.	Building Easy to Identify	Newness of Materials	Interlibrary Cooperation	Free-ness of Services
25.	Special Group Services	Goal Achievement	Building Suitability	Amount of Planning and Evaluation
26.	Support of Intellectual Freedom	Staff Suited to Community	Users' Evaluations	Building Easy To Identify
27.	Interlibrary Cooperation	Staff Morale	Staff Suited to Community	Materials Expenditure
28.	Staff Morale	Building Suitability	Number of Visits	Staff Suited to Community
29.	Circulation	Interlibrary Cooperation	Staff Contact with Users	Handicapped Access
30.	Staff Contact with Users	Total Expenditures	Goal Achievement	Total Expenditures
31.	Users per Capita	Users per Capita	Circulation	Efficiency*
32.	Goal Achievement	Program Attendance	Building Appeal	Staff Contact with Users
33.	Building Appeal	Materials Owned	Efficiency*	Written Policies, etc
34.	Number of Materials Owned	Support of Intellectual Freedom	User Safety	Building Suitability
35.	Program Attendance	Efficiency*	Public Relations	Staff Expenditures
36.	Total Expenditures	Staff Contact with Users	Users per Capita	Inter-Library Cooperation
37.	Efficiency*	Amount of Planning and Evaluation	Amount of Planning and Evaluation	Public Relations
38.	Reference Fill Rate	Library Products	Materials Owned	Materials Owned
39.	Amount of Planning and Evaluation	Building Appeal	Other Collections	Parking
40.	Relations with Community Agencies	Materials Expenditure	Materials Expenditure	Newness of Materials
41.	Library Products	Safety of Users	Board Activeness	Staff Continuing Education
42.	Materials Expenditure	Reference Fill Rate	Voluntary Contributions	Safety of Users
43.	Info. about other Collections	Community Analysis	Relations with Community Agencies	Staff Size
44.	In Library Materials Use*	In Library Materials Use*	Program Attendance	Reference Fill Rate
45.	Community Analysis	Voluntary Contributions	Equipment Usage	Program Attendance
46.	Public Relations	Relations with Community Agencies	Total Expenditures	Community Analysis
47.	Equipment Usage	Inter-Library Loans	Inter-Library Loans	Equipment Usage
48.	Inter-Library Loan	Equipment Usage	Reference Fill Rate	Building Appeal
49.	Voluntary Contributions	Public Involvement in Library	In Library Materials Use*	In Library Materials Use*
50.	Safety of Users	Info. About Other Collections	Staff Continuing Education	Variety of Users
51.	Staff Continuing Education	Staff Size	Staff Size	Board Activeness
52.	Staff Size	Public Relations	Public Involvement in Library	Relations with Community Agencies
53.	Variety of Users	Staff Expenditure	Staff Expenditure	Voluntary Contributions
54.	Public Involvement in Library	Variety of Users	Library Products	Inter-Library Loans
55.	Staff Expenditure	Staff Continuing Education	Variety of Users	Info. About Other Collections
56.	Volume of Ref. Questions	Board Activeness	Community Analysis	Library Products
57.	Library Use Compared w/Other Services Events*	Volume of Ref. Questions	Written Policies, etc	Volume of Ref. Questions
58.	Board Activeness	Library Use Compared w/Other Services Events*	Volume of Ref. Questions	Public Involvement in Library
59.	Written Policies, etc	Written Policies, etc	Library Use Compared w/Other Services Events*	Library Use Compared w/Other Services Events*
60.	Materials Turnover*	Turnover of Materials*	Turnover of Materials*	Turnover of Materials*
61.	Energy Efficiency*	Energy Efficiency*	Energy Efficiency*	Energy Efficiency*

Note: Bold indicators are ranked in the same sextile by four or more constituent groups.
Bold and asterisked (*) indicators are ranked in the same sextile by all seven groups.

USERS	MANAGERS	SERVICE LIBRARIANS	
Convenience of Hours*	Convenience of Hours*	Staff Helpfulness*	1.
Range of Materials*	**Staff Helpfulness***	Range of Services*	2.
Range of Services*	Range of Materials*	Range of Materials*	3.
Staff Helpfulness*	Services Suited to Community*	Convenience of Hours*	4.
Materials Quality*	Range of Services*	Services Suited to Community*	5.
Convenience of Location	Circulation	Circulation	6.
Materials Availability	Public Opinion	Materials Quality*	7.
Free-ness of Services	**Materials Quality***	Staff Morale	8.
Services Suited to Community*	Number of Visits	Awareness of Services	9.
Newness of Materials	**Awareness of Services**	Staff Quality	10.
Parking	Convenience of Location	**Public Opinion**	11.
Speed of Services	**Staff Quality**	Number of Visits	12.
Interlibrary Cooperation	Users' Evaluation	Convenience of Location	13.
Handicapped Access	Users per Capita	Users' Evaluation	14.
Awareness of Services	Materials Availability	Materials Expenditures	15.
Staff Quality	Materials Expenditures	**Managerial Competence**	16.
Special Group Services	Staff Morale	Users per Capita	17.
Support of Intellectual Freedom	**Speed of Services**	Materials Availability	18.
Building Suitability	Building Easy to Identify	Materials Owned	19.
Staff Morale	Reference Fill Rate	**Contribution to Community Well-being**	20.
Building Easy To Identify	Contribution to Community Well-being	Reference Fill Rate	21.
Flexibility of Library	Total Expenditures	Support for Intellectual Freedom	22.
Staff Suited to Community	Managerial Competence	**Staff Contact with Users**	23.
Contribution to Community Well-being	**Flexibility of Library**	Building Easy To Identify	24.
Managerial Competence	New Materials	Flexibility of Library	25.
Staff Contact with Users	**Staff Contact with Users**	Staff Size	26.
Users' Evaluation	Support of Intellectual Freedom	Special Group Services	27.
User Safety	Materials Owned	Total Expenditures	28.
Building Appeal	Free-ness of Services	Speed of Services	29.
Info About Other Collections	**Staff Suited to Community**	Written Policies, etc.	30.
Efficiency*	Goal Achievement	Handicapped Access	31.
Library Products	Staff Size	Free-ness of Services	32.
Inter-Library Loans	Special Group Services	Goal Achievement	33.
Materials Owned	Building Suitability	Newness of Materials	34.
Reference Fill Rate	Written Policies, etc	Interlibrary Cooperation	35.
Goal Achievements	**Efficiency***	**Efficiency***	36.
Public Opinion	Volume of Ref. Questions	Staff Suited to Community	37.
Materials Expenditure	Parking	Public Relations	38.
Staff Continuing Education	Handicapped Access	**Amount of Planning and Evaluation**	39.
Amount of Planning and Evaluation	**Amount of Planning and Evaluation**	Building Stability	40.
Public Involvement in Library	Variety of Users	Volume of Ref. Questions	41.
In Library Materials Use*	Public Relations	Staff Expenditure	42.
Relations with Community Agencies	**In Library Materials Use***	Variety of Users	43.
Equipment Usage	Building Appeal	Program Attendance	44.
Circulation	Staff Expenditure	Parking	45.
Public Relations	**Program Attendance**	**Staff Continuing Education**	46.
Staff Size	Inter-Library Cooperation	Building Appeal	47.
Number of Visits	**Relations with Community Agencies**	**Relations with Community Agencies**	48.
Total Expenditures	**Staff Continuing Education**	**In Library Materials Use***	49.
Written Policies, etc.	Community Analysis	Board Activeness	50.
Voluntary Contributions	**Turnover of Materials***	Inter-Library Loan	51.
Staff Expenditure	Board Activeness	Equipment Usage	52.
Board Activeness	Inter-Library Loan	Safety of Users	53.
Users per Capita	Equipment Usage	Community Analysis	54.
Community Analyses	Safety of Users	Info. About Other Collections	55.
Variety of Users	**Public Involvement in Library**	**Turnover of Materials***	56.
Program Attendance	Info. About Other Collections	Library Products	57.
Number of Ref. Questions	Voluntary Contributions	**Public Involvement in Library**	58.
Library Use Compares w/Other Services Events*	**Library Use Compared w/Other Services Events***	Voluntary Contributions	59.
Energy Efficiency*	Library Products	**Library Use Compared w/Other Services Events***	60.
Turnover of Materials*	**Energy Efficiency***	**Energy Efficiency***	61.

The Most Important Indicators

Returns were tabulated separately for each constituent group, and the constituent groups were compared. Because of the varied nature of the seven constituent groups, each group was sampled in a different way. That is, different proportions of their total populations were studied (for instance, all four top-ranking library managers, but only six users drawn quasi-randomly from a very large number of users). Thus, the samples are too heterogeneous and their sizes too variable to tabulate all their data together.

All 61 indicators were found to have some importance in describing a library's effectiveness. Specifically, of the 427 scores (seven constituent groups x 61 indicators), 97 percent were above the midpoint on the one-to-five scale.

Six indicators scored in the top nine for all constituent groups. 1. Convenience of Hours; 2. Range of Materials; 3. Staff Helpfulness; 4. Range of Services; 5. Services Suited to the Community; and 6. Materials Quality. All six can be interpreted as client-centered and service-centered. They deal with the nature and quality of service offerings and client access to services. Internal processes (such as management activities) or institutional inputs (such as expenditures or the number of staff) do not figure in the high-scoring six. Note that two of the top six are related to materials.

Three indicators scored in the bottom 11 for all groups. They can be considered "universally" the least important of the 61 for describing a public library: 1. Library Use Compared with Use of Other Community Services/Events; 2. Turnover of Materials; and 3. Energy Efficiency. An additional five indicators were scored in the bottom 11 by four, five, or six constituent groups. They are widely, although not universally, considered least important: 1. Variety of Users; 2. Public Involvement in Library; 3. Staff Expenditures; 4. Volume of Reference Questions; and 5. Board Activeness. Remember that, while relatively low, the scores of these indicators rarely fell below the midpoint on the scale, indicating that they were considered "important to know" to some degree. This is not surprising, since almost all of the indicators on the questionnaire had been drawn from literature that asserted their importance.

Turnover of Materials is equivalent to "turnover rate," a measure of collection viability included in *Output Measures*. Surprisingly, both librarian groups—managers and service librarians—relegated this to their bottom 11 indicators.

Like the highest-ranking indicators, the lowest-ranking include concern with services and clients: Volume of Reference Questions, Public Involvement in Library, Variety of Users, Library Use Compared . . ., and Materials Turnover. However, in contrast to the highest-ranking set, the lowest-ranking set also includes indicators focused on the running of the institution: Energy Efficiency, Staff Expenditures, and Board Activeness. To some extent, Materials Turnover and Public Involvement in Library can be considered institution-oriented.

Indicators that scored between the top and bottom sets also contrast with the top set in including institution-oriented concerns: management matters (such as Managerial Competence, Goal Achievement, Efficiency and Flexibility of Library); and external nonclient relations (Relations with Community Agencies, Public Opinion, and Contribution to Community Well-being). With these, the bottom and middle ranges include a large number of service and client-centered indicators.

It is natural to ask if there is a relationship between the size of the library and the way constituents of that library ranked the indicators. One could suppose, for instance, that respondents from a larger library might put more emphasis on service to special groups or interlibrary loan; or that a smaller library might stress the helpfulness of staff. When analysis-of-variance tests were run, the answer was no. The size of their library did not seem to influence the importance they attached to the various indicators.

Across Constituent Groups

Another natural question is, "Do different types of constituents attach importance to different indicators?" Do constituents view the library differently? There are prima facie arguments on both sides of the question. On the "Yes" side, one can claim that different constituents play different roles vis-a-vis the public library. Therefore, they heed different things about a public library. For example, a library director might be concerned with internal efficiency and fiscal and personnel resources; a library service professional, with materials and service provision; a city official and library trustee, with the way a library fits the community and overall quality of library management; and so on. The argument is not that a group would be *un*concerned with any of the indicators in the study, but that each group would *emphasize* certain indicators over the others.

On the "No" side is the argument that there is a pervasive idea of what a public library is—at least for the United States—and that that idea will dictate the responses of all constituent groups. Their scores for indicators would be more alike than unlike. For the first time, this study explored the differences in perception of the public library on a national level by various groups of people. Whether differences or samenesses were found, the results could be important. The study revealed that groups are remarkably similar, as the table shows. The six indicators that scored in the top nine did so for *each* separate constituent group. Moreover, Convenience of Hours scored highest for *all* constituents except the Library Service Staff, for whom it was fourth.

Three more indicators—Materials Availability, Awareness of Services, and Convenience of Building Location—were scored in the top ten by at least four constituent groups. Put another way, four or more constituent groups agreed on *nine* of the *ten* most important indicators. Four or more groups agreed on eight of the ten least important indicators. The picture is clearly one of more similarity than dissimilarity.

A Broad Definition of Library

For decades the profession has tried to conceptualize the public library in various ways, employing objectives, output measures, role statements, standard statistics, etc. There have been virtually no attempts to define the library empirically. The data of this study were used to ask, "What view is useful in defining the library, in order to measure it, set its objectives, or evaluate it?"

People's preferences on indicators were used to identify *dimensions* of effectiveness. The dimensions are groups of indicators. The indicators in each dimension are pointing to a common element, which the researchers try to characterize in the name of the dimension. By performing factor analysis of the study data, we identified indicators that were grouped by the respondents, tending to get similar "importance" score from a given respondent.

Using the data for all constituent groups, the following dimensions were developed. Below each dimension are listed the indicators most influential in forming that dimension, statistically. The indicators that scored among the top six by all constituent groups, as discussed above, are indicated by an asterisk.

Dimension 1: Outputs and Inputs; 16 indicators
  Users per Capita
  Number of Visits to Library
  Reference Volume
  Circulation
  Variety of Users
  Materials Turnover
  Materials Expenditure
  Total Expenditures
  Program Attendance
  In-library Use
  Materials Owned
  Staff Size
  Reference Fill Rate
  Staff Expenditures
  Equipment Usage
  Use of Library Compared to Other Services/Events
Dimension 2: Internal Processes; 9 indicators
  Managerial Competence
  Staff Morale
  Staff Quality
  Efficiency of Library Operations
  Written Policies
  Goal Achievement
  Staff Helpfulness*
  Safety of Users
  Support of Intellectual Freedom
Dimension 3: Community Fit; 11 indicators
  Community Awareness of Offerings
  Users' Evaluation

Contribution to Community Well-being
Services Suited to the Community*
Public Opinion
Flexibility of Library Management
Relations with Community Agencies
Community Analysis
Staff Suitability to Community
Public Relations
Staff Contact with Users

Dimension 4: Access to Materials; 6 indicators
Information About Other Collections
Interlibrary Loan
Cooperation with Other Libraries
Speed of Service
Materials Availability
Extent Services Are Free

Dimension 5: Physical Facilities; 5 indicators
Building Appeal
Convenience of Building Location
Building Easy To Identify
Parking
Building Suitability

Dimension 6: Management Elements; 7 indicators
Board Activeness
Voluntary Contributions (Gifts, Money, Time)
Library Products (Booklists, Guides, etc.)
Energy Efficiency of Building
Continuing Education for Staff
Planning and Evaluation
Public Involvement in Library Decisions

Decision 7: Service Offerings; 5 indicators
Range of Materials*
Range of Services*
Convenience of Hours*
Materials Quality*
Newness of Materials

Dimension 8: Service to Special Groups; 2 indicators
Handicapped Access
Special Group Services

By using the many individual responses, one can identify clusters of related indicators, revealing the broad underlying themes of a phenomenon such as library effectiveness. Success of the analysis lies in the coherence of elements in each dimension, and a good test of coherence is the nameability of the dimension.

For the most part, the elements make sense in their dimensions. Although the sixth, "Management Elements," contains a number of disparate indicators (Board Activeness, Energy Efficiency of the Building, and Voluntary Contributions) and thus forced a general name, the dimensions are relatively coherent. For all constituents, these are the major themes of public library effectiveness.

The View of the Public Library

The description of an organization's effectiveness—such as its price/earnings ratio, number of prescriptions dispensed, market share, or the grandeur of its main headquarters—is made from a particular vantage point. That description is equivalent to a *view* of the organization and to *what the speaker values* about it. This is the case for public libraries as well as for other types of organizations.

In the current study, the complex nature of effectiveness has been demonstrated in several ways. First, all 61 proposed indicators of effectiveness were seen as valid by all constituent groups. The indicators are wide-ranging, expressing or implying political, functional, social, economic, aesthetic, philosophical, and other considerations. Moreover, the indicators and the dimensions derived from them include not only service elements, but also aspects of management and internal operations, physical plant, and relations with the community.

Second, the dimensions reflect all four of the models of organizational effectiveness described at the beginning of this article. The goal view, the process view, the open systems view, and the multiple constituencies view are useful in evaluating the library and all four are embedded in one or another of the dimensions.

The "view" of a public library turns out to be not singular, but plural and complex: "views."

The views imply many areas of decision-making related to the public library organization and the information that may be useful to library constituents in making decisions about the library. For example, most of the indicators suggest one or more *measures* that could serve the decision-making process.

Although public librarianship has made substantial strides in developing measures, the job is far from complete. We have long known that existing measures must be fine-tuned and tested before their meaning is clear and their data reliable. But this study makes it clear that at a more elementary level, the field probably needs additional measures. To wit, none of the six indicators that were in the Top Ten category for all constituent groups is matched in practice by a clear and widely shared measure. While the field measures some things related to hours, materials, staff, etc., there is no measure for the indicators as they are stated in that list.

The Grail is not yet in our grasp. This study proposes challenges for the future: validate the dimensions and indicators further; rank the importance of the dimensions in the field; develop multiple measures for each dimension; and define the effectiveness of other types of libraries.

References

1. Buckland, Michael K. *Library Services in Theory and Context*. 2d ed. Pergamon, 1988, p. 241.
2. Palmour, Vernon E. & others. *A Planning Process for Public Libraries*. ALA, 1980; McClure, Charles R. & others. *Planning and Role Setting for Public Libraries*. ALA, 1987.
3. Zweizig, Douglas L. & Eleanor Jo Rodger. *Output Measures for Public Libraries*. ALA, 1982; Van House, Nancy A. & others. *Output Measures for Public Libraries*. ALA, 1987.
4. One of his most important works in this area is Cameron, Kim, "Domains of Organizational Effectiveness in Institutions of Higher Education," *Administrative Science Quarterly*, 1978, p. 25–47.
5. Sponsored by the U.S. Department of Education, Office of Educational Research and Improvement.

CAN WE SAVE THE PUBLIC'S LIBRARY?

Charles Robinson

I believe in public libraries and what they can do to contribute to our quality of life and to our democratic society. (I hate using phrases like that, because they make me sound like the Council of the American Library Association.)

Most of the world gets along just fine without public libraries and most people in this country rank them in their importance to quality of life above symphony orchestras and art museums and a long way below local theaters or bowling alleys.

Public libraries are pretty much an American phenomenon, and their development is almost completely restricted to Western countries like Australia, New Zealand, Canada, the United Kingdom, the Scandinavian countries and, somewhat spottily, on the continent.

Inherently Dangerous

Why is public library development restricted to the West? Obviously because public libraries are an inherently dangerous institution, or at least have the potential to be. That means they are inimical to the interests of government. Few governments, local, state, or national, are really comfortable with freedom of information. Public libraries, to the everlasting credit of librarians and trustees, are really dedicated to freedom of information about 38 percent of the time. That is enough to scare the daylights out of anyone involved in government.

Academic libraries are something else. There isn't a country in the world that doesn't have academic libraries. They all try to be the biggest, with the full support of their government, whether it is democratic, socialist, communist, fascist, or has some other kind of power over the people. This is because education is important to every government and to every economy, as long as the education you get is carefully controlled to serve the interests of the government—the government, not the individual. Government control is what you don't have, and shouldn't have, in a public library.

Educational, But Not Academic

In simple terms, the public library is an educational institution in the broadest possible meaning of that term, but it is *not* an academic institution. Trying to make it academic will endanger the existence of the public library. Academic libraries are absolutely necessary to support the curriculum of their institutions and to support the immense amount of research done there—but their primary function is to serve formal, class-oriented, pedagogically controlled courses of study.

School libraries are also academic libraries, although school librarians never describe themselves as "academic" since that term has been confined to institutions of higher education. Like the confusion between academic and public libraries in the minds of public library administrations, trustees, and the public, there is similar confusion regarding the roles and functions of public and school libraries.

Academic and school libraries have books, buildings, and librarians, just like public libraries. This leads to that massive confusion among trustees, librarians, appropriating authorities, and, sadly, among the people who use public libraries and who have the most to lose as they become more and more like academic libraries or, God help us, "research libraries."

This confusion is not new. Early in my career, as administrative assistant to the director of the Free Library of Philadelphia, Emerson Greenaway, I did a certain amount of speech writing. This necessitated a lot of reading about the history of libraries, and I have kept it up since. One of the most interesting and well-written books on the subject I have read recently is Wayne Wiegand's *The Politics of an Emerging Profession: The American Library Association 1876–1917* (Greenwood, 1986). The founders of ALA were concerned, with the words of the motto of ALA proposed by Melvil Dewey (and recently readopted): "The best reading for the largest number at the least cost." These founders included prominent public librarians from Chicago (William Poole), Boston (Justin Winsor), and Indianapolis (Charles Evans).

Their discussion at the first and later ALA conferences didn't seem to address directly the difference between the role and function of public libraries and that of academic libraries. Perhaps it really wasn't necessary at the time because the real growth of public libraries, supported by tax dollars, was yet to come. After all, all libraries had books, and to one degree or another, they were all interested in the "best reading" which was easily defined by a librarian from the "cultivated" classes.

Pathetic Attempts to Be All Things

As far as I can tell, since the founding of ALA in 1876, public librarians really never have faced the challenge of clearly defining the role of the public library as it differs from that of the academic library. That's not a problem for academic or school libraries. They know exactly what they are about. Public libraries don't, as evidenced by our pathetic attempts to be all things to all people—pathetic because our limited financial resources assure us of failure in any one area of service as a result of trying to be successful in all.

Joey Rodger, executive director of the Public Library Association, who has her own professional problems with being "all things to all people," has characterized the historically perceived responsibilities of public libraries as institutions designed "to save and to share" books. Pretty clear, pretty basic, and, in my view, pretty wrong. Saving books for future needs, needs which cannot in any way be clearly seen and clearly delineated, is the responsibility of academic libraries and, obviously, the Library of Congress, insofar as it serves as the national library.

Saving books is absolute poison to effective public library service. Yet many of us, trustees, librarians, and members of the public, see that warehouse function as a primary function of public libraries. They see it as a function of libraries of all types (with the possible exception of school libraries) and of all sizes. Perhaps this was not a problem in 1876, given the relative scarcity of books and funds in those days. It certainly is a problem now, as a larger and larger portion of public library funds goes to the care, housing, heating, and cooling of millions and millions of volumes which the public doesn't want now (at least in numbers which make their availability affordable), and may not have even wanted when they were published.

We not only save third-rate novels from the 1930s and radio repair books from the 1940s, but even in the present day we dilute our inadequate book funds by trumpeting our duty to be, in the immortal words of Marvin Scilken, "kennels for the publishers' dogs."

Practically no one has ever given any thought to differentiating between collection development for public libraries and that for academic libraries. That is collection development relating to the materials which the public wants, rather than those which librarians divine as "the best reading." That is the part of the ALA motto which has contributed the most confusion, confrontation, and sanctimonious prattle over the history of public libraries.

Guaranteed Alienation

After all, who's in charge of "collection development" in the American Library Association? The Library Administration and Management Division (LAMA) and the Association for Library Collections and Technical Services (ALCTS), that's who. (ALCTS used to be called the Resources and Technical Services Division or RTSD.)

LAMA and ALCTS are made up chiefly of academic librarians. When the collection development concepts and practices of these academics are adopted by public librarians they guarantee the alienation of their libraries from all but the college students in their communities, taking the load off the academic libraries. No fools, these academic librarians! No wonder they get paid more than public librarians. They ought to. They are serving their public. We are not.

The academic library building and most of the equipment in it is totally and absolutely inappropriate to a public library. Yet in many cases public libraries continue to replicate these buildings for general public use. I often run into architects who cite their experience with a library building —almost always it is an architect who has been infected by conversation with an academic librarian instead of a shopping center architect.

What about equipment? Libraries are full of shelving, and 98 percent of the public libraries have almost totally steel bracket shelving, which was designed for storage, not merchandising. Perfectly appropriate for the savers, which academic libraries are. Perfectly ridiculous for public libraries, whose responsibility is to get materials out of the building for people who are alive now, not to store them for future generations.

No bookstore interested in book distribution (for which read "sales") uses bracket shelving. Check out your local Waldenbooks.

Firing a Cannon at a Mouse

Now, let's talk about that most all-consuming subject, whether it consumes our time or our resources: automation.

Automation has, understandably and justifiably, affected almost everything we do in libraries except, of course, for the most important things—collection development, staffing, and general administration.

Where have libraries—public libraries—spent the most money for automation? Why, in all the same places as academic libraries: cataloging, interlibrary loan, and circulation control. Circulation control is certainly necessary in the high-use environment of public libraries, at least the larger ones.

Most other automation in public libraries has been like shooting a cannon at a mouse. Few people—only about 15 percent of all people using a public library—use the catalog at all, and I have never heard anyone, even a public service librarian, screaming for a full MARC entry. Just the opposite—all that stuff just confuses them. Without repeating all the reams of statistics and quotations used so effectively by Tom Ballard, few—very few, pitiably few—of our readers *ever* use interlibrary loan.

How many millions and millions of public library dollars, to say nothing of LSCA dollars spent by the states for the "benefit" of public libraries, have poured into the bulging coffers of OCLC, an organization founded by, run by academic librarians and benefiting academic libraries and those trying desperately to make public libraries become academic libraries? I wonder how the public library users would have fared during the past 20 years if all that money had been spent for collection development, adequate salaries for library administrators, and sending trustees to ALA conferences so that they could talk to other trustees.

Now we have enormous, full-MARC databases in which probably 30 percent of the location symbols point to missing books (purging databases is not considered anywhere near as exciting as building them). We have splendid bibliographic identification of books which arrive three weeks after the user has given up and lost interest. We pay for high incomes for the field engineers who fix the machines. We buy communication lines so we are looked upon with glee by the telephone companies.

Obviously, not all computers are evil—only some of the activities we force them into in the name of "serving the public." All sorts of specialized services and collections—I imagine even the Orientalia collection at Cleveland, the collection of original Dickens in parts at Philadelphia, and God knows what all in Boston and Chicago are all supported by tax funds in the name of "serving the public."

I wonder if the collections of books for preschool readers in the branches of those libraries are all sufficient to meet the demand? I hope so, because nobody serves the preschool child but us. This should be one of our highest priorities. These collections should be bought before practically anything else (except air conditioning).

I could go on and on illustrating the thesis that too many public libraries are run like academic libraries. If you think about it, you could too. Use this rule: If a policy, procedure, or activity is practiced by an academic library, it is probably bad for the public library user. You will probably be right 90 percent of the time.

Governed by the Elite

How did we get this way? If we understand that, what should we do about it? I read somewhere that a populist, one of several labels often applied to me, is neither conservative nor liberal but is anti-elitist. My picture of the public library is somewhat similar, but rather than anti-elitist, I would describe the proper posture of the public library as pro-nonelitist.

Boards and commissions, whether self-perpetuating or appointed, and particularly boards of cultural institutions rather than, say, liquor boards, are generally drawn from the ranks of the elite. "Elite" in this case may or may not refer to wealth, but certainly to education and some position in the community. Most public libraries are guided by the policies —and in some cases, actual administrative decisions—of these boards.

The larger the library, the more "elite" the board. In the largest libraries wealth and social position are almost prerequisites for gaining a seat on the board. Rarely does a library board represent a cross-section of the community. Interest in the public library as an institution is generally limited to those with a college education.

Board members, at least initially, don't know much about the library, and seldom are they clear about the public library's role in the community. This is not surprising since neither the profession nor the public is clear about it either. Thus, as good, responsive citizens, the board tries to make a library be all things to all people. This is a difficult, if not impossible, mandate, but it avoids having to say "no" to a friend at a cocktail party.

Most dangerous is the fact that a board member, probably a college graduate, is likely to have had the most experience with an academic rather than a public library. Without information to the contrary, the average board member will act on his or her perceptions of what a "library" should be doing, not specifically a public library which is tax supported to serve all the people, not just the 20 percent who are college graduates.

Much worse, however, is the library administrator, who should have developed a clear perception of the public library's role in the community —all of the community—but didn't do so. In defense of administrators, I have to say that several factors have prevented them from developing this clear philosophical perception concerning the role of the public library.

From the first days of public library service confusion has existed and most public library administrators follow the original ALA leadership, who, as Wiegand points out (p. 234) had "convinced themselves that they were helping to create 'arsenals of a democratic culture' ready to wage war against ignorance. But they did not realize that they were also self-appointed 'apostles of culture' who were members of a patronizing elite concerned over a perceived lack of domestic order caused by the pressures of pluralist society."

The public themselves, influenced by libraries, the American Library Association, and not least of all the media (all of whom can be described to some extent as representing the elitist element), have *believed* these self-appointed "apostles of culture," insofar as they think about public libraries at all.

Boards of trustees tend to retain library administrators who fulfill their views, however elite, however illogical, however academic in origin these views may be. Several years ago I was approached to apply for the directorship of a large, old, hidebound, eastern public library. Interested to see whether the board really intended to change their focus to that of an institution which would be truly the public's library, I agreed. Before the interview, I toured several branches and the massive central library. I saw pathetic basic collections in the branches and hordes of college students in the central library—a central library in a city with at least four academic institutions of the first rank. In my opening statement to the search committee I stated that I thought the library was giving the taxpayers of the city five cents of value for every dollar (and they were lots of city and state dollars) spent on the library.

The interview lasted another hour; my candidacy, and in my opinion the possibility of an exciting reform of that library, ended at that moment.

The larger the public library, the more likely it is to name an elitist board, a board likely to contribute by its actions toward the decline of the public's library, adding but another psuedo-academic library to their community. For good or ill, and even with the fervid justifications likely to be offered by well-meaning boards, examples of this tendency are increasing. Look at New York, Chicago, and St. Louis, all headed by recently hired directors whose experience is from the academic field.

The Fundraising Mirage

Another recent development to affect library boards and administrators across the country has been the phenomenon ALA's Art Plotnik called the "Vartanization" of public libraries. This new dance, done to the tune of a Gregorian chant, is fundraising from the private sector.

Now that we are finally getting governments to recognize that support of public libraries is a basic responsibility, the notion that fundraising from the private sector is a proper solution to funding problems is a mirage rather than a reality. However, the process is infinitely attractive to the many library board members and is a case of elitism run rampant.

In a society where wealth is often seen as the measure of a man or woman, board members and administrators—especially the kind of administrator these boards tend to hire—now get a chance to mix with the rich, who often prefer to give to a glamorous cultural institution at chic parties. Public libraries, unlike some academic libraries, shouldn't have to be glamorous—they should be effective service agencies well-supported by the public. Good support depends upon board members and directors with demonstrated skills in the political process. Increasingly in modern government, they should have the management skills to run a responsive public agency.

Subverting the Mission

It is in collection development that we find the most insidious, long-term effect of academic thinking on the public library, draining us of the ability to be really responsive to our readers. Academic institutions are supported because they teach the young what we think they ought to know—oft defined by the indefinable term "social value." Let me quote from the March 9, 1989 Board minutes of a prominent large public library, discussing the videocassette collection:

> The director began his presentation by stating feature films are used primarily for entertainment. He feels that the library is not justified to spend tax money strictly for entertainment. Entertainment is something people should pay for without government subsidy. Only if there is a concurrent social value should tax money be used to subsidize it. He said that the reading materials that are in the library that are purely for entertainment can be justified because practice in reading is good for everybody, especially children. So he would not be in favor of doing away with entertainment reading. However, he does not feel that watching movies on television (video) offers any such benefit, and therefore, it does not warrant subsidy from taxpayers monies.
>
> He does not think the library should be offering free service that has little or no social value and that competes with the video rental businesses. Feature films are available from rental stores throughout the city at low prices.

I know the director who made these comments. I'm a great admirer of his interpersonal skills. He is bright, he's a nice guy, but he's an academic librarian by training and by inclination—he shouldn't be in a public library at all. The quotation from his board minutes proves it. I don't need to list the internal inconsistencies and poor reasoning he gives to justify his cultural elitism—they are obvious.

Incidentally, someone else has made the observation that while some of us are eager to apply "social value" to reading or audiovisual materials, we don't apply this to answering information questions, an infinitely more expensive service, since it is supplied by a professional staff. Can you imagine saying to the telephone caller from the bar, "I'm sorry, your question has no social value!"?

The point is, this library is being run for the few at the expense of the many, under the apparent assumption that "social value" is something defined by English literature professors or perhaps sociologists, neither of whom is interested in the distribution of information. Incidentally, information can be found in both fiction and entertainment videocassettes—*D-day, the Sixth of June*, for example, which is found in both formats.

The point of view expressed here, however, is readily acceptable to many board members, people who look upon the library as a sort of ill-defined cultural institution, and who have never really considered the mission and function of a public library.

Who Will Tell These Boards?

These same board members hire the library director, and unfortunately many administrators looking for a position will quite understandably give such board members just what they want. It comes down to a lack of understanding by board members and a lack of commitment to the validity or worthiness of service to ordinary people—people who are served only by the public library—by an administrator who should know better. It's akin to hiring a creationist to teach evolution or a Marxist to run your school of business administration. They are often perfectly honest, perfectly dedicated, and perfectly wrong for the job.

Who will tell these boards that they are subverting the public's right to their own library? Boards have only two chief functions anyway, to hire and to fire the director. The high-priced headhunting firms won't tell them. Those firms don't know anything at all about public libraries. The American Library Association won't tell them, it is dominated by academic librarians in both membership and staff. Not governments, who know and care little about their libraries.

Bridget Lamont of the Illinois State Library had a splendid idea—maybe the state library should set up its own headhunting service for public libraries. Consulting in this area is a full-time job, and expertise not only in search practices but in the philosophy of public library service is a lot more important in the long run than consulting in buildings, staff training, and so on. With over 500 public libraries in Illinois, it would be a full-time job for one or more people.

Questionable Hiring, Low Expectations

Boards have a questionable track record in hiring administrators, just as too many administrators obviously have a questionable track record in identifying and carrying out the mission of public libraries. They get away with it because public libraries are not very important in the governmental scheme of things and the public doesn't really know what's going on. There is a very low expectation for public library service anyway, based on generations of poor leadership.

A state-supported consulting firm, so to speak, could not only eliminate outrageous fees from private firms, but also would bring a knowledge of the philosophy of public library service, possible candidates, and information on prevailing salaries and benefits to the search. Private firms promise this service but seldom deliver it. To private headhunters, unfortunately, a librarian is a librarian even if he or she is an academic. Board members often feel the same way. this is a real contribution to the decline of the public's library.

How are we to assure that public libraries serve all the public, since the trend seems to be more and more that they serve only a small proportion of the public—the highly educated elite? Realistically, the leadership of public libraries is pretty firmly in the hands of boards of trustees and the directors of public libraries. Where boards don't exist, or are advisory, leadership, at least in the important areas of service and collection development, is with the director.

City or town authorities seldom know or care about anything other than budget increases and the lack of complaints. The possibility that lack of complaints may be due to lack of users doesn't really concern them very much.

Dilemma: Trustees/Directors

Almost everything that prevents or endangers the development of truly user-oriented policies is a responsibility of trustees and/or directors. It is with them that remedial action must be taken if improvement is to come. We are victims of bad management, management which is bad because we don't pay attention to the bottom line—which is providing information and materials to "the greatest number."

It's not surprising that boards and directors don't really know what they are doing. They certainly don't teach it in library schools, where any interest or concern with public libraries is pretty thin on the ground. We desperately need a common vision of public library services—a vision which might come from ALA, but hasn't in the past, probably because interest, leadership, and power in that organization is either academic or from large public libraries pretending to be academic.

In recent years the situation is starting to change, with the development of what can become a clearer vision of public library service germinating in the Public Library Association, which, after all, is a division of ALA. PLA, unlike other divisions like LAMA, ALSC, and the rest, is a generalist rather than a specialist division and therefore is better equipped to deal with an overall perspective in this area. Additionally, it has not been overwhelmed with library directors from the old city libraries, libraries which over the years have lost their users as a result of sticking with the conventional patterns of service—service which no longer serves the needs of their constituency, if it ever did.

The hope and promise of public libraries is in the smaller libraries— or those large libraries which are really consolidations of small service outlets for reasons of efficiency and economy. Few of these librarians have the stultifying influence of a large central library full of specialists (academic librarians for all intents and purposes). The "central library syndrome," which has affected almost all large public libraries, like Chicago, is simply a collection of all the ills I have mentioned, making it a powerful force working against the future of the public's library.

The small libraries, and almost all American public libraries are "smaller libraries," have nearly cornered the supply of innovation, service orientation, and response to user demands in the field—although those characteristics are far from prevalent even among smaller libraries.

Tools For a New Vision

Starting with *A Planning Process for Public Libraries*, an almost unreadable but very important document, and picking up speed with the publication of *Output Measures for Public Libraries*, the Public Library Association has taken up the leadership in the development of a new vision of service based on user demand as well as perceived need.

The state library agencies of this country, which have, for good or ill, the most influence on the development and progress of public libraries, to their credit have largely supported and implemented these important new tools to improve public library management. PLA has recently produced not only a second edition of the very widely used *Output Measures* (Nancy Van House et al., ALA, 1987), but also a new and significantly more realistic *Planning and Rolesetting for Public Libraries* manual (Charles A. McClure et al., ALA, 1987) which breaks new ground in a fundamental area, that of determination of roles of a particular, individual public library.

With these tools, trustees working with the staff of a public library can attain a new clarity about their mission—a mission which is always very different from that of an academic library. If the identification of roles is followed up by assignment of financial priorities to the *support* of those roles, we will be on the way to recognition of the bottom line for public libraries.

Failure to follow such a course, failure in planning, failure to manage with an eye toward the basic mission, will bring more of the fuzzy, sentimental, institution- and book-centered thinking so inimical to the interests of the public and their library.

Lutece or McDonalds?

There is a great future for the public's library. That future will be impossible to achieve without a more critical, hard look at the conventional wisdom which too many of us, trustees and librarians alike, are so happy to accept. That conventional wisdom leads us to anoint ourselves as "apostles of culture," to see ourselves as arbiters of values, as definers of access, as keepers of order, as true intellectuals, and as controllers of supply and interpreters of demand.

We are attempting to be the French restaurant of institutions rather than the McDonald's of information and materials distribution.

The future lies in responsiveness to the very people our libraries were created to serve, the people who provide the funds to serve their interests, not ours. Responsiveness demands those traits of good management such as informed opportunism. In libraries it demands collection development for users, not librarians. It demands selection of directors who understand the purpose of public library service, the motivation of staff, and the construction of facilities aimed in only one direction: at providing service to the people who support us, service in the public's interest through the public's library.

SERVING YOUNG ADULTS: WHY WE DO WHAT WE DO

Dorothy M. Broderick

Reading Enriches Life

Reading provides an enrichment to life. For example, in May, McGee, my dippy Dalmatian, and I were camped in a KOA in North Carolina that had a small lake. The first sight I saw was a mother duck with her 12 ducklings swimming all bunched behind her. Later, she took the ducklings on a complete tour of the campground. I don't know what other campers felt as they watched this marvelous performance, but in my mind's eye, I saw the beautiful sepia drawings in Robert McCloskey's *Make Way for Ducklings* and I felt all over again the joy of that warm, loving book, with the added benefit of recalling all those bright-eyed preschoolers to whom I introduced the book during preschool programs.

Early in June I was privileged to hear Walter Dean Myers speak at the ABA meeting in Washington, D.C. Myers was trying to make some connection in his own mind between his life in Harlem and those of the boys involved in the "wilding" viciousness. One of the points he made beautifully was that reading allows one to engage in life and that he was at a loss to know how one could get these kids to "re-engage in life." Reading enriches us by engaging us in life—not just our own, but all of humankind's.

Now, what we read determines the possible impact we can have on others. Diane Goheen and Mike Printz wrote about how their reading experience influenced an entire school. Moved deeply by Hazel Rochman's superb collection, *Somehow Tenderness Survives*, they gained an entire

---

"Serving Young Adults: Why We Do What We Do," by Dorothy M. Broderick in *VOYA* Vol. 12, no. 4 (October 1989), pp. 203–206; reprinted with permission from Scarecrow Press.

school's cooperation in devoting this year's Multi-Ethnic Week to the subject of apartheid. Two people read a very fine book and while they may never know how many lives were changed by the emphasis the school put on apartheid, the chances are high that more than one or two students, teachers, and even administrators, will never again be indifferent to the plight of the black majority in South Africa.

By stressing reading, I do not mean to disparage other media experiences that can be equally enriching. Many years ago I saw a 16mm film called *Seconds to Play* that showed how ABC televised the college football game of the week. That experience has made me a much more informed viewer of television sports programs. So, I am ignoring other media experiences here only because there is not enough time to cover the entire field.

Ideal Adolescence

Let me begin my talking about young people in general; the audience we wish to reach, to serve, to enrich, to engage in life.

When I was teaching Young Adult Literature and/or programming, I always began each semester by asking the class the following question: "If you could relive your adolescence all over again, not knowing anymore the second time around than you knew the first (in other words, no bringing to it the adult insights you may currently have), would you do it?" Only once in all those years did a student reply in the affirmative, and I knew from that first day that here was a young lady in awful trouble. Clearly, anyone who would give up adulthood to relive adolescence has problems.

Let me hypothesize an as close to perfect adolescent experience as I can imagine. You are the adolescent in this portrait.

You have wonderful parents. They love each other, they love you, and your sibling. They work at jobs that pay very well (if mother doesn't work outside of the home, it is by choice and not some societal imposed role, and she likes it that way); the jobs are satisfying, and do not impose undue stress on them. Both parents have outside interests of their own that add another layer of fulfillment to their lives.

Your sibling, who may be older or younger than you—your choice—and either same gender or opposite, again as you choose, is more like your best friend than sibling. You have separate interests, but each of you is very good at what you do, whether that be sports or working on the school newspaper, or whatever you want your competence to be.

You live in a stable neighborhood where the neighbors are more like loving grandparents or doting aunts and uncles than strangers. They don't threaten to shoot you or call the police when your generally well behaved dog chases a squirrel across their yard. They are there when needed but are not busy-bodies or otherwise intrusive.

You go to a high school where everyone, beginning with the principal, genuinely likes teenagers and is caring and supportive. There are no in and out groups, greasers and socs as in *The Outsiders*. Students are allowed to be individuals, but always work as a team for the good of the school and the student body as a whole.

You are well liked by your classmates; you always have a date for the big dance or game with someone you really like. You may not be Hollywood beautiful or handsome, but you are not too fat or too thin, too short or too tall, and your complexion glows. And, of course, you are white.

Enough already! Dare I ask for a show of hands from those of you who recognize yourself?

But even if everything I described was true for an individual, adolescence is not, and cannot be, a time without stress.

First of all, there is the matter of hormones. Even without those awful sex education classes the conservatives rant and rage against, your hormones will do their own thing. Your body is changing; there are growth spurts for some while others are labeled late bloomers; male voices change; females begin menstruation; hair grows in new places; and you think and feel differently about the opposite sex.

Then there is the process of becoming independent of your parents, a process made easier when there is true love within the family, but which is never as easy as one would like. You have to learn how to set your own limits rather than having them imposed; you have to learn to internalize values rather than mouthing them by rote.

If you are a "normal" adolescent, you probably have a period where you want to be a member of your religious community—rabbi, priest, minister, nun—or spout unadulterated atheism. You become a member of the Young Republican or Democrat club, or decide that no problems can be solved except through revolution.

In other words, even normal adolescence is a time of great change. That doesn't make it psychopathic or outrageous; it just is.

As Piaget discovered many years ago, an adolescent who does not question, does not grow into a productive, creative adult. It is the time to dream large dreams. And for most adolescents, the time period coincides with the middle aged blahs their parents are experiencing, so often, even with the best of parents, they cannot be as stable as one might wish. A parent who has reached the point of asking, "Is this all there is to life?" is not able to be as supportive as we'd like.

Adolescent Reality

But today most adolescents do not come close to resembling the portrait I've painted. Even when white, and we'll get to being non-white in a while, you stand a good chance of living in a single parent home. Your father left for another woman and has new children; he doesn't always send his child support payments on time and you don't have the right brand of sneakers or cords to start school. Mother doesn't have any work skills and is working for peanuts as a check-out lady at a supermarket. She's too tired and hurt and filled with a deep sadness to be able to give you the love and support you need when you need it.

At school you're considered a nerd. Your complexion looks like a Martian landscape; your social skills are nil.

All that would be bad enough, but suppose you are black and poor and living in an urban ghetto, going to a run down school staffed by beaten down, underpaid teachers. Your trip from home to school is almost as dangerous as living in Beirut. Drug dealers, crack houses, prostitutes, rule the neighborhood.

But despite it all, you survive. You're 15 and a good kid and you work and save your money and the allowance your father gives you, even though he doesn't live with you and your mother. When you have the $115 needed to buy a pair of Air Jordan sneakers, you buy them and wear them with pride. You earned them. Two blocks down from you is a 17 year old who covets your sneakers so he strangles you and steals the sneakers. A true story from the mean streets of our nation's capital!

Or maybe you're a really smart kid. You do well in school. You have college aspirations. But as a black, you find your teachers, whether they be black or white, don't really expect much of you. It is a constant struggle to break down their low expectations because, among other things, if you answer too many questions in class or get straight A's, your black peers accuse you of wanting to be white. Sad to say, too many of your peers will have absorbed the racist measure that intellectual achievement is not a characteristic of the black community. The only time you find yourself on the pages of your local newspaper is when you graduate with honors, and there is usually a subtle tone to the story that conveys surprise that the valedictorian of the school is black.

Before leaving the subject of lifestyle, let me add one more. A recent television documentary on U.S. education showed one young man with his pickup truck, girlfriend, and playing on the football team. His quote was "I don't want to graduate. It's fun. I like it." That young man is as hooked as the kid on crack: his hook is "fun." Yet if adolescence is to mean anything, it must mean a conscious striving to become an adult and to become a responsible citizen capable of contributing not only to society, but to their own interpersonal relationships. Would you like your daughter to marry a young man whose focus in life is fun?

I could go on and on about the various lifestyles facing the adolescents of today, but let me move to the major point: it isn't easy growing up in modern North America. Try to always keep in mind that the adolescents you meet are facing great challenges, some you may never know about, so be kind.

The Realistic YA Novel

My second point has to do with the literature produced for them, the young adult novel, so often maligned by critics. I want to deal with only one of the charges often expressed by the ultra conservatives, namely, that young adult novels are not uplifting. Why, oh why, cry these critics, do the authors have to deal with such depressing subjects? Why can't we go back to the good old days?

As one who has spent six decades on this planet, let me tell you an important fact: *there were no good old days.* Every problem confronted in a young adult novel today (with one exception I shall spell out in a minute or two) not only existed during my childhood and adolescence, but was known to most of us. There were drunks in families, there were wife abusers, there were child molesters, divorce, certainly death and dying, mental illness, premarital pregnancy, and, yes, abortions if you were among the elite. In high school, one of my classmates went home one day to find his father had hanged himself in the garage; a couple of weeks later he went home to find his mother had done the same thing.

Earlier I said we never know what challenges the young are facing so we should be kind. We should also avoid, at all costs, attributing motives to the young when we lack the necessary background to make informed judgments. The event from my own life that still rankles, can never be totally resolved, occurred in January 1942. My mother was mentally ill as well as racked with many physical ailments, but she was, to the adults who knew her a charming, vivacious person. When my grandmother could no longer cope with the erratic, violent, self-destructive behavior of my mother, she threw us out of the house in the spring of 1941. Not quite one year later, we found ourselves living in a summer cottage on the shores of Long Island Sound, being supported by food stamps and my mother's current lover, a married man. When Ed came less and less to spend the night, my mother became more and more upset.

On the day in question, I awoke to find her screaming and carrying the pot of corn soup from the iron bellied stove to the bathroom. It was all there was to eat in the house and she was going to throw it in the toilet. I stopped her, but as I carried the pot back to the stove, she put on her heavy winter coat and fled the cottage. She crossed the street, walked between the empty summer homes, and plunged into the freezing water. I had no choice but to plunge in after her and drag her to shore. It took monumental effort to get her back to the house. I told my younger brother to get the school bus while I stayed at home to watch over my mother.

After school was over, my best friend Alicia came to see how I was. I left my brother to watch my sleeping mother, with orders to call me if she got up, and went outside to play catch with Alicia. As we were tossing the ball back and forth, the Woodmont bus went by and my homeroom teacher, Mrs. Halloran, saw us. The next day, without asking any questions (not that I would have told her the truth), she sentenced me to two weeks detention. Shortly after that, my mother disappeared and I did not see her again until eight years later when she was on her death bed. Could anyone have helped me through the torment of that event and those years? I shall never know. What I do know is that there were no supportive adults.

Oh, no, ladies and gentlemen, there were no good old days. In my small town of 4,000, I knew all these awful, depressing, life-threatening behaviors. And if we did not talk about them and people did not write about them, that changed nothing—they still existed and because of the silence, we were each left to cope as best we could, believing we were alone, we were unique, no one else experienced what we were experiencing. There is no more damaging psychological experience than being faced with the conspiracy of silence.

The one terrifying experience that others were not aware of, only the person experiencing it knew of, was sexual assault by a family member or close friend of the family. We now know it happened, even then, in the good old days, because older women have begun to speak out and share with therapists and counselors, the guilt and filth they have carried with them through the years. This has been the last deep, dark, secret to creep out of the closet.

One point to keep in mind: we didn't always know the words for the behaviors I have outlined: people, mostly men, were not alcoholics—they were drunks. There were two kinds of drunks, happy drunks and mean drunks. Child molesters were simply dirty old men. Etc. etc. Terminology changes; human behavior does not.

The best of the young adult authors, and there are too many to name them all, are writing to help adolescents understand the world in which they live. Perhaps understand is not quite the correct word: ponder may be a better choice. For example, one of the best young adult novels begins with a poster inside a locker reading: "Dare I disturb the universe?" For Jerry Renault in *The Chocolate War*, it is a very real question, as it is for thousands of other adolescents. Most people never even ask themselves the question: how often has someone said, either to you, or in your presence: "To get along, go along." Only the movers and shakers of our world ask the question and answer it in the affirmative.

Now, the censors of this world do not even want the question asked, never mind ponder what the answer might be. I never cease to be amazed at the number of adults who truly believe that simplistic values can be ordered into children and adolescents. Values that cannot be internalized are not values, they are rote dogma.

Compare Cormier's question with the following paragraph from *Chinese Handcuffs*, Chris Crutcher's stunning new novel. Dillon, our central character, has taken his problems to the woman basketball coach, who tells him:

> "You have no control over the world. You have no control over anyone but you. You can't control how Stacy feels about you or whether she had your brother's baby. You can't control what's gone on in Jennifer's life or how she's reacting to that. There's nothing in the world outside yourself you can control. Winter's cold, summer's warm. Things fall from high places, they break. You lie, trust goes. Truth stays the same, Dillon. Truth is simply what is. It doesn't have to be believed to exist. Only our responses change."

Eventually, Dillon learns that lesson. If more adults would learn that lesson in relationship particularly to the young, we would all be better off. Expending energy trying to control others is wasted energy, and ultimately ends in failure.

The Role of Adults

Which leads to my third point in all this: guidance, not control, is the secret to helping young people move into adulthood. In *The Chocolate War*, Cormier has painted us a portrait of a young man totally devoid of adult support, and it is that lack that leads to Jerry's disaster and disillusionment. In *After the First Death* we see not just a lack of support, but an outright betrayal by a father.

Crutcher, on the other hand, always provides his character with some adult who helps. The adult both challenges and comforts the young person. But, and this is vital, particularly for well meaning librarians: the adult never becomes absorbed with the young people with whom he or she is working, nor has any desire to be part of their intimate lives. By intimate, I do not mean sexual, I mean intimacy as it ought to be used: a mutual sharing of deep feeling in a caring relationship.

A measure of how really good many young adult novels are is to find their basic themes verified by research. In the February 1989 issue of *The*

Ford Foundation Letter, a report called "Public/Private Ventures: The Next Step" spells out the importance of adults in the lives of young people, most particularly the impact on that group we call "at risk." The insight into the role of adults in the lives of these young people emerged from failure: why did so many at risk young people drop out of programs designed to help them succeed? Summer job programs, remediation help in academics, etc. still resulted in a high drop out rate.

Let me spare you all the details and get to the conclusions: first, there are two kinds of supportive adults who make a difference in young people's lives: primary and secondary. I quote: "A primary relationship was one where the older person came to assume a role in the life of the kid like that of an extended-family member." It was characterized by a "considerable amount of intimacy" and a willingness on the part of the elder to take on the youth's full range of problems and emotions. "One where, when the kid was in trouble, the elder might be the first person he or she would call to help them out."

In the secondary relationships, the older person took an interest in the young person's life, but there were certain lines that weren't crossed. They were more like helpful neighbors in these cases, trying to provide some real assistance but maintaining more emotional distance.

Young people benefited from both types of relationships. Obviously, those lucky enough to have a primary relationship benefited more, but both groups benefited.

Are there those of you out there thinking, "Oh, God, she's going to tell us we have to be social workers." Relax. Librarians should be librarians —I just may have a slightly expanded view of what a librarian is while on the job. Librarians who work as big brothers or big sisters on their own time are to be applauded, but here I want to speak only about our on-the-job responsibility to young people.

There is a terrible tendency in our society to allocate responsibility by job title rather than by humane ideals required by all. The schools, and no one else, should educate the young; houses of religious worship should inculcate morality and no one else; and in libraries, only those people designated as children's or young adult specialists should concern themselves with the young. It is this attitude that makes the work of youth specialists, regardless of their jobs, harder if not impossible.

Personally, I get awfully tired of adults who treat young people as dirt, roaches to be sprayed with lethal pesticide, complain about the lack of respect they receive from the young. Respect is a reciprocal action—give it and you get it. Every library should make respect for all patrons, regardless of age (and all those other identifying characteristics such as race, creed, country of national origin) the first statement in what I would like to see developed, namely, "A patron's library bill of rights."

Adults have only two roles they can play in the lives of young people: we can be constructive or destructive. At first, I thought there might be a third, namely being ciphers, a zilch, but I realized one does not have to be actively destructive: nothingness will do nicely, thank you. The very best book I have read in living memory is *Heartbeats and Other Stories* by Peter Sieruta. Not only is there not a wrong word in it, not a false note, but every word, every sentence is vital to the story being told. In the title story, one paragraph reads:

> Mr. Minotti emerges from behind his newspaper to say, "Be back by eleven." To be perfectly truthful, I've forgotten he was even in the room. It happens a lot. He seems to get swallowed up by all the Minotti women.

Skip that paragraph, fail to grasp its importance, and you just may miss the whole point of the story. Nothingness imposes a price on the lives of the young.

In "The Substitute," the story that will have all librarians talking, particularly those who work in the schools, we are offered the most devastating portrait of an adult destroying a young person that I have ever read. I say no more about that, except to plead with you not to rush to read only that story. It comes in the middle of the book, and the arrangement of the stories is as important as the stories themselves. It is, in my opinion, a totally perfect book.

Finally, a small word about *No Kidding* by Bruce Brooks. As one of five people in the country who really likes the book [following the talk, there was a rush by colleagues to proclaim their enthusiasm for the book], let me just say this here: Brooks is showing us a world that is inevitable if adults do not meet their responsibilities toward the young. In the absence of adult responsibility, children must be in charge. It isn't good for either generation, but someone has to be responsible if society is to survive.

Read. Ponder what kind of adult you are and what you offer the young with whom you work. Don't strive to be their buddy; strive to show them that the pain of adolescence can lead to the serenity of adulthood. It is not enough for me to tell you to "Go forth and do no harm." You must be willing and able to "Go forth and do good."

THE PUBLIC LIBRARY & THE LATCHKEY PROBLEM: A SURVEY

Frances Smardo Dowd

Today, the majority of public libraries are being used, at least to some extent, for a function other than their traditional purposes—that of caring for children during the after-school hours. In increasing numbers, elementary age-level children, locked out of the house, wait unattended in the children's room until a parent returns home from work. Librarians are certainly aware of the problem created by unsupervised children in the library, commonly referred to as "library latchkey children," and are trying to cope with this phenomenon.

Although many believe the problem of latchkey children was widespread, no research was conducted to investigate the issue until the summer of 1988, when the Services to Children Committee of the Public Library Association (PLA) published a position paper on the topic in collaboration with the Library Service to Children with Special Needs Committee of the Association for Library Service to Children. The report, *"Latchkey Children in the Public Library"* (ALA Publishing Services) is a comprehensive document which discusses appropriate programs for latchkey children and their families, networking and advocacy measures, and policy development. The writers emphasize that latchkey children offer an unparalleled opportunity for public libraries to become part of their community service network advocating attention to the welfare of children.

Independently and concurrent with the writing of the PLA position paper, I conducted research on the topic and, based on empirical evidence,

---

"The Public Library & the Latchkey Problem: A Survey," by Frances Smardo Dowd in *School Library Journal* Vol. 35, no. 11 (July 1989), pp. 19–24; reprinted with permission from Reed Publishing, USA, copyright © 1989 Reed Publishing, USA.

* The author is currently writing a book on this topic, entitled *Latchkey Children in the Library and Community* to be published by Oryx Press in 1991.

arrived at the five recommendations for libraries which appear at the end of this article.

Description of the Research

The goals of the research were to assist public libraries in clarifying their appropriate role in serving latchkey children and to develop recommendations for more effective service to this user group. A preliminary questionnaire was developed and pilot tested for appropriate wording and content validity by nine librarians throughout the United States—children's coordinators, library directors, or salaried officials in the American Library Association—with expertise in research and/or children's services. After revising the preliminary questionnaire to incorporate the recommendations of the majority, a final three-part questionnaire was constructed, consisting of multiple choice and open-ended questions. The first section addressed the description of, magnitude of and explanation for the existence of library latchkey children. The second part focused upon the content and extent of written or unwritten latchkey library policies and procedures, while the third portion dealt with programs and services recommended or provided for this clientele.

The questionnaire was mailed with assurance of anonymity to a random sample of 125 children's librarians and children's coordinators among the 425 listed in the directory, *Coordinators of Children's and Young Adult Services in Public Library Systems Serving at Least 100,000 People*, published by the Association for Library Services to Children, a division of ALA. This sample included 42 states and the District of Columbia, since eight states did not have public libraries serving populations over 100,000 people. Ninety-one usable questionnaires were received from each of the 43 geographic areas identified, with approximately one-third representing one facility and the remainder responding for between two and 86 facilities. Data analysis for the multiple choice questions utilized the SPSS–X Statistical Package, which converted responses into frequencies and percentages.

Latchkey Children Situations

"Have you found," our survey asked, "that latchkey/unattended children are using your library for child care purposes after school on weekdays?

On weekends?" A majority responded affirmatively to the first question. Sixty-nine respondents (75.8%) reported unattended children after school on weekdays, while 45 respondents, just under half of the 91 participants (49.5%), reported unattended children on weekends.

Sixty-one of 91 participants completed at least some portion of a chart "estimating the number of latchkey children present in their public library during a typical week between 3 and 6 p.m.," and "considering each category (i.e., 1 day a week, 2 days a week, etc.) as exclusive and independent." As Table 1 depicts, the number of children using the library regularly for child care purposes increases with the age level of the child, until peaking for 10- to 12-year-olds, with an average of 21 children present at least three days per week.

Participants were asked to indicate specific problem areas relating to latchkey children. They were asked to select the term which most accurately described their situation. Data in Table 2 reveal that the majority either "sometimes" or "always" encountered all but one of the eight problem situations listed, including "some difficulty in performing regular library services effectively for other patrons," "uncertainty regarding how to best deal with unattended latchkey children," and "vandalism/destruction of library property." "Disturbances due to inappropriate behaviors (as running, moving furniture, etc.)," "limited or unavailable seating," "delays or difficulty in closing the library when a child is left unattended," and "patron complaints" were also problem situations the majority encountered. However, the majority (72.2%) do at least sometimes perceive the situation of latchkey children as a positive one, in that this presents staff with "an opportunity to develop new methods of effective service."

Several questions dealt with respondent's opinions as to why latchkey children use the public library in lieu of after-school child care, and asked participants to "check as many as apply." An examination of Table 3 indicates that while the majority checked every option, participants almost unanimously felt that the reason is because "their parent(s) perceive(s) the library as an appropriate facility where children can safely spend a few hours after school."

As to possible factors which may aggravate the library latchkey situation, exactly half of the respondents perceived that the "architectural design and layout of the library building" exacerbated the problem, while 69.4%

TABLE 1
Estimated Number of Latchkey Children Present in Public Libraries

	Under Age 6	Avg. No.	Ages 7–9	Avg. No.	Ages 10–12	Avg. No.	Over Age 12	Avg. No.
3 days per week	22	.04	176	2.89	218	3.57	240	3.93
4 days per week	37	.61	205	3.36	438	7.18	362	5.93
5 days per week	91	1.49	496	8.13	609	9.98	585	9.59
TOTAL	150	2.14	877	14.38	1265	20.73	1187	19.45

TABLE 2
Description of Public Library Situation Due to Latchkey Children

	NEVER	SOMETIMES	ALWAYS
DIFFICULTY in serving other patrons	12 (16.7%)	56 (77.8%)	4 (5.6%)
UNCERTAINTY as to how to best serve latchkey children	8 (11.1%)	53 (73.6%)	10 (13.9%)
VANDALISM of property or furniture	23 (31.9%)	46 (63.9%)	1 (1.4%)
OVERDUES/LOST MATERIALS borrowed by latchkey children	35 (48.6%)	27 (37.5%)	2 (2.8%)
DISTURBANCES due to inappropriate behavior	5 (6.9%)	58 (80.6%)	9 (12.5%)
PATRON COMPLAINTS due to inappropriate behavior	16 (22.2%)	53 (73.6%)	1 (1.4%)
LIMITED SEATING due to large numbers of latchkey children	26 (36.1%)	39 (54.2%)	7 (9.7%)
DELAYS AT CLOSING TIME due to unattended children	12 (16.7%)	59 (81.9%)	1 (1.4%)

TABLE 3
Why the Public Library Is Used in Lieu of Child Care

	YES	NO
Parents can't afford child care	51 (70.8%)	21 (29.2%)
Parents lack child care information	31 (43.1%)	41 (56.9%)
Parents perceive library as safe/appropriate	71 (98.6%)	1 (1.4%)
Parents perceive library as educational	43 (59.7%)	29 (40.3%)
Library philosophy welcomes children	48 (66.7%)	24 (33.3%)
Library near school	54 (75.0%)	16 (22.2%)

felt that limited personnel worsened the situation. Just over half (51.4%) cited limited seating or space as a worsening factor.

The majority of participants who completed the statement, "The main challenge that public libraries have in serving latchkey children is . . .", referred to their attempts of achieving a balance between meeting the needs of latchkey children and maintaining an effective library climate and service to other patrons. Thirteen respondents primarily expressed the library's main challenge in terms of what they felt the library is not (i.e., not a daycare center, drop-off center for children or a babysitting service). An equal number cited the library's main challenge in regard to latchkey children as being able to deal with medical emergencies, children's safety and security, or the library's liability and legal responsibility. Coping with inadequate staff, training, or funding while attempting to serve latchkey children was noted ten times.

Library Policy/Procedures

In order to obtain an accurate description of current library policy and procedures about latchkey children, participants were asked to check the statement from a list of six alternatives which identified their library's situation. As a study of Table 4 reveals, less than one-third (30.8%) have policies/procedures in effect, while 17.6 percent are developing them; an equal percentage recognizes the need for them, and the same percentage follows unwritten rules.

The questionnaire listed six possible reasons why written library policies/procedures concerning latchkey children are/would be important and instructed participants to "check as many as apply" to their library's situation. A large majority (between 64.8% and 83.5% of the participants) felt that such policies/procedures would standardize what should be done at closing time, explain or clarify appropriate staff responses, boost staff confidence, state concern for children's safety, express the library's position, and maintain equitable library use.

Libraries not having policies/procedures for latchkey children were asked to skip the remainder of this section; therefore, the findings in Tables 5 and 6 do not reflect data from 59 respondents. Data in Table 5 reveal that the majority of those responding to this section have developed written policies/procedures for latchkey children "after experiencing a problem," while the minority develop them after reviewing those of other libraries, after discussing the topic with community agencies, or after formulation of a committee. Over two-thirds (68.8%) reported additionally that their policies/procedures are adequate in meeting their needs, and a full 87.5% indicated that their policies/procedures "had been used/followed at least once."

TABLE 4
Status of Library Policy/Procedures About Latchkey Children

Has written policies/procedures	28 (30.8%)
Is developing written policies/procedures	16 (17.6%)
Is considering written policies/procedures	6 (6.6%)
Follows unwritten policies/procedures	16 (17.6%)
Needs but doesn't have written/unwritten policies/procedures	16 (17.6%)
Doesn't have or need written/unwritten policies/procedures	7 (7.7%)

TABLE 5
Circumstances Influencing Development of Library Policy/Procedures for Latchkey Children

Respondent libraries' policies/procedures were developed:	YES	NO
Before experiencing problem?	7 (21.9%)	21 (65.6%)
After experiencing problem?	19 (57.6%)	10 (30.3%)
After reviewing other libraries' policies/procedures?	14 (43.8%)	14 (43.8%)
After discussion with community agencies?	12 (37.5%)	16 (50.0%)
After committee made recommendations?	11 (34.4%)	17 (53.1%)

TABLE 6
Content/Inclusions of Library Policy/Procedures for Latchkey Children

	AGREE	DISAGREE
Specific aged child should not be left unattended	17 (53.1%)	13 (40.6%)
Library not responsible for specific aged child unattended	12 (37.5%)	18 (56.3%)
Parents/guardians responsible for behavior of child in library	22 (68.8%)	8 (25.0%)
Action specified if child left unattended at closing time	22 (66.7%)	9 (27.3%)
Action specified if child is disruptive	20 (60.6%)	11 (33.3%)
Action specified if child identified as latchkey	5 (15.6%)	25 (78.1%)

Participants were given three options regarding potential methods in which the public might be informed of their library's policies/procedures for latchkey children and were asked to "check as many as apply." While none of the three methods—a sign, talks to community groups and schools, or printed material given to patrons—is utilized by the majority, most frequently a sign is posted in the library (34.4%).

The final questions in this section pertained to the actual content of the policies/procedures concerning latchkey children. Six specific statements or actions were listed and participants were instructed to "check as many as apply." Data in Table 6 reveal that library policy/procedure statements dealing with latchkey children most frequently include a statement to the effect that "parents or guardians are responsible for the behavior of their child while in the library," but rarely specify the action to be taken if a child is identified as a latchkey youth. The majority usually contain statements which are negative in nature.

Programs/Services

All respondents—regardless of whether or not they found that latchkey children were using their library, and regardless of whether or not their libraries had written policies/procedures for dealing with them—were instructed to complete the next section in its entirety. Participants were instructed to indicate whether their library provided each of 12 recommended library programs/services for latchkey children, or whether they recommended that their library provide it. Data in Table 7 indicate that the service most frequently recommended (and the only one provided by a majority) is that of "information and referral services for parents regarding available licensed child care in the area." For almost all of the programs/services the percent of respondents recommending provision was higher than the percent actually providing the program/service. The service with the greatest discrepancy in this regard was "an on-line computer database community resource file listing activities for latchkey children and their parents." Conversely, in three instances a greater number of respondent libraries offered a service/program in comparison to the number who believed that it should be offered. Included in this category were "after-school child care services"; "drop-in activity programs such as arts and crafts projects"; and "special security guards on monitors to supervise unattended/latchkey children in the library."

Each of the final five items of the questionnaire were open-ended and were designed specifically to gather creative, positive, and effective methods for dealing with latchkey children to assist libraries experiencing similar

TABLE 7
Library Programs/Services Provided and Recommended for Latchkey Children

	PROVIDED	RECOMMENDED
After-School Child Care Services	5 (5.5%)	2 (2.2%)
Self-Help Survival Skills Workshops	31 (34.1%)	50 (54.9%)
I & R for Parents about Child Care	61 (67.0%)	65 (71.4%)
Computerized Resource Database for Latchkey Services in Community	6 (6.6%)	48 (52.7%)
Drop-In Activity Programs as Arts & Crafts	40 (44.0%)	39 (42.9%)
Volunteer Opportunities for Latchkey Children	38 (41.8%)	39 (42.9%)
Warm-Line Telephone Service	5 (5.5%)	19 (20.9%)
Story Hours, Book Clubs, Films, etc.	42 (46.2%)	50 (54.9%)
Tutoring in Homework/Reading by Volunteers	17 (18.7%)	43 (47.3%)
Paired Tutoring: Older/Younger Latchkey Children	7 (7.7%)	25 (27.5%)
Special Programs/Services Not Provided for All	18 (19.8%)	22 (24.2%)
Special Security Guards/Monitors to Supervise Latchkey Children	18 (19.8%)	13 (14.3%)

situations. Participants were asked to complete this sentence: "An additional program/service which I would recommend public libraries provide for unattended/latchkey children is . . .". Although no more than two respondents cited the same suggestion, among the inclusions were a free house phone for children's use in calling home; snacks or a break room for nutritional after-school foods, and additional staff or volunteers to allow more after-school programming.

A second open-ended question pertained to whether respondents felt interaction between libraries and other community agencies, in regard to dealing with latchkey children, was important. A clear majority —68 librarians (or 74.7%)—indicated "yes," while ten stated "no"; three "partially agreed" and ten left this item blank. In clarification of their affirmative responses, eight participants stated that they felt libraries should serve as advocates for children, belong to or form coalitions for better child care, or network with other community agencies in behalf of children.

Respondents were asked to complete this statement: "The role of the public library in regard to latchkey/unattended children is . . .". Forty-seven respondents (51.6%) indicated that the library's role is to provide normal effective service just as is given to any other user group. However, they qualified this by noting that this role was only feasible by working within the limits of funding and staffing so that other patrons' services are not adversely affected. While 17 participants defined the library's role in negative terms, almost an equal number believed that it involved working with parents or community agencies. Six felt that the library had *no* role in regard to unattended/latchkey children, and another six felt that their role is unclear or undefined.

Respondents were then asked: "Is your library successful in dealing with latchkey/unattended children?" Forty-seven respondents (51.6%) stated "yes," 13 "no," and 13 "partially agreed"; the remaining 18 left this item blank. Although the majority considered their library to be effectively serving this clientele, there was no consensus as to the reasons for this estimation. While 12 librarians attributed their accomplishments to their staff's positive attitudes or constant supervision, ten considered activities or programs to be the reason for their success, and 11 noted community support and communication/publicity as key factors.

In their general comments concerning latchkey children, 15 participants remarked upon the pervasiveness and permanence of this phenomenon. A few respondents commented on policy development, differences between the terms "latchkey" and "unattended," or stated that latchkey children are not a new phenomenon. Some expressed concern about negative publicity from the media and from restrictive library policies, as well as concern for children's safety and for the library's liability.

Summary

Almost unanimously, librarians perceive that the library latchkey phenomenon is primarily due to parental attitudes (i.e., parents' perception that libraries are safe and appropriate places for unattended children after school). Librarians feel that additional staff would lessen the negative effects of this situation, since the majority stated that inadequate staff was the most aggravating factor. Most librarians are frustrated or ambivalent about how to handle latchkey children, as they responded that this situation creates "uncertainties" and "difficulties" for them in serving other patrons, yet at the same time they perceived the existence of latchkey children as "an opportunity" for developing innovative methods of effective service. Moreover, while librarians want to serve this clientele (in that they perceive this as their role), at the same time they feel that fulfilling this role without negatively affecting service to other patrons is their "main challenge." It seems that public librarians need assistance in serving latchkey children effectively, as only about half felt that their libraries were successfully dealing with the situation. In addition, the majority did recognize that libraries alone cannot effectively deal with latchkey children, in that they affirmed the importance of interacting with other community agencies.

It appears that the majority of respondent libraries may not consider policies/procedures for latchkey children essential, since less than one-third have developed them. Most librarians believe that these written documents pertaining to latchkey children are as beneficial to staff as they are to these youth. Libraries have been reactive rather than proactive in developing written policies/procedures for this group, and a majority have not devoted particular thought, time and attention to their formulation, in terms of reviewing those from other libraries, discussing the topic with other community agencies, or establishing a library committee to gather facts and make recommendations. Developing policies/procedures for latchkey children seems well worth the time and effort, however, as almost all who did so have used/followed them at least once, and the majority find them adequate for their needs.

Libraries are not in agreement as to the most effective method of informing the public about the content of these written guidelines, since no single technique is utilized by the majority. Libraries are anxious to disclaim any potential liability for unattended children, as most incorporate in their policies/procedures for this clientele specific statements which place responsibility for the behavior of children upon the parent/guardian. Adults may perceive most library policies/procedures for latchkey children as being restrictive, since many libraries express these official statements largely in negative terms.

Apparently librarians recognize that their services/programs for latchkey children are inadequate, since traditional library information and referral services were more often recommended than provided—especially the online computer database community resource file listing activities for latchkey children and their parents. In contrast, librarians consider having special monitors and providing child care services inappropriate library activities, even though some do provide these.

Recommendations

Based upon these findings, here are five recommendations to help public libraries clarify their appropriate role in serving latchkey children and facilitate more effective service for this clientele:

- *Public library personnel should be better educated regarding appropriate services to latchkey children.* Preservice preparation could be included in the content of library courses dealing with children's/youth services or programs, library management, or public libraries. In-service preparation could be offered via an in-house staff development workshop, a program session at the Annual Conference of the American Library Association, or through a correspondence course such as those published in *American Libraries*, which require participants to read certain materials and complete written assignments.
- *Public libraries should develop and publicize specific non-negatively worded written policies and procedures for dealing with latchkey children.* They ought to do this whether or not they presently encounter this phenomenon.
- *Public libraries should re-evaluate their present programs/services available for latchkey children and their parents.* This should be done with the goal of providing additional traditional library-related services—including, on a trial basis, information and referral services for latchkey children and their families via an online computerized community resource database. Non-traditional services, such as security guards or monitors and after-school child care services, should be eliminated.

- *Public librarians should become actively involved in some type of community-sponsored committee/board/task force composed of representatives from neighborhood agencies.* Its goal should be to explore and provide appropriate services/programs for latchkey children during the after-school hours in order to meet the local area's particular needs.
- *Additional research on the topic of latchkey children in public libraries is warranted.* I make this recommendation not only because no studies other than this have investigated this topic, but also because the online computerized latchkey community resource database merits implementation on a broad scale. Ideally research will involve demonstration sites at several various-sized public libraries throughout the United States where there are a significant number of library latchkey children, and the evaluation will be qualitative, including pre- and post-testing.

MITCH SNYDER ON THE HOMELESS IN AMERICA

Mitch Snyder

The Homeless in America

I am a member of the community for Creative Non-Violence in Washington, a group that came together in 1970 in response to the war in Vietnam. We figured out after about two years that there was a domestic counterpart to the violence of Southeast Asia and for us that was manifested most clearly in the existence of hungry and homeless people within just a few blocks of the White House. We opened a soup kitchen in 1972. With the opening of the kitchen we began to work more closely and to serve to advocate on behalf of, and fairly quickly live with, people who are very poor and destitute.

During those antiwar years some of us used to travel around the country and say to folks like you all, "The war is going to come home. You can't do that kind of violence with impunity somewhere else, and at some point the implications of that will turn on us and the violence will return to us." And people would say, "Well, what does that mean? What do you mean by that?" And we would say, "Well, we don't know for sure. We just know that as the night follows the day, that this war will come home." Now we have a better understanding of what this means. We have a half million automatic weapons floating around in this country, many of them in the hands of children. We are the murder capital of the Western world and

---

"Mitch Snyder on the Homeless in America," by Mitch Snyder in *Public Libraries* Vol. 22, no. 5 (September/October 1989), pp. 283–291; reprinted with permission from the American Library Association, copyright © 1989 by ALA.

The editor and the jury regret the recent death of the author, whose work on behalf of the homeless in America will be long remembered.

our capital, which is in fact the capital of the Western world, has how many murders per year now? I live there and I can't even keep count any more. They come too quickly. We live in a country that is about as drugged up as it is possible to be and still be functioning.

I drove into Fort Wayne, Indiana, right in the middle of the heartland, and the first sign I saw when I got into town was "Got a problem with crack or cocaine? Call this number." I was shocked. It is one thing to see that in Washington or New York or Chicago. It is another to see it in a moderate-size city in the middle of the Midwest. But that is what it means when war comes home.

You Can't Let Millions of Human Beings Live This Way

Some of us travel around the country and we say, "You know, you can't let millions of human beings live this way. Especially you can't do this to the kids because allowing three quarters of a million or more children to grow up out of the backs of cars or under bridges or in abandoned buildings or in apartments with three, four, five other families or in welfare hotels is going to do really terrible things to those kids." And people say, "Well, what does that mean?" And once again we are forced to answer we don't know exactly what this means but we can guarantee you one thing—don't walk into a dark alley with one of those kids ten or fifteen years from now, because you won't walk out the other side. And you probably won't fully understand what hit you but that kid has turned into an adult with no hope and no future and you will feel the pain and the anger that that kind of deprivation produces.

I would like to address two things. One is the programmatic. Why are there lots of homeless people? The second is more difficult to come to grips with and that is the systemic. Why is all this happening beyond the obvious, beyond the programmatic, beyond the fact that roughly 80 percent of the housing budget has been cut over the last eight years? This is the primary cause of homelessness in America. And whether you are poor or whether you are working and not making very much money or whether you are mentally or physically disabled, *your bottom line is that you don't have a place to live.* And there is a crisis in housing that didn't drop from the sky. The budget was cut by $25 billion a year between 1981 and 1989. We were spending $32 billion a year on housing programs and now we are spending well under $8 billion and Mr. Bush and Mr. Kemp in a fit of kindness and gentleness have suggested bringing it down closer to $6 billion.

We have many homeless people because we don't have affordable housing. When the federal government doesn't build affordable housing, nobody builds affordable housing. Anyone that tells you that the private sector can pick up the slack is either an idiot or a liar. The private sector ain't going to build affordable housing when the private sector can build condos, co-ops, office buildings, shopping malls, and high-ticket housing. There is just no reason to do it. They are in the business to make money. It is unrealistic and absurd to suggest that people in the private sector are going to start building affordable housing just as it is ridiculous to suggest that if the federal government stopped putting all the money into interstate highways, that the private sector would pick it up.

You have Habitat for Humanity—that is a wonderful thing. Habitat for Humanity would probably take three or four thousand years at their present rate to make up the current housing shortfall, which is going to double in fifteen years. The same thing would happen with interstate highways. If the feds stopped putting money into interstate highways, within about seven or eight years, whenever you left a major city you would be driving on a dirt road. The same, of course, is true of the defense department. Nobody is suggesting seriously that the private sector take over and people get together in their backyards and start building howitzers. It is not going to work this way for DOD, it doesn't work that way for the highways, *and it doesn't work that way for housing.*

When the federal government walked away from the responsibility to build, maintain, and encourage the construction of affordable housing, affordable housing disappeared. It is a reflection of the shift of priorities in this country that it's only funds for affordable housing that have disappeared. Just as with the larger budget has been this dramatic shift of resources, our nation's wealth, from legitimate human needs—health care, day care, assistance to older folks, the children, to the disabled, to pregnant women, veterans—all of those resources have been shifted massively to the service of essentially very wealthy and powerful people and corporations. This is reflected by the fact that right now the federal government spends less than $8 billion on all housing programs—moderate-income, middle-income, low-income—and at the same time it spends a great deal of income subsidizing housing for people who are essentially upper-income.

Is there anyone in the audience who owns their own home? Do you write off your mortgage interest? Your property taxes? Then why the hell don't you assume that that is a subsidy? It costs the federal government $46 billion a year to cover the cost of your write-offs. The majority of people who avail themselves of these tax write-offs earn over $50,000 a year. So on the one hand we are spending more than $46 billion a year, up about 50 percent since 1980, to subsidize housing for predominantly upper-income people, and on the other we spend less than $8 billion a year to subsidize housing for predominantly lower- and moderate-income people, down from $32 billion a year. This is the kind of economic justice that has developed over the last eight years, and nothing has taken a harder hit than housing, which is why there are all those folks out on the streets. Yes, it is true that people have been displaced by deinstitutionalization, which I am sure many of you as public librarians would be very familiar with, but it is not deinstitutionalization that put the people on the streets. It is the absence of community-based housing. Where are people supposed to live? Dumping them out of the institutions, putting them on the street, providing them no mental health services of any consequence, no housing that is in any way either appropriate or available is guaranteed to cause people to be homeless. So whether they are there because they are mentally disabled or whether they are there because the minimum wage really doesn't sustain them is not the point. In most parts of this country you just can't live on $3.35 an hour.

A Million People to Washington, D.C.

The underlying cause of homelessness is the absence of housing. Again, this is the programmatic. And this is the easy one to deal with. It is easy in the sense that in October 1989 we are going to bring a million people to Washington, D.C., and we are going to force Congress to put the money back in the budget and if they don't put the money back in the budget, we will tell Congress we will tear their building down one brick at a time and hand it back to them because we will not allow them to walk away from that obligation that was articulated when I was five years old back in 1949. A conservative Republican senator, Senator Taft of Ohio, introduced a bill that committed the federal government to the creation of safe, decent, affordable housing for every citizen, and we intend to get Congress and the federal government back to that commitment. Whether this will take three months or two years or five years I don't know, but I assure you that we *will* make them do it because there are enough of us. If there were two, that would be enough because the truth is so blatantly clear and the injustice is so profoundly obvious. At some point we will understand what is going on. And by "we" I mean this nation, this country of ours.

Why Do We Allow This to Happen?

But again this is the easy part. The hard part is *why*? Why does this happen? Why do we allow this to happen? You all deal with information, right? I have no interest in information. Information is neutral. I am more interested in the context within which it lives and the reality within which it functions. You take information to do all kinds of interesting things with it. Of and by itself it is valueless. The context is what interests me because the context is what has driven 3 million people to the streets and what has eliminated 80 percent of the housing budget while we have nearly doubled the defense budget during this same period of time. It is the context which interests me because I always wonder why, when I go to every major city that I have ever visited, the nicest part of town is the cemetery. Well-manicured lawns, beautiful area. Everybody there is dead. And then you go to the ghetto where everybody is alive and there are rats and roaches and things are falling down, and so it is the context and the reality that I find far more interesting because that, in fact, is what governs our lives and our futures.

I moved to the streets of Washington for the second time in 1980 on the first day of winter. I remained there till the last day of winter, and I took up residence on a heat grate in the middle of downtown Washington, D.C., just a few blocks away from the monument and right across the street from the Interior Department. Occasionally at night I would leave that grate on which I slept and I would walk to what at that time was the only public bathroom in D.C. at night, one by the Washington Monument. It has since been closed because it was used. Now there are no bathrooms in Washington at night available to anyone and of course it is a crime to defecate or urinate in public and there are at least 15,000 people who are homeless in Washington and there are 5,000 beds which means at least 10,000 people are forced to commit crimes virtually every day, but at that time there was this one bathroom. And I would occasionally go there at night, and particularly on nights when the weather was bad, the scene would be a very amazing one. I would walk in and there would be dozens of people in that bathroom. People would be sitting up on the stalls snoring. People would be hunched in corners and propped up against the walls, curled up on the floor, and occasionally the police would come and they would shuffle everybody out, and as inevitable as the tide, everybody would flow back as soon as the police left because the alternative to being in the bathroom was to be nowhere and when the weather was bad, you might die or you might lose limbs because of frostbite and gangrene.

It just finally distressed the police sufficiently to cause them to shut down the bathroom and so now nobody uses it. Some of those folks froze to death. Closing that bathroom killed them. But back in 1980 the bathroom was open and I would go there and I found the sight to be disgusting. Not the people, they weren't disgusting. What was disgusting was that dozens of human beings were reduced to living in a bathroom, many of them eating out of trash bins during the day, and for me the most distressing part of the whole experience was when I would walk out of that bathroom, and I would look up and in front of me was the Washington Monument, the symbol of our power, our majesty. And I would turn to the right and there would be the White House and I would turn around and back there was the United States Capitol looking probably like the Senate looked in Rome, very powerful, very brightly lit, very imposing, and for me the most difficult part of all of that was the contrast, the contradiction. And the contradiction, of course, was that the bathroom in the midst of all of those trappings of power—economic, political, power of empire—in the midst of all of that were dozens of human beings whose only sin or common bond was that they were in some way temporarily or permanently disabled either economically or physically or emotionally, desperately and legitimately in need of help and reduced to living in a bathroom and eating out of trash bins.

Now one can look at that sight and without a great deal of intellect understand *something is wrong*. The dilemma is that good people spend considerable amounts of time and energy thinking and talking about and attempting to discern the root causes of that kind of injustice and, in fact, in almost every instance what people are looking at are the branches, never even coming close to what is really responsible.

Everything Ain't Going to Get Better

The truth is that neither the existence of those folks in that bathroom or the millions throughout our country in every town, city, and rural community that I ever visited, and I have been in more than 100 communities in the last several weeks alone, the existence of those people is not an accident. The kind of violence and injustice that exists within our nation and our world—every minute about forty-five people starve to death or die at least as a consequence of malnutrition, the majority of them children under five. The squandering of the wealth of our country and the wealth of our world on instruments whose only function and purpose is to destroy humankind and the planet, the desecration of the environment—the destruction of the land, the air, and the water on which we as a species rely for our continued existence—none of these outrages is temporary. It is not as though if we just had a couple of Ralph Naders tinkering here and adjusting there everything would get better. *Everything ain't going to get better.* Everything is going to continue to get worse because all these things are not temporary aberrations. They are the logical and predictable consequence of our effort to build a livable society on a foundation of unbridled competition and individualism and greed. I said that to a group of folks in Detroit a couple of months ago and somebody ripped up and said, "Aha, you are a Communist." And I said, "No, aha, I am a Christian, and isn't it sad that you can't tell the difference between the two?" The truth is that we are reaping what we have sown. *And it is not going to get better.* It is not going to get better for you. It is not going to get better for your kids. We can slow it down a little bit from time to time with a burst of energy or a massive display of instinct for survival, but it is not going to be reversed until all of us do and change a couple of things. It seems to me, and I will easily accept that while all five billion human beings on the face of the earth are all individual like snowflakes, there ain't no problem, but we also share certain basic needs and aspirations and drives and have certain basic responsibilities that have to be fulfilled.

We Are All Members of One Family

Until we acknowledge that there is in fact a just and living God and call it whatever you will, think in whatever terms are comfortable or fit within your brain, there is something that is everywhere. This universe is very large. There may even be more than one universe. All is bound together with a very impressive display of harmony, and the existence of that harmony, the existence of that God implies inexorably that all human beings are brothers and sisters to one another. All people, regardless of nationality, regardless of economics, color, or race, are members of one family, equal members of one family—very large and beautiful and coherent creation and anything that disrupts or denies that oneness is wrong. What I just said is an abstraction. And we can take it out of the abstract real quick. Anyone in this room who has got two pair of shoes is a thief because there are folks barefoot and if you think there is no connection between your shoes and their feet, you are wrong. You are either wrong, or you are functioning in a reality that bears no relationship to that which exists. If you have a room in your house that isn't being used, you are killing folks because they are outside freezing to death, not because the federal government isn't doing their job. They're not. But they're not doing their job because we are not doing our job and because we fail to hold others to the same level of accountability that we would wish to be held to and we make it easy for institutions to walk away *because we walk away*.

Five Percent of the World Consuming 50 Percent of the World's Wealth

There is a direct correlation and relationship between the food that we stuff in our mouths in this country to the point of causing illness among many people in America—many of us are not properly nourished, not that we are inadequately nourished—we are improperly nourished. We consume and suck up all of the resources of this planet and what, 5 percent of the world's population consuming somewhere around 50 percent of the world's wealth? I heard an interesting statistic the other day and it involved China and obviously they have their problems over there. And people are paying a high price in trying to solve some of them but one of the problems is not homelessness. There are no homeless Chinese. A nation of 1.2 billion people and they don't have any homeless folks. They are a very poor country and they don't have any homeless folks. And they are so poor, in fact, that—and this was the interesting statistic that I read, we feed so much protein, so much grain to our cows, to our livestock to try and marble them and do all kinds of interesting things with the meat so that we can consume it and enjoy it that the animals are not capable of digesting the vast majority of what they consume. It comes out the other end unprocessed. It is still raw protein. There is more protein that comes out the other end of our cows than is consumed by all of China every year; *1.2 billion people eat less protein than our cows shit every year.* That's the reason people are starving throughout this world, and so we need to take concepts like God and justice and truth out of the abstract and apply them to the way we live and to the way we use the resources we have and to the way we treat our neighbors and to what we declare a priority.

We Have Allowed So Much Distance to Develop Between Ourselves and Others

Now what takes priority when somebody who is homeless walks into the library? If you say the priority is anything other than the well-being of that human being whose life and health is in direct jeopardy at that moment in time, I would say you are culturally inept, which is why we step over the broken bodies of our neighbors and go about our business and continue to stuff ourselves while thirty-five people are permitted to starve to death, most of them children under five. And the reason all of that goes on is not because we are inherently evil. We are not. We are inherently good. That's my belief and no one will ever sway me, but we have allowed so much distance to develop between ourselves and others, particularly those that don't look or act or smell like we do, that the gulf, that distance, that space is the space within which all of the evil of the world fits neatly and comfortably. This is why we are able to go to war with people and blow them away—we don't see them as human beings. They are the enemy. It's why we can allow those thirty-five people per minute to starve to death, most of them children under five. It's not because we lack compassion, but because we lack vision. We don't see them as human beings. They are not, not for us. They are something other than human beings because if they were human beings, we wouldn't let them starve to death.

If we saw and understood and felt the humanity of those folks, we would do whatever it takes to enable them to come inside because we couldn't let them be outside. We would understand that in looking at them, we are looking at us and that we are looking at all that is important to us and dear to us, those we love, those we know, those that are familiar to us, but because they are not familiar and they are not known and they are not loved, we are prepared to abide all kinds of evil and it grows worse and worse and we grow more and more distant and the walls and the barriers that we have erected become increasingly complex and sophisticated and increasingly difficult to take down, so we need to reduce that distance and we need to respond to the situations that confront us such as homelessness.

If tonight there were 50,000 people burned out of their homes in New York City, you and I know what would happen. The governor and the mayor would declare a state of emergency and the Red Cross and the Salvation Army would rush in personnel and supplies and school buildings and churches would throw open those doors and all 50,000 people would be inside tonight, and before the morning came, people would set in motion the process that would guarantee those folks permanent housing before too long—and yet there are at least 100,000 people homeless in New York City right now. Where are the Red Cross and the Salvation Army? Where is the state of emergency? Where are the churches and the school buildings throwing open their doors? And where is anyone in this room who can explain to me what in God's name the difference is whether you got there under that bridge or on the street because of a fire or flood or an earthquake or unemployment or mental disability or minimum wage? The answer is that there is no difference, at least not for those folks out there, and that is why people in the shelter where I live, and I live in a shelter with 1,400 people, were very angry when they watched some months back as airplanes started taking off from every major country in the world heading to the Soviet Union to bring supplies and resources to people who have been devastated by an earthquake. They weren't angry and upset because they couldn't emphathize with those folks—they could emphathize better than most could—but they were angry because they didn't understand why all the airplanes were going the other way. They watched as anchormen and women would tell them that half of a million people had been blown out of their homes, that the temperature was dropping rapidly and it was getting down to freezing and there was a real danger that people would start dying out there, and they were angry because they knew damn well that at exactly that same moment in places like Minnesota and Wisconsin freezing would be considered tropical and they understood that there were six times that number of people destitute in our country and no planes heading this way, no supplies and resources coming this way. All going the other way. That is a problem with proportion, it is a problem of vision, it is a problem of our having grown to accept the kind of misery and pain that 3 million people living in our streets represent and our ability to have insulated ourselves sufficiently to bury those feelings except when it is an emergency, a catastrophe, when it attacks people who weren't that way yesterday and hopefully won't be that way tomorrow.

And openly and lastly we have to understand the nature of change if we are to have any hope at all of effecting it in either a positive or predictable way. I have a friend, a Jesuit priest named Ned, who is a very simple fellow (which, if you know Jesuits at all, you would understand is an inconsistency), but he has reduced things down to their basics and Ned, who runs the soup kitchen, which generally helps you get simple, Ned would say, "Envision if you would an infinitely long table and on that table are arrayed all of the finest foods that you can imagine and stretching out in front of that table of equally infinite length is a line of people, each of whom has one hand securely tied behind their back and in the other they hold a fork for feedings and for eternity these poor souls exist in a hell of their own creation because try as they might they can never get that food into their mouths because the fork is just too long," and so Ned would say, "How long do you think it would take if just one of those people would put some food on the end of that fork and turn and serve the person next to them?" How long would it take before the simple liberating truth of that act that it is better to serve and be served than to starve in the face of plenty, made its way up and down that line and the answer is, a relatively short period of time because as damaged as we have been by this culture, we can still recognize the truth when we see it. We can still intuitively understand that something is happening which is right and reasonable and so Ned would say we teach by example and we change the world by example, not by words. Words are cheap instruments. We cheapened them in places like Vietnam where we talked about protective reactive strikes and pacification programs which were in effect annihilation programs. And ultimately we are called on to do our share and that's it. We are called on to do our share in the creation of a decent, just, sane, and equitable world, the world in which we don't stand at each other's throats with loaded revolvers, a world in which we don't tear away the resources that each of us needs to live and survive. All we need to do, Ned would say, is our share.

What Does It Mean to Do Our Share?

And so the question, at least for me, the ultimate question, in fact the only question that is even worthy of addressing is *what does it mean to do my share*? And what does it mean for you? Unfortunately, I have no answer to provide you, and in fact, if I could provide you an answer, I would suggest that you leave the room quickly because either I would be insane or lying to you or trying to trick you because the nature of liberation is that no one can provide it for anyone else. No one can offer anyone any kind of magic answer, a little pearl that can be taken that will make everything right and clear and beautiful and wonderful again. The process of liberation is a personal one, an individual one. Theologians would say that there is no heaven, there is simply the journey to it. It is in the struggle that you find heaven and that you find truth, not in the destination because you never arrive and it is the same with the struggle for personal liberation and for personal justice. That's an individual struggle and we have to wrestle with the kinds of questions that we address on a daily basis. I hate to keep harping on it, but you've got a real live one, and that is what librarians do when people come in who are smelly or crazy or taking up space and aren't there to use the books but just to get in out of the elements? That's just one of the questions that we face. We face questions like that every single day. We have to wrestle with those questions because our salvation and probably the salvation of the world is dependent on our willingness to do that and our success, not at achieving some goal, but our success at making sure that we are constantly less than comfortable and constantly challenging our own suppositions and the parameters within which we are bouncing all the time.

But while I can't offer you the answer to the question, what I can share with you in closing is a personal experience that I found helpful in getting a better understanding of the nature of the question where the answer might lie.

I said earlier, I think, I live in a shelter with 1,400 people and it is a very nice place. We convinced the government to spend $14 million renovating it and making it the largest and most comprehensive facility of its kind in the country, and as shelters go it is about as good as you are going to find and it should be closed tomorrow. The place has no right to exist because it is a shelter and not a home, and we are too wealthy and too powerful to be throwing shelters out to our citizens. But a couple of years ago there was not a $14 million shelter, it was a hole in the wall. It was a place that had holes in the wall literally so large that you could go in and out without ever using the door, the windows were either missing panes or missing windows and so the wind and the rain and the snow would howl through the building. For extended periods of time we had only two toilets and two showers. A building of 180,000 square feet with a thousand people in it doesn't work real well with two toilets and so the older folks particularly and the more disabled people, they would defecate and urinate where they were and so the place looked like and smelled like and was in fact a sewer, a human sewer, and yet a thousand people squeezed into that place because the alternative was so much worse. And at least they weren't freezing to death in there, and I used to stand on the front steps of that building in the evening as hundreds of people would come pouring in and the feelings that I experienced were very similar to the feelings that I experienced when I walked in and out of that bathroom by the Washington Monument, only 50-fold, 100-fold, because there we were talking about dozens of people; here I watched hundreds and hundreds of people, physically disabled people, people with no legs who left them in Vietnam, patriots who came back to live on the streets of their country—I don't even believe in war and I think that it is irrational not to take care of those who are going to fight them if you do. But we don't. We treat our soldiers very badly. Women, little old women seventy, eighty, ninety years old getting physically abused, raped repeatedly, going in and out of that building, children, people who are obviously senile and mentally disabled, just kind of mumbling and drifting on by, and I would stand there every night, every evening that I did that and I would watch in silence because there is not really a lot you say in the face of all of that as there is not a lot to say when you walk into a bathroom with dozens of people living in it. Inside I would conduct the same dialogue every single time. And actually it was a monologue, it wasn't really a dialogue. I would look out over this mass of human misery pouring into that building and I would say, "God, this is insane. You can't let this go on. This is wrong. It just isn't right. Look at the little old lady. What in God's name did she ever do, what in your name did she ever do to deserve this? And the guy with no legs and the person who is blind." And to this day I can't comprehend how you can live on the streets and be blind and I am really grateful that I have never had a chance to find out, but there are and there were blind people living in that building wandering in and out every day. And so I would say, "God, do whatever you got to do to make it right, to make it better, stop it because it is wrong. You just can't let it go on."

And again and again it would be the same monologue and then one evening not all that long before we finally convinced the government to renovate the building, it finally dawned on me. What dawned on me was that it was and is in the existence of those hundreds of people pouring into that building and millions of others just like them in this country and hundreds of millions of others far worse off than them throughout this world and the existence of all those people, that God was saying to me exactly what I was saying to God, which is look at all these innocent people. What did the guy do who left his legs in Vietnam, who was stupid enough to be a patriot and to take it all seriously and to go over there and fight and to lose parts of his body and then come home and be given the streets as a home? And the little old lady and the kid and the blind person, what did they ever do to deserve any of this and why don't you do whatever you have got to do to make sure that that doesn't happen and that doesn't go on because I didn't make it. I didn't create it. You did and so now you uncreate it and you make it better and you end it because it is a blasphemy. It is an insult to the truth to allow millions of human beings to live and die that way in a country of our wealth and power.

A Final Message of Urgency

The one thing that I always bring everywhere I go is a final message of urgency. Unless you have been outside, you have absolutely no comprehension of what it is like to be outside. You can't. It is a horror. It is an absolutely disgusting, inhuman way to live and whatever you have got to do and whatever you can do to guarantee those folks who are your sisters and brothers and your mothers and fathers and your son and daughters, whether you understand it or not—and in fact, those folks are you, whether you understand it or not, and you will never be whole as long as they are cold and alone—whatever you have got to do to get those folks inside, do it. People have a desperate need for shelter, no matter what it is—to get in out of the elements—and we have got to provide it. People have got even more desperate need for homing and it ain't going to come magically. It is only going to come if we force it back into existence, if we start acting like we live in a democracy and the citizens have both a right and a responsibility to show the policies and the priorities to govern our lives.

Unless we begin to take our responsibilities as citizens, as human beings, as sisters and brothers seriously, then not only isn't it going to change and get better, but it is going to keep getting worse. So it is not nice to be polite and patient in the face of injustice and evil. We should not be polite. We should not be patient. We should be screaming at the top of our lungs that something horrible is going on because human beings have been reduced to this kind of existence and we, you, I, all of us, should do whatever it takes to make sure that within a very short period of time we will be able to look back with horror and embarrassment on the fact that this country abided the existence of millions of people on the streets. If we do this with a sense of seriousness and with a sense of commitment and with an open mind and an open heart out of our proximity to our neighbors who are suffering and in pain, then it will get better, and if we don't, then it will keep getting worse and the truth is that the power is in our hands. It is not in Congress' hands. It is not in the White House's hands. It is not in the hands of people who run big corporations. Those folks have no power at all. They have the illusion of power. We, all of us, any of us have the ultimate power, which is the power to transform the world in which we live, and because so few of us take that responsibility and that possiblity seriously, the world is going to hell in a hand basket.

PART III:
POLITICAL ISSUES

THERE ARE NO NEUTRALS IN POLITICS

John N. Berry III

Herb White and Ed Holley, two of librarianship's chief worriers, are currently worried about how our professional politics mesh with the kinder, gentler administration of George Bush. They both sweat out our "errors" from vantage points in the groves of academe.

Holley wants us to take seriously the badly flawed, half-hearted Bush administration proposal for a "Library Service Improvement Act" (*American Libraries,* June 1989, p. 525–528). The bill is a thinly disguised attempt by a Republican administration to escape from or reduce funding for that long-established, bipartisan in origin, federal responsibility for library support negotiated back in the Fifties.

White is afraid that if we continue to support causes that are "invariably espoused by liberal Democrats" (White Papers, *Library Journal,* June 15, p. 40–41), we will offend Bush Republicans.

The two agree that we're stuck with the current political situation, so we must, as White put it, "play the hand we're dealt."

In fact, librarianship and especially the American Library Association have done exactly that. We have played our hand with consummate skill and great success.

ALA forged bipartisan alliances that gave us a successful White House Conference on Libraries and Information Services in 1979. White's critique of that conference fails to report that more than 75 percent of its recommendations have been enacted into law. That alliance gave us the Library Services and Construction Act (LSCA) plus the library titles of the Higher Education Act and the National Defense Education Act. It was ALA's very effective efforts that brought nonpartisan victory.

We librarians join professional associations to add collegial voices to our views on a host of issues. Although those issues are not acted out in libraries, they have impact on libraries. We couldn't care less whether this conscientious taking of positions by our association offends White, Holley, or even Lyndon Johnson, Jimmy Carter, Ronald Reagan, and George Bush.

ALA has won bipartisan support for library legislation even though ALA supported the Equal Rights Amendment and opposed the Vietnam War, AIDS testing, and racial and sexual discrimination. Support for libraries was, and in the current Congress still is, bipartisan, maybe even better, nonpartisan.

Despite that nonpartisan support, White blames us for "polarization." Despite ALA's success in getting funding for the nonpartisan LSCA, Holley asks us to support the first truly partisan library legislation ever proposed.

It is not we librarians who are partisan. Political parties take partisan stands. One party opposed funding for the federal responsibility to libraries for the eight years it was in office. We were forced to oppose that partisan position. In our opposition, we won support for that library funding in Congress.

The new Republican administration apparently got our message. It has moderated that opposition to federal library support. To cut its losses on this issue the Bush administration has even proposed legislation. Holley tells us to take that legislation seriously, even though the Bush administration only barely takes it seriously. The drafter of the bill has left the government.

Don't be afraid to vote for ALA to push for continued federal funding of library programs that work like LSCA because Ed Holley says they are obsolete. Obviously Congress disagrees.

Don't be afraid to vote for ALA to support causes because White labels them partisan. ALA has supported causes since the Fifties. This has never harmed our legislative efforts in any way. We librarians have been very successful in our political battles. These exhortations to neutrality by our chief worriers offer far less promise for success. As Herb White put it in that same column: "There are no neutrals in the political process."

TOWARD A NATIONAL INFORMATION POLICY: WHAT SHOULD WE EXPECT FROM A SECOND WHITE HOUSE CONFERENCE?

Patricia W. Berger

In 1987, the National Commission on Libraries and Information Sciences (NCLIS) announced the theme for the second White House Conference on Libraries and Information Services—"Productivity, Literacy, and Democracy." In 1988, President Reagan signed Public Law 100-382, which provided for a second conference and authorized (but did not appropriate) $6 million to cover part of the expenses. The law directed the President to convene the conference not earlier than September 1, 1989 and not later than September 30, 1991. It stated that the conference shall be "planned and conducted under the direction of NCLIS."

As was true for the 1979 conference, there will be an advisory committee of 31 members, which will include the Librarian of Congress and the Secretary of Education. The chair of NCLIS will serve as the committee chair. The purpose of the conference is to "develop recommendations for the further improvement of the library and information services of the national and their use by the public in accordance with the findings set forth in the preamble to this [law]."

As you might expect, the preamble constitutes a laundry list of those information access issues that librarians hold dear, including:

• The belief that "access to information is indispensable to the develop-

---

"Toward A National Information Policy," by Patricia W. Berger in *Bottom Line* Vol. 3, no. 2 (1989), pp. 11–17; reprinted with permission from Neal-Schuman Publishers, Inc.

ment of human potential, the advancement of civilization, and the continuance of enlightened self-government"
- The tenet that "the economic vitality of the United States in a global economy and the productivity of the work force of the nation rest on access to information in the post-industrial information age"
- The fact that "library and information service is essential to a learning society."

Because:

- "Social, demographic and economic shifts of the past decade have intensified the rate of change and require that Americans of all age groups develop and sustain literacy and other lifelong learning habits."

And because:

- "The growth and augmentation of the nation's library and information services are essential if all Americans . . . are to have reasonable access to adequate information and lifelong learning."

The preamble also declares that:

- "The future of our society depends on developing the learning potential inherent in all children and youth . . . ."

The precise composition of the delegates is set out in the law:

- One quarter must be individuals from the library and information profession,
- One quarter must be persons who, at the time of the conference, are "active library and information supporters including trustees and friends groups,"
- One quarter must be federal, state or local government officials,
- One quarter must be selected from the "general public."

In addition, delegates must be members of one of the following groups:

- "Representatives of professional library and information personnel"
- "Individuals who support or furnish volunteer services to libraries and information services centers"

- "Representatives of local, statewide, regional, and national institutions, agencies, organizations, and associations which provide library and information services to the public"
- "Representatives of educational institutions, agencies, organizations, and associations (including professional and scholarly associations for the advancement of education and research)"
- "Individuals with special knowledge of, and special competence in, technology . . . for the improvement of library and information services."

Clearly, the time has come for librarians, their supporters, patrons, and library associations to spell out what they wish the conference to accomplish. During the months ahead, conference agendas—public and hidden—will be crafted and lobbied. We must be involved in that process. First of all, while I am sure the second conference's advisory committee will be dedicated and hard-working, I suspect that some of the appointees will find it difficult to spend long hours on conference matters, due to the press of their other duties. This is a common weakness of advisory committees, and I believe some of us may be asked to assist committee members with their pre-conference work.

Second, it became evident during 1988 that not all NCLIS commissioners are friends of libraries, of librarians, or of library patrons. Indeed, NCLIS's description of itself as an "honest broker" in library matters no longer fits. When NCLIS met with a representative of the Federal Bureau of Investigation in January 1988, several NCLIS commissioners vociferously defended the FBI's attempts to persuade science librarians to report the reading and research habits of their patrons "with foreign-sounding names."

Both NCLIS's chair and one commissioner-librarian went so far as to excoriate science librarians in general and the staff of the American Library Association's Office of Intellectual Freedom in particular for insisting that library patrons have a right to read what they want, when and where they want to read it, without fear of scrutiny by any outside agent. There is a danger, then, that what John Berry has called the "Politicization of NCLIS" could cause a skewing of the White House Conference agenda in destructive, non-productive ways.[1]

The 1979 Conference

The first White House Conference on Libraries, held in 1979, evolved around the theme "Bringing Information to People." I was a conference delegate for the federal library community. Conference preparation by the White House Conference on Library and Information Services (WHCLIS) staff was extensive. Weeks before we convened, I received an array of background materials—some in print, some on tape—on the role of information in various facets of our society. My two most pervasive conference recollections are, first, of a vast amount of time spent discussing the role and potential of the public library and, second, of multiple sessions exploring more creative ways to relieve the federal government of money. Because these two matters dominated so much of the agenda, delegates for academic, school, and special libraries as well as minority delegates felt that their needs and those of their patrons were ignored.

The Washington, D.C. staff of the American Library Association will tell you that the 1979 conference was a great success. Further, the White House Conference Task Force (WHCLIST), which organized as a result of the conference, would agree with ALA's assessment. I do not share that view, for, while the conference generated good will and financial help for public libraries, it did little to articulate the issues those libraries and their communities would face throughout the 1980's, including financial issues, nor did it identify the information problems other types of libraries, as well as other professions, vocations, and institutions, would encounter. In vain will you search the conference proceedings for in-depth discussions of the nation's literacy and minority populations' problems, or of how libraries should position themselves to assist new immigrants. Although there are some exceptions—such as the omnibus education resolution for Native Americans, which the delegates passed—many significant issues facing America's libraries were never discussed.

Finding the Focus

So, given my perception of the constraining process called a White House Conference, why would I opt for another? It was precisely because I was disappointed in the outcome of the first conference that I lobbied hard and successfully for a resolution, which I brought to the Conference from the Federal Library Community. That resolution calls for a second conference in ten years. I believed then and believe now that many of our problems will be solved only when substantial national attention is focused on them—attention from a diverse group of men and women who care about this country's intellectual, educational, economic, political, and ethical health and progress.

We must try again to articulate a broader national agenda for all libraries. We dare not do otherwise for two reasons: first, the United States lacks a rational, coherent body of national information policies. Second, we are faced with the very real and unpleasant prospect of entering the next century as productivity in the U.S., and its concomitant economic advantage, is decreasing and citizen illiteracy is increasing.

Next time, we must be sure that the conference's agenda and deliberations reflect a better balance among information issues, institutions, and constituencies. We must identify some of the causes of our more urgent information problems and intensify our search for remedies. Most of all, we must articulate a direction and focus for effective, responsive library and information services throughout the 1990s. Little progress will be made if we settle for resolutions that paper over our crucial problems by throwing more federal money at them.

I am not a Republican—I am a yellow-dog Democrat—but I have had my fill of attempts to solve society's problems, including its library problems, with dollars alone. Dollars are necessary to implement policy, but dollars can't and don't change bad policy, nor can dollars alone create good policy.

Let's focus on a single aspect of our productivity—our scientific productivity—and how access to reliable scientific information supports it. Although the question appears to be straightforward, the answer is not: How can we best maintain and increase our scientific productivity? By open exchange of scientific information and ideas, or by shrouding our scientific efforts in secrecy and surveillance?

Strong arguments continue to be advanced for both points of view. The delegates to the second White House Conference will need to pick their way through this doctrinal mine field in order to develop a rational, realistic position. The FBI defends its library awareness program by stating that it "seeks to alert librarians that they and their libraries are, and have historically been, significant . . . targets [of Soviet Intelligence services]."[2] The Bureau concedes that:

> The strength of a free society is derived from the easy exchange of information and ideas; ideas nurtured by the creativity and imagination of America's scientific, engineering and technical community. It is the very lacking of information and idea exchanges in a closed society that stifles creativity, suppresses the imagination, and acts as a barrier to social, economic, and technical progress. . . . The FBI has attempted to accomplish its objectives while safeguarding America's scientific and technical advances, recognizing that those advances flourish only in a free and open environment.[3]

The FBI argues that our scientific productivity is best protected, and therefore increased, by decreasing the number of persons with access to our science knowledge base. A similar position is enunciated by those who contend that the centuries-old scientific ethic regarding the value of rapid, open publication of new ideas and hypotheses is no longer a fruitful way to assure robust scientific progress. In a May 24, 1988, *New York Times* article, William Broad reports that:

> Dramatic increases over the last decade in scientists' ties to commercial enterprises . . . are adding to a trend toward secrecy that had already been accelerated by the rising rate of military contracts in the nation's scientific research. . . . Among the dangers . . . [are] not only productivity "breakdowns" but the tarnishing of the scientific image.
> The ethic of open scientific publication had its inception three centuries ago. . . . Reports of new discoveries are rushed into scholarly journals so insights can be widely shared. . . . In contrast, the new commercial secrecy seeks to delay publication of research findings or to eliminate it altogether so industry can use the secret research to make innovative products no rival can match. . . . Scholars say the fundamental force behind the expansion of industrial secrecy is the narrowing of the gap between science and technology. . . .
> In the early days of science, discoveries often found practical application only after the passage of decades or centuries . . . but today the delay can be as short as years and sometimes months. The result is that industry and inventors are increasingly eager to tap science as soon as possible and to monopolize its findings . . . industrial secrecy has moved

out of company laboratories and rapidly expanded into . . . the nation's system of . . . federal laboratories . . . the links between the federal labs and industry have been encouraged by congress and the administration, which are eager to increase American industrial innovation and productivity.[4]

Over the last eight years, federal efforts to increase scientific productivity and our economic base have sometimes missed the mark because administrators have misunderstood how scientific and technical information relate to scientific productivity. In April 1987, President Reagan signed executive order number 12591 "To ensure that federal agencies and laboratories assist universities and the private sector in broadening our technology base by moving new knowledge from the research laboratory into the development of new products and processes."[5]

Sounds great, except that an earlier change in federal policy had eliminated the requirement that government contractors report new technological developments. This earlier change continues to constrict our scientific and technological productivity. In a July 1986 article in *Technology Review*, M. J. Goldstone noted that by eliminating certain patent and invention reports formerly required of government contractors, the U.S. has "exchanged the future health of our nation's industry for an easier workday for federal contractors." The government claims that it gave up its first rights to new technology developed with tax dollars because it hoped contractors would do a better job of commercializing inventions than federal agencies have done. This may or may not have happened. Unfortunately, what has happened is a result predicted earlier by Admiral Hyman Rickover.

In 1980, Admiral Rickover warned that relaxing reporting requirements on discoveries would achieve exactly the opposite of what the government wanted. He said such changes "would impede, not enhance, the development and dissemination of technology; would hurt small businesses; would inhibit competition; and would be costly to taxpayers." He further commented that the new requirements would "allow contractors to use . . . technology . . . as trade secrets," which, while giving one contractor a competitive edge, would "hurt American industry in general." Moreover, he noted that a new process would benefit no one at all "if the contractor that develops it does not bother to . . . [market] it."[6]

I do not believe that these conditions result from the efforts of greedy or mindless bureaucrats who spend their days devising ways to gut government science programs of all relevant information. I do believe, however, that information policies like this one disregard the need for nurturing the rich, open archive of information and data required to increase scientific productivity. This is an important information issue with profound consequences for our long-term economic as well as scientific health; it is one which the delegates to the next White House Conference must address.

The OMB/GPO Factor

Reliable access to federal scientific information is further diminished because of radical changes in publishing technologies and in the information policies of both the Office of Management and Budget (OMB) and the Government Printing Office (GPO).

The elusive document is not a phenomenon peculiar to non-federal libraries. Indeed, the evolution of cheaper, user-friendly desktop publishing systems coupled with draconian cuts in funds for federal publishing and escalating publishing costs have persuaded many scientists in my institution to forsake formal publishing routes and produce limited numbers of camera-ready copies, which are then distributed to colleagues engaged in work similar to their own. Such redirection takes a substantial portion of the National Institute of Standards and Technology's (NIST) annual publications output out of the government's publications channels, and out of GPO's depository library dissemination program as well.

We try always to persuade our people not to forsake NIST's formal publication route, but we are not always successful. Frequently, a lack of dollars mandates a less-than-preferred publishing medium. In one instance, because there was *no* money to publish an index needed by state government officials throughout the country, it was turned over for publishing to an outside, not-for-profit, non-governmental organization. That organization simply added its own cover to the NIST index. The arrangement got the information into the hands of the state officials who needed it, and that's good; but it also took the index out of the depository library program, and that's not good at all. While we all know it's unwise to let costs drive policy decisions, costs may well continue to determine how federal documents are published and, therefore, how accessible they are, at least for as long as the National Deficit problem is severe.

Further, in recent years, changes in GPO's sales and pricing policies have persuaded many of our scientists that publishing through government channels wastes their time and money. In 1982, GPO informed us of something we already knew, that the research NIST performs rarely generates "best sellers." For example, many scientists in our center for absolute physical quantities work in esoteric research areas, which, while critically important to a limited number of their colleagues throughout the world, are of no moment to anyone else. So, when GPO staff announced that they would no longer accept our publications for sale unless they could be reasonably sure of selling at least 1,000 copies per year, we were in a pickle.

We persuaded GPO to market our wallflowers by agreeing to pay the printing costs for 100 copies of each document and then giving the copies back to GPO for public sale. Needless to say, our scientists and engineers are less than happy with these add-on costs. As a result of GPO's policy and NIST's reaction to it, the percentage of NBS/NIST publications offered for sale by GPO continues to decrease. From October 1987 through September 1988 the Superintendent of Documents accepted for sale just 34% of the reports NIST produced.

GPO's policies affect only those manuscripts which ordinarily would have or should have been issued as government documents. Every year, well over half of what NIST authors produce appears as articles in the core refereed scientific and technical journals and as parts or the whole of a book. Such manuscripts are not affected by GPO's policies or decisions.

OMB further limited access to federal scientific information when it took the position that online information dissemination by executive branch agencies should not be controlled by GPO because such dissemination is not bound by the definition of printing and binding in Chapter 5 of Title 44 of the U.S. Code. Further, OMB contended that the U.S. Department of Justice's interpretation of the Supreme Court's decision in *INS* v. *Chadba*, which declared the legislative veto unconstitutional, invalidated those parts of Chapter 5 giving GPO control over executive agency printing decisions. If OMB's position on this matter is unchanged at the time of the White House Conference, finding ways to reverse it will be a critically important task for delegates.

It is ludicrous for OMB to put forth two conflicting mandates: on the one hand, that executive agencies use the GPO Depository Program to disseminate paper copy of their organizations' documents and, on the other, that a large and proliferating body of government information is exempt from that program. OMB's position is untenable now; by 1991 it will be absurd!

In a letter written in 1822, James Madison observed that: "A popular government without popular information, or the means of acquiring it, is but a prologue to a farce or a tragedy: or perhaps both. Knowledge will forever govern ignorance. And a people who mean to be their own governors must arm themselves with the power knowledge gives."[7]

Madison considered scientific information to be popular information. But, in recent years, many policy makers have retreated from Madison's sentiment on the importance of "popular information" to a free people, even though that sentiment articulates an important measure of the value of information in a free society. Indeed, there is deep division and widespread disagreement between those who hold to Madison's perception of the value of information and those who view its worth strictly as a function of its use or cost. Somehow, some way, the value operator must reenter the information equation; otherwise, that equation is neither complete nor rational.

Keeping Science Accessible

While it is true that the present state of access to scientific information is far from healthy, strong and respected voices continue to protest the dismantling of scientific communications and the depletion and restriction of government scientific information and data. There is an ever-expanding community of critical commentators including not only the members of the American Library Association, but also legislators, members of other library and information associations, individual librarians, information scientists, journalists, authors, jurists, historians, educators, political analysts, publishers, scientific societies, and individual scientists and engineers. The problem with addressing this issue, then, is to discern patterns and intentions amid a surfeit of conflicting comment.

In 1982, a Presidential executive order clamped controls on the kinds of research that could be reported at unclassified scientific and engineering meetings attended by Warsaw Pact or Peoples' Republic of China scientists. As a result of the ensuing uproar in the scientific and engineering communities, the National Research Council convened a panel of academics, scientists, and industrialists. It was chaired by Cornell University's President Emeritus, Dr. Dale R. Corson. In October 1982, the panel issued its report, "Scientific Communication and National Security." The Corson panel found that there is "a substantial and serious transfer" of U.S. technology to the Soviet Bloc, a "significant portion" of which is damaging to U.S. security. However, the panel also found "very little" leakage of militarily significant information from open scientific research performed at universities.[8]

Perhaps the most significant conclusion of the panel was offered by Elmer Staats, a former U.S. comptroller general and a former executive officer of the National Security Council. Staats noted that: "There is a thread running throughout the whole report, [namely] a recognition that the most important idea we have had is that the strength of the United States lies in the openness of its scientific community. Over time, the Soviets can get any results from R&D that they concentrate on getting, but our strength is in keeping ahead of them by maintaining open communication and encouraging the resulting innovation."[9]

In a November 1982 article on the work of the Corson panel, Jean Coon noted that Staat's idea "formed the basis for what the panel termed 'security by accomplishment' in contrast to the current imposition of controls to enhance 'security by secrecy.'"[10]

The panel identified four criteria for defining sensitive technologies and recommended that a technology be identified as sensitive *only* if it met all four. The panel concluded: "The vast majority of university research, whether basic or applied, should be subject to no limitations of access or communications."[11]

Chairman Corson, when asked what he hoped the panel's chief accomplishment would be, replied: "If we succeed in having policy-making people in the federal establishment buy our analysis of what should be open and what is sensitive, that would be a great achievement."[12]

Protecting Information

Unfortunately, that was not to be. On September 17, 1984, National Security Decision Directive 145 was published. That directive ordered a Cabinet-level group to develop ways to protect not only government data and information, but also private and proprietary data and information in electronic databases. The directive stated that a "comprehensive and coordinated approach" is required to control "information, even if unclassified in isolation, [which] often can reveal highly classified and other sensitive information when taken in the aggregate."[13]

In addition to the President's signing of NSDD 145, the Pentagon issued an updated version of a report entitled "Soviet Acquisition of Militarily Significant Western Technology." The report stated that, in order for the Soviets to keep their military and economic systems functioning, they beg, buy, borrow, or steal U.S. science and technology, including the ideas, science, and technology created in U.S. universities. The report described 60 U.S. universities as "targets of opportunity which the Soviets have identified." Assistant Secretary of Defense Richard N. Perle said that the Pentagon hoped the report would "sensitize the scientific and technical community to the fact that there is a very large and well-organized Soviet apparatus that has targeted scientists and engineers and universities . . . [and] without intervention from the government . . . [scientists and engineers] may be more circumspect . . . [about] . . . what they publish and the circumstances in which it's made available."[14]

Perle added that "the price you pay for more classification is to narrow the circle of individuals who have access to information . . . [and who] . . . may be stimulus to research and development. . . . Striking a balance is difficult. . . . Were we to significantly restrict unclassified material, we would impair our own scientific and technical efforts."[15]

Executive Branch reassurances regarding the elimination of unnecessary restriction on unclassified scientific material seemed valid when President Reagan signed National Security Decision Directive 189. The policy section of NSDD 189 states that:

> To the maximum extent possible, the products of fundamental research remain unrestricted. It is also the policy of this administration that, when the national security requires control, the mechanism for control

of information generated during federally funded fundamental research in science, technology, and engineering . . . is classification. . . . No restriction may be placed upon the conduct or reporting of federally funded fundamental research that has not received national security classification, except as provided in applicable U.S. statutes.[16]

Dr. Robert M. Rosenzweig, who was then president of the Association of American Universities, summed up the collective reaction of scientists and engineers to NSDD 189 when he said "Those elements in the government who believe they can enhance security by keeping things from the Russians are still there and still very effective. But the new directive will provide those of us who believe in openness an important argument on our side. It helps us clear the cloudy atmosphere."[17]

Irwin Goodwin has observed that NSDD 189 established "an uneasy truce in the government's battle to keep scientific and technological secrets." He notes that "in recent years, spying has concentrated on acquiring the latest scientific and industrial information with military and economic implications."[18]

The Congress agrees with Goodwin's assessment. In a report entitled, "Meeting the Espionage Challenge," issued in October 1986 by the Senate Select Committee on Intelligence, the committee said that damage to the nation's security caused by the theft of advanced technology and incursions into electronic files "amounts to a staggering loss of sensitive information to hostile intelligence services. As an open society, the U.S. already allows its adversaries unfiltered access to vast amounts of information that must be shared widely so that our political system can function democratically and the process of free scientific inquiry can be most productive. Our openness gives hostile intelligence services the ability to focus their efforts on those few areas of our government and society where confidentiality is required."[19]

On February 23, 1988, President Reagan sent Congress proposed legislation, which he called the "Superconductivity Competitiveness Act of 1988." (I mentioned this act earlier in my description of industrial secrecy conditions in federal laboratories.) In the President's accompanying message, he advised the Congress that Title IV of the Act:

would provide protection for . . . commercially valuable scientific and technical information generated in federal . . . laboratories. . . . [such] information . . . loses potential commercial value when it is released wholesale under the Freedom of Information Act (FOIA). . . . Mandatory disclosure of such information . . . could encourage U.S. competitors to exploit the U.S. science and technology base rather than making investments in their own research. . . . Federal agencies will be required to withhold information . . . where disclosure could reasonably be expected to harm the economic competitiveness of the United States. . . . Title (IV) is not intended to end the U.S. tradition of sharing the benefits of . . . science and technology; it merely provides that the freedom of information act may not always be the appropriate or best avenue for doing so.[20]

In March 1988, William R. Graham, Jr., the President's science advisor, testified before the Senate's Judiciary Committee that "government scientists, unlike their colleagues in academia and industry, can be 'compelled' to release data, including laboratory notebooks on work in progress —even when doing so jeopardizes the government's ability to protect patent rights, copyrights or control of trade secrets.[21]

The Case for Openness

Professor Robert L. Park, of the University of Maryland, testified that one immediate effect of the proposal would be to "isolate researchers at federal laboratories from the rest of the scientific community. In a rapid moving field such as superconductivity," he said, "progress depends in large part on the informal exchange of ideas and results. Such informal channels are quickly severed if there is a perception that information from one side may be withheld. That could be disastrous," he added, "because many of the recent developments in the field have occurred outside of the United States. Clearly, we are in no position to erect a wall around this field."

Park said the restrictions could prompt foreign scientists to retaliate by withholding data and could create bureaucracies charged with censoring scientific information. "Nothing is more fundamental to scientific progress than the process of open encounter between scientists," said Dr. Park. "We read the papers of our colleagues, respond to their challenges in open debate, visit their laboratories, argue with them in the halls of our institutions. In the absence of this sort of open scientific scrutiny and debate, erroneous theories or sterile lines of inquiry become chronic."[22]

In an article in the March 30, 1988, issue of the *Chronicle of Higher Education*, Park notes that President Reagan's science advisor had been "reduced to little more than a cheerleader for the President's programs," even though "we are confronted on every hand with science-related problems that demand . . . honest technical advice even when it's not what the boss wants to hear.[23]

Park observes that Ashton Carter of Harvard argues "for greater reliance by the White House on institutions that openly publish their analyses for all interested consumers." Park concludes: "If there is one lesson we should have learned from the sad comedy of 'Star Wars'—and more recently from the Iran-Contra scandal—it is that flawed advice . . . given in secret, may go unchallenged at great cost to democracy."[24]

The ultimate irony for librarians, especially federal librarians, is that, as some government agencies work to develop ways to frustrate foreign access to unclassified information, other government agencies work to contract out their libraries to the lowest bidder, including foreign bidders.

As we all know, databases are most often accessed via an organization's library. In addition, most federal libraries include in their collections the data and information gathered or developed by their parent agencies. The relevance to the information leakage problem, of access to databases and federal library collections containing agency-specific information seems to have escaped the policy-makers thus far. It has not, however, escaped the notice of Congress.

Equally ironic are the dual efforts of the executive branch to prohibit foreign access to the document collections of NTIS while laboring mightily to contract out *all* NTIS operations and functions to the private sector.

On June 29, 1986, William Carey, who was then executive officer of the American Association for the Advancement of Science, had this to say about contracting out and privatization:

> Privatization is not a panacea . . . when it becomes a pretentious coverup for the indiscriminate dumping of public responsibilities . . . without regard for either equity or for the public interest—about which we hear next to nothing—it is not a pretty business . . . I need no instruction

about government's capacity for foulups and bureaucratization, but those scales are fully balanced by the evidence of failure and worse in the profit-making sector.

At least it can be said that government is politically and judicially and journalistically accountable when things go haywire, but we have much less assurance of that when we go the privatization route. When the apostles of privatizing [push for selling off] information services or educational services or health care services . . . what is it that would persuade private owners to bid? . . . [the most likely] motive [is] capturing a public asset which is likely to turn a profit, and a taxable profit at that.

But it's embedded in efficiency theory that whatever the acquired asset is, it must be priced and provided to maximize the economic return, and it is at that point that people like me begin to get nervous about equity considerations and the incentives for excluding access at the lower ranges of ability-to-pay.

We come back once again to how our society defines its priorities, relative to what it represents to be its values, and if the ideology of the new privatization ignores . . . [the imperative] . . . that decisions carry a moral component, our priorities will be dusty indeed.[25]

Robust scientific communications require more than just access to documents and data. Certainly in such areas of accelerating science as superconductivity, access to the scientific meeting, the colloquium, and the electronic bulletin board can be as important as, or more important than, access to the written report. This may well be the case in other areas of our national life. So the delegates to the second White House Conference will need to address the broader issue of communications access, not just the document information access issue alone.

Trying to reconcile these two fundamental national priorities—fostering scientific and technological productivity while simultaneously protecting national security interests—forces us to face the difficulties present when two objectives of our national concern collide. While the conflict is not easily resolved, reconciliation is a priority of the first magnitude if the United States is to sustain its national economic growth. If WHCLIS II is to prove worth the substantial contribution of resources it will require, it cannot fail to face this and other issues of national information policy on its agenda.

References

1. Berry, John. "NCLIS and the White House Conference." *Library Journal*, November 1, 1988, p. 4.
2. U.S. Federal Bureau of Investigation Intelligence Division. "The KGB and the Library Target, 1962—Present (effective date of study, January 1, 1988)," p. 10. Washington, D.C., 1988, 33 pp. Unclassified.
3. Ibid., pp. 32, 33.
4. Broad, William J. "As Science Moves into Commerce, Openness Is Lost." *New York Times*, May 24, 1988, p. C1.
5. "Facilitating Access to Science and Technology," Washington, D.C., U.S. Executive Office of the President, Executive Order 12591, April 10, 1987.
6. Goldstone, M. J. "How Not to Promote Technology Transfer." *Technology Review*, July, 1986, pp. 22–23.
7. Madison, James to W. T. Barry, August 4, 1822. *Writings of James Madison*, G. Hurst, Ed. New York, Putnam, 1900–1910.
8. "Reagan Issues Order on Science Secrecy: Will It Be Obeyed?" *Physics Today*, November 1985, pp. 55–58.
9. Ibid.
10. Coon, Jean. "NAS Panel: Most University Research Should Not Be Restrained." *Physics Today*, November 1982, pp. 6970.
11. Ibid.
12. Ibid.
13. "National Policy on Telecommunications and Automated Information Systems Security." Washington, D.C., U.S. Office of the President, National Security Decision Directive 145, September 17, 1984.
14. "Reagan Issues Order on Science Secrecy: Will It Be Obeyed?" Op. Cit., p. 57.
15. Ibid.
16. Ibid.
17. Ibid.
18. Goodwin, Irwin. "Making Waves: Poindexter Sails into Scientific Databases." *Physics Today*. January 1987, pp. 51–52.
19. Ibid.
20. "Superconductivity Competitiveness Act of 1988—Message from the President—PM113." *Congressional Record—Senate*, February 23, 1988, pp. 1408–09.
21. Raloff, J. "Graham Defends FOIA Exemption for Federal-Lab Research." *Science News*, March 26, 1988, p. 200.
22. McDonald, Kim. "White House Defends Proposal to Protect Data of Researchers at Federal Laboratories." *Chronicle of Higher Education*, March 23, 1988, pp. A4, A8.
23. Park, Robert R. "Is There a Science Adviser to the President?" *Chronicle of Higher Education*, March 30, 1988, pp. 81–82.
24. Ibid.
25. Carey, William D. "Setting Priorities: The Slippery Slope." *Vital Speeches of the Day*, September 15, 1986, p. 733.

LIBRARIANSHIP & POLITICAL VALUES: NEUTRALITY OR COMMITMENT?

Henry T. Blanke

When, in the original issue of *Library Journal*, Melvil Dewey proclaimed that "the time has at last come when a librarian may, without assumption, speak of his occupation as a profession,"[1] he was giving expression to what would become a leitmotif throughout subsequent library history. Over the next century librarians would energetically assert their right to be considered as professionals. Concomitant with the pursuit of professional status has been the desire of librarians to portray their profession as politically value-free. As William Birdsall has pointed out, the myth of the apolitical librarian has been persistently promulgated from the latter decades of the 19th century to the present.[2]

A scientific mode of inquiry eschewing political commitments, social ideals, or value judgments has been a desideratum of the social sciences since Max Weber. The dominant trend among contemporary social scientists is to view themselves as "value-free professionals."[3] Similarly librarianship has embraced political neutrality as a means toward acquiring professional status.[4] However, the idea that any enterprise, scientific or social, can extricate itself from the political culture in which it is embedded is dubious. Often such enterprises that strive for an ideal of neutrality will unconsciously adopt a dominant value orientation, one all the more tenacious for being unexamined.[5]

It is the contention of this article that librarianship's reluctance to define its values in political terms and to cultivate a sense of social respon-

---

"Librarianship & Political Values: Neutrality or Commitment?" by Henry T. Blanke in *Library Journal* Vol. 114, no. 12 (July 1989), pp. 39–43; reprinted with permission from Reed Publishing, USA, copyright © 1989 Reed Publishing, USA.

sibility may allow it to drift into an uncritical accommodation with society's dominant political and economic powers. Furthermore, the library profession's eagerness to be in the vanguard of a post-industrial information society may cause an erosion of its public service commitments in favor of a role as servant to a technocratic elite.

The Professional Pantheon

According to Michael Harris, "the central theme in the history of American librarianship is the librarian's self-conscious and impelling desire to gain entrance to the professional pantheon." This eagerness to be a part of America's sociopolitical elite has propelled librarianship toward a series of cultural crusades aimed at buttressing the status quo and dulling social change. "Stability, order, and moderation have always been the catchwords to the professional librarian in America, and these have always taken precedence over forceful agitation for human rights."[6]

Harris convincingly indicts American librarianship of a cynical pragmatism in allowing itself to be manipulated by the ruling elite and calls for librarians to generate socially responsible professional values and to commit themselves to the public good.[7] We are now approaching a time when Harris's jeremiad is especially pertinent. Failure to take it to heart may irreparably erode the ideals and principles which, while never adequately defined or applied, are the elan vital of the library profession.

There is ample evidence to suggest that the industrialized world is in the midst of profound socioeconomic and technological change. In 1973 Daniel Bell forecasted the emergence of a post-industrial society in which industrial manufacturing is superseded by a service-oriented economy.[8] Because information is viewed as a crucial resource in the post-industrial society, librarians have followed the prognostications of Bell, John Naisbitt, and others with keen interest. Naisbitt has argued that the so-called service economy is actually centered around the creation, processing, and distribution of information.[9] If information takes on an unprecedented importance as a vital economic resource, it follows that those skilled in its manipulation and interpretation will assume a pivotal societal role.

Redefining Roles

While librarians may not, in fact, find themselves thrust into the professional vanguard of a new information society,[10] it is likely that revolutionary changes in information technology and broad socioeconomic developments will require librarians to redefine their roles and sense of professional purpose in relation to larger societal issues. Without a willingness on the part of librarians to define their values in political terms and actively defend those values against the interests of wealth and power, such fundamental library ideals as free and equal access to information are in jeopardy. Several in the profession have already issued warnings on the dangers of their colleagues embracing opportunities to serve and participate in exclusive knowledge elites at the expense of the wider public.[11]

Historian Theodore Roszak has described the upper echelons of contemporary urban-industrial society as a "citadel of expertise" where technical experts are used as political resources to legitimate power and privilege in an increasingly complex and technological social environment.

Guided by a value-free concept of efficiency, the experts lend themselves to the consolidation of political and economic power.[12] In a society increasingly reliant on science and technology, matters involving political values are redefined as problems to be addressed by technical expertise.[13] The crucial question in such a situation becomes "who owns the experts?" Birdsall fears that librarians "in their enthusiasm to serve and join the professional elites of the post-industrial society . . . may again adopt the uncritical attitude that seemed to characterize earlier efforts to respond to social change."[14]

Seduced By Conservative Crusades

The evolution toward an information-based economy may provide a seductive opportunity for librarians to thrust themselves into yet another of the conservative crusades which, according to Harris, characterizes the history of American librarianship. In the past, America's ruling elites, under the guise of preserving the nation from ruin, have enlisted the services of librarians to combat sociopolitical developments perceived as threatening to the status quo.[15]

Today, the giants of American corporate capitalism, responding to an erosion of global power, are publicly promoting involvement in the production, processing, and transmission of information as a strategy for revitalizing the country's economy. The private agenda surrounding the information industry, however, is the insuring of private profit and worldwide corporate hegemony.[16] If Harris's reading of library history is accurate, librarians may once again allow influential segments of government and business to define their roles.

Indeed, it appears that a shift is already taking place that will align librarianship with the ethos of technocratic corporate capitalism. This shift is reflected in the language of librarianship where "patrons" become "clients," "librarians" become "information brokers," and information is no longer a public good freely accessible to all, but a commodity to be marketed. Matters of technical innovation and efficiency are increasingly overriding equity of public service as library goals.

When the director of one of the country's large urban public libraries recommends "more technology and less social experimentation,"[17] he is expressing a mood that extends beyond library circles to the highest echelons of government and business. By perpetuating the myth that their profession should be politically neutral, librarians have created a value vacuum that is easily being filled by the prevailing political and economic ethos. Neutrality, in effect, allows an unquestioned acquiescence to the imperatives of the most powerful and influential elements in society.

Challenging Ideologies

Since futurology is often more valuable for what it teaches us about contemporary sensibilities than for the insight it purports to give us into future states of affairs, it's appropriate that a forecast such as "The Reference Librarian of the Future: A Scenario" by Thomas Suprenant and Claudia Perry-Holmes should appear during the height of the Reagan era.[18] The vision presented here is in perfect accord with that administration's ideological bent. The authors set out to challenge certain principles that they feel will prevent librarians from assuming their proper status in the age of information. Chief among these outmoded principles is the provision of free information and services. "The profession will be increasingly unable to offer new innovations to any users if there is a continued insistence on maintaining services at an artificially low pricing structure centered around those least able to pay."[19]

While paying lip-service to the idea of library service as a public good, Suprenant and Perry-Holmes are willing to establish the provision of costly new information technology to those able to afford it as a priority, thus creating a hierarchy of information users. Not only does an uncritical reliance on databases and other technical innovations offered by the commercial information industry favor more affluent patrons, it threatens to establish a hierarchy of knowledge where the provision of information in less profitable subject areas such as the humanities is deemphasized.[20] The introduction of the priorities of the marketplace will distort the library's traditional function of accumulating and disseminating a wide variety of the world's knowledge as a public good.

Protecting the Library Ideal

Rather than exploring ways in which libraries may continue to serve as broad a public as possible, the authors call for fees for services as a means to enhance the library's "institutional status." Where they might advocate political activism to secure a more equitable distribution of funds between the private sector and libraries, the best the authors can do to protect the library ideal of free and equal access to information is a scheme of issuing "information stamps" to those unable to pay for services.[21] The effect of this plan would be to stigmatize an underclass of the information poor who must rely on institutional largess for what should be their right as citizens.

Suprenant and Perry-Holmes envision a future in which librarians will go directly to their clientele or establish themselves as "personal librarians" with offices and hours on the model of other professionals.

> The salary of such professionals will come directly from their clientele. Thus, the greater the expertise and level of assistance provided, the higher the salary of the librarian. In essence, the future reference librarian will act much like an individual entrepreneur. Fees will be paid for all services.[22]

If the authors' vision of the future comes to pass, a situation that pertains in this country to the provision of health care will exist with regard to information: the highest quality of services go to the rich while the poor make do with inadequate services or none at all.

Even a casual examination of recent library literature reveals a similar emphasis on the adoption of business values and methods of evaluation. David Lewis suggests the use of a market mechanism in libraries as a means to determine user needs and judge staff performance. "With a market system, we would see for the first time if what we do is really worth anything to anyone, and if it is, how much."[23] Ervin Gaines and Marian Huttner call for libraries to adopt a "tougher and more durable philosophy of service" based on fees for services.

> The new world of payment for information finally puts the information "transaction" in the marketplace. The patron is now a customer who expects results for his dollars. . . . Output measures are at long last being introduced to calculate library performance.[24]

According to these views libraries are industries the value of whose services is determined by consumer demand. Unfortunately, concern for equity of service and the needs of the poor are too often sacrificed at the altar of the marketplace. Since "the real needs of the poor citizen—emotional, financial, and physical—are forever beyond the scope of the library to solve," Gaines and Huttner argue, providing paid research "to those who are sophisticated in their information needs" (i.e., those who can afford it) does not deprive the less affluent.[25]

No Remedy for Financial Problems

Obviously, the library is not a social service agency. It is not intended to remedy the financial problems of the poor. But among the "real needs" of the poor, of all citizens in a democratic society, is information. It is true that the information needs of the poor (and those of most people) are different from those of an affluent elite. "What most people don't need most of the time is a bibliography," contends Fay Blake. "And to most librarians and information scientists, that particular nonneed translates itself into a generalized, 'Well, then, they don't need information.'"[26]

Instead of catering to an already well-served elite, librarians should be devoting themselves to finding out what types of information most citizens need and how best to provide it. Learning the "values of advertising" and the "technique of selling"[27] may enable libraries to turn a profit, but will not assure that the information needs of all people are being served.

The views expressed by these authors are congruent with a number of ominous developments occurring outside the library domain where a private information industry is working to transfer information from public custodianship to private control after which it can be marketed and sold for a profit.

Among the most influential advocates for the effort to privatize information is the Information Industry Association. It functions on behalf of some of the most powerful corporations in the United States to promote the idea of information as a commercial product and to facilitate the incursion of private enterprise into the field of information.

As Anita and Herbert Schiller explained in *The Nation*, the private information industry, with full support from the Reagan administration, set its sights on the huge and valuable stock of information traditionally handled by the federal government.[28] Heedless of social need, private information vendors are taking control of the fund of information the public has paid to have produced.

GPO: Victim

In recent years the Government Printing Office, historically responsible for providing government-generated information to the public, has been the victim of a series of budgetary cutbacks, legislative acts, and executive orders designed to curtail its role in favor of private information firms. With the encouragement of the previous administration, not only the GPO but an increasing number of public information institutions are becoming targets of the private information industry.[29]

The latest victim of the push to privatize federally produced information has been the National Technical Information Service, a clearinghouse for the collection of scientific, technical, and engineering material. The Reagan administration had been proceeding with its plans to transfer the functions of the NTIS to private firms. Once privatized, there is no assurance that ready public access to the agency's valuable collection of reports and studies would continue. When society's information needs are allowed to be defined by private interests, the public's right to know and consequently the foundations of democratic decision-making are weakened.

The rationale for encouraging the encroachment of private enterprise into the public information domain was established in 1982 when the

Public/Private Sector Task Force of the National Commission on Libraries and Information Science issued its report. Among the principles established by the task force was the following: "The Federal government should establish and enforce policies and procedures that encourage . . . investment by the private sector in the development and use of information products and services."

The task force recommended that private enterprise should be encouraged to "'add value' to government information (i.e., to repackage it . . . and otherwise enhance the information so that it can be sold at a profit)."[30] The extent to which this report, with its view of information as a "capital resource" of great value on the free market, reflects the present political climate is made clear by comparing it to an earlier document. Just three years earlier the White House Conference on Library and Information Services declared:

> Information in a free society is a basic right of any individual, essential for all persons, at all age levels, and all economic and social levels . . . all persons should have free access without charge or fee to the individual, to information in public and publicly supported libraries.[31]

Suprenant and Perry-Holmes feel that by adopting an "entrepreneurial spirit," by emphasizing efficiency, productivity, and quality control, librarians can successfully compete with private information enterprises thus ensuring the health and vitality of their profession.[32] On the contrary, accepting a business ethic and allowing librarianship to slip into an easy accord with the present celebration of market values, private enterprise, and corporate capitalism will corrode the values that allow librarians to contribute to the creation of a just and equitable society.

Librarianship Drifting Aimlessly

There are those who, clinging to the idea that the library profession should be politically neutral, would contend that contributing to social projects is not an appropriate activity for librarians. However, without a clear and vital set of philosophical and political ideals acting as a guiding beacon, the library profession will not remain neutral, but will drift aimlessly with the currents of power and privilege.

Librarians must forcefully articulate their commitment to serving the information needs of all segments of society. They must rededicate themselves to assuring the widest and most equitable access to information by opposing fees for services and the commercialization of knowledge. Furthermore, librarians must be willing to enter the political arena and advocate for these principles.

A 1970 issue of *Wilson Library Bulletin* presented a symposium in which a group of librarians responded to the question "When is a social issue a library issue?" Robert Wedgeworth's response went to the heart of the matter by pointing out that a consequence of the assumption that the library should remain neutral on social issues is to allow librarians to

> ignore or repress recognition of the political forces which impinge upon and shape the policies of public institutions. . . . Recognition of the political process involves creating allies and identifying opponents to the role of the library as an agency for facilitating the development of a well-informed public.[33]

Two years later, *Library Journal* published a collection of essays in response to an earlier article in which David Berninghausen maintained that partisanship in social and political issues is not within the province of libraries and that the American Library Association has been weakened by its concern for social responsibility.[34] Joining a chorus of disagreement, Betty-Carol Sellen explained that the movement toward social responsibility was motivated by the need to redress an imbalance of service in favor of those social groups with "the largest and most conservatively respectable power base. . . . the only partisanship on the part of the socially responsible is to insist that libraries must really serve all people."[35]

Just as these debates emerged from the social and political ferment of the 1960s, perhaps the societal shifts being wrought by the transition to a post-industrial society will spark a renewal of discussion and activism. Is information a public good to which every citizen deserves free and equal access or is it a commodity that can be bought and sold at a profit? Does the imposition of fees for service impede the library mission of being responsive to the information needs of all citizens? Is the proper role of the librarian that of the value-free technical expert or the socially committed public servant?

Some would address these questions using the ostensibly neutral criteria of efficiency and cost effectiveness. Such neutrality serves to further the interests of a wealthy and influential elite at the expense of society as a whole. These are not questions that can be approached neutrally. They are political questions with broad social implications that present librarians with ethical and political choices. The values of equity and public service not the imperatives of the technocracy and the marketplace should provide the criteria for governing access to information. Not only the health and vitality of the library profession is at stake, but that of our democracy as well.

References

1. Dewey, Melvil, "The Library Profession," *Library Journal*, 1876, p. 5–6.
2. Birdsall, William F., "The Political Persuasion of Librarianship," *Library Journal*, June 1, 1988, p. 75.
3. Gouldner, Alvin W. *For Sociology: Renewal and Critique in Sociology Today*. Basic Books, 1973, p. 16.
4. Birdsall, p. 75.
5. Sabia, Daniel R. & Jerald Wallulis, eds., *Changing Social Science: Critical Theory and Other Critical Perspectives*. State Univ. of New York Pr., 1983, p. 21–22.
6. Harris, Michael H., "Portrait in Paradox: Commitment and Ambivalence in American Librarianship, 1876–1976," *Libri*, Dec. 1976, p. 283, 284, 295.
7. *Ibid.*, p. 295, 297.
8. Bell, Daniel. *The Coming of Post-Industrial Society*. Basic Books, 1973, p. 123–164.
9. Naisbitt, John. *Megatrends*. Warner Books, 1982, p. 14.
10. Estabrook, Leigh, "Productivity, Profit, and Librarians," *Library Journal*, July 1981, p. 1377.
11. Blake, Fay M., "Let My People Know: Access to Information in a Postindustrial Society," *Wilson Library Bulletin*, Jan. 1978, p. 392–399; Braverman, Miriam, "From Adam Smith to Ronald Reagan: Public Libraries as a Public Good," *Library Journal*, Feb. 15, 1982, p. 397–401.
12. Roszak, Theodore. *Where the Wasteland Ends*. Anchor/Doubleday, 1973, p. 34–38.
13. Frankena, Frederick & Joann Koelin Frankena, "The Politics of Expertise and the Role of the Librarian," *Behavioral & Social Science Librarian*, Fall/Winter 1986, p. 38.
14. Birdsall, William F., "Librarianship, Professionalism, and Social Change," *Library Journal*, Feb. 1, 1982, p. 224.
15. Harris, p. 284.
16. Schiller, Herbert I. *Who Knows: Information in the Age of the Fortune 500*. Ablex, 1981, p. 3–10.
17. Gaines, Ervin J., "Let's Return to Traditional Library Service," *Wilson Library Bulletin*, Sept. 1981, p. 51.

18. Suprenant, Thomas T. & Claudia Perry-Holmes, "The Reference Librarian of the Future: A Scenario," *RQ*, Winter 1985, p. 234–238.
19. *Ibid.*, p. 235.
20. Schiller, Anita R. & Herbert I. Schiller, "Commercializing Information," *The Nation*, Oct. 4, 1986, p. 308.
21. Suprenant & Perry-Holmes, p. 235.
22. *Ibid.*, p. 236.
23. Lewis, David W., "Bringing the Market to Libraries," *Journal of Academic Librarianship*, May 1984, p. 75.
24. Gaines, Ervin J. & Marian A. Huttner, "Fee-Based Services and the Public Library: An Administrative Perspective," *Drexel Library Quarterly*, Fall 1984, p. 22, 20.
25. *Ibid.*, p. 21.
26. Blake, p. 396.
27. Gaines & Huttner, p. 20.
28. Schiller, Anita R. & Herbert I. Schiller, "Who Can Own What America Knows?" *The Nation*, April 17, 1982, p. 461–463.
29. *Ibid.*
30. National Commission on Libraries and Information Science. *Public Sector/Private Sector Interaction in Providing Information Services*. Report to NCLIS from the Public/Private Sector Task Force, GPO, 1982, p. 7–8.
31. Quoted in Schiller & Schiller, "Commercializing Information," p. 307.
32. Suprenant & Perry-Holmes, p. 234, 238.
33. Wedgeworth, Robert in "When Is a Social Issue a Library Issue?" Bendix, Dorothy, ed. *Wilson Library Bulletin*, Sept. 1970, p. 48–49.
34. Berninghausen, David, "Social Responsibility vs. The Library Bill of Rights," *Library Journal*, Nov. 15, 1972, p. 3675–81.
35. Sellen, Betty-Carol in "The Berninghausen Debate," *Library Journal*, Jan. 1, 1973, p. 27.

WHITTLE'S ED-TECH TROJAN HORSE

Lillian N. Gerhardt

Whittle Communications is an agency that specializes in putting advertisers in touch with target audiences. This time, the target is public school students. The coveted attention of these hard-to-reach young buyers is to be delivered to advertisers straight from their classrooms through Whittle's provision of free 25-inch TV's for every room, free VCR's and a free satellite dish. What students will see over this free closed-circuit TV system, daily, is Whittle's 12-minute "Channel One" news program, which carries two minutes of commercials for such items as shampoo, jeans, and candy bars. All it costs a school is the academic freedom of teachers to teach without interference, because this ed-tech Trojan horse is led in by some tight strings.

In order to get and to keep all these highly useful and very expensive educational tools, a school must air the program in every classroom—and Whittle's targeted teenage audience is estimated to have over $5.5 billion in loose change to spend each year. Put another way, junior and senior high school students spend more than the 73,000 public school libraries are given annually for the purchase of new library materials, including the hardware and software of educational technology.

When Whittle announced the pilot project, five national organizations involved with improving the quality of life for students and teachers promptly attacked the idea of big business tapping teen pockets on school time. Action for Children's Television (ACT) came out fighting mad against what it called Whittle's "seductive proposition." "The important thing to

---

"Whittle's Ed-Tech Trojan Horse," by Lillian Gerhardt in *School Library Journal* Vol. 35, no. 8 (April 1989), p. 4; reprinted with permission from Reed Publishing, USA, copyright © 1989 Reed Publishing, USA.

remember," ACT went on to say, "is that Whittle's primary deal is with advertisers. Giving schools a news show is secondary. Whittle has designed a clever way to assure that the school will deliver to the show's sponsors, on a 'cost per thousand' basis, students who are *mandated by law to attend school.*"

Manya Unger, president of the 6-million member National Parent Teacher Association, hacked the issue into two distinct parts. While applauding and endorsing educational technology as a "creative means of instruction," Unger put the PTA on record as opposed "to making the availability of that technology contingent on subjecting a captive student audience to the promotion of commercial products or services."

George Fowler, principal of Nathan Hale High School in Tulsa, Oklahoma, speaking as president of the 40,000-member National Association of Secondary School Principals said, "There's no need to test bad ideas in the classroom. We know selling junk food in the cafeteria is bad nutrition, and we know it's bad education to bring commercials into the classroom." Fowler invited business involvement in education but said its gifts should come with no strings attached.

The National Education Association, over 1.9 million members strong, has criticized the commercials and the 12 minutes that teachers are required to surrender each day. So has the 660,000-member American Federation of Teachers (AFT). I spoke with Bella Rosenberg, assistant to Albert Shanker, AFT's president. "Members of our executive council," Rosenberg said, "expressed dismay about this approach to using schools—especially its attractiveness to underfunded schools in areas of urban and rural poverty that hunger for the resources of educational technology. Our councilors questioned the damage enforced viewing does to teacher choice and teacher professionalism." AFT's councilors voiced "deep skepticism" about Whittle's claim that the value of the 10 minutes of current events offsets the two minutes of commercial intrusion.

I think AFT is right. While advertising is already going into schools and their libraries via newspapers and magazines, no students or teachers are forced to look at it and no teaching time is stolen by it.

It's this forced viewing/listening aspect of Whittle's project that calls to mind a great book—George Orwell's *Nineteen Eighty-Four.* On the first Monday in March, when students in six schools in California, Kansas,

Massachusetts, Michigan, Ohio, and Tennessee started watching Channel One via equipment supplied by Whittle, I re-read Orwell's dark satire of a society enslaved through technology. There was Big Brother. And, there were the daily, two-minute hate sessions, beamed full blast into every room on TV sets that could not be turned off, whipping the populace of Oceania to dementia.

Nineteen Eighty-Four provides an excellent background for any discussion of whether two minutes for Big Business really matters in a school day. Nobody's ever read it to relax. But, with Whittle Communications horsing around in American public education policy, nobody ought to relax.

INFORMATION DROUGHT: NEXT CRISIS FOR THE AMERICAN FARMER?

Nancy C. Kranich

Farmers are among the many Americans dependent upon information collected, organized, and disseminated by the federal government, e.g., timely and accurate weather, marketing, livestock, and crop reports. Such information can mean the difference between survival and default for small farmers, profit and gain for large farmers.

Recently, private firms have begun to offer the farmer information that had previously been distributed by the government. While government agricultural information is either free or has a nominal cost, private firms are charging high fees for access to these data. For many farmers, especially those who run smaller operations, these fees are extremely burdensome. Yet farmers have no choice but to pay these prohibitive fees if they are to have access.[1]

OMB's Circular A-130

Since the Reagan administration began its "war on waste" in 1981 and the Office of Management and Budget (OMB) promulgated guidelines for managing federal information resources in 1985, farmers and other citizens have had no alternative to buying their information from the private sector at far steeper prices.

OMB's Circular A-130 sharply reduced the federal government's efforts to collect and disseminate information to the public, and accelerated the trend toward commercialization and privatization of government infor-

---

"Information Drought: Next Crisis for the American Farmer?," by Nancy Kranich in *Library Journal* Vol. 114, no. 11 (June 15, 1989), pp. 22–27; reprinted with permission from Reed Publishing, USA, copyright © 1989 Reed Publishing, USA.

mation. The circular's emphasis on "maximum feasible reliance on the private sector for dissemination of [information] products or services" has also resulted in the discontinuance of distribution through the depository library system that assures public access in every Congressional district.

Because private sector firms disseminating government data are under no obligation to make government information available to the American public at an affordable price, nor to keep that information easily accessible and readily available, the American Library Association has charged that a gap between information "haves" and "have nots" will evolve.

The issues involving the role of the public and private sectors in disseminating government information are well documented in the literature. In just the past few years, reports have emanated from the National Commission on Libraries and Information Science, the Office of Technology Assessment, Association of Research Libraries, ALA, Government Documents Round Table (GODORT), and the House Committee on Government Operations.[2] These reports focus specifically on electronic access and raise several fundamental questions: What should the role of the private sector be in delivering government information in electronic format? How much should this information cost? What is the government's legal responsibility for providing this information?

Focus on the EDI database

McClure and Hernon have asserted that "there is a paucity of studies conveying 'empirical evidence'" about the effects of technology on the federal government's provision of information.[3] This article will present "empirical evidence" gleaned from a specific government database—the Electronic Dissemination of Information (EDI) database of the U.S. Department of Agriculture—and address relevant service issues of concern to librarians. This database is a good example of the issues and problems librarians face in trying to provide access to government information in electronic formats.

Background on the EDI database was difficult to obtain. Few articles describing the system have been published and agricultural librarians are generally unaware of EDI's services and status. There is no listing for EDI in the latest edition of *The Federal Database Finder,* even though it is included in the *1988 Encyclopedia of Information Systems and Services.*

A General Accounting Office report was issued on the status of the EDI system in January 1987, but distribution was restricted, although later disseminated through libraries. Information for this article was compiled from these limited sources and through interviews with Russell Forte and Roxanne Williams of the U.S. Department of Agriculture (USDA) and Jim Hawley of Martin Marietta Data Systems.[4]

EDI offers news, commodity, economic, statistical, and other reports through a computerized system operated by Martin Marietta Data Systems (MMDS) under contract to the USDA. The service provides access to crop production and other reports and releases issued by the USDA and cooperating agencies. Topics covered include commodity grading, food inspections, forestry, food stamps, school lunch programs, soil and water conservation, farm loan programs, market data, export sales, and trade leads. Most of the information, which is input by various USDA agencies, is perishable and time sensitive and is released immediately to subscribers.

Martin Marietta and EDI

In the past, the USDA released this electronic information to AGNET, a not-for-profit group stationed at the University of Nebraska, which put the information on its electronic network and made it available to the public. In 1985 the USDA signed an exclusive contract with MDDS to provide that same USDA information. Because of increased costs charged by the vendor, AGNET can no longer afford to provide these data to its customers without raising its fees.

Forte, of the USDA's Office of Information Special Programs Division and coordinator of the EDI database, indicated in January 1989 that the system had 34 Level 1 subscribers, 17 of which are multipliers or news services (with thousands of subscribers), while the rest are big businesses interested in commodities.[5] Level 1 users include such organizations as Drexel-Burnham, E. F. Hutton, W. R. Grace and Company, Knight Ridder Financial News, the Quaker Oats Company, and Washington Press Text.

Level 2 users are those to whom Martin Marietta, by contract, must give limited access at a subsidized rate. These users include USDA agencies, Agriculture Extension Services and other groups that work with the USDA, and the CIA. According to a General Accounting Office (GAO) Report, the system users include the public, which it defines as "agricultural information retailers, publishers, the news media, agribusiness establishments, etc., and several Department of Agriculture agencies." That report goes on to say that "the contract is unrestrictive with respect to who can access the system as a public user, [as long as they are] technically capable of receiving the electronic data and willing to pay for the service."[6]

The role of Martin Marietta is strictly technical, leaving the USDA to coordinate data entry and user services. Substantive questions about data are referred to the supplying USDA agency. The USDA retains total control over its data including selection and retention. Martin Marietta simply provides a host computer and communications system to mount USDA information.

According to a USDA fact sheet on the EDI service, "an important feature . . . is the automatic transmission of reports while they are still current to users virtually anywhere in the world immediately upon release by the USDA." Yet when some of the Level 1 users redistribute those data, such as pioneer Hi-bred International, Inc., which includes them in its AGRIBUSINESS database available through Dialog, they are loaded only every two weeks. Hence, Dialog, a major source available to the general public, provides this timely information as much as two weeks late. Moreover, Dialog, in its "Database Supplier Terms and Conditions," claims that, "This database is copyrighted by Pioneer Hi-bred International, Inc. No part of AGRIBUSINESS U.S.A. database may be duplicated without the written authorization of pioneer Hi-bred International, Inc."

When the USDA originally proposed creation of this database, it was with the intent of discontinuing print versions. Nevertheless, most print counterparts are still issued simultaneously with the electronic version but are distributed through postal delivery. According to Forte, the USDA could save at least $10 million of its $50 million annual postage costs by ceasing to mail news releases.

What This Government Info Costs

Formerly, the USDA distributed this information free or at nominal cost through the Government Printing Office to depository libraries, farmers, and others. AGNET used to get the electronic version free from the USDA, then charged $50 a year plus 50¢ per minute for access. Martin Marietta now gets the information free from the USDA. But the contract between Martin Marietta and the USDA does not specify charges to public users; rather, they are established by Martin Marietta in separate contracts with each user.

Generally, these charges are $45 per hour plus a minimum use/subscription fee of $150 per month for Level 1 users. (USDA providers are not charged the monthly minimum use/subscription fee.) Once this information becomes available through Dialog, one of several commercial vendors, it costs $96/hour, 60¢/full record offline, and 50¢/full record online. While Dialcom and Agridata offer cheaper rates, they are not so widely available.

At the same time that costs have increased for public access, unforeseen expenses have been incurred by USDA agencies. Although Martin Marietta receives the government information free, it charges agencies for loading and storing the data entered and retrieved from the system. When the USDA's Marketing Service considered placing all its information on the EDI system as a possible alternative to its own network, it found the cost of entering data to be seven times higher than the initial estimate. At first, the Marketing Service was allotted $1,500 per month to load all its reports. Its actual cost for the first three months was approximately $10,000 per month. Unwilling to increase its commitment to covering the cost of loading all its data into the system, the Marketing Service reduced its data loaded into the system by 90 percent.[7]

No matter what the rationale for privatizing the wholesale component of the USDA's information services, giving the private sector a monopoly in distributing this information has caused prices to soar.[8] The cost is passed from the government to host computer company to multipliers and information brokers and then to the user.

Not-for-profit AGNET still exists but can no longer afford to load this information; it is too expensive from Martin Marietta. Hawley of Martin Marietta claims it makes no profits on the service but hopes the company will attract additional government business. By contract, Martin Marietta is prohibited from charging more than time-sharing costs to information vendors. But there are no controls over fees information vendors may charge for public access to this information, and during the three years of service, the USDA's costs for accessing it from Martin Marietta have soared.

Forte has stated that Martin Marietta was not contractually obligated to control prices for individual farmers because "contractors can only be asked to jump through so many hoops." He went on to add that "farmers who are really making it are the ones who have gone after this technique" of accessing information and are, in fact, "the more efficient farmers." Yet, as of the mid-1980's, U.S. farmers lagged well behind their nonfarm counterparts in the adoption of microcomputers. Case and Rogers, in their study of information technology and agriculture, have indicated:

> that larger sized farmers are especially likely to adopt, thus widening the socio-economic and information gaps among U.S. farmers. Because the information technologies are usually fairly expensive, relatively elite farmers tend to adopt first—a critical circumstance in these days of farm bankruptcies.[9]

In the past, the nation's 1,400 depository libraries have served as a safety net, providing the American people with the cost-free information they need to know in order to govern themselves and to ensure political and personal independence. Once essential information is no longer published by the government, no such safeguards will exist for the small farmer lacking direct access to new technologies. The USDA has not developed policies to deal with the information poor. Martin Marietta is not in a position to even offer general public access, let alone reduced rates. Information vendors such as DIALOG are simply not in business to provide two-tiered services, although their prices are generally half for government data provided directly to them.

Martin Marietta's Hawley thinks the EDI service is a good way for government and therefore the taxpayer to reduce costs. Nevertheless, like librarians, he feels strongly that the government must find a way to provide this electronic service to depository libraries, at no cost to either the library or the user. While he sees such a service as no threat to either his or other vendors' market, the official position of the OMB and the Information Industry Association is that such a safety net provided through depository libraries will result in unfair competition with the private sector.

Martin Marietta has excelled in offering the USDA the electronic dissemination of information databases according to the agency's specifications. Building upon the company's excess computing capacity, the EDI service has provided wider distribution of information in a timely fashion but with no foreseeable profit. Yet, Martin Marietta has not added value to the USDA data; instead, it has served as a secondary wholesaler, adding one more link in the information chain, and therefore multiplying the cost to the end user. Even if the contract is saving the taxpayer funds at the USDA, it has passed additional costs on to the consumers. By contracting out a system based on efficiency criteria, the USDA has recast government information policy in a way that has serious consequences on equal and ready access to public information.

Access to Info Electronically

Since Martin Marietta began operating, several other databases have been contracted out including the Securities and Exchange Commission EDGAR system and the Patent and Trademark Office PTO system. Like the USDA system, these databases promise speed and efficiency for "public" users. They have, however, raised serious concerns for librarians: bibliographic access, physical access, standards, cost and equity, proprietary control, intellectual freedom, expert assistance, public access and dissemination, continuity, currency and scope, format, user profiles and feedback, confidentiality, and database security.

Bibliographic Access—There is no government-sponsored central source for listing databases. Those that exist are only published by the private sector, even though OMB's proposed revisions to Circular A-130 call on government agencies to produce computerized inventories of these products. Because machine-readable data files and other non-paper formats are not generally considered government publications, the government has, until now, made little attempt to bring them under bibliographic control. Timothy Sprehe of OMB's Office of Information and Regulatory Affairs, has commented that:

> rarely do agencies have budget lines for making machine-readable data files accessible. The policy on this issue in the government is confusing and contradictory and there is no clear sense that government considers bibliographic control of machine-readable data files its responsibility.[10]

Physical Access—In the case of the EDI database, there are only some 50 organizations with Martin Marietta accounts. In the case of the SEC database EDGAR, there are only three public reading rooms in the entire country. While librarians and library users have enjoyed broad access to such government databases as Medline, ERIC, and the GPO Monthly Catalog, the bulk of government-produced electronic databases are virtually unavailable to the general public, either directly or through commercial vendors. Those that are available are often not affordable to most potential users.

Standards—For all intents and purposes, the federal government has no standards for database development—not for data elements, not for record formats (except MARC), not for retrieval protocols. Agencies are developing uncoordinated, incompatible systems and they are not working together, which results in wasteful spending. OMB is supposed to regulate information in the federal government; instead it serves as a promoter of privatization, not a coordinator of information activities. Private sector firms are even less likely to adopt common data elements and command language.

Cost Factors and Equity—Many printed documents are distributed free to depository libraries, and free or at low cost to the general public. In contrast, electronic databases are provided at least on a cost-recovery basis, in order to avoid unfair competition with the private sector. When government databases are provided directly to a vendor, they cost an average of $45.70 per connect hour on DIALOG. That is less than half of the $93.26 per connect hour charged when government databases are provided to DIALOG by the private sector.[11]

The few government databases that can be accessed directly from the government as well as through a private vendor have an even greater disparity in user cost. For example, a recent Joint Committee on Printing report indicated that the cost to the federal government of delivering Energy Research Abstracts online to the user would be $16/hr., while access to older titles in that database offered through a commercial vendor would be $85–$120/hr.[12]

Proprietary Control—Works created by U.S. government employees in the course of their employment are in the public domain. As a result, any individual or company is free to reproduce government documents. If they add value, they can copyright those enhancements, although not the information itself. In electronic formats, it is difficult to separate the proprietary component of a database from the public information. As a result, companies like Pioneer Hi-bred International attempt to restrict reproduction of public information that is available with enhancements in their AGRIBUSINESS database. So vendor proprietary control over their added value to government information can inhibit researchers and others from downloading and analyzing data that is in the public domain.

Intellectual Freedom—The private sector has numerous examples of databases that favor certain vendors, ranging from securities investment to airline scheduling. Examples include a bond price database that tenders advantage to those companies listed first and an airline booking system that prompts travel agents to choose that company's flights over its competitors. Once government information is privatized, similar developments can occur. Contractors should not receive unfair advantage over the flow of information. In the case of the SEC database, critics including consumer advocate Ralph Nader have questioned whether the contractor, the Bechtel Group, Inc., has a "government-sanctioned de facto monopoly on the timely provision of [SEC documents]."[13]

Censoring by Omission

In addition, the private sector has a tendency to censor information on the basis of the marketplace. Vendors such as Dialog are free simply to drop databases that are used infrequently. Aside from those popular government databases already widely available through private vendors, most government-produced databases are unlikely to be commercially viable. As a result, the public is threatened with the complete elimination of access to specific segments of data with limited commercial value but with substantial significance in terms of policymaking, research, scholarship, and accountability.

Other kinds of censorship related to electronic databases have plagued consumers of information. Those libraries using the NASA Recon database (supplied by RMS Associates) have had stipulated in their contract that "Access is permitted only within the United States, and to United States citizens, unless specifically authorized by RMS. If citations are printed out, they must be similarly restricted."

This means that if catalog cards from the NASA Recon database are filed in a library's card catalog, foreigners cannot look at those particular cards. While the University of California system has dropped use of that database, the principle of open access is not resolved. In another case, Dun & Bradstreet blocked labor union access to its corporate database on DIALOG. Actions such as these cannot be ignored as the government moves forward with privatization of public information.

Expert Assistance—For government-produced databases, most expert assistance is available at the agency level. Unfortunately, when vendors provide information, they can tell you how to search the system using their protocols but they are rarely familiar with the content of the databases they offer. Furthermore, federal agencies that create information will often search that information on their internal databases for the public. Agency personnel help guide users to the actual information sources cited; provide the documents listed in their databases; provide additional materials; and may give suggestions and referrals to other sources. This expert assistance is very important to users as well as to librarians who are working on behalf of those users.

Public Access and Dissemination—The private sector is under no obligation to make government information available to the American public at an affordable price, nor to keep that information easily accessible and readily available. Furthermore, OMB's policies on how to administer government information set up artificial distinctions between dissemination and access. Under the OMB guideline, dissemination is considered the distribution of government information to the public, whether through printed documents or other media. This is the activity that OMB has encouraged agencies to contract out, thereby abrogating government's dissemination responsibilities.

Access, on the other hand, is providing to members of the public, *upon their request,* the government information to which they are entitled under law. This is the activity that OMB officials regard as passive and can be accomplished simply by placing information in one location only. An OMB official has stated that as long as the information is available in an office in Washington, the government has satisfied public access requirements. These definitions were cited repeatedly as problems by librarians in their comments on the 1985 draft of OMB Circular A-130, but were not corrected in the final policy.

Continuity—This concern was justified recently when the GPO's microfiche vendor stopped production; no fiche were delivered for almost a year to depository libraries. Consequently, huge gaps developed in depository collections unless libraries searched, ordered, and paid for the corresponding documents from the Congressional Information Service.

Archiving—Electronic technology makes it possible to erase documents long before a cumulative record can be assembled or before the historical value can be ascertained. Obsolete electronic equipment can also impede retrieval of government records. As more data are computerized, the public record will be imperiled unless appropriate action is taken to assure the preservation and retention of electronic records for future inquiry.

Currency and Scope—The EDI database is not loaded onto a widely available vendor service immediately, nor does it have the breadth or the scope of data that is available from the government. For EDI's commodities information, two-week out-of-date information is not helpful for many potential users. Moreover, the data are not cumulated.

Format—Currently, electronic government information comes in formats ranging from CD-ROM to magnetic tape and from dial-up to floppy disk. Different operating systems and different software packages are used. The new Census CD-ROMs are to be used with dBase III. If R-Base or another version of dBase is used at a particular library, it is simply not compatible with the census product. Other government databases will not necessarily run with dBase so libraries will be forced to buy not only a variety of software packages but also learn how and teach others to use them.

User Profiles and Feedback—There is very little user input into how government databases are being constructed and developed. When they are privatized, it is likely to get worse. User profiles are proprietary and therefore unavailable to system designers. Furthermore, information on use and users that vendors are collecting is not analyzed for purposes of service improvement. Hence, it is virtually impossible to identify farmers using the USDA information and the benefits and problems they encounter with that data.

Confidentiality and Database Security—Although librarians promote public access, they guard against disclosure of personal data. Just because the government collects certain personal data does not authorize public access or misuse. In addition to protecting data related to specific individuals, every attempt must be made to secure the integrity of databases from computer viruses, tampering, and unauthorized entry.

Shortcomings of Government Info Policy

Technology has outpaced the laws that govern federal information policy. With few exceptions, statutes predate electronic dissemination developments. Today, government information policy relative to electronic formats is nothing less than chaotic. Moreover, the federal information system has evolved toward a cost-driven rather than user-oriented model. The public access vacuum this model has created cannot be filled by the nation's libraries, which are not funded to insure that the public has adequate access. Even if the government provides electronic information through the depository library system, it is unlikely to offer any additional assistance, particularly for the purchase of hardware.

The government's attempts to deal with information policy are at best contradictory. While OMB has limited public dissemination of the government's data, the Joint Congressional Committee on Printing has recommended the distribution of electronic databases through the depository library system and proposed (in June 1988) to distribute five databases. This proposal followed a hard-fought battle by librarians to test the utility of such distribution networks.

When the House Appropriations Committee was asked to reprogram GPO funds for a pilot project in 1987, it deferred action until completion of a study by the Office of Technology Assessment (OTA), *Informing the Nation: Federal Information Dissemination in the Electronic Age.* That report was released in fall 1988.[14] The information industry also claims that it wants more opportunity to react to the proposal even though several of its members sat on the committee that initially recommended the pilot project. As of March 1989, only one of the five databases—the Census CD-ROM—has been received by depository libraries.

On a more positive note, Congress has passed significant legislation to guarantee the public's right to know about toxic wastes in their communities. With authorization through Title III of the 1986 Superfund legislation, the Environmental Protection Agency is responsible for distributing information to the public about toxics through an online computer database, the Toxic Release Inventory (TRI) (Automation Roundup, *LJ*, October 15, 1988, p. 19). This legislation promises to be the most powerful right-to-know tool citizens have to protect public health and environmental quality in their community. It should serve as a model for legislation in other areas. The TRI is one of the five databases proposed to be distributed to depository libraries as part of the demonstration project.

Finally, because there is no provision in the Freedom of Information Act (FOIA) for electronic formats, many rulings have denied access as long as a database has to be reprogrammed, claiming that the government is not responsible for giving that information because it is considered the creation of new data. A recent case appealed by the National Security Archive in conjunction with ALA won on that issue, however, and forced the Department of Energy to reprogram a database for a list of "limited reports" emanating from DOE's Oak Ridge nuclear facility. While the case is not necessarily precedent-setting, it is a crucial change in the public's effort to attain access to government information in electronic format.

Libraries on the Front Line

In conclusion, librarians must recognize that they are stationed on the front line of the fight for public access to electronic information produced by the government. If they are to win the battle, librarians must stand firm and be persistent as well as consistent on this issue. They must urge federal action on depository libraries, the Paperwork Reduction Act, the Freedom of Information Act, government regulations, and right-to-know provisions. As Fred Wood of the OTA recently stated,

> the fundamental crosscutting issue is public access to government information. Debate over the rise of electronic formats, privatization, and the like is obscuring the commitment of Congress and state legislatures to public access. These bodies have expressed through numerous public laws the importance of government information and the dissemination of that information in carrying out agency missions and the principles of democracy and open government. A renewed commitment to public access in an electronic age may be needed.[15]

The example of the EDI database case study helps to illustrate librarians' concerns. It would be far more useful if it also cited how a disenfranchised farmer could not afford crucial agricultural information due to the vagaries of privatization. Congress, the press, and the public want anecdotes. Unless they have stories about the human effects of public policy, they rarely take action. Consequently, librarians must continue to search for that farmer if they are to alert the American public to the importance of public access to government information. Only then will we be certain to convince the OMB, Congressional policy makers, and the general public of the value and importance of public dissemination of government information in all formats.

References

1. For more information about farmers' limited use of new information technologies, see Tracy L. Myrup, "Dishing It Out to Farmers," *Washington Journalism Review*, Dec. 1988, p. 14; Donald Case & Everett Rogers, "The Adoption and Social Impacts of Information Technology in U.S. Agriculture," *The Information Society*, 5, 1987, p. 57-66; Raymond D. Lett, "Computers: The Newest Technology for American Farmers," *The Information Society*, 2, 1983, p. 121-129; and, Andy Jacobitz, "Slowing Down High Tech: All but a Few Farmers Fight Information Advances," *Farmfutures*, Jan. 1989, p. 34D.
2. See U.S. National Commission on Libraries and Information Science. *Public Sector/Private Sector Interaction in Providing Information Services*. GPO, 1982; U.S. Congress. Office of Technology Assessment. *Informing The Nation: Federal Information Dissemination in the Electronic Age*. GPO, 1988; Information Industry Association. *Meeting Information Needs in the New Information Age*. Information Industry Association, 1983; U.S. Congress. Joint Committee on Printing. *Provision of Federal Government Publications in Electronic Format to Depository Libraries*. GPO, 1984; Association of Research Libraries. *Technology and U.S. Government Information Policies: Catalysts for New Partnerships*. Association of Research Libraries, 1987; American Library Association. *Less Access to Less Information by and About the U.S. Government*, ALA, 1981-1988; Commission on Freedom and Equality of Access to Information. *Freedom and Equality of Access to Information*. ALA, 1986; American Library Association, Government Documents Round Table. *Government Information Technology and Information Dissemination: A Discussion Paper*. American Library Association GODORT, Dec. 1987; and U.S. Congress. House. Committee on Government Operations. *Electronic Collection and Dissemination of Information by Federal Agencies: A Policy Overview*. GPO, 1986.
3. McClure, Charles & Peter Hernon. *Federal Information Policies in the 1980's*. Ablex, 1987, p. 164.
4. Telephone interviews conducted by Nancy Kranich with Russell Forte, USDA Office of Information, Jan. 27, 1989; Roxanne Williams, USDA, Jan. 22, 1989; and Jim Hawley, Martin Marietta Data Systems, Feb., 21, 1989.

5. For a list of subscribers, see Forte, Russell, "Letter to Subscribers to USDA's EDI Service," U.S. Dept. of Agriculture, Office of Governmental and Public Affairs, Sept. 12, 1988.
6. U.S. General Accounting Office. *Data Processing: Status of Agriculture's Electronic Dissemination of Information System*. GAO, Jan. 1987, p. 14.
7. *Ibid.*, p. 4, 18, 14.
8. For a more extensive discussion of the private sector's prices for providing public data, see Frances Seghers, "Computerizing Uncle Sam's Data: Oh, How the Public Is Paying," *Business Week*, Dec. 15, 1986, p. 102–103.
9. Case & Rogers, p. 64.
10. Sprehe, Timothy, "A Federal Policy for Improving Data Access and User Services," *Statistical Reporter*, March 1981, p. 323–344.
11. Shill, Harold B. Testimony before the U.S. House Subcommittee on Science, Research and Technology on Federal Information Policy, Washington, D.C., July 14, 1987, Appendix E.
12. U.S. Congress, Joint Committee on Printing. *Dissemination of Information in Electronic Format to Federal Depository Libraries: Proposed Project Descriptions*. JCP, 1988.
13. Sugawara, Sandra, "Seemingly Perfect SEC Deal Stirs Controversy for Bechtel," *Washington Post*, Oct. 31, 1988, p. 1, 20.
14. U.S. Congress, Office of Technology Assessment. *Informing the Nation: Federal Information Dissemination in the Electronic Age*. GPO, 1988.
15. Wood, Fred W., "Statement on 1989 Directions in State Information Dissemination Policy," before a hearing of the Joint Committee on Information Technology Resources, Florida State Legislature, Jan. 19, 1989.

PART IV:
PROFESSIONAL ISSUES

INFORMATION MALPRACTICE: SOME THOUGHTS ON THE POTENTIAL LIABILITY OF INFORMATION PROFESSIONALS

Martha J. Dragich

For several years librarians and other information professionals have speculated about malpractice liability. Although many of us find it hard to believe that we will be faced with lawsuits filed by dissatisfied clients, the trend toward greatly increased malpractice litigation involving other professionals[1] gives us pause, especially as the commodity in which we deal—information—has taken on enormous value in our times.[2] To date we have only speculated about, and not actually faced, malpractice suits. This article examines the hypothetical cases of library malpractice posited in the literature. It then suggests other hypothetical situations in which information providers might face ethical dilemmas or charges of negligence. Finally, it discusses a few cases arising in other contexts that shed some light on how courts would react to malpractice suits against information professionals.

The classic hypothetical library malpractice case was put forth by Alan Angoff more than ten years ago. In Angoff's hypothetical, a public library patron sued the library for $250,000 for "injuries to his home and personal injuries to himself and his family as a result of . . . inaccurate information contained in a book recommended to him" by the reference librarian.[3] The patron had wanted to build a deck on his house and went to the library to find a how-to book. Although he followed the instructions

---

"Information Malpractice: Some Thoughts on the Potential Liability of Information Professionals," by Martha Dragich in *Information Technologies and Libraries* Vol. 8, no. 3 (September 1989), pp. 265-272; reprinted with permission from the American Library Association, copyright © 1989 by ALA.

in the book, the deck collapsed, injuring him and his two sons and damaging part of the house. The book recommended by the librarian was about ten years old, and the publisher was no longer in business. The patron claimed that the library was "grossly negligent" in circulating an antiquated book.

Law librarians have also speculated about malpractice liability.[4] Even law librarians who very carefully avoid giving legal advice wonder whether they could be charged with malpractice for recommending an outdated or inadequate law book. Typical examples include the patron who needs to find out the length of the statute of limitations that would apply to his legal problem, and the patron who wants to write his own will or do her own divorce.

Angoff's hypothetical was based on the traditional library setting where a brief, often anonymous transaction takes place and where the librarian's involvement in actually solving the client's problem is quite limited. The charge against the librarian rests on faulty information contained in the book itself. In order for the librarian to be found liable in such a case, the librarian's duty to the client would have to include verification of all the information in every book before recommending any book to the patron. Although it is a librarian's duty to build a good collection of sound materials, and to know the collection well, it is clearly impossible to undertake independent verification of the informational content of the collection.

Therefore, we should forgo further speculation about malpractice liability in cases such as those posited thus far. No actual case on similar facts has been reported to date, and they are unlikely to arise in the future. We should turn our attention instead to the rather different situations in which we as "information providers" find ourselves and explore the possibilities for malpractice liability there.

Malpractice

One writer on the malpractice liability of librarians defines malpractice as "any professional misconduct or unreasonable lack of skill in the performance of professional duties through intentional carelessness or simple ignorance."[5] The legal requirements for a charge of professional negligence are that there be a duty owed by the professional to the client which was breached, causing actual damage to the client.[6] The scope of a professional's duty to her client does not extend so far as to guarantee a satisfactory result in the provision of every service.[7] Thus, each situation must be examined to see whether the professional had a duty to perform a particular action in a specified manner or, to put it another way, to determine whether the professional's actions constituted breach of her duty. The balance of this article focuses on the elements of duty and breach of duty as they might apply to information professionals, particularly in light of the challenges we face in dealing with an ever-expanding universe of print and online resources. We will assume that the element of damage is satisfied.

Professional-Client Relationship

First, we must consider the concept of duty by examining the relationship between the information professional and the client. The duty of a professional to the client arises out of the relationship between the two parties.[8] The client entrusts his/her needs to the professional because the professional has knowledge or expertise the client lacks. This places the client in a vulnerable position and the professional in a corresponding position of power and responsibility. Although our transactions with library patrons were often anonymous, we are moving closer to the consultative model of other professionals.[9] Librarians traditionally provided access to sources of information in which patrons could find for themselves the information they needed. While in the past the librarian may have been the "organizer and dispenser of books and documents," the role of information providers today is more often to advise the client on information needs.[10]

Today, information professionals often provide either raw data or synthesized information to clients.[11] Anne Mintz, who writes on information malpractice, states that while in our earlier role it was improper for a librarian to interpret information for a patron, information professionals now are required to evaluate requests for information, determine the best databases for searching, translate the request into the appropriate search language, evaluate the results during and after the search, and decide whether the results are appropriate.[12] It is clear that a professional-client relationship does exist in the circumstances under which many independent information professionals currently practice.[13] This relationship results from the provision of more extensive services to clients and from the imposition of fees for services.

The "information profession" includes independent information brokers who specialize in conducting online research for clients in certain technical areas, operators of legal research services providing manual and online legal research for attorneys and law firms, and many other nontraditional roles. Clients retain information professionals to conduct research for them—not merely to direct them to sources of information in which they could do research themselves. The information provider is expected to find the information the client needs, not merely to recommend an item from a preexisting collection of materials. The information provider in these instances has taken on a more active role in solving the client's problem. The client likely has sought professional help precisely because the client's own skills do not enable her to undertake the kind of sophisticated research needed.

Other information professionals work as information consultants, whom law firms or businesses might hire to recommend and set up a litigation support system or business records management system to meet certain objectives. Here again, the professional possesses knowledge and expertise the client lacks and is expected to study the client's needs and come up with an appropriate solution for them. In all of these situations, the client pays for the services rendered. While this factor alone is not determinative, it goes a long way toward suggesting that a different relationship exists here than in the traditional library setting.

The client's increased reliance on our knowledge and judgment increases our duty to assume responsibility for the accuracy of the information we provide and for the manner in which it was obtained.[14] Even though we gather and use data originating with an author, database producer, publisher, or agency, we are called upon specifically to employ our knowledge and judgment to retrieve accurate and up-to-date information relevant to the client's information needs. We are not only the finders but also the evaluators and interpreters of the information—roles formerly performed by the client. Thus, it will be much easier for courts to find a duty sufficient to sustain liability in cases filed against us by disgruntled clients.

Having established that the relationship that exists between an information professional and the client is likely to give rise to a duty to act responsibly, we must define the scope of that duty in order to determine what would constitute its breach. One component of a professional's duty to the client is the need to act in an ethical manner. The second component of the professional's duty is the need to exercise reasonable care in the performance of professional services. Many professional codes of ethics include both provisions related to ethical behavior and provisions related to care, knowledge, and skill.[15] Library-based codes have focused almost exclusively on the former.

Ethical Issues

Several library associations have formulated codes of ethics by which to judge professional conduct.[16] Some of the more common provisions of these codes relate to the need to respect the privacy of the client and the need to be impartial in providing information. These codes, however, grew out of and still reflect the traditional library setting—that of the librarian dealing primarily with books and journals. Information practice today draws professionals from a wide variety of backgrounds who work not only in libraries or for corporations but also as solo or group practitioners.[17] They deal with information in diverse formats. Not all share a common educational preparation, and there is no single professional organization to which all belong. As Shaver noted, no license is required for the "practice of information."[18] Thus, the application of library-based codes of ethics to the "new breed" of information professional can be problematic.

For information professionals in the online environment, breaches of confidentiality and the misuse of information gained in the course of professional employment are the most likely ethical dilemmas. While traditional codes of ethics considered confidentiality mainly in the context of protecting circulation records, online searching has added a whole new dimension to the problem. For billing purposes, most search-intermediaries keep detailed records of the searches performed for clients, and the bills themselves often show the client's identification and the files searched, if not the actual content of the search. In addition, the use of online SDI services makes it possible to monitor and record a client's ongoing research. Ethical precepts designed to foster intellectual freedom and to protect the freedom to read do not adequately account for the competing concerns these situations present.

The following hypothetical case illustrates some of the ways nontraditional information providers run into problems with confidentiality issues. An independent information broker recently completed a project for Client A, for which A paid a fee. The broker kept extensive records and files of the search process and results. Today prospective Client B requested that the broker take on a substantially similar project for him. Clients A and B could be competing corporations, law firms representing opposing parties, or simply unrelated persons engaging in similar research. They happen to have consulted the same information broker.

Can the information broker accept the assignment, and if so, can the broker make any use of the information in A's files? The mere resale of information prepared for Client A to Client B would clearly be improper. As professionals, we have a duty to perform for B the services for which the client is paying. We also should recognize that even similar requests may require different search strategies to fulfill the client's particular needs, and by simply giving the previously compiled information to B we have failed to consider his needs fully.

The more difficult question is whether we can make any use of what we did for A—surely there is a profit-motivated desire to do so, and reference back to an earlier successful search may even improve our service to B. But any reference to A's request may raise questions about the breach of client confidentiality or even conflicts of interest. The Congressional Research Service of the Library of Congress has established a policy for this very situation. If two members of Congress make similar research requests, each request must be treated independently.[19] Breaches of confidentiality and conflicts of interest are matters typically governed by professional codes of ethics. We as a profession must ensure that our codes cover these issues, as they occur outside the traditional library setting.

A related problem is the misuse of information gained in the course of rendering professional services to one's client or employer. About two years ago, a former librarian at a New York law firm was charged by the SEC with violating the insider trading laws.[20] The librarian was responsible for files containing confidential information concerning the takeover plans of certain corporate clients of the law firm. According to the SEC, the librarian "routinely performed computer research on target companies and obtained documents and information for . . . attorneys working on proposed business combinations involving clients of the firm."[21] The SEC stated that the librarian's "position and assignments caused him to be entrusted with or enabled him to gain access to highly confidential information."[22] The suit alleges that the librarian leaked this confidential information to family members who used the information to make profits of over $400,000 trading in the stock of the companies concerned. This is a clear example of the increased economic value of information and the temptations that value might pose to information professionals.

These examples illustrate a few of the ethical dilemmas information professionals might face. Although code revisions might provide better guidance, ethical conduct ultimately must rest on the individual determination of the professional. This is especially true in an unlicensed profession whose codes of ethics typically have no enforcement mechanism.

Reasonable Care

That brings us to the second component of a professional's duty, the requirement for exercising reasonable care, skill, and diligence in the rendering of professional services. Problems related to the lack of reasonable skill are more difficult to define than ethical problems, in part because the concept of "reasonable skill" itself is hazy. The standard courts use to judge whether or not the professional breached a duty is what a member of the profession in good standing would have done under the same circumstances.[23] The members of any profession are expected "to possess a standard minimum of special knowledge and ability" not shared by the general public.[24]

Two additional hypotheticals further explicate the application of these concepts of breach of duty to information professionals. In the first, an information consultant was retained to advise a law firm on litigation support systems for a complex class action lawsuit it is handling, perhaps a case like the Agent Orange or Dalkon Shield litigation. The client's two main objectives were that information entered into the system be retrievable and that information about trial strategy and the like not be subject to discovery by the other side. As it happens, the system has not performed well in retrieving documents, and the entire database has been held discoverable.

In terms of retrieval ability, the consultant should have known the relative merits of the available systems, as well as any unique features of the data the client intended to include in the database that might have affected retrieval. The consultant should also have known that systems frequently have not performed to clients' satisfaction[25] and that fulltext-only systems, at least, have been shown by some studies to retrieve as little as 20 percent of the relevant documents in the database.[26]

As regards the discovery issue, the consultant should have been aware of rulings on the discoverability of information contained in various types of litigation support systems.[27] If the consultant recommended a fulltext-only system, for example, the consultant should have advised the client that the work-product exception to the discovery rules likely would not protect information in the database.

It's difficult to tell, of course, from these limited facts, whether the consultant failed to exercise reasonable knowledge and judgment in the selection of a system or merely failed to advise the client adequately about the expected performance of such systems in general. Either way, it is possible that the consultant could be found negligent if expert testimony by other information professionals convinces the court that his/her performance was not "reasonable."

In the second hypothetical, the information professional runs a legal research service for law firms. The researcher assigned to a particular project failed to locate a recently decided case that bears directly on the issue to be researched. Certainly this is a serious failure, but we cannot determine whether it was the result of negligence without knowing what steps the researcher took and where the information could have been found.

Let's consider a few possibilities. The case might have been available either online or in print, and the researcher simply missed it. Although this is the easiest case, it may still be difficult to prove that the researcher failed to exercise reasonable care in the search. Or, the case might have been available online but not yet in print. The researcher had access to the online systems but did not consult them. Was the researcher required to do so? Conversely, the researcher might have used only the online services, not realizing that some concepts are more easily or reliably located through controlled and coordinated indexes than by means of fulltext searching.[28] Or, the recent case might have been available on either Lexis or Westlaw but not both.[29] The researcher has access to both systems, but since they generally contain the same information, the researcher only searched one, in this case the one that didn't include the relevant case. Should the professional have searched both? Or, the case might have been available on both systems, but on one system the case contained a typographical error that prevented retrieval.[30] As it happens, this is the only system the researcher tried. Was the researcher negligent in failing to consult both systems?

The information profession has not articulated standards by which to judge this researcher's performance. We must define acceptable practice for information providers, not only in terms of ethical standards, but also by establishing procedural guidelines to ensure the quality of our services. That won't be easy, especially in the online environment. New databases appear almost daily, contents change, search logic and communications methods are improved. Clearly, we must stay on top of these changes by reading the literature, obtaining continuing education, and the like. But in the midst of such changes, who can say what a reasonable search might have been on a given day?

Court Cases

The traditional library malpractice hypotheticals failed because no professional-client relationship sufficient to give rise to a legal duty existed. But the problem they posed was, ultimately, whether the librarian could be held responsible for the information contained in the sources the professional recommended. Similar problems may face information professionals in many situations where there is a duty. We are all aware, for example, of inaccurate or "dirty" data online.[31] In fact, the problem of assuring the accuracy or validity of information provided to clients may be more acute in the online arena because our knowledge of and ability to access online information so far outstrips that of most clients. Our duty to the client requires that we exercise our professional knowledge and judgment. The question is whether we can be held responsible for retrieving information that is itself inaccurate.

There are no reported cases addressing this issue. Three cases arising in very different circumstances may nevertheless offer some guidance to information professionals. In *EWAP v. Osmond*, a defamation case, a video store was held not liable for disseminating libelous information contained in a video tape by showing that there was no reason for it to believe that the information was libelous.[32]

The court stated that "one who merely plays a secondary role in disseminating information published by another, as in the case of libraries, news vendors, or carriers," could not be held liable for defamation unless it knew or had reason to believe the information was libelous.[33] The court further stated that when the books of a "reputable author or publishing house" are offered for sale or free circulation, the vendor or lender is not required to examine them to determine whether they contain any defamatory information. But if a particular author or publisher "has frequently published notoriously sensational or scandalous books," a shop or library that offers them to the public may run the risk of liability to anyone defamed by them.

Although the law of defamation has many special rules, this holding suggests that information providers might not be found liable for malpractice in cases where the faulty information originated elsewhere. We cannot be held responsible for knowing and verifying the contents of all the sources we use, whether in print or online. We should heed carefully, however, the caution regarding the reputation of the authors or publishers of the information we provide. Information professionals are in a position in most cases to make some judgment about the general quality and reputation of the sources of information, and in our role as consultants on the information needs of our clients we should apprise them of the source and reputed quality of the information we provide.

In *Brocklesby v. Jeppesen*,[34] a $12,000,000 verdict was upheld against Jeppesen, a company that publishes aeronautical charts based entirely on data provided by the Federal Aviation Administration. The FAA data are originally published in tabular form; Jeppesen converts it into graphic form. In *Brocklesby*, a pilot used one of Jeppesen's charts to make a landing and crashed into a mountain, killing the entire crew and destroying the plane. The chart was followed correctly but provided erroneous instructions. It was stipulated that the inaccuracies were contained in the original FAA data, not created by Jeppesen.

Jeppesen is an information provider. It gathers data, repackages it, and sells it. If it merely passed on erroneous data provided by the government, how could it now be required to pay $12,000,000 to the survivors of the crew members? The court treated Jeppesen's chart as a product, thus allowing the case to be considered under the strict liability provisions of products liability law. This determination turned mainly on the fact that Jeppesen's charts are mass-produced, not developed at the request of an individual client.[35] The court emphasized that Jeppesen had a duty to test its product and to warn users of its dangers.[36]

The *Osmond* and *Brocklesby* rulings pose an apparent conflict on our duty to test or verify the information contained in sources we use. The distinction turns, I think, on our role vis-a-vis the originator of the data. The video store in *Osmond* was merely a disseminator of information produced by someone else. Jeppesen, on the other hand, used information published by the FAA to produce a conceptually different package of information. Most of our practice falls somewhere between these two extremes. Taken together, these cases suggest that our potential for liability increases significantly as we become more active in providing raw data and especially in synthesizing the data into information useable by the client, rather than merely leading the client to sources of information.

In both *Osmond* and *Brocklesby*, the information was produced for the mass market. A third case, however, comes closer to approximating the situation of information professionals who provide information to specific clients. In *Dun & Bradstreet, Inc. v. Greenmoss Builders*,[37] the credit reporting agency erroneously reported to subscribers that Greenmoss had filed for bankruptcy. Dun & Bradstreet's employee had mistakenly attributed to Greenmoss a bankruptcy petition filed by one of its former employees. The jury awarded $50,000 in compensatory damages and $300,000 in punitive damages. Dun & Bradstreet moved for a new trial on the ground that punitive damages cannot be awarded absent proof of actual malice. The request for the new trial was granted but later reversed by the Vermont Supreme Court.

The United States Supreme Court agreed that a new trial was not required. The Court held that "permitting recovery of . . . punitive damages in defamation cases absent a showing of 'actual malice' does not violate the First Amendment when the defamatory statements do not involve matters of public concern."[38] The Court's focus on the law of defamation, along with the convoluted procedural history of the case, obscures the critical importance of this case to information professionals. Of the cases discussed in this paper, the facts of this case are most closely analogous to the practice of information professionals. Dun & Bradstreet's business is to research various records to find information on the financial status of companies. It is also a database producer that could face liability for erroneous information contained in its database and used by others. It should be of great interest and concern to us that a jury saw fit to award $300,000 in *punitive* damages for the provision of erroneous information, and the Supreme Court held that knowledge of or reckless disregard for the falsity of the information need not be proved to sustain the award.

Conclusion

The most fascinating and vexing aspect of the online environment is that the information universe with which we deal is invisible to us. This would make the independent verification of data exceedingly difficult. We cannot examine the source as a whole; we can only retrieve bits of it. The invisibility of the source also impedes judgments about the quality of our service. While it is relatively easy for doctors or lawyers to determine the state of medical or legal knowledge at a particular point in time so as to judge the performance of a peer in a particular case, information providers often cannot know what was in a database at a given time. The information in many databases is not "date-stamped," and even more importantly, changes in the data can be made without a trace.

Still, we as a profession can and should work towards a collective judgment about our standards of practice. Some of the questions we might consider are: What kinds of education and training do our present and future circumstances demand? What are the qualitative differences between print and online versions of the "same" source, and when should we use one format over the other? What role does cost play in that determination? How far should we go in analyzing, synthesizing, and repackaging, rather than merely gathering, information for clients?

To sum up, our concerns about malpractice may be speculative, but we do not engage in idle speculation. The incredible economic value of the information industry, the increase in malpractice suits against other professionals, and the suits against disseminators and producers of information in other contexts are ample evidence of the potential for liability on our part.

References and Notes

1. See "The Professionals' Liability Reform Act of 1988," remarks of Rep. Don Ritter, 134 *Congressional Record* E919 (3/31/88), 100th Congress 2d session, p. E.919.
2. As an example of the worth of the information industry, *Business Week* reported that Mead Data Central, the provider of Lexis and Nexis online services, had revenues of $154 million and before-tax profits of $20 million in 1986. "The Information Business," *Business Week*, (Aug. 25, 1986), p. 82. Dialog was sold in the summer of 1988 for $353 million. "The Media Business: Knight-Ridder to Buy Lockheed's Dialog Unit," *New York Times* (July 12, 1988).
3. Alan Angoff, "Library Malpractice Suit: Could it Happen to You?" *American Libraries* 7:489 (Sept. 1976).
4. See, for example, Gerome Leone, "Malpractice Liability of a Law Librarian?" *Law Library Journal* 73:44–65 (1980); and Robin Mills, "Reference Service vs. Legal Advice: Is It Possible to Draw the Line?" *Law Library Journal* 72:179–93 (1979).
5. William Nasri, "Malpractice Liability: Myth or Reality?" *Journal of Library Administration* 1:3 (1981).
6. *See Prosser and Keeton on the Law of Torts*, ed. W. Page Keeton (St. Paul, Minn.: West, 1984), p. 164–65.
7. Ibid., p. 186 (discussing physicians).
8. Ibid., p. 356.
9. See Durrance, "The Generic Librarian: Anonymity versus Accountability," *RQ* 22:278.
10. See, for example, Lancaster and Smith, "On-line Systems in the Communications Process: Projections," *Journal of the American Society for Information Science* 31:194, 199 (May 1980).
11. Kathleen Nichol, "Database Proliferation: Implications for Librarians," *Special Libraries* 74:116 (April 1983).
12. Anne Mintz, "Information Practice and Malpractice," *Library Journal* 38 (Sept. 15, 1985).
13. Ibid., p. 41.
14. Ibid., p. 38.
15. See, for example, the American Bar Association's Model Rules of Professional Conduct, adopted in 1983.
16. See, among others, the American Library Association Statement of Professional Ethics 1981, *American Libraries* 12:335 (June 1981); and the American Association of Law Libraries Code of Ethics, *AALL Newsletter* 10:43 (Jan. 1979).
17. See Donna Shaver, Nancy Hewison, and Leslie Wykoff, "Ethics for Online Intermediaries," *Special Libraries* 76:238, 239 (1985); Lancaster and Smith, "Online Systems," p. 199.
18. Shaver, "Ethics Revisited: Are We Making Progress?" in *The Information Profession: Facing Future Challenges* (Washington, D.C.: Special Libraries Association, 1988)

p. 103, 106.
19. Telephone conversation with Roberta Shaffer, former special assistant to the Law Librarian of Congress, Oct. 4, 1988.
20. "Librarian Accused of Insider Trading," *Washington Post*, Dec. 25, 1986.
21. *BNA Daily Report for Executives*, 1/6/87, p. A-6.
22. Ibid.
23. Prosser and Keeton, p. 175.
24. Ibid., p. 185.
25. See, for example, Rudolph Peritz, "Computer Data and Reliability: A Call for Authentication of Business Records under the Federal Rules of Evidence," *Northwestern Univ. Law Review* 80:856, 993–99 (1986) for an account of the problems several firms have encountered with computer systems.
26. David Blair and M. E. Marron, "An Evaluation of Retrieval Effectiveness for a Full-Text Document Retrieval System," *Communications of the A.C.M.* 28:289, 293 (March 1985).
27. See Edward Sherman and Stephen Kinnard, "The Development, Discovery, and Use of Computer Support Systems in Achieving Efficiency in Litigation," *Columbia Law Review* 79:267 (1979) for a discussion of this issue.
28. See Mary Jensen, "Full Text Databases: When to Use Them and When Not to Use Them," *Law Office Economics & Management* 27:77, 81–81 (1986).
29. See Kelly Warnken, "A Study in Lexis and Westlaw Errors," *Legal Economics* 13:39 (July/Aug. 1987).
30. Ibid., p. 58.
31. See C. A. Cuadra, "Database Producers, Online Services, and Custom Information Services—Who Will Survive?" in *Information Policy for the 1980's: Proceedings of the Eusidic Conference, 5 October 1978* (Learned Information, 1979) p. 23, 28.
32. Osmond v. EWAP, Inc., 153 Cal. App.3d 842,200 Cal. Rptr. 674 (1984).
33. Ibid., p. 680.
34. Brocklesby v. Jeppesen, 767 F.2d 1288 (9th Cir. 1985), *cert. den.*, 474 U.S. 1101 (1986).
35. Ibid., p. 1295.
36. Ibid., p. 1297.
37. Dun & Bradstreet, Inc. v. Greenmoss Builders, 472 U.S. 749 (1984).
38. Ibid., p. 763.

RECRUITING, RETAINING, AND REWARDING RESEARCH FACULTY: ART OR ATMOSPHERE?

Richard W. Budd

Successful recruiting of strong faculty, particularly those who can make major research contributions to the field, requires some conceptual and mythical "blockbusting." It requires some drastic shifts in thinking about what we are as a discipline as well as how we go about implementing that in an academic setting. A key issue is viewing ourselves as *academic* programs serving a variety of professional fields. Another is valuing research as the equivalent of teaching—and supporting that activity with grant assistance, equipment, internal funding, external contacts, and a strong sabbatical leave program. An essential underlying ingredient is the creation of a lively intellectual environment with the proper balance of tenured and younger faculty with complementary research interests.

The Prerequisites

There is neither art nor mystery about successful faculty recruiting programs. Successful recruiting of strong faculty, particularly those who can make major research contributions to the field, does however, require the establishment of a particular set of conditions—none of which can be instituted overnight. That combination of circumstances includes program, environment, resources and incentives, a vision of the future, and some demonstrable movement toward the goals that vision articulates. Although, in my view, these conditions represent a *systemic unity*, I will attempt to describe each of these as they have been obtained at the Rutgers School of Communication, Information and Library Studies (SCILS) and the impact I believe they have had upon our recruiting efforts.

Program

The underlying stratum of program is to be found not in courses and sequences, but simply in recognizing who we are and where we are. That, I fear, is easier said than done. The reality is that we are academic programs situated in the context of universities. The extent to which we subscribe to that concept and all that it implies is, in my judgment, directly related to our ability not only to attract top-flight faculty members but also to produce meaningful and significant research for our discipline. Our acceptance of that notion also bears importantly upon the valuation of our membership in the university community of which we are a part and, therefore, the extent to which we will share in the overall resources of that institution. I might note that efforts to establish ourselves as something other than that not only will detract from such status but constitute, in my judgment, less-than-responsible behavior for those who choose to view themselves as educators.

Universities have a unique role in our society. They provide both students and faculty alike with the freedom to dissect, study, critique, and reformulate our social institutions—to challenge conventional wisdom and practices and, hopefully as a result, to foster change and provide leadership for every aspect of our society. Those conditions apply equally to all corners of higher education—the arts and sciences as well as to the professions, to philosophy as well as engineering, to psychology as well as library and information studies. Academic programs are not the baggage cars of the fields of endeavor they represent but are in fact the engines that drive them toward the future.

Operationally, that means designing programs of intellectual substance which by their nature raise critical questions and challenge current philosophies and practices. That, in my judgment, is the fundamental prerequisite for establishing a vital research program. Programs that present mundane issues in static learning environments will produce mundane and repetitive research findings—not likely to prove very attractive to top-flight scholars.

Environment. Program alone, however, will not get the job of recruiting high-powered faculty done. To succeed, programs of worth must be situated in *growth-inducing environments.* Being located within a research university, at least for SCILS, is a great asset. In articulating criteria for promotion and tenure, Rutgers University makes no distinction between programs, professional or otherwise. Research and scholarship have no substitutes, no approximations, no field-related exceptions. If you are not actively engaged in advancing your field through original research, peer reviewed and promulgated in refereed scholarly publications of national and international reputation, you will have a limited career at Rutgers. Neither does this policy discount strong, effective teaching or professional activity and public service—and substantial evidence of all three are basic requirements for promotion. I am one of the few deans of a professional school at Rutgers who strongly endorses these standards.

Why, and what does this have to do with establishing an environment that facilitates recruiting? First, it presents a clear and powerful message that says SCILS places a high value on research; that we view it not as a concern nor as an issue separate from what we do, but as a *way of life* for the members of our academic community. Second, it means that only those persons with a desire to pursue such a course will join our faculty; others, perhaps among them some very talented teachers, will locate elsewhere. Third, such a faculty consistently produces research of such quality as to place our school in respectable parity with other units of quality within the university (determined by interdisciplinary peer evaluation as opposed to self-assessment).

Finally, it means that when we pursue more senior scholars, they will find themselves surrounded by colleagues who share the research ethic and are capable of providing the intellectual climate that is attractive to them. There can be nothing less appetizing or lonely than a highly productive scholar being offered a position in a program to become its resident researcher, expected to carry the research banner for a program that places its values elsewhere.

In addition to benefiting from a pervading research ethos, the environment for recruiting is immeasurably enhanced by the presence of a vital, research-oriented Ph.D. program. I realize such a statement is technically redundant, since the Ph.D. *is* a research degree. Unfortunately, much of what emanates from many such programs is often considerably less than that, reflective of the esteem with which research is held by the collective. Few things are more attractive to research-active scholars than to have bright, young students to share their work.

Yet another part of the mosaic is a program closely allied with related disciplines—either formally or informally—but significantly related. Our field is presently one of the most rapidly changing domains of study. While that fact can partly be attributed to the technology underlying much of what we do, considerably more must be credited to the increased interest by other fields in the impact of information in a variety of arenas. Unfortunately, we do not find ourselves in the fore of much of this work (as any cross-disciplinary citation analysis will demonstrate), but if we are to understand the phenomenon in greater depth than we do, as well as to apply it to our own area of focus, we need to connect solidly with those who are pursuing such study. We must cease to view our intellectual isolation with some sense of misguided pride and take positive steps to alter the situation. This is a particularly important and vital aspect of providing an attractive landscape for a prospective senior research scholar.

There is no one model for achieving this goal. Most of you are familiar with what we have done at Rutgers—where we have formally incorporated several information-oriented disciplines within a single school. While we think there is considerable to be gained by allowing such disciplines to retain their separate identities while at the same time cooperating in research and new program development, it is clearly not the only approach. Several programs are moving toward a similar goal by appointing scholars from allied disciplines to a single existent faculty. While such an approach may be somewhat more difficult to execute effectively—particularly if the content of the program itself does not reflect course work that takes advantage of such appointments—it nonetheless reflects a growth-inducing strategy which augurs well for change.

A third, although less desirable, model for formalized relationships involves joint appointing program faculty members with allied disciplines. In my experience, such appointments most usually do not yield the intended results. However, any of the three formal approaches just noted, in my view, are superior to loose liaisons with other disciplines—which have a tendency to come and go with given individual faculty members.

In any event, the more interdisciplinary the program and its faculty, the more likely distinguished researchers will find it attractive. Indeed, several candidates that we have identified over the past few years have themselves been ensconced in a variety of nonlibrary or noninformation programs.

The Basics

So much for the prerequisites. Let us turn now to a review of some of the basics also necessary to successful recruiting. It is perhaps too obvious to mention compensation as a key ingredient in the process, but it needs emphasis. Another advantage to being part of a research university is the willingness of the parent institution to support highly competitive salaries for outstanding candidates. Rutgers University has been most supportive in this aspect of recruiting. It needs to be noted, however, that if the prerequisites were not first in place, SCILS most surely would not be the recipient of such a response. Rutgers internally grades all of its units based upon regular external program reviews, the quality of their academic offerings, the caliber of students enrolled in their programs, the quality and volume of faculty research publications, the number of grants won and the significance of the granting agencies, and so forth. These assessments translate into an internal grading process that determines ongoing budget support and university willingness to contribute to meeting salary offers. In addition, units that measure up can also expect cooperation in developing startup packages to support an individual's research activities.

For beginning tenure-track candidates of high quality, there are also available two-year research fellowships that guarantee beginning assistant professors half-time off for research as well as provide them significant funds for supporting their research. SCILS has been most successful in competing for these fellowships for qualified new appointments. The university also supports a World Class Scholar program for exceptional senior appointments, providing them with dramatically high salaries as well as research and facilities support.

At the school level, we mirror the university policy of rewarding departments with respect to demonstrable research activity. We have also developed a set of policies and mechanisms to support and encourage a scholarly research environment. Perhaps the most difficult phase of our school effort was shifting from a *teaching load* to a *workload* concept. We have retreated from the prevailing notion that views faculty assignments principally in terms of teaching assignments with research relegated to whatever is left over. Our approach views the notion of "released time" for research or other nonteaching activities as a debilitating concept—one that does not value research on a par with teaching, administrative activity, or professional service. The most difficult aspect of this approach is that it permits differential assignments among faculty and lays to rest the myth of equal teaching loads.

Established in conjunction with department chairs to cover the entire coming academic year, a given faculty member's workload might look like any of those in Table 1.

The requirement is that workloads for individual faculty members should reflect their strengths, interests, and demonstrated performance in relation to teaching, research, and service in accordance with program and school priorities and needs. Clearly there is less flexibility in such

TABLE 1
Workloads of Three Faculty Members

	Faculty Member No. 1	Faculty Member No. 2	Faculty Member No. 3
Research *specific project(s)*	10%	60%	30%
Teaching *specific courses* *dissertation committee(s)*	65	25	45
Advising	10	5	5
Governance *particular committee assignment(s)*	5	5	5
Professional service *particular service activity*	10	5	15

arrangements for faculty working toward tenure, who, by the nature of the institution, must maintain a workload strongly biased in favor of research. Grants or other sources of outside funding can, of course, alter these pre-determined assignments.

There are a multitude of other policy issues that reward research activity such as travel funding, availability of a grants officer to assist with developing proposals for funding, flexible arrangements for research collaboration and/or work with the corporate sector, a generous sabbatical program that even embraces untenured faculty during their first appointment, and mechanisms for facilitating contacts with corporations, foundations, or other outside agencies. Our school also maintains an internal research council, which has funds at its disposal to award internal research grants in support of research proposals on a competitive basis. Finally, the dean has at his disposal a discretionary merit program that permits selectively upgrading the salaries of faculty with active ongoing research programs. Indeed all these basics assist greatly in our recruiting process, particularly for established scholars, who find in us a coordinated program that will facilitate the continuance of their research program.

A Vision of the Future

Perhaps it would have made more sense to begin with what I call a vision of the future, but I elected to make it my endnote. One cannot, I feel, underestimate the potency of having such a vision in the process. I will not profess to our possessing a highly detailed, finely tuned blueprint of what our school will look like in the year 2000. On the other hand, we have developed a master plan that acknowledges our entrance into the Information Age and recognizes that its major characteristic is the evolution of a more complex information and communication environment. Further, the convergence of new technologies and the growing importance of information and its effective communication for economic growth and the achievement of social, organizational, and personal goals has made it essential that communication and information professionals and scholars develop a more sophisticated understanding of the nature and function of information and communication processes and the impact of the new technologies on systems, policy, management, and, most especially, human behavior.

In short, we are dedicated to the creation of instructional and research programs focusing on a wide spectrum of information phenomena and communication processes—a spectrum that clearly cannot be encompassed by any single discipline or existing program. We are, both programmatically and in our research, committed to looking at interpersonal communication processes and interaction analysis on the one hand and distributed expert systems, organizational communication and behavior of human systems on the other. How and in what particular order we pursue this agenda is unspecified—and as such, it extends a very serious invitation to scholars to join us in the process of giving specificity to that vision. It is clearly an invitation that prospective faculty—both new as well as established—find powerfully attractive and exciting, one that provides them an opportunity to participate in the creation of their own work environment. At the same time, the contributions of persons who have come to our faculty under that invitation have invariably added new and dynamic dimensions to our programs—and have served to stimulate and rejuvenate faculty who have been in the school for several years, revamp arcane programs and initiate new ones, and raise the level of student interest as well as the quality of their work.

As I noted previously, a successful recruiting program is more than a matter of setting out a laundry list of essential ingredients. It is a matter of establishing clear expectations and working to ensure that they are met as fully as possible. Beyond that, it involves the collective creation of an environment and atmosphere that speaks for itself and that manifestly bids others to join it and, more importantly, to take up permanent residence in it.

"WOMEN'S WORK" WITHIN LIBRARIANSHIP: TIME TO EXPAND THE FEMINIST AGENDA

Suzanne Hildenbrand

Library feminists searching for equality for women librarians have concentrated their efforts on pay equity and on increasing the number of women in managerial positions in large libraries. While encouraging progress has been made in these areas, though much remains to be done, it is time to ask if there are not other fronts on which to wage the battle for gender equity in librarianship.

"Women's Work"

The literature on "women's work," including the so-called women's professions such as librarianship, nursing, and elementary school teaching, stresses that such work is usually devalued. The pay, status, career opportunities, and working conditions in these occupations are generally lower for both the men and women in them than they are in occupations requiring similar levels of education and responsibility but not typed as women's work.[1] Another characteristic of these female-intensive professions is that the male minority is overrepresented in the top positions and the better-paying areas. In contrast, in male-intensive occupations the female minority is clustered in the worst areas and in the lowest-rated slots.[2]

It is clear that librarianship fits the model of a female-intensive profession. But are there areas of librarianship that are likely to employ more

---

"'Women's Work' Within Librarianship: Time to Expand the Feminist Agenda," by Suzanne Hildenbrand in *Library Journal* Vol. 114, no. 14 (September 1, 1989), pp. 153–155; reprinted with permission from Reed Publishing, USA, copyright © 1989 Reed Publishing, USA.

women than the profession as a whole? If so, it can be predicted from the literature on female-intensive professions that these areas would trail the profession as a whole on salary, status, career opportunities, and working conditions. That is, these areas would have a relationship to librarianship as a whole similar to the one librarianship has to male-intensive professions.

Children's Librarianship

Many studies illustrate that children's librarianship is more female-intensive than the profession as a whole. (This holds true for public library service to children and school library service. School librarians, however, have careers that resemble those of teachers and so will not be considered here.)[3] It is also the lowest paid specialty listed in the latest *ALA Survey of Librarian Salaries*.[4] Children's librarians bear a double burden: located in an institutional setting, the public library, that is low paying in comparison to academic and most special libraries and in a service that is paid less in comparison to others in that institution.[5]

Turning from salary to status, the little research that exists tends to confirm the view that within librarianship, children's librarianship does not enjoy a good reputation or high status. Professor Roma Harris and colleagues at the School of Library and Information Science of the University of Western Ontario found that graduates of that school ranked children's services consistently low in "prestige."[6] Ironically, although the librarians surveyed in this study devalued the work of children's librarians, another study done at Western Ontario showed that the public devalued the work of librarians.[7] Mary Somerville, children's coordinator of the Broward County Public Library (Fla.) and past president of the Association for Library Service to Children (ALSC), found that there were "many subtle and not so subtle prejudices against children's librarians" within the profession.[8]

Career opportunities are another area often singled out as one in which children's librarianship trails behind other specialties.[9] More data on career opportunities are needed: for example, how long does it take to move from Librarian I to Librarian II in children's work in contrast to reference work? How many directors or other managers have come from children's work in comparison with other specialties? What opportunities do children's librarians have to transfer to other services if they wish? How does this compare with librarians in other specialties?

Comparative working conditions are also in need of assessment, although they may be the most difficult of all to evaluate. They include level of supervision or degree of personal autonomy, privacy, workplace isolation or lack of interaction with the rest of the professional staff, and input on automation plans. There appear to be virtually no data on these questions.

Cataloging, too?

Although there are even fewer figures on cataloging than on children's work, several studies suggest that it too may indeed be more female intensive than librarianship as a whole. Harris, for example, found that within library education the teaching of cataloging has been a more female-intensive activity, over the period for which there are records, than has library education as a whole.[10] Harris also reported that women graduates of her school were more likely to catalog on either the first or current job than were men.[11]

The data on salary and status are sparse. However, the ALA salary study found catalogers trailing all specialties surveyed, except for children's and young adult librarians.[12] San Jose State University Library Director Ruth Hafter, in a study of six academic libraries, found catalogers to have low status within their institutions.[13]

It is difficult to find evidence on career opportunities or working conditions in cataloging and one must rely on impressions. Herbert White's observation that students reject cataloging careers because they know what goes on in cataloging departments may be relevant, however.[14] The lack of privacy, coupled with high noise levels and production quotas found in many catalog departments, suggests white-collar sweatshops.

The Research Agenda

There are no large data sets available to researchers reviewing the relationship between sex and variables such as salary and career opportunities in different library specialties. The literature consists either of studies of small populations or impressionistic accounts. Both have been cited in this article but the time has surely come to go beyond these.

The American Library Association and its divisions should be encouraged to collect data by task as well as by institution. Such an approach will not only make for more meaningful studies of who does what and for how much in the library world, but may help to explain the current shortages in some areas, notably children's and youth services and cataloging. Such data may also help with the restructuring of jobs that automation is predicted to bring.

While waiting for more complete statistics for the entire profession, however, studies of individual institutions or jurisdictions can be initiated. Although salary is the most fundamental variable to investigate, numerous others including status and career opportunities are important to a full assessment of the relationship between sex and specialization in librarianship.

The Political Agenda

If research does indeed establish that the familiar link exists between a higher percent of women and inferior conditions of employment within librarianship, library feminists will have to expand their agenda. For neither of the items which they currently champion will offer equity to those librarians who suffer the most from sex discrimination: those in the most female-intensive specialties. For example, a pay equity suit will raise the salaries of all librarians in the jurisdiction involved, but it will not affect inequities within librarianship in that jurisdiction.

Similarly the feminist emphasis on moving women into management will not remedy the problem. Most library women will never be directors and although they may be heartened to see some women achieve top slots, that does not improve their pay or working conditions. In addition, many women directors are tokens with little power to effect change.

What then can feminists do to remedy the inequities faced by those in the female-intensive specialties? First and foremost, begin discussion of the issue and promote research into it. Secondly, encourage the use of mechanisms already in place to redress these injustices. These include affirmative action channels available in many organizations that employ librarians and union contract negotiations.

A Greater Direct Impact

While library feminists are not to be discouraged from pay equity actions and promoting the movement of women into management, they need to work toward programs that will have a greater direct impact on the inequities faced by more library women. A good place to start would be with the conditions in those specialties in which women are concentrated in even greater numbers than they are within the profession in general. That is, we need a kind of internal sex equity movement to bring salaries and conditions within the most female-intensive specialties up to the standard of the profession generally.

References

1. Stromberg, Ann Helton & Shirley Harkess, eds. *Women Working: Theories and Facts in Perspective.* Mayfield Pub., 1988, p. 208.
2. Williams, Christine L. *Gender Differences at Work.* Univ. of California Pr., 1989, p. 9, 132.
3. See for example, Carol Learmont & Stephen Van Houten, "Placements and Salaries 1987: The Upswing Continues," *LJ*, Oct. 15, 1988, p. 33 or Loriene Roy, "A Survey of Children's Librarians in Illinois Public Libraries," *Library and Information Science Research*, Jul.–Sept. 1987, p. 189.
4. *ALA Survey of Librarian Salaries, 1988.* American Library Association, 1988, p. 27.
5. Roy, p. 191.
6. Harris, Roma M., Susan Monk, & Jill T. Austin, "MLS Graduates Survey: Sex Differences in Prestige and Salary Found," *Canadian Library Journal*, Jun. 1986, p. 152.
7. Harris, Roma M. & Christina Sue-Chan, "Cataloging and Reference, Circulation and Shelving: Public Library Users and University Students Perceptions of Librarianship," *Library and Information Science Reserarch*, Jan.–Mar. 1988, p. 105.
8. Somerville, Mary, "Facing the Shortage of Children's Librarians," *American Libraries*, Jun. 1987, p. 421 and Roy, p. 202.
9. Somerville, p. 421; Roy, p. 202.
10. Harris, Roma M., B. Gillian Michell, & Carol Cooley, "The Gender Gap in Library Education," *Journal of Education for Library and Information Science*, Winter 1985.
11. Harris, Monk, & Austin.
12. *ALA Survey.* . . .
13. Hafter, Ruth. *Academic Librarians and Cataloging Networks: Visibility, Quality Control and Professional Status.* Greenwood, 1986.
14. White, Herbert, "Catalogers—Yesterday, Today and Tomorrow," *LJ*, Apr. 1, 1987, p. 48.

RESEARCH AND THE USE OF STATISTICS FOR LIBRARY DECISION MAKING

Peter Hernon

In the social sciences, there are three types of research: basic, applied, and action. *Basic* research concerns the pursuit of knowledge for its own sake and may or may not immediately contribute to the theoretical base of a discipline or a profession. *Applied* research validates theory and leads to the revision of theory. *Action* research is usually applied research conducted with regard to an immediate problem by someone having a direct interest in that problem. Librarians often conduct *action* research and generate data to which they can apply judgments. In other words, they produce data useful for local decision making concerning library programs, collections, services, operations, staffing, and so forth.

The library profession is statistics oriented (numbers and percentages), but not fully committed to gathering data that lend themselves to inferential statistics. Library research and the use of statistical analyses have grown in sophistication over the years. This is "partly because of the availability of computer programs which can analyze large amounts of data in complex ways and solve complicated problems quickly and efficiently, without enormous investments in manual labor."[1] Many discussions of statistics, or the reading of a research article for that matter, seem to require "mathematical sophistication" on the part of the reader.[2] Statistics are often cast in terms of mathematics, the calculation of formidable appearing formulas, and a dry, and highly formal, writing style. Many

---

"Research and the Use of Statistics for Library Decision Making," by Peter Hernon in *Library Administration & Management* Vol. 3, no. 4 (Fall 1989), pp. 176–180; reprinted with permission from the American Library Association, copyright © 1989 by ALA.

research articles therefore reach only a limited audience, presumably one with a background in research and statistics.

More librarians ought to become familiar with research and statistics, both as consumers and as participants in the research process. To aid them, this article highlights information contained in two recently published books concerning statistics and the role of microcomputers in number crunching.[3]

An important question is, "How much research and statistical competence should library managers and decision makers have?" This is a hard question to answer because so many factors must be taken into account. The larger and more complex the library and its environment, the greater the research and statistical skills that the library staff need for decision making and planning. As Swisher and McClure suggest, "by understanding basic research and statistical techniques, utilizing research to support decision making and planning, and encouraging the development of research competency in the librarians, the library will be better able to increase its effectiveness, respond to the information needs of its clientele, and assume a leadership role for accessing the information environment."[4]

Data collection and the interpretation of statistics should come from librarians who have knowledge of the research process, who can relate that process to decision making and planning, and who are change oriented. Without an interest in decision making, research, and measurement of the extent to which formal objectives are met, library staff will be unable to respond effectively to the changing environments affecting the library. Further, they will not be able to demonstrate accountability and to justify the existence of actual or planned programs and services. In effect, the staff might continue to do well (efficiently) activities that need not be done (ineffectiveness).

By understanding fundamental research and statistical techniques, utilizing research to support decision making and planning, and encouraging the development of research competencies in the professional staff, managers will be better able to increase the effectiveness of library collections and services, and to respond to the information needs of current and potential clientele.

Planning and Evaluation

Planning is the process of setting goals and objectives, developing programs and activities to accomplish those objectives, and evaluating the effectiveness and efficiency of those programs in context of the goals and objectives. Evaluation results in accumulation of "information for . . . decision making," is the accountability aspect of planning, and represents a measurement of library effectiveness in reaching a predetermined goal.[5] The complexity and uniqueness of existing administrative techniques, local situations, and the resources available in a particular library preclude "cookbook" recipes for how to prepare every organization for the implementation of every type of *formative* and *summative* evaluation. The purpose of summative evaluation is to determine the success or failure of a program or service, while formative evaluation seeks to improve an ongoing program or service. Both types of evaluation have a role in the planning process, and one is not necessarily better than the other.

Library managers must recognize existing conditions and constraints in the library, determine their knowledge and competency about planning and evaluation, and analyze the administrative assumptions under which libraries organize and service information resources. They should also assess the overall willingness of the organization to change. Recognizing and addressing these contingencies, librarians can develop administrative strategies to create an organizational climate that encourages the planning and evaluation of information collections and services.

Areas Amenable to Data Collection

Research can be conducted in almost all phases of library work. Hernon, for example, illustrates the facets of reference service that lend themselves to the development of performance measures.[6] Librarians can evaluate both the *direct* (personal assistance, effectiveness and efficiency of bibliographic instruction, etc.) and *indirect* (collection development, etc.) aspects of reference service. Topical areas that they might examine include the:

- Staff themselves
- Clientele
- Library's capacity to provide service
- Reference questions asked

- Resources needed to answer questions
- Answers given

Bommer and Chorba identify specific performance or effectiveness measures for different aspects of reference service.[7]

Data Collection Methods Amenable to Statistical Analysis

Employing a variety of methodologies, librarians can collect data that can be subjected to statistical analyses using a mainframe computer, microcomputer, or hand calculation. Some of the methods for quantifiable data collection represented in library literature include:

- *Expert judgment.* For example, staff might evaluate the collection, according to written procedures, to gather data for the identification of strengths and weaknesses.
- *Retrieval of items from a database and evaluation of their usefulness and relevance.*
- *Testing (standardized or locally developed tests).*
- *Self-rating of a project's impact from participants.* The success of numerous conferences and programs is often determined from the opinions of participants about sessions and the elements they either liked or disliked.
- *Response to a questionnaire or interview.*
- *Observation of behavior and the impact of that behavior on programs and services.*
- *Unobtrusive evaluation* (the testing of staff members unaware that they are test subjects).
- *Obtrusive evaluation* (the testing of staff members who are fully aware that they are the test subjects, or an examination of how staff members work).
- *Content analysis.* Documents representative of an issue or topic are gathered and their contents classified and analyzed.
- *Analysis of historical and current records.* Studying statistical or other records for patterns may be simplified by placing such information onto diskette, magnetic tape, and so forth, for computer manipulation.

- *Queuing* (or the monitoring of traffic patterns, such as observing the flow of traffic at reference, periodical, and circulation desks).
- *Transactional analysis* (for example, the analysis of circulation records or records resulting from participants' use of online catalogs). Technology captures each transaction (or use), and researchers analyze patterns in the records.
- *Bibliometrics and citation analysis.* Bibliometrics studies investigate the structure of published literature and its usage: patterns in "authorship, publication, reading, and citation." Bibliometrics includes studies relating to "the growth of the literature on a given subject," "patterns in the distribution of publishing productivity by individual authors," "how articles on any subject are dispersed across journals," "the 'obsolescence' of literature," "the epidemiology of ideas as reflected in scholarship as evidenced by analyses of who cites whom."[8]

Lancaster identifies and describes a number of studies that have used the above-mentioned methodologies and that have produced data amenable to analysis on microcomputers.[9]

Resistance to Data Collection

The library director might support data collection and decision making based on "hard evidence" and might assume that the staff shares this enthusiasm. In fact, other managers might not be supportive. They might believe in their intuitive ability to recognize "poor quality" and "inefficiency" and resist data collection because the data might conceivably be used against the library—to argue against a program or service favored by the library. Staff might view data collection as a distraction; research takes them away from the provision of services and programs. McClure's discussion of the use (or, more correctly, nonuse) of performance measure data illustrates internal resistance to data collection and a distrust of the utility of such data.[10] Further, the "identification of 'poor' performance on a specific service would require a remedial action and would represent a change in the status quo."[11]

Performance measures represent a broad managerial concept that encompasses both *input* (indicators of those resources essential to library services) and *output* (indicators of the services resulting from library activities) measures. Such measures depict the extent, effectiveness, and efficiency of library operations, services, and programs. Yet, even middle management might have little understanding of such measures—their purpose and relationship to planning. They might also surmise that performance measure data will not alter the decision-making process and that a complex and time-consuming data collection process far exceeds the value of the resulting data.[12] McClure discovered instances in which department heads kept two sets of records: one for submission to the director and the other for internal use.[13]

The McClure essay indicates that organizational change must be acceptable throughout the library. There must be a strong commitment to change, a sense of purpose, and a willingness to conduct research that has an impact on local decision making and the profession, and improves the quality of library collections, operations, programs, and services.

Measurement and Level of Significance

Measurement provides a means for quantifying variables and making comparisons among them. It "is the process through which observations are translated into number."[14] There are four levels of measurement: nominal, ordinal, interval, and ratio. Prior to data collection, librarians should determine which levels of measurement to use and if those levels adequately address study questions or hypotheses.

Swisher and McClure provide an excellent discussion of the levels, with examples drawn from librarianship.[15] Suffice it to say, nominal measurement, which is the least useful, classifies observations, objects, or individuals into different or mutually exclusive categories. It identifies observations, objects, or individuals and places them "into categories which are qualitatively rather than quantitatively different."[16] For example, the variable of gender is represented or distinguished by the categories of female and male. Librarians then count and report the number of female and male respondents. They do not manipulate (add, subtract, multiply, or divide) the numbers. Nonetheless, they may report the proportion or ratio of one responding gender to the other.

With ordinal or the second level of measurement, librarians place observations, objects, or individuals in ascending or descending order, without either specifying or knowing the magnitude of the difference between them. Consequently, "we know more about a variable than that it is present in an object or person as one of the mutually exclusive categories of the variables."[17] For example, survey respondents might check "never," "sometimes," "frequently," or "always" to a particular question. There is an ordering of response options from "never" to "always." However, the difference among the response options does not have precise meaning. The size of the interval between categories is unknown or unequal.

Interval measurement classifies observations, objects, or individuals on an ordered series of points that are equally spaced. There is "some sort of physical unit of measurement which can be agreed upon as a common standard and which is replicable, i.e., can be applied over and over again with the same results."[18] Interval measurement therefore "possesses the properties of nominal and ordinal measurement, and adds the property of equal intervals to its meaning."[19] With interval measurement, staff members can "determine amounts or quantities much more precisely."[20] However, there is no absolute value for zero; rather, the zero is arbitrary. The Fahrenheit scale of temperature is an example of interval measurement.

Ratio measurement has all the properties of an interval scale and adds an absolute (not arbitrary) zero point. Library staff can compare scores by computing their ratios. For example, if respondents were asked to report their actual age (as of their last birthday), the "zero-point" becomes absolute. A response of 80 is twice as much as one of 40, and a mean could be computed for the sample. A question such as "How many years of school have you completed?" could also yield ratio level data.

The level of significance is the predetermined level at which a null hypothesis is rejected.[21] The level is an arbitrarily chosen probability that is used to decide whether a given sample is likely to have come from a given population. The most common levels are .05 and .01. Staff members should select a level of significance prior to data collection after evaluating the consequences of making a Type I error (rejecting a true null hypothesis) or Type II error (accepting a false null hypothesis as true). They then either support or reject a null hypothesis on the basis of that level. For example, if the level is set at .05, libraries reject the null hypothesis if the probability is less than .05. The probability level may be reported at $p < .05$, with p meaning probability and the symbol $<$ standing for "less than."

Choosing the Appropriate Statistical Test

Statistical tests aid in data interpretation. Researchers use statistical testing to compare data and to determine the probability that differences between groups of data are based on chance. To decide on the appropriate statistical test, library researchers must determine the number of independent (the experimental or predictor variable that the researcher manipulates and that presumably produces change) and dependent (influenced by the independent variable) variables, whether they are willing to risk a Type I or Type II error, whether the distribution has one- or two-tails,[22] as well as the measurement scale. They must also decide whether parametric or nonparametric tests are more appropriate. Nonparametric tests make fewer assumptions about the distributions, do not require a normal distribution (or population) or equal group variance, and are based on nominal or ordinal measurement. They are useful for large samples not meeting the assumptions of parametric tests.[23]

Other considerations include whether researchers are analyzing one group, or two or more groups. Further, the researchers must decide if they want to characterize respondents or cases (provide descriptive statistics) or draw inferences to the population (inferential statistics).

The selection of statistical tests, and the interpretation of the results, should be done after careful review of the conceptual underpinnings of the objectives and hypotheses, as well as other steps in the research process. It is important to remember that: "a statistically significant result is not necessarily socially or practically significant. Differences of a few thousand volumes between two university library collections could produce significant statistical differences, but in terms of multimillion volume collections, such differences hold little if any practical significance."[24]

Researchers should exercise caution in making interpretations when they deal with "weighted data, small sample sizes, complex sample designs, and capitalization on chance in fitting a statistical model. . . ."[25]

Research Statistics and Opportunities for Their Use

In preparation of the book *Statistics for Library Decision Making*,[26] six doctoral students and I examined an enormous number of library research studies using statistical analyses that might have value to library decision making. As might be expected, the majority of writings used elementary statistics such as descriptive statistics, in particular percentages. The next greatest number of writings employed lower ordered statistics, meaning correlations, chi-square test of independence, etc. The smallest number used more complex statistics such as analysis of variance, regression analysis, and factor analysis.

It is not within the scope of this paper to even briefly highlight statistical applications discussed in *Statistics for Library Decision Making*. However, it is worth noting that descriptive statistics organize data in a convenient form that makes it easier for researchers to characterize the dataset and communicate the results of the characterization. Inferential statistics is a set of procedures used in drawing inferences and generalizations based on a sample of cases from a population. Generally, hypotheses and/or research questions guide data collection, analysis, and interpretation, as well as the statistical applications which are selected. Among the most useful for library research and decision making are frequency distributions, the chi-square test of independence, t-tests, correlation, analysis of variance, and regression analysis.

As already mentioned, librarians collect large amounts of data, which might be digested into monthly and annual reports, or reports to accrediting bodies. At the same time, they might conduct online database searching or have online catalogs and circulation systems. They might also be developing an automated decision support system. Where computers automatically capture transactions or are programmed to record the types of information sought by decision makers, there are increased opportunities for compiling data subject to statistical analysis.

In addition, many libraries conduct community analyses and surveys. It would seem that managers should reassess how they want the data reported. Do they want staff to incorporate statistical analyses and the graphic presentation of data? It is my hope that library managers will give this question an affirmative response.

References and Notes

1. Maurice P. Marchant, Nathan M. Smith, and Keith H. Stirling, "SPSS as a Library Research Tool," Occasional Research Paper no. 1 (Prov, Utah: Brigham Young University, School of Library and Information Sciences, 1977), p. 1.

2. "The Usefulness of Fill Rates: Research and Debate," *Public Libraries*, 27:15 (Spring 1988).
3. See Peter Hernon and John Richardson, *Microcomputer Software for Performing Statistical Analysis* (Norwood, N.J.: Ablex, 1988); and Peter Hernon and others, *Statistics for Library Decision Making* (Norwood, N.J.: Ablex, 1989).
4. Robert Swisher and Charles R. McClure, *Research for Decision Making: Methods for Librarians* (Chicago: American Library Assn., 1984), p. 20.
5. *Evaluating Bibliographic Instruction: A Handbook* (Chicago: American Library Assn., Association of College and Research Libraries, Bibliographic Instruction Section, 1983), p. 9.
6. Peter Hernon, "Utility Measures, Not Performance Measures, for Library Reference Service?," *RQ*, 26: 449–59 (Summer 1987).
7. Michael R. W. Bommer and Ronald W. Chorba, *Decision Making for Library Management* (White Plains, N.Y.: Knowledge Industry, 1982), Chapter 1.
8. Michael K. Buckland, *Library Services in Theory and Context* (New York: Pergamon, 1983), p. 166.
9. F. W. Lancaster, *If You Want to Evaluate Your Library* . . . (Champaign, Ill.: University of Illinois, Graduate School of Library and Information Science, 1988); and *The Measurement and Evaluation of Library Services* (Washington, D.C.: Information Resources Press, 1977).
10. Charles R. McClure, "A View from the Trenches: Costing and Performance Measures for Academic Library Public Services," *College & Research Libraries* 47: 323–36 (July 1986).
11. Ibid., p. 329.
12. Ibid., p. 326.
13. Ibid., p. 327.
14. Donald Ary, Lucy C. Jacobs, and Asghar Razavich, *Introduction to Research in Education*, 3d ed. (New York: Holt, 1985), p. 95.
15. Swisher and McClure, p. 75–80.
16. Ary, Jacobs, and Razavich, p. 96.
17. Swisher and McClure, p. 76.
18. Hubert M. Blalock Jr., *Social Statistics* (New York: McGraw-Hill, 1972), p. 18.
19. Swisher and McClure, p. 78.
20. Ibid.
21. A null hypothesis states that no difference exists between the populations being compared. For a discussion of hypotheses, see Ary, Jacobs, and Razavich, Chapter 4.
22. In estimating the value of the population mean, researchers might believe that the population mean is on one side of the sample mean. In such cases, they are dealing with only one tail of the sampling distribution. When the hypothesis does not predict the direction of the difference, researchers only discover that the sample results differ from the null hypothesis. See Hernon and others, p. 84–86.
23. Parametric statistics make assumptions about population parameters. One assumption is that population scores are normally distributed about the mean, and another is that the population variances of comparison groups in a study are similar. When research data deviate substantially from these assumptions parametric statistics are not appropriate.

24. Ronald R. Powell, *Basic Research Methods for Librarians* (Norwood, N.J.: Ablex, 1985), p. 159.
25. Frank M. Andrews and others, *A Guide for Selecting Statistical Techniques for Analyzing Social Science Data* (Ann Arbor, Mich.: University of Michigan, Institute for Social Research, Survey Research Center, 1974), p. 2.
26. Hernon and others.

NETWORKS AND SCHOOL LIBRARY MEDIA CENTERS

Phyllis J. Van Orden and Adeline W. Wilkes

Over a decade has passed since the 1978 publication *Role of the School Library Program in Networking* recommended that "library networks in which school library media programs are full participating members be established and operational in every region, state, and area in the nation."[1] During that decade the number of school districts participating in networks has increased. Yet in 1988 the goal of schools as full partners in the networking of our nation's resources has not been realized. Patricia Glass Schuman stated in a February 1987 article, "Over 80 percent of our librarians work in school libraries, few of which currently participate in networks. Only about 7,000 U.S. libraries do participate in networks, mainly medium to large academic and public libraries."[2] A manual search of *Library Literature* and online searches of *ERIC, LISA, Dissertation Abstracts Online,* and *Information Science Abstracts* databases revealed numerous articles about the barriers and benefits of networking for school library media centers. Other articles reported on individual school districts and individual networks. None of the articles presented a national overview of the networking activities of school districts or the effect of network membership on school library media centers.

The concepts of networking and resource sharing are not new to the world of school library media centers, as exemplified by the 1975 guidelines *Media Programs: District and School*.[3] The involvement of school library media centers with other types of libraries, regardless of location, is a newer phenomenon. Telecommunications connection is just one of

---

"Networks and School Library Media Centers," by Phyllis J. Van Orden and Adeline W. Wilkes in *Library Resources & Technical Services* Vol. 33, no. 2 (April 1989), pp. 123–133; reprinted with permission from the American Library Association, copyright © 1989 by ALA.

the developments that has opened the way for schools to participate in today's networks.

The term "networks" can be interpreted in different ways. Susan K. Martin's explanation guided this study: "In modern usage, a network can be defined as a group of individuals or organizations that are interconnected to form a system to accomplish some specified goal. This linkage must include a communications mechanism."[4]

THE STUDY

The purpose of this exploratory, descriptive study is to share the networking experiences of school districts in order to identify the services and implications of networking for the collections and technical services of school library media centers. A questionnaire was used to survey network members' insights into the benefits and barriers of networks; the implications of networking on cataloging, classification, and processing practices; interlibrary loan patterns; and resource sharing.

Earlier claims about what schools could do for and how they would benefit from participation in networks served as a framework for our investigation to ascertain if these predictions had come true; e.g., the 1978 report of the Task Force on the Role of the School Library Program in Networking noted that school library media centers are capable of making contributions by sharing specific resources.

The population was composed of school library media districts holding membership in one or more networks based on the "Directory of Networks and Members" appendix in Martin's book. Additional school districts were listed in "Elementary/Secondary Schools and School Systems Using OCLC" in the *School Library Media Annual, 1985*.[5]

After reviewing the literature, talking with individuals involved in networking, and listening to presentations on the development of networking systems in a number of states, the authors identified the areas in which they sought information. The investigation followed the design recommended by Dillman in *Mail and Telephone Surveys: The Total Design Method*.[6]

The questionnaire was designed and field tested through the cooperative efforts of school library media specialists and a state consultant for school library media services. The initial letter and questionnaire were sent to seventy school district media centers with three follow-up letters, prior to June 1, 1987. Of the fifty-seven responses, forty-nine met the criteria for use in the study, providing a response rate of 70 percent.

RESPONSES

The network membership reported by the respondents differed from the information obtained prior to the mailing. School districts reported participating in one or more of the following networks:

Online Computer Library Center (OCLC)	21
Michigan Library Consortium (MLC)	8
Illinois Library and Information Network (ILLINET)	2
Indiana Cooperative Library Services Network (INCOLSA)	8
Western Library Network (WLN)	4
plus one read-only level	
Bibliographic Retrieval Services (BRS)	4
Bibliographic Center for Research (BCR)	4
Area Library Services Authority—Indiana (ALSA)	2
The AMIGOS Bibliographic Council, Inc. (AMIGOS)	1
Federal Library and Information network (FEDLINK)	1
OHIONET	1

In many cases the statewide network, such as INCOLSA or ILLINET, is the broker for OCLC. A pattern emerged revealing that school districts belonging to national networks tend to belong to other networks at the local, state, and regional levels.

Fifteen of the responding school districts had electronic networking capabilities within the school districts. None of the respondents reported this capability for *all* the media centers in their districts.

The student populations for these school districts ranged from eight districts in the 0—4,999 category to two districts with more than 100,000 students. None of the responding school districts fell in the 30,000—39,999 category. The districts included 43 with high schools, 40 with middle or junior high schools, 42 with elementary schools, 18 with vocational/technical schools, 16 with adult schools, and 3 with special education schools. Also included in the districts were one each of a nonpublic regional center, a private school, a preschool center, a science and mathematics center, and an alternative high school.

Staffs for the centralized services and operations in these districts varied, having a maximum of 5 administrators, 24 professionals, 49 clerks, 24 technicians, and 200 volunteers.

Six of the school districts use CD-ROM and online bibliographic services including *Books in Print Plus*. Six use vendor- or jobber-produced programs including *Lasercat WLN, Bibliofile,* and Brodart's *ACCDESS, PA*. Three schools use *Wilsonline*, but only one school uses *Wilsondisc*.

NETWORK BENEFITS

Commonly cited benefits of network membership include those aimed at specific audiences. Students can access information located outside of the schools. Teachers have available an increased range of materials and information about materials, including human resources. Administrators can use data collection agencies and information services. Specialists can obtain professional materials, such as public health and guidance materials. Parents can access information about children's emotional and intellectual development. A further benefit claimed for the school library media specialist is more time to work with teachers. *Information Power*, the 1988 national school library media program guidelines, indicates that one of the missions of the school library media center is to provide "access to information and materials outside the library media center and the school building through such mechanisms as interlibrary loan, networking and other cooperative agreements, and online searching of various databases."[7]

Some of the advantages of networking memberships are the services and products offered. School districts identified newsletters (31), directories (29), training packages (27), and guidelines about copyright (14) as products received. Other products used by at least one school district included microdisks of word processing programs, equipment, microsoftware, 16mm films, videotapes, catalog cards, current awareness services, union lists, and bibliographies. Twenty-six of the school districts reported access to online databases through the networks.

Twenty-seven school districts used the network's technical consultant services and twenty-five used the staff development and in-service activities. Thirteen schools used consultant services dealing with database management assistance. Thirteen schools received public relations services, ten utilized curriculum planning for teaching online searching, and one school used workshops for network users.

Networks are making an impact on the joint purchase of materials. Eleven school districts jointly purchased equipment, ten supplies, five audiovisual materials, and one serials. Five placed cooperative book orders and three coordinated acquisitions.

Examination centers and previewing arrangements were available in eleven school districts, while twenty-three districts had cooperative film libraries.

According to Sorensen, "As more and more library media specialists who are involved in interlibrary cooperation come to recognize that no collection can be truly comprehensive, they have come to concentrate more on building complementary collections rather than having a little bit of everything. The aim is to develop within a reasonably large geographic area a comprehensive selection, with each library or media center holding a portion."[8]

Resource sharing is taking place in a variety of ways. Seven districts had coordinated collection development programs and four had coordinated materials selection programs.

Primary collecting responsibility has been assigned to individual media centers and to individual school districts for specific materials: audiovisual (12), career education (10), children's (9), computerized instructional (9), those for students with special needs (9), ethnic (8), high interest/low vocabulary (8), professional (8), young adult (8), and also for instructional equipment (8).

Schools had responsibilities for the following nonbook formats: 16mm films, kits, filmstrips, models, video materials, realia, charts, maps, study prints, and transparencies. One school reported its extensive special education professional materials as its unique responsibility. Other examples of materials for special clienteles include those for and about visually impaired, gifted, hearing impaired, native American, bilingual, mentally impaired, learning disabled, and academically talented persons.

A distinction between coordinated collection development and interlibrary loan (ILL) is noted by Fiels:

An interlibrary loan is reactive, coordinated collection development is proactive—its goal is to have the item there *before* [italics in original] it is requested. Coordinated collection development may include a number of related activities, including coordinated planning; collection analysis; standardization of policies; establishment of shared databases; and coordinated or joint acquisitions, retentions, storage, and preservation.[9]

Four of the school districts reported they do not participate in ILL. Seventeen of the schools used manual ILL systems, 9 were online, and 13 used a combination of manual and online. Thirty-eight school districts borrowed books, but only 34 lent them. Seventeen school districts borrowed audiovisual materials; 14 lent them. Twenty-two of the school districts borrowed serials; 16 lent them.

Four types of borrowing practices were used by the school districts. Twenty-nine borrowed from other schools in the district, 29 from nonschool libraries, and 30 from members of the networks, as compared with only 23 who borrowed from schools in other districts. Lending practices included 30 school districts who lent to other schools in the district, 28 who lent to members of the network, and 26 who lent to schools in other districts and to nonschool libraries.

Delivery systems included 32 with school system couriers. Twenty-two school districts used the post office, 17 multitype library couriers, 14 United Parcel Service, one personal delivery, and one an interdistrict courier.

Borrowing privileges had been extended to teachers by 40 school districts, to administrators by 35, high school students by 31, to elementary and middle school/junior high students (24 each), to school board members by 23, to parents by 15 and to other community members by 14.

Twenty-four school districts were involved with ILL systems with formalized procedures through the network. Eleven had formalized ILL procedures through the state library. Four districts only lent materials through reciprocal borrowing agreements.

In eighteen school districts no charges were made for interlibrary loan materials, while three districts charged on a per item basis. Other districts included mailing costs and one district determined fees on an informal basis.

NETWORKING BARRIERS

Barriers to establishing networks are commonly cited in the literature. The report of the Task Force grouped in the possible problems under five headings: psychological (including attitudes), political and legal, funding, communication, and planning.

Thirteen of the schools mentioned inadequate fiscal commitment. Eight indicated barriers created by a lack of understanding of the concept. In seven school districts individual media specialists were unwilling to share, while six school districts faced lack of staff commitment. Only three school districts responded that they had faced restrictions based on the range of their collections. Two school districts indicated they had overcome the inhibition of free exercise of professional judgment.

How did school districts overcome these barriers? As one respondent wrote, the barriers were overcome "with time, establishment of trust and relationships, taking small steps, showing results, developing administrative support, information and directing," or through, to use another respondent's word, "persistence."

A chief argument used by respondents was based on the premise that increased fiscal commitment would address the problem of the cost of telecommunications, which leads to more consistent and efficient operations. A further argument presented was that the provision of microcomputers in all school library media centers would provide automated management of library routines and greater student access to information. Workshops and discussions of the advantages and applications of administrative authority have helped staff and funding sources understand the concept of networking and thus support it.

Two school districts reported that some individual media specialists were still reticent about sharing, while in another district the skeptics became enthusiastic.

When asked what advice the respondents would offer to those considering participation in a network, a common reply was that one can learn from the experiences of others. Other suggestions addressed how the school districts had overcome specific types of barriers.

Psychological Barriers

For a network to succeed, overcoming psychological barriers is an important step. Sorensen states:

> The most dramatic change has been in the attitude of the individual school library media specialist. This change is important because it directly affects service to users. The media specialist who has become involved in networking is conscious of the need to look beyond the building-level collection. The reference interview doesn't end with "I'm sorry, we don't have what you need." It continues, "But I think I know where we might find it."[10]

Respondents' advice regarding staff commitment was mixed. Some warned that the process must be mandated. Several felt that a positive commitment must be developed by moving slowing but deliberately. An individual advised that one should "involve people at every step, let them assume responsibilities and establish ownership, be visible and make frequent visits to local school libraries." Others wrote "explain thoroughly all implications."

Opinions differed about the impact on staff time. One useful suggestion was to prepare staff "to understand the rearrangement of work and work flow and that pressure times will change as will the load balance." Staff hours were rotated to utilize non-prime time on the networks. One person wrote, "when we joined MLC and OCLC we were able to reduce that cataloger's position from full-time to half-time. For this reason we were able to justify the move because personnel is so expensive."

Political and Legal Barriers

Political and legal barriers need to be removed. The respondents agreed that it is important to have legal advice and avoid as much contractual matter as possible. One individual wrote, "only develop contracts where a proven need has been determined—beware of 'maybes and what ifs' and wait until there is a real 'problem' to fix before devising rules and regulations." Another person wrote that one should not only read the existing contracts carefully and solicit the school attorney's opinion, but also "be actively involved in governance and daily use of the network."

Fiscal Commitment Barriers

Planning for funding is another key element. While agreeing that networking is cost-effective, the respondents noted that an ongoing fiscal commitment is necessary. A recommended way to achieve that goal is through the development of "a strong rationale to show need and increase library output for student achievement to present to supervisors, the superintendent, and board of education." One individual advised presenting "a breakdown of costs compared with your current operations." Or, to use another person's words, "be prepared, services are money, professional development excellence, *but* nothing is free" (original italics). Another respondent noted that while "the services, particularly meetings that enable us to be up to date and workshops that enable us to have 'hands on' activities, are invaluable" and that while high school students and staff make good use of ILL, "going online and/or networking is expensive."

Another respondent posed questions that more school library media specialists are facing: Who will use the services, and at what cost? She wrote:

> We have not yet committed to a CD-ROM service. *Magazine Index* seemed a natural combined with online access (classroom rates) through DIALOG until I got down to dollars and cents and that terrified me (MAG Index most particularly). That requires more analysis when time permits this summer. I wanted kids to be able to search on CD without the cost and personnel interface needed for DIALOG online, but this will have major budget impact which will perforce affect collection development.

Communication Barriers

Communications can be a barrier. To communicate members need telephones and other delivery systems. Communication between network members was via terminals at the district level for seventeen of the respondents. Five of the districts had terminals at the building level and six districts reported terminals at both district and building levels.

Telephones were available in nineteen of the districts at both the district and building level; while ten districts reported having telephones only at the district level, eight had them at the building level. The lack of a telephone at the building level has been documented by Miller and Moran in their study of 1,500 school library media centers, where they observed that

> one of the most startling facts to arise from the data is that 48 percent of the LMCs [school library media centers] do not have telephones, that most-basic of all communications technology. . . . any hope of being involved in resource sharing, inter- and intralibrary cooperation . . . is doomed to failure.[11]

Telex was available in four district-level offices, and one school district reported having telex available at both the district and the building level. Other means of communication reported by one school district each were community television cable, electronic mail, and daily courier serving U.S. mail.

Planning

The planners of network arrangements may find themselves agreeing to practices and procedures of benefit to the network, even though they are inconvenient for their own media centers. Many writers agree that representation on the planning and policy board of the network is important if the network is to succeed. School districts reported representation in the governance of formal networks through a variety of positions:

board representative	13
membership council	4
voting member	4
through member of central staff	2
elected representative to network	2

Other forms of representation were by type of library, school district, and advisory committees.

IMPLICATIONS FOR CATALOGING AND CLASSIFICATION

The cataloging and classification process was handled in various ways by the school districts, as shown in Table 1. District-level staff handled the greatest amount, the network was the second most heavily used method, and outside agencies such as Brodart ranked third. Building-level staff and intermediate units serving more than one school district were the least used methods.

TABLE 1
Methods of Handling Cataloging and Classification Activities

	25%	50%	75%	100%
By the network	5	3	5	5
By an intermediate unit serving more than one school district	1	0	1	12
By district-level staff	9	5	1	1
By building-level staff	7	1	1	1
By use of outside agencies (e.g., Brodart)	1	5	5	0
By other arrangements	3	0	0	0

Processing materials (including labels for spines, cards and pockets, ownership stamps, bar codes for circulation systems, and sensing devices for security systems) was handled at the district level for thirty-one respondents, at the building level for thirteen, by outside agencies for six, and by an intermediate unit serving more than one school district for four.

The classification system used by most of the districts was the Dewey Decimal Classification. Forty-two respondents used Dewey, one used the Library of Congress Classification, and two used some other method of classifying materials.

Bibliographic records were customized for twenty-seven districts. Nineteen respondents indicated that records were customized for individual schools within their districts. Customizing included truncated classification numbers for twenty-five respondents, locally created subject headings for twenty-two, and other special treatment for eight.

An authority file for names was maintained at the district level by twenty districts. One respondent noted that the authority file was limited to artists, musicians, illustrators, and well-known authors. Eighteen districts maintained a subject authority file: eighteen did not.

Sears List of Subject Headings was the subject authority used most frequently. Twenty-three respondents used Sears, eight used the *Library of Congress Subject Headings*, and thirteen used more than one subject authority.

Thirty-nine districts used *Anglo-American Cataloguing Rules*, 2d. ed. (*AACR2*) as a standard; one did not. Fifteen districts reported that they used the first or minimum level of cataloging, twelve used the second level, two reported using the third level, and three used more than one level. One district used only commercial cataloging, and others used a combination of *AACR2* rules and past practices.

Thirty-seven of the districts used the same cataloging standards for both books and audiovisual materials; seven did not. Differences included the use of locally developed subject headings, using KT as a classification symbol for kits in order to locate them in one section on the shelves, using additional codes for a film library, and the use of a state system.

Twenty-eight of the school districts used the network in cataloging operations, including activities such as preparing union lists of books (19 districts), audiovisual materials (15), serials (13), and the entire collection (9); and maintaining bibliographic records (16), authority files (13), and online catalogs (11). Only four of the responding school districts offered contractual cataloging services to other libraries. Fifteen of the school districts use the network in their processing operations.

Respondents offered advice relating to cataloging operations. One who "feels very positive about OCLC" wrote that in "joining the network, cataloging via OCLC does not cut down on staff requirements, but it does help to catalog and process books more rapidly." From his overall perspective, an individual wrote that "we have no way of knowing whether kids will actually plan ahead far enough to use this service [access to network] or even if our faculty use resources other than those in their own studies at home." Another warned prospective networkers to be prepared for the individuals who will complain about how the catalog cards are done. A fourth noted that retrospective conversion takes time, but in the long run saves time.

Eighteen school districts received funds to prepare for retrospective conversion of their records; nine did not. For five school districts the conversion was handled by the intermediate unit serving more than one school district. The regular school district staff handled the conversion for eight districts. In one school district, the district-level staff did the conversion for the elementary schools, while the building-level personnel did the conversion for the secondary schools. One school district contracted through another agency for the conversion; one school used OCLC.

Funding for the retrospective conversion came from several sources, including the district budget process, local school boards, LSCA, block grants, special grants, statewide funding programs, state libraries, and New York State Regional automation grants.

As preparation for the conversion, fourteen of the collections were weeded, thirteen by building-level media center staff, four by district-level staff or centrally appointed teams, and two by intermediate units serving more than one school district. Seven school districts did not weed their collections in preparation for the conversion.

FURTHER RESEARCH

This exploratory study can serve as a beginning step in recording the developing role of school media centers participating in networks and the impact upon their collections and practices. Further studies are needed. While this investigation focused on the district level, the field needs information about the impact at the building level as well. Such an investigation could be further expanded to compare how informational needs are being met by schools belonging to networks with those who are not members. Such studies need to expand upon this preliminary work and address issues related to governance, operations, and, most importantly, how effectively informational needs are being met.

Correlations to be explored include the availability of forms of communication necessary for networking activities: telephones, telex, etc. Other studies could focus on the relationship of staffing patterns at the school district level to network membership. Further investigation also needs to be conducted in examining the influence of outside funding on the growth of networking activities at both district and building levels.

Although this investigation did not examine why school districts followed certain practices, such as the variety of approaches to resource sharing, the results do indicate that some school districts are taking greater advantage than others of the opportunity to address local informational needs through interlibrary loan.

The current study did not examine the relationship of the leadership role and responsibility of the central staff in terms of guiding the practices used in the system. If such responsibilities are not handled at the district level, on what basis are decisions being made about the level of involvement by individual schools?

The idea of individual schools lending and borrowing materials may be so new that discrepancies in practice may be the result of the untried, rather than lack of desire to participate.

As this study shows, there are many issues and practical matters on which school library media specialists must be prepared to make decisions. School library media specialists at the district and building levels need information to help them in their decision making.

CONCLUSIONS AND RECOMMENDATIONS

Findings of this study reinforce those of Miller and Moran,[12] which determined that school library media centers, particularly at the building level, lack the communication mechanisms to handle the linkages described by Martin as being a necessary element in a networking effort.[13] Without these basic tools, building-level programs are unable to take advantage of the district's participation in a network. Schools contemplating membership in networks need to address this basic means of participation.

The favorable response to our questionnaire is only one indication of the widespread interest in networking. The positive replies indicate that schools are able to overcome the barriers commonly mentioned in the literature. The respondents' comments on their experiences will provide practical advice for schools facing similar situations. Their remarks indicate they are willing to share their experiences with others. If a school is considering joining a network, it is recommended that the staff speak to and visit school districts that are participating in such activities.

This research has provided both questions and answers. The authors hope that through sharing what others have experienced, readers will find, in the words of one respondent, that "the benefits are enormous—both tangible and intangible—and the problems few," and will be led to share her "opinion [that] school library systems/networks represent the legacy this generation leaves to the profession."

References and Notes

1. Task Force on the Role of the School Library Media Program in the National Program, *The Role of the School Library Media Program in Networking* (Washington, D.C.:

National Commission on Libraries and Information Science, 1978), p. 34.
2. Patricia Glass Schuman, "Library Networks: A Means, Not an End," *Library Journal* 112:33 (February 1, 1987).
3. American Association of School Librarians, American Library Association, and Association for Educational Communications and Technology, *Media Programs: District and School* (Chicago: American Library Assn.; Washington, D.C.: Association for Educational Communications and Technology, 1975).
4. Susan K. Martin, *Library Networks, 1986-1987* (White Plains, N.Y.: Knowledge Industry Publications, 1986), p. 2.
5. "Elementary/Secondary Schools and School Systems Using OCLC," *School Library Media Annual, 1985*, v. 3 (Littleton, Colo.: Libraries Unlimited, 1985), p. 432-35.
6. Don A. Dillman, *Mail and Telephone Surveys: The Total Design Method* (New York: Wiley, 1978).
7. American Association of School Librarians and Association for Educational Communications and Technology, *Information Power: Guidelines for School Library Media Programs* (Chicago: American Library Assn.; Washington, D.C.: Association for Educational Communications and Technology, 1988).
8. Richard J. Sorensen, "Changes in School Media Programs Resulting from Participation in Networking," *School Library Media Annual, 1984* (Littleton, Colo.: Libraries Unlimited, 1984), p. 436-42.
9. Keith Michael Fiels, "Coordinated Collection Development in a Multitype Environment: Promise and Challenge," *Collection Building* 7:26 (Summer 1985).
10. Sorensen, "Changes," p. 436-37.
11. Marilyn L. Miller and Barbara Moran, "Expenditures for Resources in School Library Media Centers FY '85-'86," *School Library Journal* 33:41 (June-July 1987).
12. Ibid.
13. Martin, *Library Networks*, p. 2.

PART V:
REFERENCE
AND COLLECTION
DEVELOPMENT ISSUES

REFERENCE SERVICES: A MODEL OF QUESTION HANDLING

Barbara M. Robinson

Demand for greater accountability and quality control in the delivery of reference service is a timely and difficult issue. In an era of tight budgets, how can library managers ensure greater accountability and quality control on the part of reference staff without stifling creativity and independent decision making? Reference is really an art, not a science. There are no simple formulae which standardize the level of reference resources and effort required to address the multitude of questions received from a wide variety of clientele. Yet, given the importance of reference services in most libraries, managers must attempt to relate levels of service to resource requirements, and to consider the appropriate mix of resources that can and should be employed.

One option is to provide reference librarians with a planning and decision making tool which provides a framework for: (1) developing strategies for handling questions; (2) evaluating the appropriateness of the strategy; and (3) allocating staff and information resources. A conceptual framework and a vocabulary which can be used to discuss strategies and choices involved in question handling are presented. There are other models which have been developed to describe reference services.[1] These models examine the reference process and do not focus as much on issues of resource allocation.

This question handling model presents a snapshot of the series of decisions which librarians automatically make every day as they handle client questions and try to match the level of resources to the level of service which they have chosen, in order to satisfy client expectations.

"Reference Services: A Model for Question Handling," by Barbara M. Robinson in *RQ* Vol. 29, no. 1 (Fall 1989), pp. 46–61; reprinted with permission from the American Library Association, copyright © 1989 by ALA.

There is a parallel with the idealized doctor-patient relationship. The doctor interviews the patient to determine the nature of the problem and then formulates a diagnosis and a strategy for how best to treat the problem. The patient's statement of the problem, however, may differ from the doctor's perception, in which case the doctor explains to the patient what the diagnosis is and why the strategy selected is appropriate. The doctor may also choose to consult with a colleague or to refer the patient to another doctor for a second opinion. If the doctor fails to spend the time bringing both sets of perceptions into line, the patient may leave the office unconvinced, dissatisfied, and frustrated. Needless to say, the doctor benefits not only from having good listening and verbal probing skills, but also from having been trained to diagnose.

In the case of reference, the perception and expectation of what type and level of service are appropriate are sensitive points. Since there are always two parties involved in question negotiation, the client and the librarian may have very different perceptions regarding the characteristics of the question and what constitutes an appropriate answer. Ultimately, however, it is the reference librarian who meditates the question for the client and selects the level of service to provide.

Making this assessment is key to success in tailoring the answer to fit the question. It sets the terms for handling the question and meeting client expectations. Given the need for dialogue and negotiation, questions which are conveyed by a third party are likely to have an unproductive outcome. Using the doctor-patient analogy again, how can a third party (for example, the boss's secretary) describe accurately where it hurts? Clearly, the reference librarian should make every effort to deal directly with the patron and not with intermediaries.

The question handling model was developed and tested in 1988 for a study funded by the New Jersey State Library.[2] Reference librarians in two libraries in New Jersey used the model to identify the time spent on question handling and other reference activities. Reference staff at the National Gerontology Resource Center of the American Association of Retired Persons in Washington, D.C., provided substantive comments during the development of the model, tested the model on questions they handled during the year, and used the model as a training tool.

THE QUESTION HANDLING MODEL

The question handling model describes the reference librarian's interaction with the client during the reference interview. It also shows options made by the reference librarian regarding the choice of internal and external information resources to be applied in handling the question. These decisions determine in what way, and with what mix of resources, the librarian chooses to answer a question.

"Question handling" is the major function of reference service. The process is called question handling, rather than question answering, because every question received by a reference librarian is mediated, whether or not it is answered.[3] Mediation implies that the reference librarian will make a series of informed choices on behalf of the client. Reference librarians also perform "other reference" services, which include "developing specialized resources" such as union lists, bibliographies, as well as collection development; "education and training" of library staff; and "quality control" of reference services.

The librarian's success in matching the appropriate level of question handling service to the availability of reference resources depends on the choices and decisions made. It is this matching process which makes it so difficult to evaluate the quality of question handling. Judgments made regarding the appropriate level of service, how much time to spend, and what level of reference resources to deploy are hard to define and difficult to quantify.

Figure 1 provides a schematic of the question handling model. The model consists of five phases: Phase I, Conducting the Reference Interview; Phase II, Formulating the Question Handling Strategy; Phase III, Handling the Question; Phase IV, Reporting the Results; and Phase V, Evaluating Service Delivery. While the diagram suggests that the decision-making process is linear, there are often times when a librarian may step through the question handling process only to find that judgments made at a previous step have proven incorrect or inappropriate. As a result, the librarian may need to loop back to a previous step, or go back to the beginning of the process, talk with the client, and reformulate the strategy for handling the question.

The model is built on several premises. First, reference librarians are

Figure 1
A Model of Question Handling

I. Conducting Reference Interview		II. Formulating Question Handling Strategy	
(1) Client's perception of question and answer:	(2) Librarian's assessment of question and answer:	(3) Evaluate difficulty of handling:	(4) Estimate resources required:
Q: simple/ complex A: simple	Q: simple/ complex A: simple	easy	1. Garden variety 2. State of practice
Q: complex/ simple A: complex	Q: complex/ simple A: complex	difficult	3. Advanced state of practice 4. Super reference 5. Resources not available locally

Notes: The terms *simple* and *complex* describe whether the question and/or the answer are perceived to be single-faceted (i.e., simple) or multifaceted (i.e., complex). The librarian then determines how "easy" or "difficult" it will be to handle

paid to exercise professional judgment and to make conscious choices when handling reference questions. Secondly, a client's initial perceptions and expectations regarding the nature of a question and the outcome of the question handling process are likely to differ from the reference librarian's initial perception. Third, the outcome of the question handling process is far more likely to be viewed as a success by both parties if the client and the librarian can arrive at a common set of perceptions and expectations regarding the question handling process.

PHASE I: CONDUCTING THE REFERENCE INTERVIEW

In this first phase, the reference librarian interviews the client, either in person or by telephone, and negotiates the terms of handling the question. Step 1 starts the process. A client asks a reference librarian a question. The client may perceive the question to be either simple or complex

	III. Handling Question	IV. Reporting Result	V. Evaluating Service
(5) Decide level of service:	(6) Action:	(7) Deliver product:	(8) Assessment of service:
1. Ready reference 2. Reference 3. Research 4. Research 5. Client referral	1. Find answer 2. Find answer 3. Conduct research 4. Conduct research 5. Refer client	1. Report 2. Report 3. Report 4. Report	a. Client satisfaction b. Appropriateness of chosen strategy c. Service quality

the question. In making that decision, the librarian assesses a variety of factors relating to the client, the reosurces required, the level of service, and the appropriate output.

and may expect either a simple or complex answer. The client may also perceive that the level of effort required by the librarian to handle the question and to find an answer will be either easy or difficult.

In an ideal world, the client not only states the question clearly and directly, but also has a clear idea of what kind of response is appropriate and feasible. In fact, in many cases, the librarian must determine what specific question the client is asking by posing a series of escalator questions. The librarian listens to the client's statement of the question and attempts to determine specifically what kind of a response the client expects.[4]

In order to assess how much effort and what kind of resources are needed, the first step is to ask clients why they seek the information. Asking why has long been a source of controversy in the profession. Some practitioners believe that probing is an infringement on client privacy. Others maintain that not understanding the client's motivation in asking a question hampers the librarian's ability to determine how to handle the question appropriately. The model supports the latter view. The issue is deciding what resources to apply in handling the question.

In step 2, the librarian makes a judgment based on an initial assessment of the question. As the reference librarian listens to the client frame the question, the librarian is mentally taking the measure of both the question and the client. This initial assessment involves the librarian in making choices regarding how best to handle the question considering the following factors:

1. The client's perception of the question, the answer, and the level of effort required to handle the question which, in turn, provide an insight into the client's conceptual framework;[5] and
2. The external variables associated with the client which might affect the question handling process.

It is important to acknowledge that external variables affect the question handling process. A partial list of external variables relating to the client includes: age; educational level; ability to read; native language of the client and resulting communication barriers if the client and the librarian do not speak the same language; ability to express the question clearly; physical disabilities of the client (e.g., deaf or blind); status (e.g., elected officials, donors, board members, or other influential citizens); and urgency (e.g., time constraints and deadlines).

Once the reference librarian has assessed the client's perception of the question and answer and has taken into consideration the external variables associated with the client, there are four major decisions to be made: Is the question simple or complex and is the answer anticipated to be simple or complex? How easy or difficult is it anticipated to be to provide an answer? What level of resources will be required to handle the question? And what level of service will be provided?

The focus of Phase I is to decide whether to treat the question as simple or complex and whether to provide a simple or a complex answer. The three other questions are addressed in Phase II. The terms, "simple" and "complex," "easy" and "difficult," "levels of resources," and "levels of service," are part of the formal vocabulary used in the model. Consequently, they require formal introduction. The paired concepts, simple and complex, are defined at this point.

"Simple" and "complex" are terms used to describe the characteristics of a reference question and an answer. If the question is simple, it is single-faceted. If it is complex, it is multifaceted. In other words, if the question is short and has only one part, it is a simple question. If the question is long and contains many parts, such as clauses, it is complex.

Sometimes what sounds like a complex question turns out to be a simple question expressed in a complicated, convoluted way by the client. On the other hand, as a result of the reference interview, sometimes a simple question evolves into a complex question. And sometimes a compound question, a nest of either simple or complex questions, is mistaken for a single complex question. A reference librarian must help the client to define each question, so that each can be appropriately handled. It is also important to identify how many questions are being asked by one client for the purposes of maintaining accurate reference statistics.

"When was Abraham Lincoln born?" "When was Chaucer born?"[6] "How many fish are there in the sea?" "At what altitude is the sky no longer blue?"[7] Each of these questions provides an example of a simple, or single-faceted question. In contrast, the question "What were the conditions in Iran which caused the Ayatollah Khomeini to come to power?" is a complex or multifaceted question.

The characteristics of an answer may also be either simple or complex. The simple answer to the Lincoln question is "Abraham Lincoln was born on February 12, 1809." But the answer to the simple question "When was Chaucer born?" could be handled either as a simple answer ("Chaucer was born in 1340") or a complex answer requiring explanation: "According to the following historians, Chaucer's birth is thought to be 1340 because . . ."[8] In discussing the issue of accuracy and completeness, using the Chaucer example, Lancaster says "One library might answer '1340,' while another might respond 'It is thought to be about 1340 but it is not known for sure.'"[9] Lancaster goes on to ask:

> If the second answer is correct, does the first library get any "points" for its answer? Another factor is whether or not the librarian quotes the source from which an answer is drawn. An answer with source may be considered more complete than one with no source supplied.[10]

In response to the simple question on the number of fish in the sea, the complex answer is to report on statistical methods used by researchers to calculate fish populations and to provide the client with a range of estimates. The simple answer is that no one knows precisely how many fish there are in the sea. Similarly, the blue sky question has no simple answer. The librarian at the Goddard Space Center library called three of America's leading experts who work at the Center to get their answers. The result was three different estimates.

In the case of a complex question, it usually follows that a complex question requires a complex answer. For example, to answer the question relating to the Ayatollah Khomeini, the librarian will supply a complex answer by including such factors as the prevailing political, economic, and social conditions in Iran at that time. In this case, rather than being able to provide an answer, the reference librarian will be reporting on secondary research findings based on the use of primary and secondary sources.

The terms "simple" and "complex" are not to be confused with the level of effort required to handle a question or provide an answer, which will be discussed in Phase II. "Simple" is never used in the discussion of the model to connote "easy." It is important to reserve the terms simple/complex for describing the characteristics of the question and answer, and easy/difficult for describing the client's and librarians' assessments of the level of effort anticipated or required to handle a question.

In Phase I, in the course of conducting the reference interview, the librarian must exercise judgment and make choices which will shape the formulation of the question handling strategy in Phase II. As the librarian assesses the client's perception of the question and the answer, and takes into consideration external variables, negotiation may be needed with the client to restate the question so that it requires a simple answer rather than a complex answer. If, after gaining the simple answer, the client still wants more information, the librarian can then seek to provide a complex answer. Providing too much information can be just as wrong as providing too little information. It shows poor judgment on the part of the reference librarian and a misallocation of a professional's time.

This incremental approach may be more appropriate, in some cases, than information overload. Simply because a client poses a complex question, or a simple question requiring a complex answer, does not mean that the librarian must take the question at face value. For example, in response to a question from a fourth grader, embarking on a lengthy research effort to explain why 1340 is thought to be the year of Chaucer's birth is most likely inappropriate. On the other hand, it is inaccurate to report that year to the student as if it were fact when it is only an estimate. If an author is writing a book on the middle ages and specifically asks why Chaucer's birth is thought to date back to 1340, however, it would be appropriate to treat the answer as complex.

Obviously, librarians sometimes understate or overestimate complexity when sizing up a question or anticipating an answer. Every experienced librarian can provide favorite examples of a simple question which turned out to have an unexpectedly complex answer. For example, the question regarding at what altitude the sky is no longer blue caught the Goddard Space Center librarian off guard. She assumed that a simple answer was available.

Children provide an endless source of examples of simple questions with complex answers. Parents usually redefine the question so that a simple answer is provided, even if the answer is simply "Because!" There are fewer stories told in reference circles regarding complex questions which turn out to have simple answers. One simple answer is "I'm sorry I can't help you," a response which may be appropriate, given the library's mission and policy statement.

Written mission statements can be very helpful to reference librarians who need clear priorities when they handle competing demands from clients of all types. For example, policy statements in many libraries define topical areas which staff are not to handle, such as legal, medical, or consumer questions. Ultimately, the clearer the reference staff are regarding the library's mission and priorities in serving clientele, the more easily they can apply the question handling model.

To summarize: some simple questions may require complex answers. Usually, complex questions require complex answers. Simple answers require much less time to provide than complex answers. The client's perception of the question and the anticipated answer should not prevent the reference librarian from redefining the question and the answer in order to provide an appropriate match between the client and the information provided.

By the end of Phase I, the reference librarian and the client have arrived at an agreement regarding whether to treat the question as simple or complex, and whether to seek a simple or a complex answer. There is also an understanding regarding the amount of time anticipated. A complex question, or a simple question requiring a complex answer, are likely to need substantial time and information resources. The probability of gaining an answer within a few minutes or hours, or even within the same day, is low.

On the other hand, if the question is simple and requires a simple answer, then both parties should expect to have the answer in hand within the same day or even within minutes. If a client requires an answer quickly, the best the reference librarian may be able to do is to provide a simple answer, regardless of the complexity of the question.

Depending on the client, the question, and the librarian, Phase I may take five minutes or less, or it may require a good deal more time. Time spent in this first phase of the process is worth the investment. It improves the librarian's ability to make decisions regarding how much time to spend on a strategy which is appropriate for the particular client and question. The net effect should be improved user satisfaction, as well as increased librarian satisfaction at the end of the question handling process.

PHASE II: FORMULATING THE QUESTION HANDLING STRATEGY

In this second phase, the reference librarian formulates the question handling strategy in steps 3 to 5. Step 3 determines the level of difficulty required to handle the question. Step 4 estimates the level of resources required to handle the question, provide an answer, and decide whether the internal resources are appropriate. Step 5 decides what level of service to provide, given the assessment of the complexity of the question and answer, the anticipated level of difficulty, and the appropriateness of the match with internal resources.

In effect, the librarian carries on an internal dialogue as follows: "How easy or difficult do I think it will be to provide an answer?" "What level of resources do I need to handle the question?" "What level of service will I provide?" An experienced reference librarian, who knows the internal library resources well, can move through this evaluation process quickly.

A less experienced librarian, or one who is new to a collection, may require more time to determine the level of difficulty involved. Determining the level of difficulty involved in handling a question may require preliminary examination of the internal resources and/or consultation with other reference staff. Consequently, the activity of evaluating the difficulty of handling the question (Step 3) may recur after estimating the resources required (Step 4), and even after deciding the level of service (Step 5). For the purposes of discussion, however, Steps 3 to 5 are discussed in sequence.

Characterizing the level of reference resources available, both inside and outside the library, is a key element in the reference librarian's decision-making process. The reference librarian must estimate what resources are required to handle a given question and then decide what to do if the desired level of resources is not available internally. The first step involves evaluating the degree of difficulty anticipated in handling a given question.

Evaluating the Difficulty of Handling the Question

Having defined the question and the answer as either simple or complex, the librarian must then evaluate the level of difficulty involved, which, in turn, may influence the decision made in Step 2 regarding whether to treat the question as simple or complex and the answer as simple or complex. This evaluation of the level of difficulty, anticipated in Step 3, might cause the librarian to go back and redefine the complexity of the question and/or the answer in Step 2.

The level of difficulty involved in handling a question can be expressed in terms of a continuum. "Easy" is the beginning of the continuum, which shades from very easy, moderately easy, easy, moderately difficult, difficult, to very difficult. Level of difficulty—whether easy or difficult—is a function of the effect that external and/or internal variables have on the librarian's ability to handle a given question. Level of difficulty expresses the level of effort anticipated before handling the question, as well as that actually required by the librarian to handle a given question.

Clearly, the perception of level of difficulty will vary depending on the individual reference librarian's past experience and expertise, familiarity with resources available internally, and the level of resources available. In general a simple question requires fewer resources to handle than a complex question, although as the examples above show, simple questions may indeed require complex answers which are very difficult to provide. Complex questions are more difficult to handle and require more resources, particularly staff time. There is certainly a relationship between the availability of levels of resources and the perceived level of difficulty.

A cluster of internal variables may affect how easy or difficult it is to handle a question. They include: the level of education, experience, and/or expertise of the staff member fielding the question and of other reference staff who could be consulted; the level of information resources available in the library, including online databases; the format and ease of accessing the material (e.g., microfiche housed in the sub-basement of a very large library is a barrier); the reference librarian's knowledge of internal and outside reference resources (i.e., experts as well as external information resources); and the overall mission and policy of the library.

Two of these internal variables can have a very significant effect on the decision-making process. If a librarian enjoys handling a complex question, and has time to do so, there is a higher probability that the question will be categorized as complex, regardless of how difficult it will be to handle. For that librarian, it will provide a stimulating challenge. For another librarian, who perhaps does not enjoy digging for information as much, or simply does not have the time to do so, there is a higher probability that a given question will be categorized as simple requiring a simple answer.

As librarians are not prescient, it is not always possible for them to predict accurately how easy or how difficult it will be to handle a question. Sometimes a question may look easy/difficult to handle, but may be either more difficult or easier than anticipated. If, for example, a colleague on the reference staff has answered a similar question recently and the answer is readily available, then the question is easy to answer the second time around because all the work has already been done.[11] The characteristics of the question have not changed, but the level of effort needed to handle the question has. Perceived difficulty in handling the question is also shaped by the next two steps; that is, the librarian's estimate of the reference resources required given the selection of the appropriate level of service.

Estimating Resources Required

In step four, the model shows four levels of reference resources: garden variety, state-of-the-practice, advanced-state-of-the-practice, and super reference.[12] Reference resources are the inseparable combination of reference resources which are used to provide reference service. The indispensable element in the mix is the librarian. If a librarian is not involved, then clients are not receiving reference service. Rather, they are handling their own questions by drawing on information resources in the library and not on staff resources.

This concept of "reference resources" differs from other measures of collection strength, such as the Research Libraries Group's special database, the *Conspectus*, or the *Guidelines for Collection Development*, which focus on objective assessment of the breadth and depth of information resources.[13] They do not assess staff resources. In the question handling model, the collection is one of several components of the stock of information resources. The collection represents only part of the reference resources in any given library because reference resources always include staff resources as well as information resources.

The definition of reference staff includes subject specialists on the reference staff in a given library as well as general reference staff. Depending on the size, budget, and/or mission of the library, the reference staff may be either partially or fully dedicated to the question handling function. The remainder of their time may be divided between other reference functions and/or nonreference-related functions. Attributes of the reference staff include: whether they have an M.L.S.; the extent to which they have received post-master's training through workshops, in-service training, and formal academic course work; the number of years of on-the-job experience; and subject expertise gained through course work or on-the-job experience.

This definition of information resources includes the reference collection; the periodicals collection; the government documents collection; the general collection; specially developed resources such as vertical files, union lists, bibliographies, and card files; as well as access to online databases and outside resources and expertise which are tapped by telephone, electronic mail, or conventional mail. To define further some of these resources:

1. The reference collection includes those materials housed in a designated area which usually do not circulate, or circulate only under special conditions;
2. The ready reference collection includes those materials, such as almanacs, housed adjacent to the reference desk for quick consultation, as well as home-grown resources such as files of frequently asked questions and the answers;
3. The general collection includes the circulating collection of books and periodicals which cover both fiction and nonfiction; and
4. Outside expertise refers to individuals with a great deal of knowledge in a particular field or subject area, who are based outside the library and often provide a shortcut for information gathering. These experts may know the answer to a question or know where to obtain the information. They may be located in the library's parent organization or in another public or private institution.

In determining the level of resources available in a given library, the competence of the staff may be viewed as offsetting deficiencies in the collection. The net effect is that highly competent reference staff can make a state-of-the-practice collection perform as if it were at a more advanced level, because they know how to "mine" it and to supplement it with outside resources.

For example, large urban public libraries have experienced severe acquisitions constraints in recent years. They have managed to continue to deliver service which they perceive to be at the advanced state-of-the-practice thanks to the experience of their long time staff. There is a point, however, beyond which the competence of staff cannot compensate for the deficiencies of the internal information resources.

There appears to be a natural balance between staff and information resources. A given library may have exceptionally strong staff in charge of declining internal information resources, which were once also very strong. This library may still be considered at the high end of the reference resource continuum. Another, much less likely scenario, is that of the exceptionally strong collection which is served by a weak staff. In this case, even the best information resources are going to be ineffective if the staff

Reference and Collection Development Issues

do not know how to use them. And since question handling is a mediated service, if the staff cannot use the information resources effectively, the client will be poorly served.

Levels of Reference Resources

The characteristics of reference resources vary depending upon whether the level of resources are garden variety, state-of-the-practice, advanced-state-of-the-practice, or super reference. Describing levels of reference resources involves being able to make comparisons. It requires positioning a given library's reference resource (i.e., the combination of staff and information resources) on a continuum of libraries of the same type, or with the same subject emphasis, to gain a sense of where a given library, or subject collection, fits.

During the course of the New Jersey study, staff participated in an informal exercise in which they were asked to define the level of their respective collections in the subjects designated under the NJSL contract. Using a worksheet developed during the study, staff at both libraries compared the reference resources in each designated subject area to resources in the same subject which are held by other libraries in New Jersey and in neighboring states.

In order to make this comparison, staff identified reference resources (i.e., a particular collection and staff) which they viewed as representing the highest standard in that subject in the state or the region. They then compared their own reference resources to the standard and to other reference resources which are at the same level as their collection or at a lower level. Terminology used by respondents to characterize the composition and level of reference staff and information resources is defined below.

Garden Variety: Staff have some reference training to handle questions. The time of the staff is not dedicated solely to question handling or necessarily to other reference functions. Information resources are those commonly found in a small reference collection (e.g., an almanac, encyclopedia, unabridged dictionary). No database searching and little-to-no long-distance telephone inquiry are used.

State-of-the-Practice: Staff usually have a master's in Library Science (M.L.S.), are trained to handle reference, and have some reference experience. Their time is not dedicated solely to question handling, or necessarily to other reference functions. Staff work with a moderate-sized reference collection, periodicals collection, and general collection. They may have access to online searching for commonly-held databases. They make moderate use of telephone inquiry for tapping outside expertise and resources.

Advanced-State-of-the-Practice: Staff are very experienced professionals with M.L.S. degrees. They may have expertise in a subject area as well, though not necessarily a second master's degree. Their time is dedicated solely to reference functions and predominantly to question handling and collection development. Staff work with large or very specialized collections which have depth as well as breadth and are current. They have funds available to access specialized as well as commonly-used databases. They make moderate-to-extensive use of telephone inquiry and advanced document delivery techniques, such as telefacsimile, dial order, and full-text retrieval online.

Super Reference: Staff are very experienced professionals with M.L.S. degrees. They usually have subject expertise as well, though not necessarily a second master's degree. Their time is heavily dedicated to question handling, although they may perform other reference functions to a limited extent. Staff work with very large or highly specialized collections. They have funds available to access specialized as well as commonly-used databases and make extensive use of the telephone for tapping outside expertise and resources.

If a question requires advanced-state-of-the-practice reference resources, but the home library's resources are garden variety or state-of-the-practice, it might be better to refer the client to another information source outside the library, rather than try to make a match using resources which are not at the appropriate level. Calculating the trade-offs in handling the question locally versus referring either the question or the client to an outside resource is part of the decision-making process.

Selecting Level of Service

Once the reference librarian has determined what resources are required to handle the question as it has been framed, the next step is to select the level of service to provide. There are four options: ready reference,

reference, research, and client referral. While these terms are familiar to reference librarians, they tend to be used rather casually and interchangeably. For example, a reference librarian might not differentiate between reference and research.

Each of these four terms are used in the model to describe discrete service options. Each level is described as being mutually exclusive, although, in reality, ready reference, reference, and research shade into one another along a continuum. Each is described in terms of time required, turnaround time, the mix of reference resources, and the anticipated outputs.

Ready Reference: Ready reference involves handling a question in less than five minutes from start to finish. In most cases, the question is handled while the client is waiting. Reference staff make use of a small, carefully chosen collection of garden variety information resources, which are commonly called "the ready reference collection." The result is always an answer unless the service level required was misjudged.

Reference: Reference usually requires from five to thirty minutes. Reference may take longer if there are no limits imposed on the time spent per question. Unlike ready reference, reference service may not be provided within one day. Usually, however, reference is provided within one to two days. The result is usually an answer (which may include a negative answer) or a client referral.

Research: Research is very labor intensive. It can easily consume a day to a week of staff time if no ceilings on the amount of time allocated to each research question have been established. The term "research" here refers to reference staff conducting secondary, not primary research. By secondary research, we mean an extensive and systematic effort to uncover knowledge derived from primary sources. The result is an explanation of research findings rather than a clear-cut answer. This level of effort is sometimes called extended reference.

Referral: There are two kinds of referral: question referral and client referral. In this article, "reference referral" is called "question referral" in order to distinguish it from "client referral." Each is discussed below.

Question referral is a process which usually involves a professional reference staff at Library A referring a *question* to professional reference staff at Library B in order to bring additional reference resources to bear in handling the question. Library A retains control of the client and does not pass the client on to Library B. Question referral takes place between libraries or between a library and a resource other than a library (e.g., an individual expert or a social service agency). Question referral is simply another option for bringing reference resources to bear in question handling.

Client referral is a process which usually involves a professional reference staff member at Library A referring a *client* to an alternative source of information, whether Library B, another institution, or to an outside expert. Once the librarian in Library A makes a client referral, both the client and the question are no longer the responsibility of the staff member at Library A, and therefore that librarian is out of the loop.

Client referral may involve providing a lead or making a contact. Reference librarians may suggest to clients that they handle the question by drawing on particular reference resources which are located outside of the library, either by writing, visiting, or using a Regional Contract Library on a "walk-in" basis. A more labor intensive approach involves the librarian who received the question either calling or writing to other reference resources to introduce the client.

In summary, in referring either the question or the client, the librarian decides to enlist the help of another individual. The librarian can choose to ask for assistance from an individual who is internal to the library (usually another reference librarian); internal to the organization (e.g., an expert in a subject area); or external to the organization (e.g., a librarian, a generalist, or a specialist in another organization).

An internal referral involves passing on a client or a question to another member of the reference staff who has more experience or more expertise. If an external referral occurs, either the question or the client is passed to an outside resource person—whether a librarian, a generalist, or a specialist. The choice depends upon the judgment of the librarian handling the question.

If librarians decide to provide simple answers to simple questions, it will be easy to do so, provided they are knowledgeable on the subject, have handled a similar question recently, or have the appropriate level of reference resources to tap in their own library. In this case, the level of service selected is likely to be ready reference or perhaps reference. The librarian would plan to spend less than five minutes and no more than thirty minutes. On the other hand, if librarians decide that questions require secondary research to produce some findings, they should anticipate spending a good deal more than thirty minutes using the reference resources they have judged to be appropriate.

To a generalist librarian working with a garden variety collection, a complex question, which requires at least state-of-the-practice reference resources, might appear very difficult to handle and be viewed as requiring effort at the research level. To a specialist librarian, working with an advanced state-of-the-practice collection, the same question may be viewed as easy to handle, requiring effort at the ready reference or reference level.

To summarize, there is a need to match the level of resources to the level of service. Ready reference is deployed when the question is simple. It will take little time, requires quick access to ready reference materials, and usually involves looking up factual information. It is usually initiated and completed while the client is waiting.

Reference level service is deployed when the question is simple. It will take reference staff a half hour or less, on average, to handle the question using information resources which are more sophisticated than ready reference tools, but which still involve looking up information rather than analysis. It is not necessarily initiated and completed within one day.

Research comes into play when the question is complex. Reference staff require more than thirty minutes, on average, to handle the question and usually make use of a number of resources. Handling the question involves analysis by the reference staff and is seldom completed the same day as received.

Client referral is provided when the librarian decides that the question will be better handled by another information provider. If this option is selected, the librarian identifies alternative information providers outside the library and may, in some cases, call or write the provider to smooth the way for the client. The client is sent to a resource outside the library. Client referral may occur immediately after the client has posed the question, or after reference staff have devoted time to trying to handle the question.

PHASE III: HANDLING THE QUESTION

At this point, phase three in the process, much of the planning and decision making has been accomplished. What remains is for the librarian to handle the question. In Step 6, the reference librarian sets out to find an answer if the targeted level of service is ready reference or reference. If the level of service is at the research level, the librarian will be involved in conducting secondary research and reporting findings.

In the course of handling the question, the librarian may decide that the question has been incorrectly categorized and that a different mix of resources is needed to deliver a different level of service. If this is the case, the librarian goes back to Phase I and starts the process over again. Ideally, the client should be interviewed again before the librarian restructures the strategy for handling the question.

If internal resources do not match the level of service required to handle the question, the librarian may opt for referral. Referral, in fact, allows for two options: either refer the question and then replay the answer/information back to the client; or refer the client together with the question to another source and withdraw from the question handling process.

PHASE IV: REPORTING THE RESULTS

Having completed the action selected, the librarian moves on to Phase IV, reporting back to the client. If an answer has been found, the librarian provides the information to the client. If the librarian has conducted research in response to a question, the research findings are reported. If the librarian has failed to find an answer, or has exhausted the time available, it is necessary to report back to the client on the lack of success and make a referral, if appropriate.

PHASE V: EVALUATING SERVICE DELIVERY

This is the fifth and last phase of the question handling process. At this point, the librarian may take the final step of evaluating whether the question was handled successfully. The problem, however, is how to measure success. There is a great deal of literature on measuring reference performance. There are no easy ways to evaluate the quality of service delivered. The objective measures commonly used are accuracy and turnaround time. The Lancaster discussion of accuracy and completeness, for example, captures some of the problems involved in quantifying reference.[14] It lists some of the key studies evaluating reference service over the last twenty years. Overall, these studies report that questions are answered accurately, on average, only 50 to 60 percent of the time.

Ongoing research being conducted by staff at the Division of Library Development and Services of the Maryland Department of Education suggests that much of the success in reference service is attitudinal and behavioral.[15] One way to gain feedback is to ask users and librarians if they were satisfied with the outcome of the question handling process. A difficulty with user surveys, however, is that most users have a very imperfect concept of what to expect from reference assistance and usually are relatively easily satisfied. Another approach is to ask librarians to evaluate their own work. The two approaches are not mutually exclusive.

APPLYING THE MODEL

The question handling model can serve as a diagnostic and training tool which helps reference librarians to analyze and evaluate their success in question handling. It can also provide a vehicle for documenting question handling and a conceptual framework for evaluating the appropriateness of the strategy. The very act of applying the model (or, for that matter, any workable model) helps reference librarians better understand the process of question handling.

Once librarians are aware of the range of decisions which they must consciously make, they can monitor their own performance more closely. They can also benefit from group discussions, peer coaching, direct oversight by supervisors, and/or formal training sessions in which they learn to refine their diagnostic skills and develop new strategies for question handling. The medical analogy used earlier is again apt. Doctors have developed formal peer-review procedures for evaluating the appropriateness of diagnostic and treatment choices. Such review, however, requires a shared understanding of the process and a common vocabulary on the part of participating doctors.

Using the schematic in Figure 1, reference librarians can physically map the choices made in handling a given question. By circling an option at each phase and step of the process, the schematic of the model becomes a form. Used in this way, the marked-up diagram provides a visual summary of the highly abstract decisions reference librarians make when they handle questions. It can then be duplicated and discussed with other members of the reference staff. Seeing how a colleague approached a question within the same schematic framework enables other reference librarians to present the decisions they made. In addition, other reference staff can map the route they would have taken, thereby introducing the possibility of alternative strategies to handling a given question.

The question handling model can also serve as a management tool for gathering information needed to make decisions regarding the allocation of staff time and the use of information resources. It can be used to relate levels of services to levels of resources required. The activities identified in the model provide a framework for costing reference services. Data collected on time spent performing reference activities, as described in the model, provide an essential building block for calculating costs.

Finally, the model can be used to characterize the types of questions asked, answers provided, and the mix of resources applied in a given library. The result is a much more refined picture of the nature of reference service. If libraries were to generate statistics using the concepts presented in the model, we would have a clearer understanding of how reference staff spend their time and the level of information resources they deploy.

Notes and References

1. In particular, see Robert S. Taylor, "Question Negotiation and Information Seeking in Libraries," *College and Research Libraries* 29:178–94 (May 1986); Karen Markey, "Levels of Question Formulation in Negotiation of Information Need During the Online Presearch Interview: A Proposed Model," *Information Processing and Management* 17: 215–25 (1981); and Marilyn Domas White, "The Reference Encounter Model," *Drexel Library Quarterly* 19:38–55 (Spring 1983).
2. Barbara M. Robinson, *Costing Question Handling and ILL/Photocopying: A Study of Two State Contract Libraries in New Jersey* (Trenton, N.J.: New Jersey State Library, Jan. 1989).
3. Many of the concepts discussed in this paper are described in Barbara M. Robinson, *A Study of Reference Referral and Super Reference*, (Sacramento, Cal.: the California State Library, June 1986). The concepts were tailored to describe public library reference resources, although librarians drawn from all types of libraries helped to formulate the definitions. If the definitions were to be applied to other than public libraries some refinements might be necessary. For example, bibliographic instruction might appear as a component of education and training under the "other reference" function.
4. See Marilyn Domas White, "The Dimensions of the Reference Interview," *RQ* 20:373–81

(Summer 1981). She characterizes four dimensions of interviewing: structure, coherence, pace, and length.
5. Brenda Dervin and Doug Zweizig, "Public Library Use, Users, Uses: Advances in Knowledge of the Characteristics and Needs of the Adult Clientele of American Public Libraries," *Advances in Librarianship* 7:231-55 (1977). They define a variety of client conceptual frameworks.
6. This example appears in F. W. Lancaster, *If You Want to Evaluate Your Library* . . ., (Champaign, Ill., Graduate School of Library and Information Science, University of Illinois, 1988), p. 112.
7. Example provided by a librarian at the National Aeronautics and Space Administration, Goddard Space Center, Washington, D.C., during a workshop held by B. Robinson for the D.C. Library Association, Dec. 1988.
8. Lancaster, *If You Want to Evaluate Your Library* . . ., p. 112.
9. Ibid.
10. Ibid.
11. The creation of "ready reference" files of answers to questions which reference staff anticipate will recur can save staff a great deal of time if the same question is indeed asked again. Developing this type of specialized resource is part of the "other reference" function which supports question handling. Examples of other specialized resources include the creation of other homegrown finding tools such as bibliographies, guides to subject collections, and the creation and maintenance of vertical files.
12. The levels of resources and service which are presented here are described in more detail in Robinson, *A Study of Reference Referral and Super Reference in California.*
13. *The Conspectus* is a special database produced by the Research Libraries Information Network (FLIN), Menlo Park, California. David L. Perkins, ed., *Guidelines for Collection Development*, Collection Development Committee, Resources and Technical Services Division (Chicago, American Library Assn., 1984).
14. Lancaster, *If You Want to Evaluate Your Library* . . ., p. 113.
15. Ralph Gers and Lillie J. Seward, "Improving Reference Performance: Results of a Statewide Study," *Library Journal* 110:32-35 (Nov. 1, 1985).

LITERARY STYLE IN REFERENCE BOOKS

David Isaacson

Definition of Reference Books

Most reference librarians would hesitate to disagree with Isadore Gilbert Mudge's classic distinction between nonreference and reference books:

> From the point of view of use, books may be divided into two groups: those which are meant to be read through for either information or enjoyment, and those which are meant to be consulted or referred to for some definite piece of information. Books of this second class are called *reference* books, and are usually comprehensive in scope, condensed in treatment, and arranged on some special plan to facilitate the ready and accurate finding of information.[1]

Reference librarians concur so readily with Mudge because this distinction is practical and utilitarian. Reference sources, by this definition, are tools to be used, not books intended for consecutive reading. Through training and experience reference librarians have learned to look at books differently than other people. When the book is supposed to have reference value we are critical if it does not present its information clearly and quickly. While we recognize that many books are not intended as reference sources, as soon as they *are* put in that category for various practical reasons, all but utilitarian considerations are usually ignored by the busy reference librarian. Thus, while acknowledging that *Moby-Dick* is a novel, as soon as someone asks a reference question that only the novel itself can answer, reference librarians may be forgiven in wishing that Melville had included an index in order to facilitate their work.

"Literary Style in Reference Books," by David Isaacson in *RQ* Vol. 28, no. 4 (Summer 1989), pp. 485–495; reprinted with permission from the American Library Association, copyright © 1989 by ALA.

Reference Books Are Not Usually Read at Length

Fortunately, while any book may at times be used to answer reference questions, most of the sources we recognize as conventional reference tools are organized, as Mudge describes them, to facilitate locating information in them. With the possible exception of some special librarians or research analysts, most reference librarians do not engage in prolonged study of the content of reference sources. In short, because of the compact way most reference books are organized, because we may lack appropriate subject expertise, and because we usually lack the time, reference librarians *qua* reference librarians consult, browse, scan, or refer to these books, rather than read them at length. Moreover, we don't usually think about *how* a reference book is written. Like the contents of reference books, we don't usually regard literary style in these sources in anything but a utilitarian way. As long as the style conveys information clearly, there is no reason to pay attention to how the effects are achieved. In fact, to pay special attention to the personality of the writer of a reference book is usually to cast suspicion on that book as a reference source. We expect reference books to be objective, reliable, and impersonal. As far as most reference work is concerned, the more factual a source is the better. Reference work gets messy when facts are hard to establish or verify. So authors of reference works who make a special effort to display wit, humor, irony, opinion, and other indications of individuality, personality, or subjectivity are suspicious. Such writers may be diverting and even enlightening, but they are not always useful from the point of view of conventional reference work. Most reference librarians are too busy to be entertained by their reference books. Even when we are not so busy, I suspect that most of us, given the prevalence of the work ethic inherent in our culture, make a sharp distinction between work and pleasure. If a reference work gives pleasure can it also be a useful tool? Typically, when a reviewer praises the author of a reference book for a style that entertains, the reviewer regards the entertainment value as something additional, not integral to the book. A reference book may be praised for being a diverting browsing source—that is, pleasurable to read at random. This is, however, clearly not a primary concern in a reference work.

Personal Expression Is Sometimes Useful

This essay seeks to examine the conventional assumption that reference books ought to be written in an objective style, or at least in a style that places much more emphasis on the impersonal transmission of information than it does on the personal expression of feeling. I will argue that personal opinion is sometimes functional, not merely diverting, in a reference work. I will also argue that the pleasure a reader may derive from a writer's style in a reference work may enhance the informational content in that reference work. I am not arguing that personal expression is ipso facto desirable in a reference work, only that reference librarians have overemphasized objectivity at the expense of other valuable qualities in reference works. In considering style in reference books, I will apply the following definition from a standard literary handbook:

> [style is] the arrangement of words in a manner best expressing the individuality of the author and the idea and intent in the author's mind. The best *style*, for any given purpose, is that which most nearly approximates a perfect adaptation of one's language to one's ideas. Style is a combination of two elements: the idea to be expressed and the individuality of the author.[2]

This definition of style would seem to exclude most reference books. While it is true that reference librarians need to be concerned with "the idea to be expressed" element of the above definition of style, it is difficult to see why we should concern ourselves with the second element, "the individuality of the author." While it is obvious that people expect writers of fiction and poetry to express their individuality, we don't expect writers of reference books to do so. Individuality suggests feelings, and feelings, in turn, suggest a subjectivity that would work against the objective presentation of information essential to reference books. However, there are different ways of being objective, and not all of them necessarily exclude expressions of individuality or feeling. Let's examine, for instance, the sentences from Isadore Mudge quoted earlier. Mudge's prose is a fine example of clear, impersonal, objective writing. It is difficult to see how the ideas could be expressed any better. Mudge was an authority on reference books not only for her bibliographic expertise but also because she wrote so well. This style is notable for its crispness: there are no unnecessary words. The style here is dignified and formal without being stilted. Mudge writes with restraint and detachment, but not without feeling, as is evident in the following sentence, taken from the same preface quoted above:

> The possession of the right books and the knowledge of how to use them are two things essential to the success of a reference department, and the latter is no less important than the former. The ignorant assistant can render comparatively useless the finest collection of reference books, while the skilled assistant, who knows how to get from each book all the varied kinds of information that it is planned to give, can show astonishing results even when limited to only a few basic tools.[3]

Mudge doesn't lecture us here about the failings of the ill-trained librarian. She simply shrewdly notes the paradox that even a small reference collection can out-perform a large one if an able librarian is in charge. Although no very overt feeling is expressed here until the emotive "astonishing" at the end of the passage, we know that Mudge feels deeply about this subject. Sometimes quiet understatement can be more effective rhetorically than obviously emotional language. A writer less in command of the subject might have diminished the effect here by calling explicit attention to the shameful waste an ill-trained or poorly motivated librarian can make even of a very well stocked reference collection. Mudge makes us feel this waste all the more strongly by not straining to make her point.

Objectively Versus Subjectivity

In contrast, all too often what passes as an objective style in reference books and in many other types of formal writing reads as if a machine, rather than a human being had written it. Inflated, prolix, and jargon-filled sentences seem to indicate objectivity and authority, but really indicate a poor or ineffective writer. Generally speaking, literary style in a reference book should not call attention to itself. It is simply a medium for conveying information. Just as a skilled writer, like Mudge, happily marries style and content, an unskilled writer divorces them, as we see in the following passage, which is the first sentence of the article, "Popular Culture and the Library," from the *Encyclopedia of Library and Information Science*:

> The first and, therefore, foremost problem confronting the proposed

acceptance of popular culture into the institutional framework of contemporary society as a first-class citizen (i.e., the formal teaching of this discipline in the nation's secondary schools and higher institutions of learning in addition to the development of comprehensive and well-balanced collections in libraries and archives) is the necessity of lucidly defining the boundaries of this area.[4]

The author of this article may know much about his subject but he does not seem to know how difficult it is for his audience to follow his thought. This sentence, especially as the first one in an essay, is too long. Much worse, this sentence, which is obviously preliminary to something more important, makes us impatient. Parenthetical remarks can sometimes be very effective, but this one is confusing, unnecessary, and over-long. The passive voice seems to lend scholarly authority to this sentence, but the active voice would communicate more immediately and directly. The metaphorical use of "first-class citizen" to refer to popular culture may be a forceful image for a moment, but unfortunately the special feeling the writer wanted to convey is rendered anemic by the time we finally finish the sentence. The writer is so caught up in the complexity of his subject that he seems to forget that it is his duty to communicate with readers, not confuse or annoy them.

Other writers in this encyclopedia, however, do keep their readers in mind. Here, for instance, are the first two sentences of the article on "Alphabetic Indexes": "Indexes guide users to documents and other things; they are not, however, the material itself. Index entries are not intended to describe the material indexed."[5] The author of this article, unlike the writer on popular culture quoted earlier, seems to have a more orderly mind and the grace and good sense to remember that most readers do not want, especially at the beginning of an essay, to untangle a knot of twisted prose. The writer on indexes actually says a great deal in a few words, managing a compact definition and a rather surprising distinction in the first sentence. Many readers may never have thought about the difference between an index and the document it indexes. But the distinction is an important one, as the second sentence suggests. Anyone who is interested in this topic will probably be hooked after the second sentence. If index entries do not describe the material, then what is it that they do? The rest of the article goes on to answer that question.

In another quotation from the *Encyclopedia of Library and Information Science*, we see how the careful choice of images not only makes a subject more interesting but also informs the reader more exactly. Here are the first two sentences of the article on "Friends of Libraries": "Organized bodies of friends are not peculiar to libraries. There have been Friends of the Cabildo, Covent Garden, French Opera, the middle border, truth, and the National Zoo, but their mission is usually the same: to further the development of the program in which they have an interest."[6] This writer manages both to define Friends groups at the same time she invites readers to enjoy her essay. Instead of simply saying there are many different kinds of Friends groups, this writer provides specific examples that let readers draw this conclusion for themselves. These examples are thought-provoking, including political institutions like the Cabildo, cultural institutions like Covent Garden and the French opera, a geographical boundary like the middle border, the abstract concept of truth, and finally, back to the concrete, with a reference to the National Zoo. The writer assumes the reader has some knowledge of history in order to appreciate these allusions. She also teases the reader rather slyly by mixing in truth with the other, concrete allusions. Such a juxtaposition is far more effective in establishing the great variety of Friends groups than a declarative statement without illustrations. If one argues that the reader of a reference work only wants information stated as plainly and simply as possible, then these examples may be seen as adornments. The reader who is not familiar with these allusions or who is not sensitive to the comic disparity between Friends of Truth and Friends of the National Zoo will not appreciate the sophisticated, ironic, learned perspective the author has toward her subject. If reference books sometimes are meant to help further understanding and appreciation of a subject, writing like this is exemplary. If, on the other hand, reference books are meant *only* to provide facts for quick assimilation, such writing may seem superfluous.

Providing More than Information

All too often users of reference books assume that these sources are simply information containers. It may never occur to such users that some reference books should be interpreted and examined critically, not just consulted. Most reference librarians know better than this, but unfortunately they often do not have the time, opportunity, or inclination to help patrons discover the most reliable sources of information. Sometimes the most reliable sources are the ones most vividly written, sources which ought to be read, not simply consulted. One of the most engaging as well as informative articles in the fifteenth edition of the *Encyclopaedia Britannica* is the one on "Humour and Wit," written by Arthur Koestler. Here is a typical paragraph:

> Why tickling should produce laughter remained an enigma in all the earlier theories of the comic. As Darwin was the first to point out, the innate response to tickling is squirming and straining to withdraw the tickled part—a defense reaction designed to escape attacks on vulnerable areas such as the soles of the feet, armpits, belly and flank. If a fly settles on the belly of a horse, it causes a ripple of muscle contractions across the skin—the equivalent of squirming in the tickled child. But the horse does not laugh when tickled, and the child not always. The child will laugh only—and this is the crux of the matter—when it perceives tickling as a *mock attack*, a caress in mildly aggressive disguise. For the same reason, people laugh only when tickled by others, not when they tickle themselves.[7]

This is a superb example of formal writing that avoids pedantry without sacrificing scholarly objectivity. This writing is accessible to a general audience, while at the same time it is not so oversimplified as to offend the specialist or distort the truth. These sentences sparkle with apt images and analogies. The comparison between a tickled horse and child charms with its gentle sense of the absurd and at the same time it instructs. We understand the phenomenon of tickling much better because of this comparison: a merely physiological explanation would not stick in our minds as easily, or, I think, inform as well.

Turgid Writing Impairs Comprehension

By contrast, try to decipher this passage, which comes from the article "Humor Development in Children" from the *International Encyclopedia of Psychiatry, Psychology, Psychoanalysis, and Neurology*:

> While empirical demonstrations of particular levels of cognitive mastery or development as prerequisites for comprehension or appreciation of

particular types of humour have been difficult to achieve, some positive support has been obtained (McGhee, 1974). More commonly demonstrated is the fact that a child must be familiar with the content of a humour stimulus before some discrepant depiction of that content may be seen as funny.[8]

Even when one acknowledges that the author of this article assumes he is addressing fellow specialists, and that certain conventions of scholarly writing therefore ought to be observed, I question the effectiveness of writing like this for anyone who might try to translate this turgidity. Surely this prose needs to be translated from the abstruse level of abstraction into something that makes some concessions to the empirical world the author refers to in his first sentence. I suspect that even fellow scientists need to be very patient with writing like this. This prose, like the passage quoted earlier on "Popular Culture and the Library," may be criticized for being written in an unnecessary and obstructive passive voice, having too many words, and not using any concrete examples.

Humor

Sometimes a wry observation, levity, and other forms of humor enhance the informational value of a reference book, rather than simply provide color or incidental entertainment. Here, for instance, are the last sentences of the entry on John Asgill in Palgrave's *Dictionary of Political Economy* (1926):

> Asgill was born at Hanley Castle, Worcestershire, 1659, called to the English bar 1692, expelled from the Irish House of Commons 1703, and from the British Parliament 1707, for an eccentric pamphlet contending that man could be translated to heaven without dying. He left this world in the ordinary way, 1738.[9]

The ironic understatement of this last sentence is, of course, much more devastating as a comment on the eccentric opinions of John Asgill than the direct statement that he died without proving his unusual contention. Nevertheless, some might argue that expressions of opinion and feeling, however quiet and subtle, have no place in reference books. This position assumes that information is always objective and factual, needing no interpretation or context. Someone who wants information about a minor figure in economic history like John Asgill needs to know that one reason he is a minor figure is for the eccentric views he held. If an ironic comment reinforces this fact, then an apparently subjective observation actually contributes to a better objective understanding. Unless the reader shares Asgill's eccentricity, the witty observation here returns the reader from a metaphysical flight to heaven with Asgill to the factual, common sense world of ordinary living and dying.

Sometimes much more direct and personal expressions of opinion may also be useful in reference books. Take, for example, this typical passage from David Thomson's *A Biographical Dictionary of Film*, excerpted from an entry on the actor Vincent Price:

> Disenchantment and sweetness together made Vincent incredulous at his own nightmare and so he found himself as the hideously scarred owner of *House of Wax* (53, Andre de Toth). He surveyed the horror genre as if it were a tray of eclairs. Nothing has since distracted him from the feast, no matter that the delicacies never satisfy him. It is a paradox that he should be the king of the genre in that he knows no one is really frightened by such an old humbug—the softie who is also art adviser for Sears Roebuck and the author of several cookery books.[10]

Interpretation and Presentation of Information

Clearly, writing like this is interpretation, not just the presentation of information. Thomson does not offer a studied, carefully reasoned, balanced assessment of Vincent Price here. He offers opinions, instead, delivered in a provocative mixture of slang and formal language. But Thomson's opinions, however snide, are often more informative than other writers' careful, tactful, "objective" judgments. The references to sweetness and eclairs here, for instance, continue a series of other allusions in the article, beginning with the fact, noted in the first sentence, that Price was the son of the owner of the National Candy Company. Thomson imaginatively uses this fact about Price as a controlling metaphor that acquires through repetition progressively more analytical force. The "sweetness" of Price is a constant throughout his career, leading Thomson to say also "for they had seen that Vincent was a good-natured man; a fruit drop melted slowly in his mouth,"[11] and later, "working largely in England, he found himself involved in some vulgar confections. . . ."[12] Yes, Thomson does take liberties other more sedulous writers would not risk, but the objective information he provides cannot be separated from his subjective expressions of opinion. To anyone who has watched a number of Price's most characteristic films, a cloying sweetness, combined with a mocking recognition that the sweetness is a joke Price intends, describes accurately an essential characteristic of his acting style.

Misinformation Is Sometimes Valuable

One might even argue that some reference books which actually present misinformation have a place on our reference shelves. If we really do believe in supporting intellectual freedom, we need to be humble enough, on the one hand, to recognize that truth and error are sometimes difficult to distinguish, and confident enough, on the other hand, to let opposing points of view be represented in the reference as well as the circulating collection. Some dogmatic idealogues who claim to have the true and the last word to say about various subjects ought to be represented in our reference collections, if only as examples of extreme points of view. Thus, for example, reference librarians might welcome works like Francis X. Gannon's *A Biographical Dictionary of the Left* because Gannon's virulent right-wing opinions are an instructive foil to equally extreme left-wing opinions. It seems clear to me, for instance, that passages like the following are not simply examples of vivid expressions of feeling and opinion, such as those of David Thomson, but are also prime examples of prejudice and bigotry. Here is a typical example of Gannon's style, from the article on James Baldwin:

> In his writings, Baldwin is preoccupied with themes revolving around sexual perversion and his pet hatreds: Christianity, America, American customs, and white people. William F. Buckley, Jr. has called Baldwin an "eloquent menace" and his attitude "morose nihilism." The descriptions are certainly appropriate as far as they go.[13]

If a reference collection is to include sources like this with a pronounced right-wing bias, it ought also, in the interest of balance, to include other sources representing an equally strong left-wing bias. Here for example, is a typical passage from the *Labor Fact Book*, a Marxist publication claiming, as the title states, to be an objective, factual discussion of world events. This is a typical passage, notable like Gannon, for its dogmatic assertions:

> The United States Government is the instrument of the American capitalist class. Through the government, the capitalist class maintains itself in power, represses the working class, pursues its ruthless course of imperialist expansion, and wages its struggles against the capitalists of other nations.[14]

Of course, there is a danger in including such obviously biased works in a reference collection. Only the most censorious of librarians would dare to label such books as factually unreliable, and yet one might sympathize with the desire to warn patrons that such books, are, to say the least, controversial. The argument I am making for the appreciation of literary style in reference books includes a recognition that some styles are inflammatory, not simply vivid, opinionated, or biased.

Individuality and Objectivity

I have been arguing up to now that there is no necessary disjunction between the expression of individuality and a writer's ability to write objectively. Quite the contrary, some of the least objective reference books are written in an impersonal, but dogmatic style such as the *Biographical Dictionary of the Left* and the *Labor Fact Book*, while some of the most authoritative reference sources are permeated with personal opinion, such as the *Biographical Dictionary of Film*. It should be recognized, of course, that many reference books do not have anything worthy of being analyzed as literary style because they consist mainly of lists of data. Unannotated indexes and bibliographies may have distinctive *bibliographic* styles, but not literary ones. Annotated bibliographies, however, are sometimes quite a different matter. Considerable literary skill is needed in order to write concise, precise, objective annotations or abstracts. The annotator or abstractor must learn to suppress any inclination to make judgments about the material being annotated or abstracted. Writers of evaluative bibliographies, and bibliographic reviews, on the other hand, are expected to give advice and make judgments. Some of the most distinctly individual literary styles, not surprisingly, are encountered in these genres of reference books. One may receive a great deal of *implicit* advice from the careful selection criteria employed in some unannotated bibliographies. But evaluative bibliographies, by definition, are written in order to provide *explicit* judgments. For example, the following excerpts from an annual bibliographic review, *American Literary Scholarship*, reveal a style quite different from what one normally expects in a reference work. Michael S. Reynolds, a Hemingway scholar, is describing here a new edition of Hemingway's book, *The Dangerous Summer*:

> Despite reviewers who found the book self-parodic (An inane response. Did they expect him to sound like someone else?), *The Dangerous Summer* is an interesting testament of what was wrong and right with Hemingway in his life's end. The book follows two bullfighters through an author-inflated duel across the Spanish summer. Perversely identifying with the younger bull-fighter, Hemingway the narrator, works imperfectly but steadily on the theme of doubleness which haunts all of his posthumous publications. The people and places, the look of the Spanish earth, the taste of the wine, the movement of the bulls and men in sunlight—all the Hemingway touchstones are included. But the book is about death, about growing old, about losing; it is about all these things even though they are mostly left out. It is not all pretty, but it is there, and we must deal with it sensibly.[15]

Clearly, Reynolds is addressing fellow scholars, not a general audience, in this passage. His allusions and tone assume the reader is not only familiar with Hemingway, but also with Hemingway scholarship. The sarcastic parenthetical remark at the beginning of the passage, inappropriate in reference sources designed simply to inform, is quite appropriate here, in a source which is addressed to readers looking for authoritative evaluations of the most recent criticism of Hemingway. As a critic and biographer of Hemingway, Reynolds, it can be assumed, has earned the right to dismiss other critics' judgments about Hemingway. Reynolds is also so comfortable with his subject that *he* parodies Hemingway here. He does not simply describe the main events in *The Dangerous Summer*; he imitates Hemingway's distinctive style, especially in the rhythms of the last two sentences, the simple diction, and the implied quote from the famous last line of Hemingway's novel, *The Sun Also Rises*. In the last few lines in that novel Brett Ashley says to Jake Barnes, "Oh Jake, we could have had such a damned good time together" and the world-weary Jake replies, resignedly, "Yes, isn't it pretty to think so."[16] Hemingway's much discussed code of "grace under pressure," a philosophy of stoicism that is sometimes just a veneer barely disguising sentimentality, is succinctly stated in these well-known last lines of his novel. It is fitting therefore that Reynolds should make an implied connection between *The Sun Also Rises* and *The Dangerous Summer* by his otherwise rather lame choice of the word "pretty" in the last sentence quoted above. Reynolds is providing more than explicit commentary on *The Dangerous Summer.* Just after criticizing some literary critics for describing this book as self-parody, in a manner which combines appreciation and criticism, Reynolds evaluates this book by imitating Hemingway himself and by implicitly comparing it to *The Sun Also Rises*, which many critics believe is Hemingway's most successful novel.

Literary Style in Dictionaries

We expect specialized bibliographic review sources like *American Literary Scholarship* to be written by scholars who themselves often have distinctive literary styles. We do not expect other kinds of reference sources to have style in this sense at all. We know, of course, that dictionaries are written by individual persons but we do not expect to read most dictionaries for idiosyncratic or personal styles. There are some exceptions however. Samuel Johnson's famous dictionary, for example, is not only useful for revealing meanings of words in eighteenth century England, but also provides clues to Johnson scholars about how he used words in his poetry and other writings. Most people who have some familiarity with Johnson's dictionary probably recognize his ironic definition of oats: "A grain, which in England is generally given to horses, but in Scotland supports the people." Somewhat less well known is the wonderfully pompous, abstruse definition of a network: "Any thing reticulated or decussated, at equal distances, with interstices between the intersections."[17] (Perhaps this is still an apt definition for very complex networks, such as OCLC.)

While Johnson's dictionary is only incidentally diverting, other, usually more specialized dictionaries, have been compiled by authors who may want to entertain at least as much as inform. John Ciardi's *A Browser's Dictionary*,[18] *A Second Browser's Dictionary*,[19] and the posthumous, *Good Words to You*[20] are good examples, as their titles indicate, of reference books that are meant to be read for pleasure, not simply consulted for information. Readers who turn to these dictionaries *only* for information will be quite surprised, for example, to read entries like the following definition:

> *kelemenopy*. The one essential trope neglected by classical rhetoricians: a sequential straight line through the middle of everything, leading nowhere. "Teddy Kennedy's career has been the classical kelemenopy of the twentieth century"—Angelo Registratore [Based on k-l-m-n-o-p, the central sequence of the alphabet, having ten letters before and after it. Hence, a strictly sequential irrelevance.] Note: Drudges lost in felonious footnotery regularly become kinkospectic if not tergivercentric. Kelemenopy is from my own psychic warp, to see if anyone would notice, and because I have always dreamed of fathering a word.[21]

Although we expect John Ciardi the poet to be somewhat present in John Ciardi the lexicographer, we don't expect to find diversion or distinctive literary style in staid and sedate unabridged dictionaries. Mammoth works like these, which are written by hundreds of people, may, nevertheless, be described as having distinctive personalities and individual styles. The new *Random House Dictionary of the English Language*,[22] for instance, may be described as having a streamlined, compact, sometimes even a rather curt style. It is certainly these things in comparison to its much more formal and long-winded rival, the third edition of *Webster's Unabridged Dictionary*.[23] We can observe these distinctively different styles by comparing the entries for many words. Let us examine, for instance, an emotionally neutral word like "paprika." *Random House* defines this word as follows:

> *n.* 1. a red, powdery condiment derived from dried, sweet peppers. *adj.*
> 2. cooked or seasoned with paprika.

In contrast, *Webster's* includes considerably more detail in its definition:

> *1.* a condiment consisting of the dried finely ground pods of various

cultivated sweet peppers (as the pimientos)—see Hungarian Paprika, King's Paprika, Spanish Paprika 2. a sweet pepper that is used for or is suitable for making paprika 3. a strong reddish orange that is yellower and slightly darker than poppy, redder and deeper than fire red or scarlet vermillion, and redder and deeper than average coral red.

The *Random House* definition is pithy and direct. It is content to describe the color of paprika with one adjective and to discriminate, as any good definition must, between the genus, condiment, of which the species, paprika, is a part, and to tell us, additionally, that paprika comes from dried sweet peppers, and that the noun may sometimes have an adjectival form. This no-frills definition ought to satisfy the needs of the average, curious, but not scholarly, general reader. By contrast, the definition in *Webster's* is more complex, and directed, presumably, at a more exacting, scholarly audience. One can argue that the definition in *Random House* is less complete when compared to the one in *Webster's*. After all, if *Webster's* is correct, *Random House* is simplistic: "dried sweet peppers" is not as precise as "dried finely ground pods of various cultivated sweet peppers." And the third definition in *Webster's* is in very marked contrast to *Random House*. *Random House* does not recognize a separate sense of the word paprika to indicate a color. It does note that the color is red. *Webster's*, on the other hand, does recognize paprika as a color, and instead of describing it as a shade of red, uses 29 words to distinguish just what kind of reddish orange is meant. For those with a finely developed visual sense, this definition is beautifully exact. For readers unable to appreciate these fine distinctions, however, perhaps the one adjective, although imprecise, is actually a better definition, because it is more accessible. The difference between these two definitions tells us a great deal about how literary style and content are inextricably interlinked, even in reference books where we are not usually conscious of style. Sometimes one must be prolix in order to be exact. And sometimes it is better to be simplistic but understandable, if the one other alternative is to be complex but hard to understand. If one of the major goals of literary style is to communicate content, then it may be argued that the third definition in *Webster's* has lost part of its potential audience. If, on the other hand, one insists that paprika cannot simply be described as red, then this definition, with its extremely discriminating distinctions, has to be preferred.

Although both of these definitions are written in objective, impersonal language, their styles are otherwise very different. If Ernest Hemingway were a lexicographer he might have written the *Random House* definition, but it would require a Henry James or Marcel Proust to write the much more nuanced definition in *Webster's*.

Literary Style of the Dictionary of Occupational Titles

We do not usually think of government publications as possessing literary style. The impersonal authority and officiousness of books like *The Dictionary of Occupational Titles*[24] suggest that its prose style could have no literary value. Yet as has been suggested elsewhere,[25] the very precise and economical prose of the thousands of definitions of jobs in this book sometimes resembles unconscious poetry, and certainly could serve as a model of the non-nonsense, waste-no-words philosophy advocated by E. B. White and William Strunk in their famous guide to writing, *The Elements of Style*.[26] Although the *DOT* definitions have to follow a rigid formula, there is something to admire in its clean, spare, very exacting definitions, such as the following definition of a librarian:

> Maintains library collections of books, serial publications, documents, audiovisual, and other materials, and assists groups and individuals in locating and obtaining materials: Furnishes information on library activities, facilities, rules, and services. Explains and assists in use of reference sources, such as card or book catalogs or book and periodical indexes to locate information. Describes or demonstrates procedures for searching catalog files. Searches catalog files and shelves to locate information. Issues and receives materials for circulation or for use in library. Assembles and arranges displays of books and other library materials. Answers correspondence on special reference subjects. May compile list of library materials according to subject or interests. May select, order, catalog, and classify materials. May plan and direct or carry out special projects involving library promotion and outreach activity and be designated Outreach Librarian (library). May be designated according to specialized function as Circulation Librarian (library); Reference Librarian (library); or Reader's-Advisory-Service Librarian (library).[27]

This definition seems to me to be a remarkably concise and accurate summary of what the generic librarian does. We might want this now somewhat dated definition to include some examples of library automation, but whether the library operations are performed with computers or manually, the *DOT* does its job in providing a definition: it describes the essential responsibilities of this job, provides precise examples of each duty, and distinguishes typical duties (the sentences beginning with active verbs) from those duties a librarian sometimes performs (the sentences beginning with the auxiliary "may"). This definition has none of the highly abstract, verbose officialese which has come to be characteristic of far too many government agencies. Quite the contrary, definitions in the *DOT*, like this one, refer to concrete things as often as possible in order to avoid vague, abstract conceptions. Instead of the weak passive voice (such as, "collections of books are maintained") so typical of bureaucratic prose, each of the first seven sentences in this definition begins with an active verb: maintains, furnishes, explains, describes, searches, assembles, answers. Combined with the preference for concrete rather than abstract words, this focus on people who do, rather than activities that are done, makes this definition vivid and easy to read. This is prose that seems to fulfill Louis Sullivan's architectural dictum of "form follows function." It is notable because of the deft way it performs its job without any wasted words. Hundreds of different people write these job titles, but all of them conform to this distinctive literary style.

Conclusion

I do not mean to suggest with these examples that literary critics ought to establish a new genre called reference source stylistics. Nor do I mean to suggest that reference librarians, who are usually too busy to read their sources at length, should try to find the time to interpret literary style in them. Because these books are primarily meant to be consulted, not read critically or at length, we should take their style for granted. We read reference books for information rather than aesthetic pleasure. But, as I trust this analysis has demonstrated, the information content of a reference book is something that is often enhanced by, and finally is inseparable from its literary style. Moreover, far from being always impersonal and objective, style in a reference book often contributes to its usefulness. Finally, it is instructive to recognize that even very impersonal sources, written by many people, such as unabridged dictionaries or *The Dictionary of Occupational Titles*, may be examined for their distinctive literary styles. We may conclude, in fact, that just as the utility of reference books is partly a result of literary style, some reference books are less useful because their writers pay little or no attention to literary style.

References

1. Isadore Gilbert Mudge, *Guide to Reference Books*, 6th ed. (Chicago, Ill.: American Library Assn., 1936) reptd. by Eugene P. Sheehy, comp., *Guide to Reference Books*, 9th ed. (Chicago, Ill.: American Library Assn. 1976), p. xiv.
2. Hugh C. Holman and William Harmon, *A Handbook to Literature*, 5th ed. (New York: Macmillan, 1986), p. 487.
3. Mudge, p. xiv.
4. Frank Hoffman, "Popular Culture and the Library," in Allen Kent and others, eds., *The Encyclopedia of Library and Information Science*, V. 23 (New York: Marcel Dekker, 1978), p. 118.
5. Charles L. Bernier, "Alphabetic Indexes," in Allen Kent and others, eds., *The Encyclopedia of Library and Information Science*, V. 1 (New York: Marcel Dekker, 1968), p. 169.
6. Sara L. Wallace, "Friends of Libraries," in Allen Kent and others, eds., *The Encyclopedia of Library and Information Science*, V. 9 (New York: Marcel Dekker, 1973), p. 111.
7. Arthur Koestler, "Humour and Wit," in *Encyclopaedia Britannica*, V. 20, (Chicago: Encyclopaedia Britannica, 1986), p. 743.
8. Paul E. McGhee, "Humor Development in Children," in *The International Encyclopedia of Psychiatry, Psychology, Psychoanalysis, and Neurology*, V. 5 (New York: Van Nostrand Reinhold, 1977), p. 443.
9. John Eatwell and others, eds., *The New Palgrave: A Dictionary of Economics* V. 1 (London: Macmillan, 1987), p. 127.
10. David Thomson, *A Biographical Dictionary of Film*, 2d ed. rev. (New York: Morrow, 1981), p. 487.
11. Ibid.
12. Ibid.
13. Francis X. Gannon, *A Biographical Dictionary of the Left*, V. 1 (Boston: Western Islands, 1969), p. 219.
14. Labor Research Association, *Labor Fact Book*, V. 1 (New York: International Pub., 1931; New York: Oriole Eds., 1972), p. 188.
15. Michael S. Reynolds, "Fitzgerald and Hemingway" in *American Literary Scholarship*, 1985 vol. (Durham, N.C.: Duke Univ. Pr., 1987), p. 170.
16. Ernest Hemingway, *The Sun Also Rises* (New York: Scribner's 1926), p. 247.
17. Samuel Johnson, *A Dictionary of the English Language* (London: W. Strahan, 1755; New York: AMS Pr., 1967).
18. John Ciardi, *A Browser's Dictionary* (New York: Harper, 1980).
19. Ciardi, *A Second Browser's Dictionary* (New York: Harper, 1983).
20. Ciardi, *Good Words to You* (New York: Harper, 1987).

21. Ciardi, *A Browser's Dictionary*, p. 217–18.
22. *The Random House Dictionary of the English Language*, 2d ed. (New York: Random House, 1987).
23. *Webster's Third New International Dictionary of the English Language* (Springfield, Mass.: Merriam-Webster, 1986).
24. U.S. Department of Labor, Employment and Training Administration, *Dictionary of Occupational Titles*, 4th ed. (Washington, D.C.: Gov't. Printing Off., 1977).
25. David Isaacson, "We're All Entitled: The Literary and Cultural Significance of the *Dictionary of Occupational Titles*," *RQ* 27:226–32 (Winter 1987).
26. William Strunk and E. B. White, *The Elements of Style*, 3d ed. (New York: Macmillan, 1979).
27. *The Dictionary of Occupational Titles*, p. 72.

LIBRARY JARGON: STUDENT COMPREHENSION OF TECHNICAL LANGUAGE USED BY LIBRARIANS

Rachael Naismith and Joan Stein

This study examines the issue of jargon in librarianship, including terminology used in the handouts written by librarians and the vocabulary used in conversations with library users, typically in the reference interview. As is true with many professions, librarianship employs many words and phrases that can be considered technical language. Technical language or jargon provides a shorthand means of labeling frequently used concepts. Librarians, in their discussions with peers, cannot redefine common terms over and over again. A label is affixed to a more complex idea, and this label takes on an everyday, understood meaning.

A problem occurs when that label is used to communicate with an audience that is unfamiliar with the specialized use of a term. To a librarian, the word *citation* may be as familiar as the word *coffee*. To an undergraduate or even graduate student, this may not be so. Can such language affect reference transactions, in a field in which "user-friendliness" is a common concern?

This study was designed to measure students' comprehension of terms derived from reference interviews and handouts. While "jargon" is not always considered synonymous with "technical language," for the purpose of this study these terms will be used interchangeably.

"Library Jargon: Student Comprehension of Technical Language Used by Librarians," by Rachael Naismith and Joan Stein in *College & Research Libraries* Vol. 50, no. 5 (September 1989), pp. 543–552; reprinted with permission from the American Library Association, copyright © 1989 by ALA.

REVIEW OF THE LITERATURE
Communication Models

A number of communication models have been proposed by researchers. In recent years, cognitive psychologists have adopted models that have added subjective components lacking in earlier models. Figure 1 is a simplified diagram of Terry Winograd's discourse model.[1]

The two participants, the speaker and the hearer (or writer and reader), each possess a set of cognitive structures, or stored schemas, some of which existed before the discourse event. Simply put, a schema is a collection of knowledge related to a concept or definition. Schemas are used in the reasoning process by which discourse becomes understood. Schemas develop over the course of the transaction through analysis of words chosen, tone used, and so on. The hearer considers the context of the spoken information and compares the data to existing schemas, noting differences between the data and the schematic structures. The hearer may refer to more than one schema in the effort to interpret the data.

In addition, each participant has a model of the other person, which develops during the conversation. The processing of the information (written or verbal) involves linguistics at a variety of levels, including syntax, conversational conventions, and word meaning. In this model, "meaning" covers all of the speaker's and hearer's goals. At the most basic level, these goals take the form of the words selected by the speaker. The hearer's comprehension of words is affected by the hearer's model of the relevant "world" and of the speaker.

Related to this model is the idea of attribution. The individual takes cues from the message or situation and judges, based on preexisting schemas, whether the situation is familiar or not. If the content of the situation seems familiar, the hearer follows the earlier path of conclusions. If the situation is not familiar, the individual attributes conclusions through abstract reasoning and inference. According to this model, comprehension is a creative process on the part of the hearer.[2]

Reference Interviews

Numerous articles have been written about the reference interview. Most of the articles stress that the reference librarian is the intermediary or

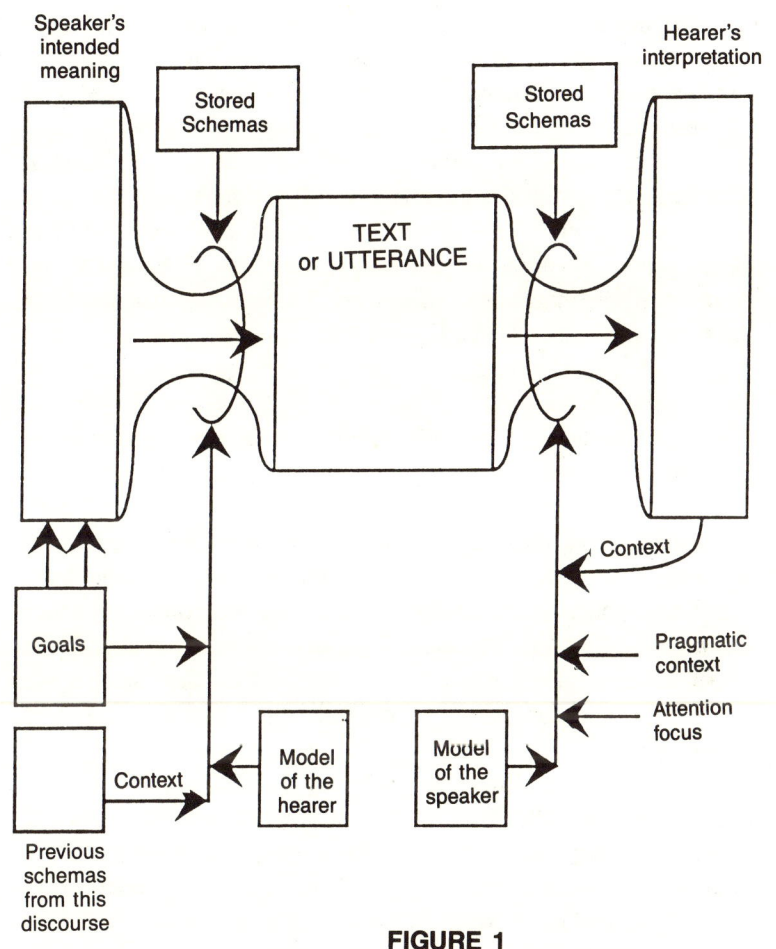

FIGURE 1
Model of Communication (Winograd)

link between the user and the information system. Articles that have been written about question negotiation tend to focus on the language used by library patrons, as opposed to that used by librarians. Ellis Mount recognized that one obstacle to a successful reference transaction is an inquirer's lack of knowledge of library terminology. This makes it difficult for the library patron to use reference tools and ask understandable questions.[3]

One article examines the use of jargon by reference staff members and users in a medical school library.[4] Library staff members were asked to record use of "short titles, terms, and abbreviations used by staff and library users to refer to any information source." The researchers conclude that jargon is used extensively in reference departments, by both staff and users. They state that jargon can be used as an effective communication tool between health professionals, who originate much of the jargon, and librarians. They recommend that library schools teach common jargon to future medical librarians.

Related to discussions about reference interviews are discussions about the language of online searching. The language of computers is now part of the language of libraries. Library users now encounter communication barriers through computer manuals, online help screens, and searching instructions provided by librarians. In one article, Bonnie Snow recommends that professional searchers customize their training methods to accommodate occasional users. She comments that "use of jargon is a habit so ingrained in most professional searchers that detecting it is one of the greatest challenges in designing handouts, visual aids, and other teaching tools."[5]

One final aspect of reference interviews that has been discussed in library literature is attitude. Librarians may assume either a vertical or horizontal relationship with library users. In a vertical relationship, an individual nurtures his or her self-concept, maintaining a superior image, with negative results for others. In a horizontal relationship, communication is positive and nonthreatening. The librarian treats the user with respect as an equal. The conversation that flows back and forth is honest, unintimidating, and noncompetitive.[6]

Written Documents

Style manuals and composition texts have defined standard rules for writing clarity. In recent years, there has been a more detailed examination of reader comprehension related to writing styles. Part of the impetus for this is the "Plain English" movement, an effort to improve the writing of public documents that were previously ambiguous or even incomprehensible to the people who used them. This movement is gaining momentum, with a number of state laws now specifying that functional documents such as insurance policies and leases be written clearly.

Many library documents are functional documents, in that they lead a person through an avenue of library research, pinpointing specific sources that must be secured and used. Because functional documents are read for use, not pleasure, they need to be written in an easy-to-follow style.[7] One principle that many advocates of Plain English feel increases readability is the avoidance of jargon.

In one research study on technical writing, David Green notes that technical terms inevitably develop with the growth of expertise in an area, and they can serve a practical function. "By using the term writers can ensure that readers familiar with its designation will understand them—that is, that they will build an appropriate mental representation."[8] Green warns against using technical terms unnecessarily or inappropriately, confronting the reader with obscure expressions rather than plain words.

In an essay on readability, Thomas Huckin stresses that the writer must consider the expertise of the audience. According to the schema theory discussed above, prior knowledge serves as a framework that makes the new information more meaningful and easier to absorb.[9] Huckin suggests that specialists can easily comprehend standard terminology in a field, even when it is long and difficult. Nonspecialists, on the other hand, need familiar concepts and require definitions, examples, analogies, and other forms of illustration. Unfortunately, as Huckin points out, writing in a way that will be optimally readable for a diverse audience is an extremely difficult task.

Several researchers have discussed the reasons why some authors adopt a tone that might be considered scholarly or aloof. This style of speaking or writing is typically impersonal, full of abstract nouns, passive sentences, and scientific-sounding technical terms. Green studied the efforts of technical writers writing for several levels of audience. He concluded that "individuals who rate their work as scientifically important are more inclined to leave technical terms undefined when they need to be defined."[10]

While articles on clear writing are available and helpful to librarians, few articles have been written about library publications *per se*.[11] In one, William Jackson states that the tone of library guides is frequently very formal, "in a style that is best understood by other librarians."[12] He advises against using words such as "stacks" to describe shelves that contain books. He also suggests that headings not merely be terms such as "Indexes and Abstracts." He points out that many of the readers who know the meaning of these terms already know how to use the reference sources. The title "Indexes and Abstracts" may alienate the library novice, discouraging him or her from reading the guide. This is obviously undesirable, since library guides are designed to teach library skills to people who need them. Jackson's preference would be the heading "Finding Journal Articles on a Topic."

This review of the literature, then, indicates concern on the part of writers and English specialists over the clarity of functional documents. Librarians have expressed a similar concern for clarity with regard to the reference interview. The communication models widely accepted within cognitive psychology, including the Winograd model, provide a context in which these issues can be examined.

EXPERIMENTAL METHOD

This study measured the comprehensibility of a list of jargon words. The list is a sample of frequently used terms culled from publications such as handouts and from reference interviews. While many of these are standard library terms, others are a reflection of the specific environment at Carnegie Mellon University Libraries. That is, some of the terms, such as "library rep," may be unique to CMU, although the concept of a departmental liaison is common to most academic libraries. In most libraries new, local terms evolve to describe services or resources.

The first part of this study determined the popularity of specific handouts, on the assumption that vocabulary used in more popular handouts would affect more students. Handouts used in this study were bibliographies on topics such as artificial intelligence, psychology, or business, and guides to resources such as the online catalog.

To measure popularity, each public service point in the Carnegie Mellon University Libraries displayed twenty-five copies of the handouts that would normally be on display, starting at 8:30 a.m. one Monday. Two days later at 8:30 a.m. the remaining handouts were counted and ranked by greatest to least number taken. From these, the ten most popular were used for the next phase of the experiment.

A class of graduate English students concentrating in technical writing was asked to identify words or phrases that they considered to be technical library terms. Aside from their availability, one reason for selecting these students was that they had had some training in editing techniques and had previous experience in identifying jargon.

The first two pages of each handout were used. For the most part, each handout was given to two students, for greater confirmation of the results. The students were asked to circle the words or multiword terms in each sample handout that they considered to be library technical language. From these results, a list of the circled terms was compiled, with a count of the number of times each word was identified. For example, if the term "viewing carrel area" was circled a total of three times, it received a score of three. Then the total number of times each word actually appeared in the total collection of handouts was counted, because many words appeared several times in the handouts. For each word, the number of times a word was identified was divided by the number of times the word actually appeared. The resulting figure, converted to a percentage, represented both degree of identification and frequency. The list could then be ranked from high to low as a means of selecting the most frequent and most identified words. A final list of ten words was derived from the written samples (see Table 1).

Using the earlier example, "viewing carrel area" appeared twice in the collection of samples distributed, once in two separate handouts. Of the four people who encountered this phrase, three identified it as being technical. The percentage 75% represented the number of times the word was identified, divided by the number of times it appeared.

An equal number of terms were sought from verbal transactions in the reference department. Four Carnegie Mellon reference librarians volunteered for tape recording of their reference interviews. They were not told the nature of the study until afterward. The tapes were transcribed and divided into two-page handouts.

The same procedure was followed for the verbal transcripts as for the written handouts. A final list of ten words was derived from the verbal samples (see Table 2).

TABLE 1
Technical Terms Derived From Written Publications

Term	Occurrences	Times Seen by Subjects	Times Identified by Subjects	% (Ident./Times Seen)
Clearinghouse	1	2	2	100
Search terms	1	2	2	100
University archives	1	2	2	100
Microform	4	7	6	86
Viewing carrel area	2	4	3	75
Catalog screen	1	2	1	50
Nonprint materials	2	2	1	50
Online database searches	1	2	2	50
Primary source	1	2	1	50
Search statement	1	2	1	50

TABLE 2
Technical Terms Derived From Verbal Transactions

Term	Occurrences	Times Seen by Subjects	Times Identified by Subjects	% (Ident./Times Seen)
Library rep	1	2	2	100
Multi-volume set	1	2	2	100
Pre-search	1	2	2	100
Call number	5	6	6	100
Citation	1	2	2	100
Command search	1	2	2	100
Proceedings	3	3	2	67
Interlibrary loan	3	5	3	60
Annual report	1	2	1	50
Bound journals	1	2	1	50

TESTING

The ten words from the written list were combined with the words from the verbal list and twenty multiple-choice questions were designed to test comprehension.[13] Each question consisted of the term followed by four possible definitions, one of which was correct. The 1983 edition of the *ALA Glossary of Library and Information Science* was used whenever possible as a basis for writing the correct definitions. Incorrect definitions were based on answers supplied by a small sampling of freshman students who were given a list of these terms and asked to define them. In addition the experimenters designed some definitions, creating logical possibilities based on their knowledge of library operations or of the words in a different context.

Subjects were informed that the terms were words or phrases used in the library. They were asked to circle the letter corresponding to the definition closest in meaning to the numbered term.

The subject group for the testing phase consisted of 100 students from freshman English classes at Carnegie Mellon. These students are required to write a research paper. Experience at Carnegie Mellon has shown that these students frequently seek the help of reference librarians and reference handouts.

RESULTS AND ANALYSIS

The tests were graded, with total number wrong noted. Table 3 shows the results, ranking the terms from least to most understood.

A social sciences statistical package, SPSS-X (release 2.0) was used to analyze the raw data. The package computed the mean and standard deviation for test scores. Also calculated were the mode and median for number of incorrect answers.

Of the total number of questions, 48.7 percent were answered incorrectly. In other words, almost half of the time subjects were not able to identify the correct definition for commonly used library terms. The mean number of incorrect answers, out of the twenty questions, was 10.290. The mode was 9 incorrect, and the median was 10. The standard deviation was 2.865. That is, the majority of results fall between 7.43 and 13.16 incorrect, which represents a normal bell curve. A breakdown of test results can be seen in Table 4.

Based on probability theory, one could expect 25 percent of the subjects to get a question right by chance if they had no knowledge of the term. If over 25 percent selected the right answer, they were performing better than chance. Conversely, one could expect 75 percent of the subjects to select a wrong answer by chance, because there are three answers that are incorrect (25 percent each).

TABLE 3
Ranking of Terms From Most to Least Understood

Term	Correct Answers
Call number	83
Bound journals	82
Interlibrary loan	75
Microform	74
Search terms	71
Catalog screen	68
Online catalog	68
Search statement	53
Online database searches	53
Pre-search	52
Library rep	47
Primary source	45
Viewing carrel area	45
University archives	41
Nonprint materials	40
Clearinghouse	38
Citation	35
Command search	25
Proceedings	20
Multi-volume set	11

N = 100 subjects.

TABLE 4
Breakdown of Test Results

Term	Correct Answers	Incorrect Answers
1. command search	25	75
2. university archives	42	58
3. catalog screen	68	32
4. viewing carrel area	45	55
5. proceedings	20	80
6. search statement	53	47
7. bound journals	82	18
8. online catalog	68	32
9. interlibrary loan	75	25
10. primary source	45	55
11. nonprint materials	40	60
12. online database searches	53	47
13. clearinghouse	37	63
14. pre-search	52	48
15. multi-volume set	11	89
16. microform	76	24
17. citations	35	65
18. search terms	71	29
19. call number	83	17
20. library rep	48	52

N = 100 subjects.
Number of questions answered incorrectly:
  Mean: 10.290
  Median: 10
  Mode: 9

LINGUISTIC ANALYSIS

Numerical data alone gave no clue as to the underlying schemas from which the subjects drew their responses. Protocol analysis was used to give an indication of the reasoning processes. This technique involves methods that attempt to determine the mental processes that a person uses to perform a task. In a verbal or thinking-aloud protocol, subjects are asked to perform a task while thinking aloud as they interact with a document. Because subjects are asked to verbalize anything that comes to mind as they work, their information is more complete and accurate than any comments collected after the task is completed. When people experience difficulty in understanding text, their comments often reveal the nature of the difficulty.[14]

In this study, four subjects, all freshmen, were given the multiple-choice test and asked to verbalize their thoughts as they selected answers. Their comments were tape recorded and transcribed. The transcripts then were coded, with phrases of verbalized thoughts assigned a category of reasoning strategy, as represented in the continuum illustrated in Figure 2. The researchers arrived at these categories by looking at each comment individually and by grouping each verbalization into classes.

The results of the protocols showed that the subjects used a variety of methods to deduce an answer. Often they admitted to simply guessing. Frequently they used standard test-taking techniques, such as comparing the specificity of the answers to the question, to make their decision.

At the other end of the spectrum, the subjects sometimes said that they knew the answer. The protocols indicated, for instance, that subjects were familiar with the concept of interlibrary loan. In one protocol a subject stated: "Interlibrary loan . . . yes, I know this . . . there we go, b, 'cause I know, we have it at school . . . obtaining items from another library system through your library."

In this case, the protocols were in keeping with the multiple-choice results, in which 73 people out of 100 answered this question correctly. In the testing, almost all *incorrect* respondents gave the answer "the ability

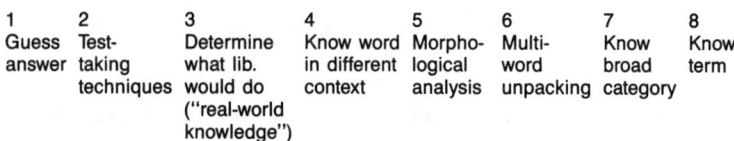

1	2	3	4	5	6	7	8
Guess answer	Test-taking techniques	Determine what lib. would do ("real-world knowledge")	Know word in different context	Morpho-logical analysis	Multi-word unpacking	Know broad category	Know term

FIGURE 2
Categories of Reasoning Strategies

to check books out *in person* from a library other than your own."[15] Both the protocols and multiple-choice tests showed that subjects connected "interlibrary loan" with obtaining materials from another library, but many subjects were unclear about the exact procedure.

Aside from subjects knowing or not knowing the answer, subjects used the other techniques pictured in figure 2 to derive their answers. These methods were of particular interest, because they give a realistic profile of how people arrive at a definition when they do not know the term. When people are unfamiliar with a term used by a librarian, they fall back on their previous knowledge, whether of semantics or of the term in another context, to select a likely answer. This related to Winograd's and Huckin's discussions of schema theory mentioned earlier.

Two semantic techniques, morphological analysis and multiword unpacking, were used to break down terms into their component parts to arrive at definitions. The remaining techniques (3, 4, and 7 in figure 2) were related to previous experience of some sort. In morphological analysis, a word is broken down into segments (prefixes, roots, suffixes). Each segment is defined individually, or, if of foreign origin, translated. The component definitions are reconstituted to arrive at a sum definition of the word as a unit. An example can be seen in this portion of a transcript:

> Microform . . . (a) a picture enlarged for an overhead projector . . . no, micro means small . . . (b) a machine that amplifies or records the voice . . . hmmm, no . . . (c) a generic term for all forms of smaller images on photographic film . . . yeah, that's possible, 'cause form is sort of general . . . (d) any library material that is not in paper form . . . Yeah, it's probably c, 'cause that . . . fits the description of micro and form.

While this subject arrived at the correct answer, some others that used this method did not. For instance, one of the four protocol subjects broke down the term "nonprint materials" into "materials that cannot be printed," presumably since "non," from Latin, has several negative meanings.

"Multiword unpacking" refers to breaking down noun compounds such as "online database searches" or "call number." The issue of how readers interpret compound nouns is complex, because the words in a string of nouns do not always modify each other in the same way. Is a "viewing carrel area" an area for viewing carrels? Or is it an area containing carrels that view, or carrels for viewing? It is even unclear whether "viewing" serves as a verb or an adjective. The reader must define the meaning of each word and then determine the connection between each word and the others, which may indicate a relationship of composition (brick house), user (student handbook), source (bank loan), purpose (calligraphy pen), and so on. One noun phrase can be potentially ambiguous in as many as twelve different ways, although some of the ambiguity is mitigated by practical considerations such as context.[16]

All of this mental unpacking is time-consuming and may not lead to a correct "translation." However, a person does get more chances to estimate a correct definition, because each word gives a clue as to the term's meaning. An example of this method can be seen in one subject's statement: "Call number. Yes, that is the number . . . each book is assigned . . . so that you can call it up."

The other method by which subjects used resources at their disposal to figure out the answer was based on context. Some subjects, though unfamiliar with a specific term, seemed to have a sense of its broader category. Answering the question "command search," for example, one subject said, "Something from a computer . . . I know it's on a computer." Closely related to this is the technique of trying to reason out how a library would actually function ("real-world knowledge"). The same subject continued, "I know it's on a computer, but checking out book on computer . . . no that's not checking it out . . . person at the desk cannot do that." While in this case the subject was wrong about library operations, he created his response by trying to match up his existing computer schema with his library schema.

The final method employed by subjects was selection of an answer based on knowledge of the word in a nonlibrary context. Many terms such as "archives," "proceedings" or "clearinghouse" have several meanings outside of the library. In choosing the answer for the term *citation*, many subjects were confused by another, nonlibrary use of this word. In one of the protocols, a subject verbalized this: "Um, citation is like a ticket or something for speeding." In a nonlibrary context, *citation* has a negative connotation, usually involving a fine. As one might expect based on Winograd's communication model, subjects took whatever exposure they had had to the term and transferred this knowledge, with incorrect results. This is confirmed by the multiple-choice testing, in which the majority of subjects, forty-four, defined citation as "a notice of overdue library materials."

SUMMARY: PRACTICAL IMPLICATIONS

Although each profession has its share of jargon, librarianship is such a heavily user-oriented field that any indication of a lack of communication should be given serious attention. The results reported here indicate clearly that there is a communications problem between librarians and patrons. Librarians cannot rely on the patrons to decipher a meaning from the context. Patrons rely on their existing schemas to help them interpret an unfamiliar term. If these schemas are lacking or incorrect, communication will be unsuccessful.

Given that patrons only understand 50 percent of what librarians say or write, what are the options available to library staff members for closing this gap? The following represents a list of options ranging from the least to most accommodating:

- use terms without defining them, and let the patron sink or swim
- use terms without defining them but be alert to verbal and non-verbal cues from the patrons indicating confusion
- solicit feedback from the user as you go along, asking, for instance, "Interlibrary loan—do you know what that is?"
- use visual aids to assist the patron, such as pointing to the components of a citation
- define terms the first time they are used in an interaction or publication, and then use them subsequently without definition
- use formal library instruction to teach library technical language
- append glossaries of terms to written publications
- avoid local terms not useful for patrons' future needs
- define technical terms whenever you use them
- avoid jargon altogether

Neither end of the continuum is ideal. On the one hand, patrons would be poorly served by totally ignoring their need for the definition of these terms. On the other hand, it is impractical, time-consuming, and unnecessary to define terms every time they are used.

The options between the extremes seem most reasonable and helpful. The best method to select will depend upon the personalities of both the librarian and the individual patron. Often a combination of methods will be effective, whereas one alone might be insufficient. For instance, if a librarian relies on his or her ability to distinguish confusion, verbally or nonverbally, there is a chance that subtle cues may be missed. However, if the librarian is also giving a visual demonstration, on the online catalog, for instance, missed communication is less likely.

While this study offers new information regarding comprehension of library jargon, there are many other avenues for further research. Not studied was the actual amount of technical language used by librarians in proportion to other language. Of further interest would be a comparison of terms identified as jargon by librarians as opposed to patrons. Other tests could also be done to extend the research on patron comprehension. It is possible, for instance, that patrons perform better in real-life situations where terms are presented in context. Mock situations could be constructed that are more realistic, or actual transactions could be monitored. It would also be interesting to see how comprehension of technical language might change as one's education progresses. A similar study would be a before-and-after testing with regard to library instruction. It would also be useful to explore the possibility of enhancing library instruction to increase patrons' abilities to interpret and use the many library terms that they obviously do not, at present, comprehend.

References and Notes

1. Terry Winograd, "A Framework for Understanding Discourse," in *Cognitive Processes in Comprehension*, ed. Marcel Adam Just and Patricia A. Carpenter (Hillsdale: Erlbaum, 1977), p. 63–88.
2. Saul M. Kassin and Joan B. Pryor, "The Development of Attribution Processes," in *The Development of Social Cognition*, ed. John B. Pryor and Jeanne D. Day (New York: Springer-Verlag, 1985), p. 3–34.
3. Ellis Mount, "Communication Barriers and the Reference Question," *Special Libraries* 57:575–78 (Oct. 1966).
4. Ruth E. Fenske and Lynn M. Fortney, "The Use of Jargon in Medical School Libraries," *Bulletin of the Medical Library Association* 74:12–15 (Jan. 1986).
5. Bonnie Snow, "What Jargon Is Really Necessary When Teaching (And Learning) Online Skills?" *Online* 10:100–107 (July 1986).
6. Nathan M. Smith and Stephen D. Fitt, "Vertical-Horizontal Relationships: Their Appli-

cation for Librarians," *Special Libraries* 66:528–31 (Nov. 1975).
7. Linda Flower, *Revising Functional Documents: The Scenario Principle*, Communications Design Center Technical Report no. 10 (Pittsburgh: Carnegie Mellon University, 1980), p. 7.
8. David W. Green, "Writing, Jargon, and Research," *Written Communication* 3:364–81 (July 1986).
9. Thomas N. Huckin, "A Cognitive Approach to Readability," in *New Essays in Technical and Scientific Communications: Research, Theory, Practice*, ed. Paul V. Anderson, R. John Brockmann, and Carolyn R. Miller (Farmingdale, N.Y.: Baywood Pub. Co., 1983), p. 92.
10. Green, "Writing," p. 371.
11. Rachael Naismith, "Establishing a Library Publications Program," *College & Research Libraries News* 2:59–60+ (Feb. 1985).
12. William J. Jackson, "The User-Friendly Library Guide," *College & Research Libraries News* 45:468–71 (Oct. 1984).
13. For a copy of the graded test, write to either of the authors at Carnegie Mellon University Libraries, Frew Street, Pittsburgh, Pa. 15213.
14. Karen A. Schriver, *Plain Language for Expert or Lay Audiences: Designing Text Using Protocol-Aided Revision*, Communications Design Center Technical Report no. 43 (Pittsburgh: Carnegie Mellon University, 1987), p. 10.
15. The actual question, with number of responses, read:
    Interlibrary loan:
    (a) book purchase funds shared by more than one library—2
    (b) *obtaining items from another library system through your library—75*
    (c) the ability to check books out in person from a library other than your own—15
    (d) obtaining books or photocopies from other campus libraries—8
16. Pamela Downing, "On the Creation and Use of English Compound Nouns," *Language* 53:810–41 (Dec. 1977).

A SURVEY OF AMERICAN ZOO AND AQUARIUM ARCHIVES

Linda Rohr

Introduction

In the fall of 1986 I conducted a survey of 161 zoos and aquariums in the United States. The purpose of the survey was to identify the presence and condition of archival material in zoos and aquariums. The survey was designed to answer the questions:

1. What type of materials exist?
2. Where is it kept?
3. Does anyone manage the material?
4. How are the materials used?

Library and Archival Collections

The 1986 edition of the American Association of Zoological Parks and Aquariums (AAZPA) Directory lists 139 accredited zoos and aquariums and 25 related organizations as members.

The oldest zoo in the United States may be the Lincoln Park Zoo in Chicago which opened in 1868. Certainly a close second and traditionally called the oldest American zoo is the Philadelphia Zoo which was chartered in 1858 and opened in 1874. A few more zoos opened to the public before the turn of the century, most notably the Baltimore Zoo (1876), Cleveland Metroparks Zoological Park (1882) and the New York Zoological Park, better known as the Bronx Zoo (1899).

Since those first zoos were founded, the role of zoos has changed greatly. Far from offering only recreational possibilities, zoos and aquariums are now involved in the conservation, education and research on a global scale of their valuable animal collections. As a result, information needs have rapidly expanded and increased.

Some zoos and aquariums established formal libraries to organize their materials and to provide access to information. According to a zoo library survey conducted in 1981, out of 157 questionnaires sent, 138 responded and 104 indicated they had a library.[1] However, "a library is not just a collection of books and serials. It must also provide information services and this involves having someone with some library skills."[2] With that standard in mind, in fact only about 42 zoo and aquarium libraries exist in North America. Collection sizes and scope vary greatly. A small zoo or aquarium library may have less than 200 monographs. The largest contains over 9,000 volumes; the majority contain fewer than 1,000 volumes. Journal subscriptions range from none to over 600. Only 4 have more than 200.[3] Less than 20 of those zoos or aquariums with a library engage a professional librarian and nearly half of those librarians are volunteers with full-time positions in another library. More likely, other zoo personnel such as secretaries, curators, or directors maintain the zoo or aquarium library.

Zoo library collections are relatively specific, and yet within a zoo library the user may have access to materials covering topics like animal behavior and natural history, conservation and ecology, veterinary medicine, zoo design and management, nutrition and horticulture. The user profile includes directors, curators, keepers, educators, researchers, veterinarian staff, docents, graphic designers and planners, maintenance personnel, and zoological society members as well as the public.

In addition to their main library materials, some zoos and aquariums have archival materials and special collections. These may or may not be included with the main collection. Archival programs are more unusual than libraries in zoos and aquariums. That is not to say that zoos or aquariums do not have archival material, but it does indicate a lack of commitment on the part of the zoo administrators concerning non-current materials. One survey respondent commented, "I've never thought of any of these things we've been storing as archives."

While the zoo or aquarium library serves the zoo staff and a wide variety of other users interested in its current information collection, the archives are important additionally for scientists, researchers, historians and other users who seek information to reconstruct the daily activities of the zoo's past. The information zoo or aquarium archives yield is important for exhibit planning, special events, public relations, promotions and publications. But its primary importance is for animal records management. As stated earlier, zoos and aquariums are more involved than ever before in conservation and research efforts to manage endangered animal species. To do this successfully, the depth of a zoo's own record system is invaluable.[4]

Relatively little is written about zoo and aquarium archives. While a survey was conducted on the condition of zoo and aquarium libraries, none prior to 1986 surveyed specifically the existence of archival material.

Methodology

A two page survey form comprised 18 questions answered by yes/no, multiple choice and short answer was sent to 161 zoos, aquariums, and "related member organizations" in the fall of 1986. A cover letter introduced me as a library science graduate student at Simmons College conducting the survey as a project for an independent study course. It also explained briefly what types of documents might be considered archival material. I suggested a deadline date, enclosed a self-addressed stamped envelope and waited.

The response rate was very high; 79 (49%) responded. Of those, 75 (95%) reported holding archival material. Two of the 4 institutions responding that they do not have archival material are privately owned institutions such as game farms or breeding farms. However, if they retain business or animal records for any length of time they probably will have archival material. I had suspected that privately owned "related member organizations" might be reluctant to disclose information regarding their records and papers; only 4 (17%) of 23 member institutions surveyed did respond and 2 thought the survey had been sent to them by mistake.

What Types of Material Exist?

As might be expected, little reported material pre-dates 1900 primarily because there were few zoos open. Only one zoo holds material from 1800–1849 (Philadelphia Zoo) and 7 (9%) have material from 1850–1900. More zoos and aquariums (43%) saved material from 1901–1950, and nearly all the respondents (99%) have material from 1951 to present.

The questionnaire requested the respondent to estimate the overall volume of material either as number of boxes or linear feet. This proved to be a difficult question to answer since most respondents are unfamiliar with judging documents in that way. Responses ranged from 1 box to 100 boxes, most saying 1 to 4 boxes (about 23%) and several estimating 10 boxes (13%). Most measured their material by boxes or file cabinets (56%) while only 20% used linear feet as a measure. Twenty-three percent couldn't give an estimate because they were unsure about measurement or simply could not identify all the material in their facility. Most institutions do not catalog or process the material (65%) and most just maintain what they already have or what comes to them by serendipity (57%).

The majority of zoos collect just about everything which will yield information about their institution (see Figure 1). Material from former and present directors (69%), from curators (63%), the veterinary staff (59%), and keeper staff (56%) are retained. In general, 57% collect correspondence of various types. Financial information (57%), library newsletters (59%), films (33%), administrative papers (61%), photographs of pertinent subjects (79%), conference papers (65%), articles written by zoo/aquarium personnel (52%), oral history tapes (12%), and maps or blueprints (37%) are saved. Only 31% felt they had "unique" collections. Some are very interesting, however; Lincoln Park Zoo has a Zoo Poster Collection comprised of over 60 posters from national and international institutions. The posters are consulted primarily by the zoo's graphics department.[5] The Franklin Park Zoo in Boston has about 30 years of diaries written by a former director.

Where Is It Kept?

Most archival material is kept in various zoo administrative offices (73%). Less than half (39%) of zoo libraries house the material and only 5% have archives to store the documents. The Smithsonian Institution Archives collects the National Zoo material as well as material from all other Smithsonian departments. Some zoos hold records in "storage" (11%) pending

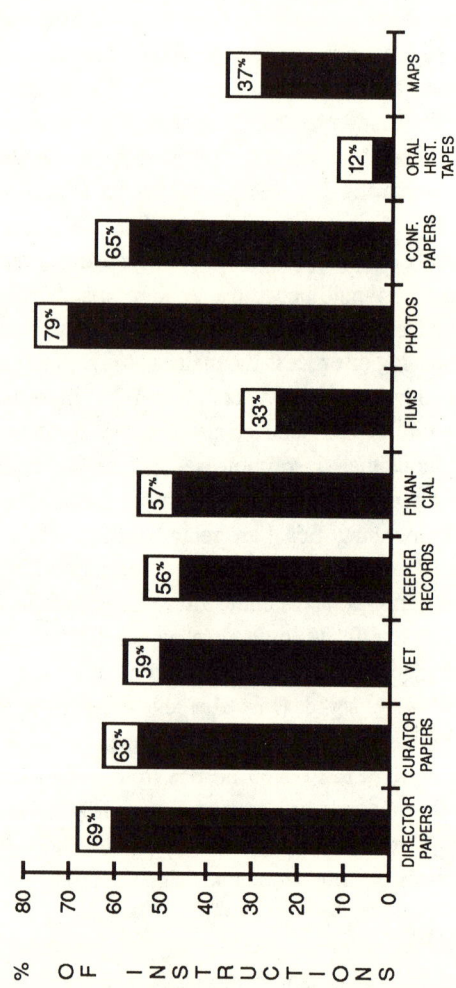

FIGURE 1. Archival Material Collected

future archives or library construction. Education departments (7%) frequently are sites for this material, as is the veterinary clinic (7%) which seems consistently to maintain its own records, both current and archival. The remaining documents can be found in local public libraries, parks department offices, or municipal offices if the institution is municipally owned. This latter example is the case for the San Francisco Zoo, which does not retain any archival material.

Does Anyone Manage the Material?

Because libraries are scarce in zoos and aquariums, it was not surprising to find that the material is kept more often by other staff (32%) than by librarians (25%). Only two zoos indicated that the archivist takes care of the material, although several librarians listed their titles as Librarian/Archivist. More frequently, the director (11%), curator (12%), secretary (12%) or the education department (13%) maintains the material. Often several people or departments ("originating office or appropriate office") are enlisted to care for the material (47%). This is an indication that documents are distributed throughout the facility and not collected centrally. However, the trend seems to be to at least engage a professional librarian or archivist in some capacity to care for the materials. Some zoos said they were looking for a retired librarian or volunteer librarian to do the work.

How Are the Materials Used?

Public access to zoo records is connected directly to the type of legal authority under which a zoo operates. Municipal zoos make their resources available to the public while those operated by zoological societies or privately owned tend to restrict the material more. However, most (65%) restrict the material to in-house use. Sometimes this is because it is too scattered for easy public access. In one instance, a zoo lost material to a user and will not make the archives available again. Many said the public may see unrestricted material and/or must make an appointment to use the archives. Since it is important to pursue ways to make the archival material available for as much justified use as possible, zoos and aquariums would be wise to open their collections to the public. It is only through increased accessibility that archivists can justify the expense, space and effort needed to make their collections valuable.

However, zoos and aquariums are not interested in advertising the existence of their material. Eighty-five percent do not do any form of outreach. Ten percent use the AAZPA and 1% advertise in local directories, NUC, Lee Ash's *Subject Collections* and International Species Inventory Systems (ISIS), which is not really advertising since it is a computer based animal records system. The Smithsonian advertises in their own publications. Some left the question unanswered, some thought advertising was "inappropriate at this time." This restrictive attitude corresponds to the response to the above question regarding public access to the material. If the public is not allowed to use the documents, there is little reason to advertise and 95% do not encourage the public to use these materials.

When it comes to funding, zoo and aquarium archives are not well supported. Ninety-seven percent of the zoos do not supply a separate budget for conservation or preservation of archival material. Sometimes money may be made available through the library budget, but more often there is only one all-encompassing budget for the entire institution which leaves little money for "extras" such as archives. As one respondent said "Information needs are current, and archival management would be an unaffordable luxury at the moment." Another said ". . . we are just beginning to have a viable library."

Conclusions

Archival materials are currently a low priority in zoos and aquariums in the United States. Minimal funding and space as well as a shortage of qualified personnel are the major problems. This survey yielded a 49% response; with over half of the institutions unaccounted for, it is difficult to make knowledgeable guesses on the condition of the archival material for all American zoos and aquariums. But it seems safe to conjecture that the state of archival material in American zoos and aquariums is precarious. Possibly much has been lost or will be unretrievable in the future if it is not properly preserved. Archival material originating from the Louisville Zoo is transferred to the city archives where it is only kept for 5 years. Certainly many people who are responsible for their institution's archival material are aware of its importance. Wildlife Safari in Winston, Oregon commented "You have opened up thoughts that perhaps we should be doing this on a more formal, organized level." Most indicated that they expect better facilities in the future. Plans for new libraries and archives were mentioned many times, and to my surprise, many were in small, less well-endowed institutions. But others said the archival material did not have priority and due to financial limitations the future does not look any brighter. Some acknowledged that space was at such a premium that they were now more selective about keeping materials, and one mentioned that keepers' records of their animals' daily lives are only kept for 2 years. Keeper diaries, in particular, are most valuable for verifying office records concerning facts about the daily circumstances of individual animals. Only keepers, with their close daily contact with the animals, can accurately report these events. Studbook keepers and researchers find the information in these diaries essential for piecing together animal genealogies.

When archival material is present and thought of as useful, another problem arises. Curators, the director, or other administrators, decline to give the material a central collection site. In some situations, as already mentioned, space is limited. However, allowing material to remain scattered in various offices, which is the predominant situation (73%) is a condition that does not encourage good archival management. Lincoln Park Zoo in Chicago applied successfully for an Institute of Museum Services Grant (IMS) for an archivist to help the library staff complete an inventory and develop an ongoing archives conservation program. The New York Zoological Society (Bronx Zoo), funded by a state preservation grant, has contracted with the Northeast Document Conservation Center for a site survey of the archives and library. The archives at Bronx Zoo supported an in-house production of a 20-minute film "depicting 90 years of wildlife conservation activity by the New York Zoological Society and a detailed chronology of that history."[6] These situations are encouraging and hopefully will inspire other institutions to follow suit.

Not every project needs to be conducted on a grand, expensive scale. The docents at St. Louis Zoo arranged for archivists at the University of Missouri-St. Louis' Western Historical Manuscript Collection to microfilm 40 years of written records through 1940. They also organized several hundred photographs. Each photograph was put in a protective sleeve, assigned a number and identified. Now with an index available, future researchers have access to zoo records that may aid the zoo in celebrating its 75th year as well as in planning its future.[7]

But, in general, the librarians and archivists already working in zoos and aquariums must become more assertive about lobbying for these kinds of programs. Every field needs proponents or lobbyists and archival work is no different. Zoo librarians and archivists and those knowledgeable about zoo history should follow the pattern being set up by other professions in creating long-term documentation strategies for their records.[8] Zoo and aquarium archivists may need to learn what their corporate and museum counterparts already know: an archivist's major task is to educate and convince the powers-that-be that the archives are a valuable component of the institution. Archives improve the zoo by increasing information availability and promoting research and conservation. San Diego Zoo responded:

> We have found that corporate use of the archives has been increasing every year. It is an area that helps to market the library within the organization and to keep a high profile, particularly with the business/administrative personnel, who usually don't use a natural history library.

Zoo archives need to be recognized and promoted as a valuable and contributing asset, rather than seen as a luxury to be supported when the institution can afford it.

Editor's Note: An issue devoted to a description of libraries maintained at zoos contains information about the role of archives to some extent.[9]

References

1. Ryan, Kathleen; Kenyon, Kay. Zoological libraries. *Sci-Tech News*. 38(2): 33–4. 1984 April.
2. Kenyon, Kay. Zoo/Aquarium libraries—a survey. *Special Libraries*. 75(4): 329–334; 1984 October.
3. Ibid.

4. Collins, Terry; Hamer, Allegra. Archive programs for zoological parks and aquariums. In: *AAZPA Regional Conference Proceedings, 1981*, p. 99–102.
5. Shaw, Joyce M. Lincoln Park Zoo Library: an introduction to the library and special collections. *Illinois Libraries*. 66(4): 164–166; 1984 April.
6. Johnson, Steve. Flood doesn't slow activities at N.Y. Zoo Society Archives. *Museum Archivist*. 2(2): 4; 1988 September.
7. Loughlin, Caroline. Dedicated volunteer team works behind the scenes to help preserve the zoo's precious archives. *ZUDUS*. 2(2): 2; 1988 May/June.
8. Hackman, Larry; Warnow-Blewett, Joan. The documentation strategy process: a model and a case study. *American Archivist*. 50(1): 12–47; 1987 Winter.
9. *Science & Technology Libraries*. 8(4): 1988 Summer.

LEARNING ABOUT CD-ROM TECHNOLOGY: AN EDUCATOR'S PERSPECTIVE ON SOURCES, ISSUES, CRITERIA, BREAKTHROUGHS, AND RESEARCH

Richard S. Halsey

CD-ROM technology is alluring but generally overpriced at this stage of its development. It can, however, offer substantial cost benefits and accelerated access to information seekers if used with full knowledge of its capabilities and limitations. Advantage will flow only to those individuals and institutions that can comprehend, weigh, and predict the economics of use that distinguish this particular information carrier from online, microform, print and other storage-access media; adversity will afflict those who are not as well informed.

It is difficult for a librarian to acquire adequate knowledge just from reading about CD-ROMs because the technical, library, and promotional literatures vary in reliability, clarity, authoritativeness, and currency. The technical literature, including such sources as the *Proceedings of the Society of the Photo-Optical Instrumentation Engineers*, various IEEE Transactions, *Applied Optics, Journal of Electronics Engineering, Journal of Imaging Technology, Journal of Applied Physics*, and reports issued by the Matsushita Electric Industrial Company, Philips, and GE give state-of-the-art information. Because at least 90 percent of the CD research is being conducted in industrial labs and schools of engineering, the technical literature is on the leading edge and can provide the best insights

---

"Learning About CD-ROM Technology: An Educator's Perspective on Sources, Issues, Criteria, Breakthroughs, and Research," by Richard S. Halsey in *Information & Technologies & Libraries* Vol. 8, no. 1 (March 1989), pp. 56–62; reprinted with permission from the American Library Association, copyright © 1989 by ALA.

regarding such factors as dimensional stability, abrasion resistance, standards, error correction, resolution, filing systems, servers, and specifications for other CD formats. For most librarians, however, these sources, because they presume their readers' command of mathematics and engineering, remain out of bounds. But is this really a critical deficiency? How many chefs know how to build and wire microwave ovens, electric ranges, and refrigerators? The technical publications are still tops in timeliness and reliability, while the derivative articles in the library literature focus on user experience and comparative costs and gloss over specifications instead of providing hard data.

Finally, and least dependable because of its self-touting nature, is that all-too-familiar literature, the writings of those affiliated with the anti- or pro-CD-ROM camps. Online promoters see problems galore with CD-ROM and vice versa.

Consequently, librarians should supplement their reading with observations, which means attending (with checklists in hand) such events as the annual CD-ROM Expo and the LITA conferences. These meetings introduce attendees to strategies and applications for library and information services and also reveal the activity in product development. Of course, wariness on the sales floor is crucial: the sellers' enthusiasm can mask the products' shortcomings.

The buyer's library is of course the best site for bringing together CD-ROM experts and librarians. The application of CD-ROM can best be judged in a real library setting, and librarians on their own turf can more freely compare the library's needs to the wonderland of technology.

Learning From Experts

Librarians cum information professionals who want to get dependable guidance from CD-ROM experts must learn how to employ two techniques, *interrogation* and *confrontation*.

The first of these uses the skill of posing questions to solicit information that is relevant and valid. What can the expert say that will justify a decision to go with or reject CD-ROM? (For example, is online, CD-ROM, print, or a mixture preferred for a particular reference source and why?) And how much confidence can be placed in what experts say? This same modus operandi applies to testimony in the courtroom, where expert witnesses are often found to be as fallible or ignorant in some respects as the questioners.

The purpose of the second technique, confrontation, is to promote discussion among two or more respected experts that generates knowledge, facts, and true cost projections rather than arguments that result merely in the exchange of more ignorance. The point is to observe how contending experts interact, incorporating information gleaned from previous interrogations. Where and why do they agree? Where and why do they disagree? The quality of answers can be assessed only if the right questions are posed, which is why this must be a two-step process. Fortunately, these skills are learnable and are common currency in our culture (see "Perry Mason," "L.A. Law"). This adversarial game may not be entirely transferable or comfortable because of librarians' inclination to be trusting, but it does make a good start and, if played right, could increase severalfold the effectiveness of technology-driven decisions in situations where dollars and knowledge of current optical disk technology and systems are in short supply.

Criteria for CD-ROM

In any case, when considering CD-ROM products, it is absolutely essential to think carefully about compatibility of the content with the disk format as well as the context and economics of use; local capacity to support CD-ROM's potential; quality and quantity of available hardware and readiness for networking; size and flexibility of budgeting; perceptions and preparedness of users, staff, and administrators; and anticipated frequency of demand. Factors relating to content are size of the knowledge base, complexity and range of subject matter, and susceptibility of the material to obsolescence. Beyond libraries, examples of successful utilization of CD-ROM include the U.S. Postal Service's national address file with 109 million delivery addresses arranged within 25 million address data records and associated ZIP+4 information. The new system will be considerably more reliable than the older online system that depended upon temperamental telephone links. Microfiche will be retained as a distribution medium.

Reference and Collection Development Issues 335

NYNEX, which has converted its 10 million telephone directory listings in Boston and New York City onto a single CD-ROM and makes the disk and search and retrieval software available, is betting that corporate customers, because of the projected gain in efficiencies of operation, will be willing to pay the annual $10,000 fee for this service, as will law enforcement and marketing agencies and firms that process credit applications for which sorting and report generation are critically important functions.

The use of CD-ROM systems for resource sharing is also becoming increasingly common. In New York State, a CD-ROM union catalog has been developed for the Long Island Library Resources Council and Nassau Library Systems to accommodate access to machine-readable bibliographic records and collections of member libraries. And in California, the Los Angeles Unified School District hopes to boost library services with an automated computer system for management, enhancement of library services, and student instruction. Similar utilization to networking and management has been reported in Missouri, Hawaii, and New York. The Fred Meyer Charitable Trust, besides issuing state-of-the-art reports, has committed money to the Washington Library Network so that nine high schools can purchase this technology. The Albany-Schenectady-Schoharie Counties School Library System (New York) is converting its union catalog to CD-ROM.

The number of basic reference works (e.g., atlases, dictionaries, encyclopedias, biographical directories); abstracting and indexing services (e.g., *Wilsondisc, Science Citation Index, PsychLIT*); and major databases (e.g., *AGRICOLA, Books in Print, ERIC, MEDLINE, NTIS, CD-MARC*) being converted to CD-ROM continues to expand. More than 500 titles for business and reference are on the market or in the planning stages. To date, several considerations taken as a whole tend to prime publishers' willingness to develop CD-ROM products. Most important among these is the assurance that urgency, irrefutable need, and purchasing power will generate sufficient income to justify investment. The medical and legal professions, financial markets, military, and, to a lesser extent, public education have the incentive and dollars to pay for the product. Without such assurance, publishers will not move into a high-risk area in which much more work must be done in the development of front-end systems minds, indexing, software programs, editing, color and resolution, networking and provision for simultaneous access, negotiation of rights and releases, and sophisticated multiformat programs. As publishers move into the CD-ROM arena, librarians should assist them in determining which reference sources are most congenial with the medium. For the reference specialist, the following three factors stand out as being critically important:

1. Ease of conversion to CD-ROM. The less the producer has to index, classify, organize, or reorganize the content, the better.
2. Longevity of the information's value. Treasuries of quotations, *Harvard Classics, Hortus II,* and *Oxford English Dictionary* contain knowledge with a very slow decay rate; in contrast, airline guides, real estate listings, social studies texts, and commodities exchange price quotations are outdated quickly. The cost of updating a database frequently is high.
3. Size of the database. Because of the extraordinary compression achievable by CD-ROM, databases exceeding 2 gigabytes are especially compatible with this medium.

Figure 1 illustrates the relative appropriateness of various reference tools for CD-ROM as a cube showing a least-likely product—a regional weather advisory service—on the lower left, inside corner; a grouping of most promising products clustered around the upper right, outside corner; and other items with varying qualifications.

Figure 2 includes some of the CD-ROM candidates shown in figure 1 as well as several additional examples of items, some already published in this format and others still in the planning stage or existing only in the mind of this writer. A rating of 8 or 9 for a real or hypothetical product indicates a promising candidate for the format; items with lower scores may also be justified if the targeted audiences are affluent and strongly motivated to use the product.

Each item is given a score of 1, 2, or 3 across each criterion dimension: ease of organization (A), usable lifetime (B), and size of database (C). The U.S. Postal Service *Zip Code Directory*; NYNEX telephone directory of Boston and New York City; a cumulation of recipes in major cookbooks with a master index of ingredients, nutritional data, nationalities, and regions, and large retrospective databases such as *AGRICOLA, CC/*

Reference and Collection Development Issues

MEDLINE, CDMARC-Subjects, and *NTIS*—all earn perfect 9-point scores, 3 being credited to each criterion.

Barriers to Realization of CD-ROM's Promise

The progress of CD-ROM is being hindered for a number of reasons so that it may not remain viable. Although lack of uniform standards is a barrier, it is a lesser one than the certain prospect of substantial research and development costs. Because of this and the attendant financial risk,

**FIGURE 1
CD-ROM CUBE OF APPROPRIATENESS**

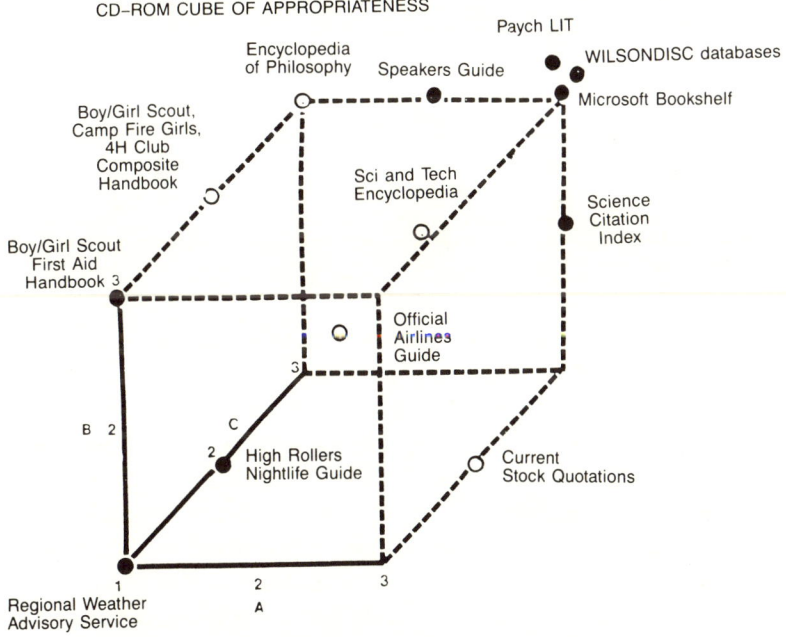

A—axis Ease of conversion or organization
B—axis Longevity of value to user
C—axis Size of database

FIGURE 2
Real and Hypothetical CD-ROM Candidates

PsychLIT	(A)-3, (B)-3, (C)-3 = 9
Retrospective indexes (e.g., *Wilsondisc* databases)	(A)-3, (B)-3, (C)-3 = 9
Ency. of American History	(A)-3, (B)-3, (C)-3 = 9
Legal Citations Index	(A)-3, (B)-3, (C)-3 = 9
Library-of-the-Month Club	(A)-3, (B)-3, (C)-3 = 9
Compact Disclosure	(A)-3, (B)-3, (C)-3 = 9
Microsoft Bookshelf (includes *Chicago Manual of Style, Roget's Thesaurus, American Heritage Dictionary, Bartlett's Familiar Quotations, National Five-Digit ZIP Code and Post Office Directory, World Almanac and Book of Facts*)	(A)-3, (B)-3, (C)-3 = 9
Speakers' Guide, an integrated "omnium-gatherum" of aphorisms, jokes, and literary quotations	(A)-2, (B)-3, (C)-3 = 8
Myth and Magic Encyclopedia	(A)-2, (B)-3, (C)-3 = 8
Science Citation Index with bibliographic-coupling feature	(A)-3, (B)-2, (C)-3 = 8
Guide to Classical Music Recordings	(A)-3, (B)-2, (C)-3 = 8
Self-help health guides	(A)-1, (B)-3, (C)-3 = 7
Encyclopedia of Philosophy	(A)-1, (B)-3, (C)-3 = 7
Auto Manual Miscellany	(A)-2, (B)-2, (C)-3 = 7
Sci & Tech Encyclopedia	(A)-2, (B)-2, (C)-3 = 7
Directory of librarians and information specialists	(A)-2, (B)-2, (C)-3 = 7
Official Airlines Guide	(A)-2, (B)-2, (C)-2 = 6
News Bank	(A)-2, (B)-1, (C)-3 = 6
Adult encyclopedia	(A)-2, (B)-1, (C)-3 = 6
Boy/Girl Scout, Camp Fire Girls, 4-H Club composite handbook	(A)-1, (B)-3, (C)-2 = 6
Current Stock Quotations	(A)-3, (B)-1, (C)-2 = 6
Electronic Yellow Pages	(A)-1, (B)-2, (C)-3 = 6
Directory of Lobbyists	(A)-3, (B)-1, (C)-2 = 6
Boy/Girl Scout First Aid Handbook	(A)-1, (B)-3, (C)-1 = 5
High Rollers' Nightlife Guide to Baltimore, New Orleans, Atlanta and Miami	(A)-1, (B)-1, (C)-2 = 4
Regional weather advisory service	(A)-1, (B)-1, (C)-1 = 3

CD-ROM products are much more pricey than they would be if the technology were settled into the marketplace. For that to happen, the following missing ingredients should be in place: (1) cheap disk servers that preclude the necessity for manual changing and the resultant wear of the medium; (2) CD-ROM drives priced below $500; (3) development of network-server capacity in a distributed online environment, allowing equilibrated access to current and retrospective information in the same and cognate databases; (4) fast access time; (5) revision programs that keep reference works on CD-ROM up-to-date; (6) training programs for users; (7) facilitation of longitudinal searches of large, chronologically arranged databases; (8) search capability that matches the capacity of the medium and is at par with that of online systems (e.g., all indexed fields

Reference and Collection Development Issues

can be simultaneously searchable, field-defined searching can be accomplished); (9) pricing that is within the reach of the typical school or public library; (10) willingness of libraries to impose a charge system that takes into account the many hidden, special-purpose expenses generated by CD-ROM (paper, printer fluid, leases, etc.); (11) equipment that can accommodate simultaneous use by six or more patrons; and (12) incorporation of an orientation to CD and other emerging information technologies into the curricula of all accredited schools of library and information science.

Technological Breakthroughs

As these ingredients are added, three breakthroughs should follow: networking, multimedia, and hypertext.

1. Networking. No new system should be brought into a library environment without the vendor's assurance of provisions for compatibility and extension of connective capacity after the system is installed. One must plan to integrate the system effectively and judiciously for multiple use, rapid response time, and a minimum number of frustrated patrons. The file server should be programmed to queue up requests.

2. Multimedia. There is a movement underway to transform CD-ROM presentations into an interactive audiovisual form akin but superior to television. Publishers have long had the hardware to accomplish this but have been stymied by (a) educators who have not designated the subject areas that have high priority and could best benefit from this approach to instruction; (b) high production costs imposed by the difficulty of devising ways in which to mix audio, video, and text in a structured mosaic that can be broken into pieces, reconstructed, and recalled by users; and (c) the "low-tech" environment of most libraries and schools.

3. Hypertext. The most significant innovation, a dramatic departure from the standard linear approach to reading, hypertext permits linkages between different but related ideas. Users can play creative games with the syndetic structure of the original reference that brings them—via light pen, icon, mouse, or megaphone symbol—combinations of recorded knowledge on people, events, and topics; excerpts from novels and poetry; reproductions of fine and applied arts; demonstrations of scientific principles; music; readings; and variant and derivative works. Apple's *Hyper-*

card is a first step in this direction. Diverse experiments with hypertext are under way: one, dealing with nineteenth-century American history, offers immediate call-up and juxtaposition of photos of Gold Rush towns and the Civil War, information on the Lewis and Clark expedition, voices of Ulysses S. Grant and Lincoln, music of the period, and Matthew Brady photographs of the Civil War. Another involves foreign-language instruction that melds the targeted nation's literature, history, art, music, landscape, and historical figures, while providing an organized sequence of language instruction. Predictably, the task of organizing, defining, and calibrating relationships between subjects and appropriate access routes is difficult and can only be accomplished by thinking, uncommonly cultured, highly skilled editors. Because editors are chronically underpaid, the talent shortfall that has developed must be redressed before hypertext can achieve its potential. Because it allows instant access to an assemblage of audio, visual, and textual presentations specified by the user, hypertext is indeed different. There are no long menus, just a mouse or light pen. The interaction is so personalized that any barrier between child and recorded knowledge seems to evaporate. This is because the system does not anticipate, coach, or force the users' moves but leaves them free to move extemporaneously. Again, as with multimedia, the dearth of current technology (e.g., lack of superior color, high-resolution monitors) in the schools could be an inhibitor of progress.

Researchable Areas

It is suggested that research focus on (1) analysis and classification of content to improve retrieval capacity, (2) human engineering problems raised by CD-ROM, and (3) a hypertext that relates to the different ways students learn as they grow older.

The philosophical dimensions should be most intriguing to the researcher. To what extent does reality generate thought? Or is reality a product of the mind? Is there a direct correspondence between reality and the mind's internal representation? Should expert systems be confined to communications enhancement and kept at a safe distance from manipulation of human thought? We periodically relearn at our peril that the attribution of human intelligence to machines is delusive, even dangerous. Human rationality is only skin deep. Below lies a secret, restive region, where the wild things are, beyond the reach of machines and numbers—the human psyche. After two decades of experimentation, artificial intelligence is still barely able to compete with the mind of a four-year-old child. It is indefensible to assume morphological correlates between the neuro-complexity of the human brain and even the most sophisticated computer.

The point is to place foremost the mission of the librarian—to transmit, interpret, and advocate recorded knowledge. Whether CD-ROM technology can be a major part of this remains to be seen.

Bibliography

Arnold, Stephen. "Electronic Information on CD—a Product or a Service?" *Online* 11, no. 6:56–60 (Nov. 1987).

Carrier, Harold D., and William A. Wallace. *An Epistemological View of Decision Aid Technology with Emphasis on Expert Systems.* Decision Sciences and Engineering Systems, Technical Report no. 37-87-140. Troy, N.Y.: Rensselaer Polytechnic Institute, 1987.

Crane, Nancy, and Tamara Durfee. "Entering Uncharted Territory: Putting CD-ROM in Place." *Wilson Library Bulletin* 62, no. 4: 28–30 (Dec. 1987).

DeBuse, Raymond. "So That's a Book . . . Advancing Technology and the Library." *Information Technology and Libraries* 7, no. 1: 7–18 (Mar. 1988).

Garfield, Eugene. "Current Comments." *Current Contents/Social & Behavioral Sciences* 22:3–9 (May 30, 1988).

Herther, Nancy K. "CDROM and Information Dissemination: An Update." *Online* 11, no. 2:56–64 (Mar. 1987).

Lowry, Charles B. "A Convergence of Technologies: How Will Libraries Adapt?" *Library Administration & Management* 2, no. 2:77–84 (Mar. 1988).

Newhard, Robert. "Converting Information into Knowledge: The Promise of CD-ROM." *Wilson Library Bulletin* 62, no. 4:36–38 (Dec. 1987).

Pearce, Karla J. "CD-ROM: Caveat Emptor." *Library Journal* 113, no. 2:37–38 (Feb. 1, 1988).

Peters, Charles. "Databases on CD-ROM: Comparative Factors for Purchase." *The Electronic Library* 5, no. 3:154–159 (June 1987).

Quint, Barbara. "How is CD-ROM Disappointing? Let Me Count the Ways." *Wilson Library Bulletin* 62, no. 4:32–34, 104 (Dec. 1987).

Reese, Jean, and Ramona Steffey. "ERIC on CDROM: A Comparison of DIALOG On-Disc, OCLC's Search CD450 and SilverPlatter." *Online* 11, no. 5:42–54 (Sept. 1987).

Rietdyk, Ron J. "Creation and Distribution of CD-ROM Databases for the Library Reference Desk." *Journal of the American Society for Information Science* 39, no. 1:58–62 (Jan. 1988).

Schwerin, Julie B. "CD-ROM: Potential Markets for Information." *Journal of the American Society for Information Science* 39, no. 1:54–57 (Jan. 1988).

Stewart, Linda. "Picking CD-ROMs for Public Use." *American Libraries* 18, no. 9:738-40 (Oct. 1987).
Valk, Anton. "Compact Disc Interactive." *Electronic and Optical Publishing Review* 7, no. 2:64-68 (June 1987).
Vandergrift, Kay E., and others. "CD-ROM: An Emerging Technology. Part 2: Planning & Management Strategies." *School Library Journal* 33, no. 11:22-25 (Aug. 1987).
Watson, Paula D. "Cost to Libraries of the Optical Information Revolution." *Online* 12, no. 1:45-50 (Jan. 1988).
Zoellick, Bill. "CD-ROM Software Architecture to Promote Interchangeability." *Journal of the American Society for Information Science* 39, no. 1:47-53 (Jan. 1988).

PART VI: CHILDREN'S LITERATURE

MERGING DREAMS AND CONSUMMATE REALITIES: THE COLLABORATIVE VENTURES OF DICK ROUGHSEY AND PERCY TREZISE

Karen Patricia Smith

When British colonizers officially established their settlement at Sydney Cove, Australia, in 1788, they went about their mission driven by very strong objectives and quite specific notions of how to achieve them. Their ideals were grounded in utilitarian principle and involved the transportation and the placement of people whose presence had been ruled "undesirable" in Great Britain. The settlers, for the most part unwilling participants, and their often less than enthusiastic overseers, found the land harsh and its climate a natural challenge to be overcome.

Some 40,000 years previous to their arrival, however, a people who came to be known as Australian-Aboriginal had emigrated to Australia from the continent of Asia.[1] Their primary concern had also been group survival and accommodation to the land. The Australian-Aboriginal people evolved a spiritual oneness with their new environment; an environment which would be at risk from them only for the provision of immediate sustenance. The two peoples, on the one hand the European, and on the other, Aboriginal, possessing as they did cultures in startling contrast to one another, were to have the expected confrontation, a circumstance which continues through the present day. The population numbers show the outcome of the cultural meeting. Currently there are 16 million poeple in Australia, only 150,000 of whom are Australian-Aboriginal.

"Merging Dreams and Consummate Realities: The Collaborative Ventures of Dick Roughsey and Percy Trezise," by Karen Patricia Smith in *Journal of Youth Services in Libraries* Vol. 3, no. 1 (Fall 1989), pp. 34–42; reprinted with permission from the American Library Association, copyright © 1989 by ALA.

History therefore, has made it difficult, and at times almost impossible, for the European Australian and the Australian-Aboriginal to accept their social and cultural differences. Politically, the European Australians lay claim to the institutions they transplanted, re-established, and developed over the two centuries, as well as most of the land upon which they sit. The Australian-Aboriginals mistrust the motives of a people who claim the land they feel belongs to those who first encountered it and whose spiritual heritage is so closely connected to the total environment. Under such circumstances, a collaborative endeavor of any type seems at best a difficult enterprise. However, the arts seem to possess that unique quality which enables those who aspire to be a creative part of the world to transcend political and social differences among cultures and cause individuals to come together, making their differences the successful basis of a shared cause. Such is the case in the artistic collaboration of Percy Trezise, a European Australian who grew up along the banks of the Upper Murray near Albury in New South Wales, and Dick Roughsey, an Australian-Aboriginal from Mornington Island in the Gulf of Carpentaria in Queensland. This paper focuses upon their meeting, friendship, and ultimate collaboration in several works for young people.

Dick Roughsey is believed to have been born in 1920, and was a member of the Lardil tribe. The family name was originally Goobalathaldin, which translated became "rough seas," a derivative of which became "Roughsey."[2] The association with the sea was to become symbolic for Roughsey for several reasons. Firstly, his upbringing took place on an island which depended on the sea for part of its sustenance, and secondly, his eventual meeting with Trezise would come about as the result of Roughsey's employment at a fishing lodge. Interestingly enough, bodies of water would also figure prominently as artistic images in the work of Roughsey and Trezise.

Roughsey had a traditional Aboriginal upbringing until the age of eight, when like so many Aboriginals, he was sent to a mission school. Here he remained until he was fourteen. At this age, Aboriginal children were generally returned to their parents, mission education considered "completed"; Roughsey had, however, acquired reading and writing skills which were to serve him well in the future. From age fourteen, he learned the ways of the bush from his family: he was taught how to fish and hunt, and for a time he worked as a cowboy.

At some point, he began to develop an interest in art. He had heard of Albert Namatjira, the most acclaimed Aboriginal artist of his time. Namatjira was to serve as spiritual role model for Roughsey. At this time while the artistic vision was very much present, a specific plan for causing that vision to become a reality had yet to emerge. Roughsey was working at a tourist fishing lodge when he met Percy Trezise—a meeting which was to cause a dream to be fully realized.[3]

Trezise grew up on a small dairy farm where the family sustenance was supplemented by hunting and fishing. He attended a primary school in the bush where he soon showed interest in, and aptitude for, writing and drawing. His ambitions exceeded the small environment in which he lived, and wishing to explore the world beyond, he became an airline pilot with Ansett Airlines and an explorer in his own right.[4]

It is perhaps artistically appropriate that on the day the two men first met in 1960, Trezise was painting a mermaid on the bottom of a pool.[5] Roughsey had heard that Trezise was a good artist and had seen a sample of Trezise's artwork done on ceramic tile. Trezise had done an illustration of an Aboriginal legend which had impressed Roughsey.[6] The two men struck up an immediate friendship which seemed to have mutual benefits leading to eventual artistic fulfillment for both. Roughsey needed a mentor, someone who was able to provide the structure upon which to develop his considerable talent, as well as someone who could provide the connections to the White Australian art world. The cultural and societal difficulties were extremely difficult for Roughsey to surmount, but far less difficult for Trezise. Trezise's assistance would gain Roughsey entree into the art world and give him an opportunity to view first-hand the conditions of Aboriginals in other parts of Australia. In his autobiography, Roughsey remarked that in travels around Australia:

> I discovered what it was like to be just a poor bloody blackfellow in a world run by whites. . . . How lucky that I was able to become an artist so that nearly everyone now treated me as an intelligent human being and an equal. Most of my poor people still have no decent homes and not enough to eat because they haven't got enough education to be able to get a job.[7]

As part of his personal plan for artistic development, Trezise suggested that Roughsey follow a ten-year plan. During the first five years, Roughsey was to perfect the art of painting Aboriginal legends on bark, a practice common to and popular within the tribes in northeastern Australia in Arnhem Land and in some other places, but not practiced by Roughsey's own people, the Lardil tribe. The second part of the plan involved mastery of the European style of painting in oils.[8] Above all, Roughsey was to concentrate upon developing his own style rather than copying that of Namatjira. Within six months, Roughsey had his first one-man art exhibit in Cairn.[9]

Trezise had long been interested in Aboriginal legend but had not been involved to any great degree in writing or illustrating any of the stories. After Roughsey's success in painting, he asked Trezise to assist him with the writing of his book *Moon and Rainbow: The Autobiography of an Aboriginal*, which was to become the first autobiography recorded by an Aboriginal. The project captured Trezise's imagination, and turned him towards thinking about recording Aboriginal legend. Roughsey assisted Trezise with his own endeavors, both in providing him with valuable information about Aboriginal lore and also in assisting Trezise in making good contacts among the Aboriginal people, particularly of the Cape York area. It was their joint exploration of the magnificent cave galleries of the area which house excellent examples of centuries-old Aboriginal rock paintings, that led to a promise by the two men to the Gugu-Yalanji people of the area, that in return for their assistance, Trezise and Roughsey would record and preserve Aboriginal lore in print. The format, a combination of illustration and text, seemed best suited to picture-book format. In all, the artistic/literary team would collaborate on six works for children. These works included *The Quinkins* (1978), which won the Australian Picture Book of the Year Award in 1979; *Banana Bird and the Snake Men* (1980); *Turramulli the Giant Quinkin* (1982); *The Magic Firesticks* (1983); *Gidja* (1984); and *The Flying Fox Warriors* (1985). Both men also single-authored a number of works. Roughsey's *The Rainbow Serpent* (1975) won the Australian Picture Book of the Year Award in 1976. For purposes of this paper, I will briefly discuss three of the coauthored works: *Banana Bird and the Snake Men*, *Turramulli the Giant Quinkin*, and *The Magic Firesticks*. These works offer excellent representative examples of the collaborative efforts of the two men.

A problem posed in cases where two author-illustrators collaborate on works is the difficulty of ascertaining exactly who is responsible for which aspect of the contribution. A 1987 videotape narrated by Trezise offers a clue regarding this question. In it, Trezise states that he usually was responsible for landscapes, while Roughsey illustrated figures, birds, and animals.[10] The texts are based upon stories contributed by the Gugu-Yalanji people of Cape York. Trezise also states on the tape: "Dick was the key to unlocking the mystery, and got the old men to tell their stories." Trezise and Roughsey are listed specifically as both authors and illustrators of the three works. It appears therefore, that these are the totally cohesive contributions of both men. The works are distinctive in many ways. The specific aspects chosen for discussion here are the compact simplicity of the vivid story line, the artistic style of the works and the emphasis upon, and portrayal of, the natural environment.

The story lines of the three works are all based on authentic Aboriginal folklore from the Cape York area. In *Banana Bird and the Snake Men*, one of the earliest of the collaborative works, the Bird men come upon the Snake men, who are cannibals. According to the lore, at this time men had the ability to change themselves at will into various types of animals. When the Bird men encounter their adversaries, the Snake men are in the form of kangaroos and therefore not immediately recognizable as Snake men. Banana Bird Man spears the largest kangaroo who is really Taipan Snake man. He is pursued by the tribe of Snake men who knock down trees in their attempts to capture him. The Snake men undergo another transformation (a recurring theme in Aboriginal lore) and now appear in the form of snakes who hide among the grass. Banana Bird Man, now hiding in a tree, comes down too soon and is captured and eaten—all except for one foot, by the Snake men. The Bird People search for Banana Bird Man and upon discovering the foot, set fire to the host of now sleeping snakes therefore killing them.

In *Turramulli the Giant Quinkin*, two children and their parents are out hunting for food when suddenly they are set upon by the hideous creature, Turramulli, the giant Quinkin, whose appearance bears a strong resemblance to the Abominable Snowman. The children become separated from their parents when they are told to hide inside a log while the parents attempt to distract the voracious Turramulli. They emerge from their hideout too soon. They are seen by the giant, and unable to find their parents, they must flee the scene. As they plummet over the edge of an unseen cliff, they are miraculously rescued by two Timara Quinkins, who are "good" Quinkins. Turramulli, however, plunges to his death. The children are safely reunited with their parents.

The Magic Firesticks is a variant of the Prometheus theme in which man desires fire, the making of which is a secret that does not belong to him. Two brothers decide to go to Fire Mountain and learn the secret of Didmunja, the old man who knows how to make fire. After crossing a broad plain with a wide river, and struggling through a dense forest, the two brothers come to Didmunja's cave. They watch him rub his firesticks together to create fire. In this manner they learn his secret. The boys wait until he is fast asleep and steal the firesticks. When Didmunja discovers the theft, he awakes in a rage and causes his mountain to spew lava and boulders. The two brothers escape and bring fire back to their tribe.

The texts of each of the stories are brief, yet inclusive. There are seldom more than four lines of text per page and sometimes there may only be one line. The reader is immediately oriented as to time, place and event. The opening text of *Banana Bird and the Snake Men*, for example, very simply establishes the situation and briefly sets up the tension which leads into the story:

> In Dreamtime, in the very beginning, people who were to become birds, animals, plants, and reptiles, were still in human form. The Snake men of the Cape York wilderness were cannibals. They would kill people, hang them in trees, and collect them later when they were hungry.[11]

The accompanying illustrated scene is peaceful, pastoral at first, until the eye of the reader shifts to the far right-hand side of the second page. Here, a body of an unfortunate victim hangs from the trees. Throughout the text, one notes the general sparsity of adjectives describing the action. The author-illustrators allow the illustrations to speak for them; there is no need to comment at length about the power of the scene; one will experience it through illustration.

The text of *Turramulli the Giant Quinkin* is a bit more descriptive, with an equally terrifying story line. The reader first meets Turramulli through his painted image on cave walls, this particular illustration showing the influence of the Cape York cave galleries. Turramulli is the biggest and most terrifying of all the drawings on the wall. (The reader does not actually know the image is that of Turramulli until the page is turned and Turramulli is revealed.) Second in size to Turramulli in the cave paintings, is the evil Imjim, a creature also capable of doing harm. Both figures are portrayed with staring white eyes, thereby setting them apart from the other figures on the wall. When next they are seen, the eyes will have changed to a glowing red. (All of the evil figures in the illustrations of all of the books, have glowing red eyes which seem to indicate their link with evil.) In the next scene, the text briefly describes the arrival of the giant Quinkin. However, the vision of Turramulli, holding a dead kangaroo upside down, with wild creatures fleeing before him (except for the Imjim who hops up and down as if in glee), serves to heighten the feeling of terror that the text only suggests. The integrative aspects of text and illustration become clear; Roughsey and Trezise have coordinated their art and also their philosophy of story telling.

The artistic style of the illustrations in the three works is distinctive. All three works make vivid use of earth tones in the style of oil painting. This lends them a startling brightness that heightens both the portrayal of the natural environment and the actions of the participants. While the setting is the Australian-Aboriginal dreamtime, that period of very productive activity of the Aboriginal ancestral beings involved in the creating of natural land features, people, and animals, the vividness of the colors portrays sharp reality. This is not merely a time envisioned and described, but rather a knowledge of the past that the tellers of the tales wish to share with the reader. The vivid quality of the illustrations is consistent throughout and is also evident in those works single-authored by Trezise and Roughsey. The colors are deep and rich and replete with the use of ochre tones, which are the primary hues the Aboriginal people would have at hand in the natural environment. The European touch comes with the addition of blues and greens to illustrate sky tones and the brightly colored birds and creatures that help make the Australian landscape so distinctive. From Europe as well is the use of the oil painting technique. Simplicity is part of the theme, but naivete is not. It is important to state this since the art of many ancient peoples is often characterized in this fashion, almost as if it is still developing, still going through the process of evolution. Thomas Keneally recently pointed this out in his extensive *New York Times Magazine* article, "Dreamscapes" which uses as a central focus the special exhibit of Aboriginal art held from October 6–December 31, 1988 at Asia House in New York. The article also quotes Peter Sutton of the South Australian Museum in Adelaide as saying that Aboriginal art is displayed without frames to illustrate its continuous and eternal qualities, part of the "dreaming" concept.[12] This quality is also illustrated in the work of Roughsey and Trezise. An illustration, for example, from *Banana Bird and Snake Man* shows a line of trees arranged across the background. The trees begin off the page at some point in time and space, span two pages and continue off the page. On the right-hand page a tree has fallen, the top of which is also off the page. This lets us know that the action continues outside of the captured segment of the story. The tops of the trees are merely hinted at, but not shown. The action continues horizontally and vertically as well. The same feeling is noted in the other works. In *Turramulli the Giant Quinkin*, a storm is advancing into view from some place outside of the immediate illustration, while four figures walk inevitably towards the margin of the page. The feeling is that perhaps when the reader looks again . . . the figures might be gone.

One notes as well, the slender and gracefully portrayed human, animal, and dreamtime figures, apparently Roughsey's contribution to the illustrations. He shows detail where he chooses to do so. In *The Magic Firesticks*, the council of old men contemplates the problem of obtaining fire. The illustrated scene shows some elders standing at attention, others sitting in a variety of poses, while in the background, two others appear to be hunting for food. Eyes and other bodily features are not emphasized; muscles are only portrayed in a limited sense. While the illustration at first seems reminiscent of some of the major differences between Medieval and Renaissance art in the portrayal of flat vs. fully developed human figures, one soon realizes that Roughsey, far from limiting his technique, is attempting to get the reader to focus upon the action and not upon the bodies of the men and creatures. Purpose appears to be at the forefront of his artistry.

In another scene from the same story, a volcanic explosion is visually portrayed. Parts of a mountain, a natural blue in color, pop off in round, cannonball-like pieces. The pieces nearest the reader have comet/tails, illustrating the speed with which they are flying down off the mountain top. In the background are smaller fragments without discernible tails, giving the feeling of depth and perspective. The contrast between the cold blue mountain and its fiery issue is dramatic—as dramatic as the rage the owner of the mountain must feel at having his precious gift of fire stolen.

The emphasis upon the natural environment is evident and quite appropriate in these stories, for it follows the life-style of the people. With the exception of several scenes taking place inside caves, and one inside a log in *Turramulli the Giant Quinkin*, all scenes are outdoors. The environment is quiet and benign in appearance. There is a feeling of harmony between men and nature which is part of Aboriginal philosophy. The intrusions upon peace are evil elements or other people. Even storms are an accepted part of the environment. In fact, people have the ability to "sing up" storms. This occurs in *Banana Bird and the Snake Men* when the Bird Men sing up a storm to put out the fire they had created to kill the Snake men.

Roughsey and Trezise liberally insert the creatures of the Australian environment into text and illustration. The reader sees brolga, emu, and kangaroo fleeing before the approaching Turramulli. Stringy bark gum trees, reedbeds, figs, and berries indigenous to the environment are present in profusion, yet do not act as story line distractions. The reader also sees other aspects of the Australian environment. In a scene in *The Magic Firesticks*, the two brothers in search of Fire Mountain enter the formidable rain forest. Presented here is a visual delight of a forest environment—the densest and richest in any of the three books. Among the luxuriant growth may be seen scrub turkeys and bandicoot. This is another world, so different from the sparse environment seen in other illustrations. Even when the landscape changes are not so dramatic, there are changes nonetheless. The introduction or rearrangement of vegetation, birds, creatures, or land forms helps to carry the action forward and avoid a static feeling.

Liberal use is made of water images in the stories. Images of lagoons and swamps are present and often become, appropriately, the place for a gathering of wild life and people. The search for water, due to the dry nature of much of the land, was continuous for the primarily nomadic Aboriginals. When Turramulli spots his quarry again, in the form of the two lost children, it is beside a lagoon where the children and various wild creatures are innocently drinking water. When Bandicoot and Curlew, the two boys in search of fire in *The Magic Firesticks*, come face-to-face with danger while crossing the wide river, the danger does not come as a result of action on the part of the cool green water, but rather from the open-jawed crocodile who emerges from its depths.

The picture book art of Roughsey and Trezise provides a clear example of synchronized collaboration not only in artistic talent, but also with artistic philosophy. The works flow easily; story lines are well balanced with illustrations, and within illustrations the natural environment and the evocation of spiritual beliefs authentically portray the vision of the Aboriginal people. The research, personal experiences, and the talent of these two men deliver to the reader a unified art.

When Dick Roughsey died in 1985, his death brought to an end an unusual friendship which had both celebrated and transcended cultural differences and which had become a vehicle for unique literary-artistic creations. Percy Trezise continues to write and illustrate works for children. His most recent books, *The Cave Painters* and *Black Duck and Water Rat*, were published in 1988. Upon the death of his friend, Trezise said:

> Dick and I always started working on a new book on the first day of January of each year. Sadly I am now working alone, for my mate Dick has returned to his Dreaming, situated somewhere on the horizon of Yilijilit-neah'. I shall have to make *Ngalculli the Red Kangaroo* . . . a very special book because I want to dedicate it to him, my bush mate of all those happy exciting years.[13]

References

1. Jennifer Isaacs, ed., *Australian Dreaming: 40,000 Years of Aboriginal History* (Sydney: Lansdowne Press, 1980), p. 11.
2. Dick Roughsey, *Moon and Rainbow: The Autobiography of an Aboriginal* (Sydney: A. H. and A. W. Reed Pty. Ltd., 1971), p. 28.
3. Margaret Dunkle, ed., *The Story Makers: A Collection of Interviews with Australian and New Zealand Authors* (Melbourne: Oxford Univ. Pr., 1987), p. 62.
4. Ibid., p. 72.
5. Dick Roughsey, p. 134.
6. Percy Trezise and Dick Roughsey, *Quinkan Country: Adventures in Search of Aboriginal Cave Paintings in Cape York* (Sydney: A. H. and A. W. Reed, 1969), p. 33.
7. Dick Roughsey, p. 153.

8. Ibid., p. 134.
9. Percy Trezise, *Quinkan Country*, p. 34.
10. Percy Trezise and Dick Roughsey, *Story Makers, Part II, Percy Trezise and Dick Roughsey: A Journey to Quinkan Country*, videocassette (Film Australia, 1987).
11. Percy Trezise and Dick Roughsey, *Banana Bird and the Snake Men* (Sydney: Collins, 1982. Reprint: Picture Lions, 1985), p. 1-2.
12. Thomas Keneally, "Dreamscapes," *New York Times Magazine*, November 13, 1988, p. 52-56.
13. Margaret Dunkle, p. 72.

Bibliography of Works Cited

Dunkle, Margaret, ed. *The Story Makers: A Collection of Interviews with Australian and New Zealand Authors and Illustrators for Young People.* Melbourne: Oxford Univ. Pr., 1987.
Isaacs, Jennifer, ed. *Australian Dreaming: 40,000 Years of Aboriginal History.* Sydney: Lansdowne Press, 1980.
Keneally, Thomas. "Dreamscapes." *New York Times Magazine* 13 Nov. 1988: p. 52-56.
Roughsey, Dick. *Moon and Rainbow: The Autobiography of an Aboriginal.* Sydney: A. H. and A. W. Reed Pty. Ltd., 1971.
Trezise, Percy and Dick Roughsey. *Banana Bird and the Snake Men.* Sydney: Collins, 1982. (Reprint: Picture Lions, 1985.)
───. *The Magic Firesticks.* Sydney: Collins, 1983. (Reprint: 1984.)
───. *Quinkan Country: Adventures in Search of Aboriginal Cave Paintings in Cape York.* Sydney: A. H. and A. W. Reed, 1969.
───. *Story Makers, Part II, Percy Trezise and Dick Roughsey: A Journey to Quinkan Country.* Videocassette. Film Australia, 1987.
───. *Turramulli the Giant Quinkin.* Sydney: Collins, 1984. (Reprint: 1984.)

THE GHOST OF NANCY DREW

Geoffrey S. Lapin

"It would be a shame if all that money went to the Tophams! They will fly higher than ever!"

Thus begins the first book in a series of titles that has whetted the literary appetites of young readers for well over fifty years. *The Secret of the Old Clock* by Carolyn Keene was to set the tone of juvenile adventure stories that is still leading young folks into the joys of reading the standard classics of literature.

Carolyn Keene has been writing the series books chronicling the adventures of Nancy Drew and the Dana Girls since 1929. With over 175 titles published, the author is still going strong, presently producing over fifteen new books each year. Her titles have been translated into at least twelve different languages, and sales records state that the volumes sold number in the hundreds of millions.

More than the mystery of the endurance of such unlikely literature is the question of who Carolyn Keene is and how one person could possibly be the author of such a record number of "best-sellers." Numerous literary histories offer conflicting information concerning the life of Ms Keene. The one common fact is that there exists no actual person by that name. Carolyn Keene is a pseudonym for the author of the series books.

Carolyn Keene was Edward Stratemeyer. Another source says that she was Harriet Adams. Yet others say that she was Edna Squire, Walter Karig, James Duncan Lawrence, Nancy Axelrad, Margaret Scherf, Grace Grote, and a plethora of others. What years of research have yielded is the fact that the one author who established both the original character of Nancy Drew and the characterization formula that has kept the young detective

---

"The Ghost of Nancy Drew," by Geoffrey S. Lapin in *Books at Iowa* no. 50 (April 1989), pp. 8–27; reprinted with permission from *Books at Iowa*. Copyright © 1989 by Geoffrey S. Lapin.

so popular is one Mildred A. Wirt Benson. Mrs. Benson had created a heroine exhibiting the values and personality that she herself had shown as a student at The University of Iowa.

I first became intrigued by the ambiguous authorship of the Nancy Drew Mystery Stories in 1963 when I was a student doing volunteer work in the public library system in Atlantic City, New Jersey. Since the library catered to the needs of vacationing families, its shelves boasted a large collection of children's books, including the Nancy Drew books. As a child I had dutifully read both the Drew and Hardy Boys mystery stories. The quaint world of roadsters, touring cars, and running boards has stayed with me into my adult years.

What aroused my curiosity was the fact that library catalogue cards for the series listed as author: Carolyn Keene, *pseudonym*. As had millions of other readers, I had always assumed that there really was a Ms Keene, regularly churning out the exploits of the teenage sleuth.

Knowing the thoroughness with which librarians catalogue information, I was surprised that the authorship information simply stopped with the word *pseudonym*. Here was the first instance where I had seen no further information given. Inquiries to the library staff were of no help: no one even seemed to care. During the next three years the only printed fact I found was one small notation in an author catalogue: Carolyn Keene, *real name unknown*.

My first big lead came in the reference department in Baltimore's Enoch Pratt Free Library. While looking through an old volume of the *Cumulative Book Index*, I found a penciled notation next to the list of books by Carolyn Keene: Mildred Augustine Wirt, see Durward Howes' *American Women 1939–1940*. Locating that volume I read, among other biographical facts concerning Wirt, that she was also author of non-Drew titles including *Carolina Castle, Sky Racers, Through the Moon-Gate Door, The Shadow Stone,* and *The Runaway Caravan*. Pseudonyms listed included Dorothy West, Joan Clark, Frances K. Judd, *and* Carolyn Keene. Returning to the *Cumulative Book Index*, I found under Wirt's name long lists of unfamiliar book titles. There were also the additional pen names of Frank Bell and Don Palmer. Checking under these two names and her other pseudonyms, I was able to compile a list of over fifty titles, not including the Nancy Drew books. Each year's edition of the CBI added titles to the already substantial list of books by this author.

Another entry appeared. This time it was not a pseudonym. Rather, it was a new surname. Wirt was now in parentheses, followed by the name Mrs. George Aaron Benson. Ms Wirt had gone and gotten married!

I diligently went through each year's volume. What information I gleaned was that this woman had written over 130 books, and, if every indication proved to be correct, was still writing. As Mildred A. Wirt she had written the Penny Parker Mystery Stories, Trailer Stories for Girls, the Ruth Darrow Flying Series, the Brownie Scout Series, the Girl Scout Series, the Cub Scout Series, an historical novel *Pirate Brig*, and numerous other nonseries mystery, adventure, and flying books. As Ann Wirt she had written the Madge Sterling Series. As Frances K. Judd, the Kay Tracey Mystery Stories; as Dorothy West, the Penny Nichols and Connie Carl books; as Frank Bell, the Flash Evans Series; as Don Palmer, the Boy Scout Explorer Series; and as Mildred Benson, *Quarry Ghost* and *Dangerous Deadline*. The latter was winner of the 1957 *Boys' Life*—Dodd, Mead Prize Competition for Children's Fiction.

My last stop that afternoon was to check the city directory for her last recorded home town, Toledo, Ohio. There, along with her address and telephone number, was listed her occupation—courthouse reporter, *Toledo Blade*.

During the next weeks I began the search for copies of Wirt's non-Drew books. With the majority being out-of-print, my visits to used book shops rewarded me with the first of many of her titles. A trip to Philadelphia resulted in my returning home with two full shopping bags. Each bookstore seemed to have some of her titles.

The next step was to start reading them. Even though author and character names were different, everything else seemed quite familiar: not just plot lines and situations, but colorful descriptions of country roads, dark passageways, and the like, all had a pleasant, readable flow. There were even roadsters and touring cars. I truly had found a gold mine—Nancy Drew was having adventures in the guise of other characters.

I met Mildred A. Wirt in 1969. I had written to her requesting an interview because of an article appearing in the January 25, 1969, issue of *Saturday Review*. "The Secret of Nancy Drew" by Arthur Prager told of the "grandmotherly lady" who was author of the Nancy Drew Mystery

Stories. Harriet S. Adams had been writing that popular series of books since its inception in 1930. She, along with four other authors, had also penned all Hardy Boys; Tom Swift, Jr.; and Bobbsey Twins books, and was yearly producing one new title per series. At that time she was working on her forty-third Drew title.

Having read the majority of books written under the name of Wirt and her pseudonyms, I was convinced that she indeed was Carolyn Keene. Therefore, why was this Adams woman being touted as author of those books?

I had since moved to Indianapolis, Indiana, which according to the map, did not seem to be too far from Toledo. I wrote to Wirt. Her response to my request was to have our meeting at her *Toledo Blade* office. She was a slight, gray-haired woman, both charming and witty. As she opened her desk drawer to put away her scarf I caught a glimpse of that particular issue of the *Saturday Review*. I knew that my decision to request the interview had been a good one.

Mildred Augustine was the first woman to graduate from the School of Journalism of The University of Iowa. She also received that University's first master's degree in journalism. While a student there she had had numerous short stories published in magazines including *St. Nicholas, Youth's Companion, Lutheran Young Folks*, and *Boy Life*. Many stories sold had been written for English class, where teacher Frank Luther Mott had said that she had no potential as an author, giving her a "B" for her course work.

Having taken a year between degrees to work as general reporter and society editor at the *Clinton Herald*, she read an ad in a trade publication requesting authors to write books for children. Traveling to New York for an interview, she met with Edward Stratemeyer, who was hiring writers to produce books in various series he was overseeing. As an editor for Horatio Alger, he had learned how to successfully glut the market with countless titles for young folks.

Augustine showed him her many published short stories, being told that he would contact her, should there be any work suited to her particular style of writing. Shortly thereafter, Stratemeyer requested that she try to breathe new life into his faltering Ruth Fielding Series. *Ruth Fielding and Her Great Scenario* by Alice B. Emerson was written at her parents' home in Ladora, Iowa, the hackneyed plot and characters fighting her all the way through. Cupples and Leon published the title in 1927.

Stratemeyer was satisfied enough to request more Fielding titles. *Ruth Fielding at Cameron Hall* and *Ruth Fielding Clearing Her Name* were both written after hours in The University of Iowa School of Journalism. The series lasted for thirty volumes, the final eight titles being written by her.

Upon completion of each title, Augustine would receive the usual payment of $100, accompanied by a short, typed document to besigned by her. This "release" relegated to Stratemeyer all claims of authorship, plots, characters, and the names of Alice B. Emerson and Ruth Fielding.

Having since received her master's degree, Augustine began work for the Iowa City *Press-Citizen*, where she met and married Associated Press correspondent Asa Wirt. With her husband's move to Cleveland's *Plain Dealer*, Mrs. Wirt started writing the first of many books to be published under her own name. The Ruth Darrow Flying Series appeared in 1930 under the publishing banner of Barse & Company. The Darrow character came about because of a new interest in women's flying exploits. The character's name was inspired by that of Ruth Elder who, in 1927, was the first woman to attempt a flight across the Atlantic Ocean. During the next two years Ruth Darrow was to have four adventures: *In the Air Derby*, *In the Fire Patrol*, *In Yucatan*, and *In the Coast Guard*. The year 1932 brought about the absorption of the Barse Company by Grosset & Dunlap. It was this same publishing house that had recently debuted the adventures of America's most famous girl sleuth.

During the time that Wirt was writing the first Darrow titles, Edward Stratemeyer contacted her asking if she were interested in beginning a new series of books for him. The Hardy Boys by Franklin W. Dixon had recently been put on the market as a new adventure-mystery series for young boys. Written for him by Canadian journalist Leslie McFarlane, the series proved to be instantly popular, warranting a similar set of books to be produced for young girls. Stratemeyer felt that Wirt's approach to the Fielding books was an indication that his new heroine would do well in her hands. The new character's name was to be Nancy Drew.

Stratemeyer's regimen for books produced through his offices was to hire established authors to write texts from brief synopses prepared by him. On index cards were listed character names, their relationships to one another, and a paragraph or two, telling the essence of the intended plot. Carolyn Keene's *The Secret of the Old Clock* was to tell of Drew's search for a missing will, hidden by one Josia Crowley. Wirt said of the plot received, "Certain hackneyed names and situations could not be bypassed. Therefore I concentrated on Nancy, trying to make her a departure from the stereotyped heroine of the day. Never was Nancy patterned after a real person. She was changeable to the reader, who projected her imagination to become Nancy. Nancy Drew represented freedom for girls which was a new concept. Girls were ready for that.

"Mr. Stratemeyer expressed bitter disappointment when he received the manuscript, saying the heroine was much too flip, and would never be well received." Wirt's manuscript nevertheless was sent off to Alexander Grosset and George Dunlap, whose publishing house aggressively had been selling Stratemeyer's Hardy Boys, Tom Swift, and Bobbsey Twins books. Not sharing the viewpoint of Stratemeyer, the publishers requested that the same author prepare two more titles for the series. *The Hidden Staircase* and *The Bungalow Mystery* were to be distributed simultaneously with the first title. The three-volume "breeder set" was published in 1930. Wirt's payment per book was $125, with all rights released over to Stratemeyer, as was required of all of his "ghosts."

Immediate sales figures foretold the financial potential of the series, prompting a need for additional titles. The books, seemingly destined for star status, almost met an early demise: Edward Stratemeyer died on May 10, 1930. His organization had been supplying all titles in Grosset and Dunlap's inventory of series starring Rover Boys, Outdoor Girls and Boys, Moving Picture Girls and Boys, Bunny Brown, Six Little Bunkers, Honey Bunch, Gary Grayson, X Bar X Boys, Ted Scott, Blythe Girls, and others. Panicking, the publishers appealed to the Stratemeyer daughters, Harriet and Edna. The women, who had not been allowed to participate in their father's business dealings, took over his operations, forming what eventually was to be called the Stratemeyer Syndicate. Original staff and ghost writers were retained at the request of Stratemeyer's principal publishing houses, Grosset & Dunlap and Cupples & Leon. Writing continuity within each series thus was assured.

Mildred Wirt received a request for the next Nancy Drew mystery story, *The Mystery at Lilac Inn*. This title most likely was the last to depend on a plot devised by Stratemeyer before his death. Wirt dutifully wrote *The Secret at Shadow Ranch*, *The Secret at Red Gate Farm*, and *The Clue in the Diary*. Requests also came for the first two titles in a new series for girls. As Julia K. Duncan, Wirt was to write *Doris Force at Locked Gates* and *Doris Force at Cloudy Cove*.

At the height of the Great Depression, Wirt received distressing news from Harriet Stratemeyer Adams: payment for forthcoming books would have to be reduced to $75 per manuscript. Wirt declined the invitation to write the next three volumes in the Drew series. *Nancy's Mysterious Letter*, *The Password to Larkspur Lane*, and *The Sign of the Twisted Candles* all appeared as scheduled. Adams had enlisted the talents of another of her ghosts to write those titles. A war historian and best-selling novelist, Walter Karig, had written several Perry Pierce, X Bar X Boys, and two Doris Force books for her organization. His schedule had permitted his producing the three Drew titles on demand.

The hiatus from the work for Adams had permitted Wirt's visiting various publishing houses to sell her independent work. Her first series to see print from the Goldsmith Publishers was the three-volume Madge Sterling Series by Ann Wirt. *The Missing Formula*, *The Deserted Yacht*, and *The Secret of the Sundial* were all shorter in length than most mystery stories of the day, having only fifteen chapters, instead of the traditional twenty-five. With the thickness of these dime store-distributed titles being less than usual, Wirt's first name could not be accommodated across the books' spines. The name of Ann was chosen arbitrarily by the publishers to replace that of Mildred.

1934 saw Wirt's return to the Nancy Drew series. The Stratemeyer organization had been able to offer acceptable payment for its contract work, and *The Clue of the Broken Locket* was published. *The Message in the Hollow Oak* was the title for 1935. It was also in that year that Wirt received a book order to continue a Stratemeyer-owned series that had been begun by someone else. The Kay Tracey Mystery Stories by Frances K. Judd had had its first two titles written by children's author Anna Perrott Wright. Wirt's first contribution to that seventeen-volume series was *The Mystery of the Swaying Curtains*. She eventually was to write the next eleven titles, ending with *The Sacred Feather* in 1940. Kay Tracey's adventures were published by Grosset & Dunlap's heartiest competitor,

Cupples & Leon.

Victor W. Cupples and Arthur T. Leon were the first major publishers to accept large numbers of books written by the Stratemeyers' most prolific ghost. Beginning with *The Twin Ring Mystery* in 1935, the firm published fifty-six independently produced titles by Wirt.

The respected Penn Publishing Company also had a 1935 Wirt title. *Sky Racers* was the first of two flying novels to come from that company. Before its later absorption by Books, Incorporated of New York, it published Wirt's first historical novel for children, *Carolina Castle*. Both *Sky Racers* and *Courageous Wings* were reprinted frequently by the latter company. *Carolina Castle*, one of Wirt's finest works, saw few print runs, now being her scarcest title.

Grosset & Dunlap had recently come out with a new girls' series by Carolyn Keene. The Dana Girls were younger versions of Nancy Drew, solving mysteries between classes at Starhurst Boarding School. Author of the first four of their adventures was Leslie McFarlane, ghost of the Hardy Boys. McFarlane said years later in his autobiography that he "was tempted to turn them loose in one of Bayport's numerous abandoned buildings with the Hardy Boys, just to see what would happen. It might have done the four of them no end of good."

Wirt was requested to write manuscripts for all Dana titles from 1936 through 1954. She also received orders for five of the Syndicate's Honey Bunch Books: *Her First Little Treasure Hunt*, *Her First Little Club*, *Her First Trip in a Trailer*, *Her First Trip to a Big Fair*, and *Her First Twin Playmates*.

1936 was the beginning of Wirt's most prolific period. Cupples & Leon were so pleased with the success of *The Twin Ring Mystery* that they advertised the new Mildred A. Wirt Mystery Series. "Mildred A. Wirt sounds a new and triumphant note in the field of mystery and adventure stories for girls with this vibrant group of stories. Told in the modern manner with a warmth of depth and feeling, and a powerful web of suspense, these stories unfold against colorful backgrounds in a panorama of excitement and mystery." From 1936 to 1940 she added eight titles to the series, including *The Clue at Crooked Lane*, *The Hollow Wall Mystery*, *The Shadow Stone*, *The Wooden Shoe Mystery*, *Through the Moon-Gate Door*, *Ghost Gables*, *The Painted Shield*, and *Mystery of the Laughing Mask*.

The Trailer Stories for Girls was yet another set published by Cupples & Leon in 1937. The "thoroughly modern series of adventure stories, unique in subject matter, precise in treatment and alive with up-to-the minute action," consisted of *The Runaway Caravan, The Crimson Cruiser, Timbered Treasure,* and *The Phantom Trailer.*

Joan Clark's Penny Nichols Series was the last series to be started during that two-year period. The four-title series was published by Goldsmith Publishers, still garnering profits from her earlier Madge Sterling Series. Under the Clark identity she also wrote that company's *Connie Carl at Rainbow Ranch* in 1939.

The years 1938 and 1939 produced two additional series from Cupples & Leon: Dot and Dash by Dorothy West and Flash Evans by Frank Bell. The five-title Dot and Dash Series told of adventures of a young girl and her dog and was aimed at much younger readers. By contrast, *Flash Evans and the Darkroom Mystery* and *Camera News Hawk* were for older boys. The latter series proved to be so impressive that producers for radio's *Jack Armstrong, All-American Boy* wrote to the books' publishers asking that they contact "Mr. Bell" concerning his writing scripts for their program.

Wirt's most significant independent series was begun in 1939, once again for Cupples & Leon. The Penny Parker Mystery Stories strove for realism. "Featuring a daring, livewire heroine—Penny Parker, daughter of a newspaper editor and a girl with a real 'nose for news'—these stories with their glamorous newspaper background unfold a series of baffling mysteries that lead the unofficial girl reporter into countless thrills and dangers." Titles such as *The Clock Strikes Thirteen, Hoofbeats on the Turnpike, Saboteurs on the River, Gilt of the Brass Thieves, Signal in the Dark, Voice from the Cave, Swamp Island,* and *The Cry at Midnight* were unusual for this genre of children's fiction. So was the often solemn approach used to stress the severity of the war years. Few books of that era dealt with black market sales, mine detection devices, and brass and gold hoarding. Penny Parker encountered them all.

Even Penny Parker could not seem to overcome the popularity of Nancy Drew. Going as strong as ever, the Drew girl was still having her adventures written by Wirt. However, there was a change that had begun to come into the texts of the books. The original volumes in the series had been written from a paragraph-long plotline that had been supplied by

Edward Stratemeyer, and later by his daughters. As the series progressed over the years, the paragraph evolved into page, pages, and finally an outline to which Wirt steadfastly complied. Character development and inventiveness were phased out in favor of what was to be known as the Stratemeyer Syndicate's "formula." Chapter beginnings and endings were specifically defined. The use of short words and sentences was stressed. The Stratemeyer sisters were becoming experts at how juvenile fiction should be written.

In the late 1940s the Nancy Drew Mystery Stories and Dana Girls Mystery Stories began appearing in print with small alterations made from Wirt's original manuscripts. The first changes were barely noticeable: discreet changes of word placement, numerous adverbs added, small deletions from the original. By the time 1947's *The Clue in the Old Album* was published, it had been altered so drastically that the entire original text had been rewritten. Someone was practicing how to write Nancy Drew.

Mildred Wirt received an order for *The Ghost of Blackwood Hall* in 1947. It would be the last title of the Drew series she would write until 1953's *The Clue of the Velvet Mask*. Four titles were to be written by Iris Vinton and others, only to have Wirt return for that one final contribution in 1953. *Mystery at the Crossroads*, 1954's Dana Girls adventure, was to be Wirt's last book written for the Stratemeyer Syndicate.

The final four series written by Wirt were all published by her principal company, Cupples & Leon. Brownie Scout, Girl Scout, and Cub Scout series had six, three, and six titles respectively. The Boy Scout Explorer Series by Don Palmer boasted three volumes. Dodd, Mead and Company's *Dangerous Deadline* (1957) and *Quarry Ghost* (1959) were the last two titles written by her.

In 1959, Grosset & Dunlap began publishing a new *The Secret of the Old Clock* and *The Hidden Staircase*. Shorter in length, they and all subsequent "updated" titles bore the inscription on their copyright page, "This new book for today's readers is based on the original of the same title." Wirt's earliest writing of the syndicate-owned titles was being phased out. On the average of two volumes per year, all original Drew titles by her have been rewritten to remove what the Syndicate called "objectionable material." The character of Nancy Drew also underwent a dramatic change: the strong-willed teen was having her personality diluted, causing her to lose her characteristic independence.

During the period of the first revisions of the Drew books, the name of Harriet Adams was beginning to be brought to the attention of the public. It seemed that for years she secretly had been writing all of the bestselling children's series books, and only now was going public. Occasional articles said that the Hardy and Drew series had had their first titles written by her father before his death, but the majority of all press releases stated that it indeed was she who was sole author. Mildred Wirt said not a word. She was legally sworn to secrecy by having signed the releases for all of her work.

Publishing history was made in 1979. All subsequent books in Stratemeyer Syndicate series were to be published by Simon and Schuster. The relationship between the Syndicate and Grosset & Dunlap, begun in 1908, had come to an end. The reason for the separation was not made public. Grosset & Dunlap sued the Syndicate and Simon and Schuster. The Syndicate sued Grosset & Dunlap.

The lawsuit did not come to trial until 1980 and publicity for it waned, for this was to be a year of celebration. Nancy Drew was fifty years old and still as popular as ever. Harriet Adams and new publisher Simon & Schuster were in the spotlight. The festivities received coverage from *Time*, *Newsweek*, and the *New York Times*. Adams was interviewed on National Public Radio. The National Endowment for the Arts was sponsoring a filmed documentary made by her grandson, because she was a "national treasure." The name Wirt was never mentioned.

The United States District Court opened the case of Grosset & Dunlap versus Gulf & Western Corporation and the Stratemeyer Syndicate in May of 1980. Present was Grosset & Dunlap's principal witness: Mildred A. Wirt. Wirt had learned of the impending trial from one of her fans. I had been told of the lawsuit during a lecture I was giving to book collectors and had passed the information along to her. During that same period of time Wirt had been contacted by an editor of Grosset & Dunlap's juvenile line. The company had recently purchased the inventory of the long defunct Cupples & Leon Company. On review of their assets they had come upon her Penny Parker Mystery Stories and felt that the books would be a good addition to their line of series books. Wirt was asked if she were interested in revising the texts for today's readers. During a telephone conversation concerning her reworking of the series, Wirt asked about the progress of the trial. When asked what her interest was, she replied: "I wrote the books."

Present in the courtroom on opening day was Harriet Adams. Upon being introduced to Wirt, her first response was, "I thought that you were dead."

While on the witness stand Wirt was presented with numerous documents and letters which had been subpoenaed by the plaintiff's attorneys. She was able to identify and verify all work releases signed by her, as well as numerous documents that proved the truth about her claims to authorship. Letters submitted included one from 1938 sent to Adams from attorneys for Warner Brothers Pictures, Inc.. It had seemed that the planned series of motion pictures about Nancy Drew could not come about unless Wirt were forced to sign a release of movie rights for her books. The original releases she had signed had made no mention of any medium, other than the written one.

Another letter was submitted as evidence. The arrival of Nancy Drew to television had prompted the Syndicate's attorneys to "remind" Wirt that should she make any claim to the Drew character, "legal or equitable action including an action for damages" would be taken against her.

The trial ended. Judge Robert J. Ward found in favor of the Stratemeyer Syndicate. While author pseudonyms and principal characters appeared in all series titles, the content of a particular book was not contingent on what had gone before in previous volumes. Therefore, Simon and Schuster was to be the new publisher of all Syndicate titles.

While on the witness stand, Harriet Adams was presented with, and questioned about the releases signed by both her and Wirt. Even though she publicly acknowledged that Wirt was author of the books, she still insisted, "I wrote the books." Adams then became so unnerved by her cross-examination that she fell out of her chair in the witness box. Judge Ward called for an early ending to the day's proceedings.

Harriet Adams died in 1982. Her many obituaries celebrated her as author of hundreds of childrens' books, including all Hardy Boys, Bobbsey Twins, Tom Swift, and Nancy Drew titles. Her work was to be carried on by her once-silent partners Nancy Axelrad, Lorraine S. Rickle, and Lieselotte Wuenn. The partnership was dissolved in 1984. All titles, characters, and properties were sold to Simon and Schuster.

Nancy Drew and the Hardy Boys have begun to appear in more titles than ever before. Each set of characters has had created an additional series written for more mature readers. The older teen market is reading the exciting adventures of a new genre of heroine. She is fiercely independent, daunted by no limitations previously endured by the Syndicate-written Nancy. Nancy Drew has once again become the Nancy Drew created by Mildred A. Wirt.

I last spent time with Mildred Wirt Benson on Thanksgiving in 1987. She is still active as a full-time reporter for the *Toledo Blade*. She swims and plays golf regularly and retains pilot's licenses for private, commercial, seaplane, and instrument flight, regularly participating in the Louisiana Air Tour.

Bibliography

The following is a bibliography of the published works of Mildred A. Wirt Benson. Series titles are listed in sequence of publication, under the various names and pseudonyms used by her. Pseudonyms followed by an asterisk (*) are those owned by Edward Stratemeyer, and later, by the Stratemeyer Syndicate. Dates are those of first publication of said titles. Numerous short stories are not included.

BELL, FRANK
Flash Evans Books
Flash Evans and the
   Darkroom Mystery   1940
Flash Evans, Camera News Hawk   1940

BENSON, MILDRED*
Dangerous Deadline   1957
Quarry Ghost   1959
Kristie at College [Quarry Ghost]   1960

CLARK, JOAN
Penny Nichols Mystery Stories
Penny Nichols Finds a Clue   1936
*Penny Nichols and the Mystery
   of the Lost Key*   1936
Penny Nichols and the Black Imp   1936
*Penny Nichols and the
   Knob Hill Mystery*   1939
Connie Carl at Rainbow Ranch   1939

DUNCAN, JULIA K.*
Doris Force Mystery Stories

Doris Force at Locked Gates   1931
Doris Force at Cloudy Cove   1931

EMERSON, ALICE B.*
The Ruth Fielding Series
*Ruth Fielding and Her
   Great Scenario*   1927
Ruth Fielding at Cameron Hall   1928
Ruth Fielding Clearing Her Name   1929
Ruth Fielding in Talking Pictures   1930
Ruth Fielding and Baby June   1931
Ruth Fielding and Her Double   1932
*Ruth Fielding and Her Greatest
   Triumph*   1933
*Ruth Fielding and Her
   Crowning Victory*   1934

JUDD, FRANCES K.*
Kay Tracey Mystery Stories
*The Mystery of the
   Swaying Curtains*   1935
The Shadow on the Door   1935
The Six Fingered Glove Mystery   1936

The Green Cameo Mystery	1936
The Secret at the Windmill	1937
Beneath the Crimson Brier Bush	1937
The Message in the Sand Dunes	1938
The Murmuring Portrait	1938
When the Key Turned	1939
In the Sunken Garden	1939
The Forbidden Tower	1940
The Sacred Feather	1940

KEENE, CAROLYN*

Mystery at the Lookout	1942

Dana Girls Mystery Stories

The Secret at the Hermitage	1936
The Circle of Footprints	1937
The Mystery of the Locked Room	1938
The Clue in the Cobweb	1939
The Secret at the Gatehouse	1940
The Mysterious Fireplace	1941
The Clue of the Rusty Key	1942
The Portrait in the Sand	1943
The Secret in the Old Well	1944
The Clue in the Ivy	1952
The Secret of the Jade Ring	1953
Mystery at the Crossroads	1954

Nancy Drew Mystery Stories

The Secret of the Old Clock	1930
The Hidden Staircase	1930
The Bungalow Mystery	1930
The Mystery at Lilac Inn	1930
The Secret at Shadow Ranch	1931
The Secret of Red Gate Farm	1931
The Clue in the Diary	1932
The Clue of the Broken Locket	1934
The Message in the Hollow Oak	1935
The Mystery of the Ivory Charm	1936
The Whispering Statue	1937
The Haunted Bridge	1937
The Clue of the Tapping Heels	1939
The Mystery of the Brass Bound Trunk	1940
The Mystery at the Moss-Covered Mansion	1941
The Quest of the Missing Map	1942
The Clue in the Jewel Box	1943
The Secret in the Old Attic	1944
The Clue in the Crumbling Wall	1945
The Mystery of the Tolling Bell	1946
The Clue in the Old Album	1947
The Ghost of Blackwood Hall	1948
The Clue of the Velvet Mask	1953

PALMER, DON
Boy Scout Explorer Series

Boy Scout Explorers at Emerald Valley	1955
Boy Scout Explorers at Treasure Mountain	1955
Boy Scout Explorers at Headless Hollow	1957

THORNDYKE, HELEN LOUISE*
Honey Bunch Books

Honey Bunch, Her First Little Treasure Hunt	1937
Honey Bunch, Her First Little Club	1938
Honey Bunch, Her First Trip in a Trailer	1939
Honey Bunch, Her First Trip to a Big Fair	1940
Honey Bunch, Her First Twin Playmates	1941

WEST, DOROTHY
Dot and Dash Books

Dot and Dash at the Maple Sugar Camp	1938
Dot and Dash at Happy Hollow	1938
Dot and Dash in the North Woods	1938
Dot and Dash in the Pumpkin Patch	1939
Dot and Dash at the Seashore	1940

WIRT, ANN
Madge Sterling Series

The Missing Formula	1932
The Deserted Yacht	1932
The Secret of the Sundial	1932

WIRT, MILDRED A.

Sky Racers	1935
The Twin Ring Mystery	1935
Carolina Castle	1936
Courageous Wings	1937
Mystery of the Laughing Mask	1940
Linda	1940
Pirate Brig	1950

Brownie Scout Series

The Brownie Scouts at Snow Valley	1949
The Brownie Scouts in the Circus	1949
The Brownie Scouts in the Cherry Festival	1950

The Brownie Scouts and Their Tree House	1951
The Brownie Scouts at Silver Beach	1952
The Brownie Scouts at Windmill Farm	1953

Dan Carter, Cub Scout Series

Dan Carter, Cub Scout	1949
Dan Carter and the River Camp	1949
Dan Carter and the Money Box	1950
Dan Carter and the Haunted Castle	1951
Dan Carter and the Great Carved Face	1952
Dan Carter and the Cub Honor	1953

Girl Scout Series

The Girl Scouts at Penguin Pass	1953
The Girl Scouts at Singing Sands	1955
The Girl Scouts at Mystery Mansion	1957

Mildred A. Wirt Mystery Stories

The Clue at Crooked Lane	1936
The Hollow Wall Mystery	1936
The Shadow Stone	1937
The Wooden Shoe Mystery	1938
Through the Moon-Gate Door	1938
Ghost Gables	1939
The Painted Shield	1939

Penny Parker Mystery Stories

Tale of the Witch Doll	1939
The Vanishing Houseboat	1939
Danger at the Drawbridge	1940
Behind the Green Door	1940
Clue of the Silken Ladder	1941
The Secret Pact	1941
The Clock Strikes Thirteen	1942
The Wishing Well	1942
Ghost Beyond the Gate	1943
Saboteurs on the River	1943
Hoofbeats on the Turnpike	1944
Voice from the Cave	1944
The Guilt of the Brass Thieves	1945
Signal in the Dark	1946
Whispering Walls	1946
Swamp Island	1947
The Cry at Midnight	1947

Ruth Darrow Flying Stories

Ruth Darrow in the Air Derby	1930
Ruth Darrow in the Fire Patrol	1930
Ruth Darrow in the Coast Guard	1931
Ruth Darrow in Yucatan	1931

Trailer Stories for Girls

The Runaway Caravan	1937
The Crimson Cruiser	1937
Timbered Treasure	1937
The Phantom Trailer	1938

FROM LABYRINTH TO CELESTIAL CITY: SETTING AND THE PORTRAYAL OF THE FEMALE ADOLESCENT IN SCIENCE FICTION

Hilary Crew

A black sand desert, a city named Carbuncle, and an asteroid spaceship traveling through time and space are some of the settings that find adolescent heroines undertaking challenging roles in science fiction novels. The female adolescent's arduous journey toward independence, maturity, and responsibility and her increasing role in shaping her own future and that of society's are often symbolized by the physical nature of the settings in which the heroine is placed.

In the genre of science fiction, particularly, setting is often far more than mere background. Details of time and space can control and determine the structure and kind of society that develops—its values and culture. On a postnuclear Earth, for example, perhaps only a mutant species can evolve. On an alien planet, a technological or patriarchal society may never have emerged. Janice Antczak, in *Science Fiction: The Mythos of a New Romance,* has written of science fiction as a "romance form of the technological age" in which the "romantic hero's quest" takes place in a setting "apart from reality," which exists as a result of some aspect of "science and technology."[1] Setting thus also becomes symbolic, an "archetypal metaphor" for an idealized world, or one which is found undesirable.[2] A "concrete" bunker and the twisting tunnels of a labyrinthine city can symbolize entrapment, and an alternative world—a pastoral valley and a "celestial city"—can offer escape into a more idyllic milieu. In the novels

---

"From Labyrinth to Celestial City: Setting and the Portrayal of the Female Adolescent in Science Fiction," by Hilary Crew in *Journal of Youth Services in Libraries* Vol. 2, no. 1 (Fall 1988), pp. 84–89; reprinted with permission from the American Library Association, copyright © 1989 by ALA.

discussed here, the authors have used, as an important element in their narrative, settings as metaphor, in which "recurring images" of "physical nature"[3] consistently depict the journey of the "heroine[s]" of the "New Romance."

A science fiction convention often used to posit a new beginning—a new society—and analogous to the "flood archetype"[4] is the setting of an earth "swept clean" by alien attack or slowly recovering from almost total devastation due to nuclear war or pollution. With the destruction of the scientific and technological societies of the nineteenth and twentieth centuries, a remnant population is able to begin life anew, often in a pastoral setting. And in this "new" world, young women claim their place as equal partners in the shaping of their environment.

Surrounded by a "grey wasteland," the walled "blue green" valley, where Ann Burden in *Z For Zachariah* demonstrates that she is capable of surviving alone after nuclear war, is a pastoral enclave with its own weather. Bees hum "in the blossoms," cress and dandelions grow in the meadows, flowers—"lilac and forsythia"—bloom, chickens scratch, and cows graze around Ann's home. Into this idyllic valley at springtime from the "grey and brown" deadness of the world outside comes the violent and unbalanced Loomis, whose intent is to exploit the earth is contrasted to Ann's own reverence for life and natural beauty. Loomis' attempted rape of Ann and his use of a rifle to maim and kill are further proof that his attitude toward life has not been changed by a cataclysmic war. But it is with Ann that the burden of the future lies as she leaves the pastoral valley—where she has proved herself to be self-sufficient—to seek an alternative life.

In *Strange Tomorrow*, the future is sealed form the past both physically and symbolically by the Clordians who have sterilized the earth, disintegrating nearly all life. As small groups of survivors begin to resettle and reseed in pastoral valleys where "the land produces trees and fruits and rabbits and chickens," Janie, fifteen years old, is a "Sustainer" responsible for the health and education of her small group. It is a traditional female role, yet Janie is also the initiator of plans for people in the different valley to communicate with each other, and Janie's future is one in which men, women, and children share equally in the shaping of their environment and culture.

Laura in *Children of the Dust* is "a golden girl with a sheen on her fur," the granddaughter of Catherine who had survived a nuclear holocaust and "had mothered mutants, fostered a new way of life" (p. 155) that was "simpler and more wholesome." Laura, "walking free in the [merciless] sunlight" perfectly belongs to the changed world of ultraviolet light. In the pastoral valley where she lives, the trees are "towers of silvery leaves," and the "bean flowers" smell "sweet." Children swim "naked" in a "small lake" where "wild ducks" nest "in the reed beds" (p. 140). And in the English countryside, surrounding the "glisten[ing] golden walls of a turreted 'Abbey,' lies a city, molten and shimmering which seems to "melt with the green-white sheen of wooded hills and water meadows until the whole valley glowed." It is a "celestial city becoming reality" (p. 174). The pastoral scene and the celestial city become symbols for the new idyllic order in which young women walk "fearless and free in the sun," and a dramatic contrast to those environments in which young women are still struggling to find their own identity and freedom.

Science fiction writers have used settings to symbolize the entrapment of the young adolescent. Barbara White writes in *Growing Up Female* that "the image of the cage, or the trap, is the most common image of female adolescence" in realistic novels.[5] In science fiction, however, the archetypal metaphor of the labyrinth and the caverns and tunnels of an underground setting symbolizing the world "of bondage and pain and confusion," and of "lost direction"[6] seem to be a recurrent image. In Vonda McIntyre's *The Exile Waiting*, the setting itself, the dismal, labyrinthine underground City of Centre, encloses the reader along with the trapped Misha and the slave society within its dark and dank caverns. The interiors of the "Three Hills" of the city are "mazes and warrens, labyrinthine beyond mythology" (p. 12). Misha, a genius, who has telepathic abilities and who must steal to live, is determined to leave an earth that is "dying," that has "stopped." Joanna Russ also uses the symbolism of the underground in *The Two of Them*, where twelve-year-old Zubeydeh, who is not allowed to "be a poet" (a male prerogative) is imprisoned with her mother and aunt in an underground "hareem" on Ka'abah. In both these novels, the females are victims of their environment. Their entrapment and their need for escape become the central issue. Ka'abah is "almost completely underground, hollowed out of the rocks," and "has no horizons." Zubeydeh cries that what she "really need[s] is to get right out of this world." Ophelia in *Children of the Dust* has been confined throughout her childhood in the sealed underground "regimented world of a "concrete" bunker, where survivors of a nuclear war have ridden out the nuclear winter. It is a "vast purpose-built subterranean city, a labyrinth of rooms and passages," where Ophelia is cut off from "scents and sights, colors and sounds." The communal city from which Liza ventures in *Ring-Rise, Ring-Set* is a drab, sterile environment cut off not only from the natural world of sun, earth, the "sweet and living waters of the creek," but also from a sense of "belonging to each other and the land."

Science fiction often opens the door for escape through the convention of an alternative setting, for example, a different planet or a synthetic world, where institutions and cultures differ in kind, and where the adolescent female will find greater fulfillment and new challenges. In these environments of the future, boundaries are pushed back, the "world" expands, and resourceful, self-reliant adolescents gain a wider vision as they grow and mature and are able to take on responsible roles in the shaping of their societies. The descriptions of alternate settings are often used to symbolize the choices that are available. Misha, in *The Exile Waiting*, escapes from the labyrinth in Centre to visit the planet Koen. From the spaceship, she sees for the first time the whole of Earth beneath her—a taste of the new vistas that will open up for her. Her friend, Jan Hikaru writes in his journal that Misha will now have "an almost infinite range of choices and can decide what she wants to do with her future and her abilities" (p. 214). Koen with its "parklike" scenery and winterless climate, whose inhabitants feel "a comradeship with the land," is an alternative to a nuclear-blasted earth with its "winter storms" and "iridescent black sand dunes." Jan compares the "tyranny" on Earth to that of the "overprotective[ness]" of Koen, where perhaps the "world was in some ways too pleasant and too easy" and "provided insufficient challenge" (p. 88).

In *The Stars Will Speak*, Lissa travels from her secure artificial satellite, "Bernal One," with its "small towns and parks, gentle sunlight and small streams" to the uncontrolled climate and "superhuman masses" of the Himalayas where she studies at the Interstellar Institute. It is here that Lissa not only studies diligently, so that she might become a valuable member of a team whose aim is to decipher an alien signal, but also learns, as she falls in love for the first time, that her feelings and emotions cannot remain ignored and are not so easily controlled—"Being a human meant not being able to know everything about one's inner self or that of another. It was hard to accept that her mind was not all-powerful over her feelings and desires." Lissa's outward journey, which subsequently takes her further into remote space, is mirrored by an inner journey of discovery.

Joan Vinge in *Snow Queen* uses different settings to portray the matriarchal agrarian society of Summers on the planet Tiamat, composed of "more water than land," and the technologically advanced planet Kharemough, with its formal gardens and "artificial beauty." Through her journeys, Moon, Vinge's protagonist, is alerted to choices that must be made in the use of knowledge and power. She becomes Summer Queen in the City of Carbuncle, a convoluted "spiral shell" with its "lowest levels" in touch with the sea but open to the heavens at its peak.

In *Moonwind* and *Earthseed*, the science fiction convention of the rocket or spaceship becomes the protective environment from which the adolescent must emerge into a hostile setting. Bethkahn, an "astral being" in *Moonwind*, is stranded on the moon for ten thousand years. During this time, the ship, which is "her only friend" and "programmed humanely to care for its crew and all life forms within it," offers "sleep and forgetfulness" to its "junior technician." However, to escape stasis and to continue to grow and mature, Bethkahn must face the threatening environment of the moonbase established during her long sleep. In Pamela Sargent's *Earthseed*, "Ship" is in effect an "artificial womb," for it had carried the genetic material from which Zoheret and her companions had been born and had overseen their growth and training. When the adolescents are ready for independence, "Ship" sends them into the wilderness of Hollow.

Pamela Sargent and other writers have used the popular male initiation theme of survival in the wilderness to test the character and endurance of their female protagonists. In *Earthseed*, Zoheret and the other girls are sent out on equal terms with the young men on the trial expedition into the uncompromising natural environment of Hollow with its "quicksand" and deep, fast-flowing river contained within their asteroid home. When the adolescents are finally released from the protective environment of "Ship" to settle first Hollow, then a strange new planet with a "yellow grass and blue-green sky," Zoheret, who has survived both the wilderness and war between rival factions, becomes the leader of her settlement.

In Piercy's *Woman on the Edge of Time,* Innocence on her naming day is taken into a "wilderness area" and left alone in the "woods" to survive for one week. It is a "rule of Passage" in which young people "transit from childhood to a full member of . . . [the] community" and is the end of "mothering." For Molly, a young clone in Wilhelm's *Where Late the Sweet Birds Sang,* an expedition into the wilderness is an "awakening"; the murmuring voices of the river and trees bring her an awareness of individual consciousness. Snake, a "healer" in *Dreamsnake* leaves the "exquisite valley" in which the "forest of trees and forest of windmills" are "harmonized" to travel the mountains and deserts of the outside world during her "proving year." Her greatest test of endurance comes in the "broken bubble" enclosing an "alien jungle" of twisted, tangled vines and trees from which parasitic plants—"crawlies"—creep and poison the natural earth. Here, she faces the twisted, deformed North, who uses the venom of "dream snakes," a drug for pleasure rather than for easing the transition from life to death. In *Return to Earth,* Samara is kidnapped and left to die in the desert with her elderly friend and helper, Galen. Samara has "no intention of dying" in the landscape of "windpolished rock and sand." Displaying the level-headed qualities that will enable her to replace her mother as director of a ruling corporation, Samara walks coolly and bravely toward the west.

Candy Foster, a sparkling personality in *Emergence* is a "singularly gifted member" of a dominant mutant species "Homo post hominen" who survive a "bionuclear" war, who walks across the devastated United States to find fellow survivors. Her control over environment and events is demonstrated in tests of survival as she drives her Chevy van across a "railroad trestle" bridge, rescues a future companion from a burning car, pilots a small, fragile plane through a clearing in sequoia trees, and survives a death ride in space after defusing a lethal bomb. High adventure—yes —but the protagonist is a female who can think logically, analytically, and in her own words is "Okay" and has "Everything. Under. Control." Candy, with Zoheret, Snake, and Bethkahn, ventures out into the uncompromising environment of the outside world and accepts the challenge with courage.

Perhaps more than most genres, science fiction has the capacity to use settings to posit a new vision. The treatment of the female adolescent's search for identity, autonomy, and a meaningful role in society is augmented in these novels by the science fiction conventions of space travel and alternate worlds. The alternative setting offers new possibilities, new choices—a way of seeing tomorrow and comparing yesterday—for these worlds in the science fiction novel exist side by side. The metaphoric use of settings, moreover, provides "familiar literary patterns" as an important element of narrative.[7] They become some of the guiding "stars" of the literary text that help the reader recreate a vision of the future.

References and Notes

1. Janice Antczak, *Science Fiction: The Mythos of a New Romance* (New York: Neal Schuman, 1985), p. 157.
2. *Science Fiction*, p. 40. Antczak has related the symbols used in science fiction to "traditional" symbols and archetypes, dividing them into "five symbol-categories" representing the "comic and tragic visions" presented in literature.
3. Northrop Frye, *Anatomy of Criticism: Four Essays* (Princeton, N.J.: Princeton Univ. Pr., 1957), p. 99.
4. Ibid., p. 203.
5. Barbara White, *Growing Up Female: Adolescent Girlhood in American Fiction* (Westport, Conn.: Greenwood Pr., 1985), p. 160.
6. Frye, *Anatomy of Criticism*, p. 147–48.
7. Wolfgang Iser, "The Reading Process: A Phenomenological Approach" in *Reader-Response Criticism: From Formalism to Post-Structuralism*; ed. Jane Tompkins (Johns Hopkins Univ. Pr., 1980), p. 62. Iser mentions "a repertoire of familiar literary patterns" as "one of the two main structural components within the text" that helps the "dynamic process of recreation" of the literary text by the reader.

Bibliography

Hoover, H. M. *Return to Earth*. Methuen, 1981.
Karl, Jean E. *Strange Tomorrow*. Dutton, 1985.
Lawrence, Louise. *Children of the Dust*. Harper, 1985.
———. *Moonwind*. Harper, 1986.
McIntyre, Vonda. *Dreamsnake*. Dell, 1979.
———. *The Exile Waiting*. Doubleday, 1975.
O'Brien, Robert C. *Z for Zachariah*. Atheneum, 1975.
Palmer, David. *Emergence*. Bantam, 1984.
Piercy, Marge. *Woman on the Edge of Time*. Fawcett, 1976.
Russ, Joanna. *The Two of Them*. Putnam, 1978.
Sargent, Pamela. *Earthseed*. Harper, 1986.
Tompkins, Jane, ed. *Reader-Response Criticism: From Formalism To Post Structuralism*. Johns Hopkins Univ. Pr., 1980.
Vinge, Joan. *The Snow Queen*. Dell, 1980.
Wilhelm, Kate. *Where Late the Sweet Birds Sang*. Pocket, 1977.
Zebrowski, George. *The Stars Will Speak*. Harper, 1987.

PART VII: READING AND LITERACY

TOWARD A HISTORY OF READING

Robert Darnton

In *The Art of Love*, the Roman poet Ovid offers advice on how to read a love letter: "If your lover should make overtures by means of some words inscribed on tablets delivered to you by a clever servant, meditate on them carefully, weigh his phrases, and try to divine whether his love is only feigned or whether his prayers really come sincerely in love." It is extraordinary. This poet of the first century B.C. might be one of us. He speaks to a problem that could arise in any age, that appears to exist outside of time. In reading about reading in *The Art of Love*, we seem to hear a voice that speaks directly to us across a distance of 2000 years.

But as we listen further, the voice sounds stranger. Ovid goes on to prescribe techniques for communicating with a lover behind a husband's back:

> It is consonant with morality and the law that an upright woman should fear her husband and be surrounded by a strict guard. . . . But should you have as many guardians as Argus has eyes, you can dupe them all if your will is firm enough. For example, can anyone stop your servant and accomplice from carrying your notes in her bodice or between her foot and the sole of her sandal? Let us suppose that your guardian can see through all these ruses. Then have your confidante offer her back in place of the tablets and let her body become a living letter.

The lover is expected to strip the servant girl and read her body—not exactly the kind of communication that we associate with letter-writing today.

"Toward a History of Reading," by Robert Darnton in *Wilson Quarterly* Vol. 13, no. 4 (Autumn 1989), pp. 87–102; reprinted with permission from *The Wilson Quarterly* and permission of Robert Darnton.

Despite its air of beguiling contemporaneity, *The Art of Love* catapults us into a world we can barely imagine. To get the message, we must know something about Roman mythology, writing techniques, and domestic life. We must be able to picture ourselves as the wife of a Roman patrician and to appreciate the contrast between formal morality and the ways of a world given over to sophistication and cynicism at a time when the Sermon on the Mount was in a barbarian tongue far beyond the Romans' range of hearing.

To read Ovid is to confront the mystery of reading itself. Both familiar and foreign, it is an activity that we share with our ancestors yet one that never can be the same as what they experienced. We may enjoy the illusion of stepping outside of time in order to make contact with authors who lived centuries ago. But even if their texts have come down to us unchanged—a virtual impossibility, considering the evolution of layout and of books as physical objects—our relation to those texts cannot be the same as that of readers in the past. Reading has a history. But how can we recover it?

We could begin by searching the record for readers. The Italian historian Carlo Ginzburg found one, a humble miller from 16th-century Friuli, in the papers of the Inquisition. Probing for heresy, the inquisitor asked his victim about his reading. Menocchio replied with a string of titles and elaborate comments on each of them. He had read a great number of biblical stories, chronicles, and travel books of the kind that existed in many patrician libraries. By comparing the texts and the commentary, Ginzburg discovered that Menocchio did not simply receive messages transmitted down through the social order. He read aggressively, transforming the contents of the material at his disposition into a radically non-Christian view of the world. Whether that view can be traced to an ancient popular tradition, as Ginzburg claims, is a matter of debate. But Ginzburg certainly demonstrated the possibility of studying reading as an activity among the common people four centuries ago.

I ran across a solidly middle-class reader in my own research on 18th-century France. He was a merchant from La Rochelle named Jean Ranson and an impassioned Rousseauist. Ranson did not merely read Rousseau and weep: He incorporated Rousseau's ideas into the fabric of his life as he set up business, fell in love, married, and raised his children. Reading and living run parallel as leitmotifs in a rich series of letters that Ranson wrote between 1774 and 1785. These letters show how Rousseauism became absorbed in the way of life of the provincial bourgeoisie under the Old Regime. Rousseau had received a flood of letters from readers like Ranson after the publication of *The New Eloise* (1761). It was, I believe, the first tidal wave of fan mail in the history of literature, although the novelist Richardson had already produced some impressive ripples in England. The mail reveals that readers responded as Ranson did everywhere in France and, furthermore, that their responses conformed to those Rousseau had called for in the two prefaces to his novel. He had instructed his readers how to read him. He had assigned them roles and provided them with a strategy for taking in his novel. The new way of reading worked so well that *The New Eloise* became the greatest best seller of the century, the most important single source of romantic sensibility. That sensibility is now extinct. No modern reader can weep his way through the six volumes of *The New Eloise* as his predecessors did two centuries ago. But in his day, Rousseau captivated a generation of readers by revolutionizing reading itself.

The examples of Menocchio and Ranson suggest that reading and living, construing texts and making sense of life, were much more closely related in the early modern period than they are today. But before jumping to conclusions, we need to work through more archives, comparing readers' accounts of their experience with the protocols of reading in their books and, when possible, with their behavior. It was believed that Goethe's *Sorrows of Young Werther* (1774) touched off a wave of suicides in Germany. Is not the *Wertherfieber* ripe for fresh examination? The pre-Raphaelites in England provide similar instances of life imitating art, a theme that can be traced from *Don Quixote* to *Madame Bovary* and *Miss Lonelyhearts*. In each case the fiction could be fleshed out and compared with documents—actual suicide notes, diaries, and letters to the editor. The correspondence of authors and the papers of publishers are ideal sources of information about real readers. There are dozens of letters from readers in the published correspondence of Voltaire and Rousseau, and hundreds in the unpublished papers of Balzac and Zola.

In short, it should be possible to develop a history as well as a theory of reader response. Possible, but not easy.

The documents rarely show readers at work, fashioning meaning from texts, and the documents are texts themselves, which also require interpretation. Few of them are rich enough to provide even indirect access to the cognitive and affective elements of reading, and a few exceptional cases may not be enough for one to reconstruct the inner dimensions of that experience. But historians of the book have already turned up a great deal of information about the external history of reading. Having studied it as a social phenomenon, they can answer many of the "who," the "what," the "where," and the "when" questions, which can be of great help in attacking the more difficult "whys" and "hows."

II

Studies of who read what at different times fall into two main types: the macro- and the microanalytical. Macroanalysis has flourished above all in France, where it has traced the evolution of reading habits from the 16th century to the present. One can follow in these studies many intriguing phenomena: the decline of Latin, the rise of the novel, the general fascination with the immediate world of nature and the remote worlds of exotic countries that spread throughout the educated public between the time of Descartes and Bougainville.

By the late 19th century, borrowing patterns in German, English, and American libraries had fallen into a strikingly similar pattern: 70 to 80 percent of the books came from the category of light fiction (mostly novels); 10 percent came from history, biography, and travel; and less than one percent came from religion. In little more than 200 years, the world of reading had been transformed. The rise of the novel had balanced a decline in religious literature, and in almost every case the turning point could be located in the second half of the 18th century, especially the 1770s, the years of the *Wertherfieber*. *The Sorrows of Young Werther* produced an even more spectacular response in Germany than *The New Eloise* had done in France or *Pamela* in England. All three novels marked the triumph of a new literary sensitivity, and the last sentences of *Werther* seemed to announce the advent of a new reading public along with the death of a traditional Christian culture: "Artisans bore him. No minister accompanied him."

Thus for all their variety and occasional contradictions, the macro-analytical studies suggest some general conclusions, something akin to what Max Weber described as the "demystification of the world." That may seem too cosmic for comfort. Those who prefer precision may turn to microanalysis, although it usually goes to the opposite extreme—excessive detail. We have hundreds of lists of books in libraries from the Middle Ages to the present, and most of us would agree that a catalogue of a private library can serve as a profile of a reader. To scan the catalogue of the library in Monticello is to inspect the furnishings of Jefferson's mind. And the study of private libraries has the advantage of linking the "what" with the "who" of reading.

The French have taken the lead in this area, too. Daniel Mornet's essay of 1910, *"Les bibliotheques privees"* ("The Private Libraries") demonstrated that the study of library catalogues could produce conclusions that challenged some of the commonplaces of literary history. After tabulating titles from 500 18th-century catalogues, he found only one copy of the book that was to be the Bible of the French Revolution, Rousseau's *Social Contract* (1762). The libraries provided no basis for connecting certain kinds of literature (the work of the philosophes, for example) with certain classes of readers (the bourgeoisie).

Seventy years later, we now have statistics on the libraries of noblemen, magistrates, priests, academicians, burghers, artisans, and even some domestic servants. Parisians were readers: Before 1789, Paris had 500 primary schools, one for every 1,000 inhabitants, all more or less free. But for artisans, reading did not take the form of the books that show up in inventories. It involved chapbooks, broadsides, posters, personal letters, and the signs on the streets. Parisians read their way through the city and through their lives, but their ways of reading did not leave enough archival evidence for the historian to follow closely on their heels.

Subscription lists and the records of lending libraries offer an opportunity to make connections between literary genres and social classes. The most remarkable are the registers of borrowings from the ducal library of Wolfenbuttel, which extend from 1666 to 1928. They show a significant "democratization" of reading in the 1760s: The number of books borrowed doubled; the borrowers came from lower social strata; and the reading matter became lighter, shifting from learned tomes to sentimental novels (imitations of *Robinson Crusoe* went over especially well). Curiously, the registers of the *Bibliotheque du Roi* in Paris show that it had the same number of users at this time—about 50 a year, including one Denis Diderot. The Parisians could not take the books home, but they enjoyed the hospitality of a more leisurely age. Although the librarian opened his doors to them only two mornings a week, he gave them a meal before he turned them out. Conditions are different in the *Bibliotheque Nationale* today. Librarians have had to accept a basic law of economics: There is no such thing as a free lunch.

The microanalysts have come up with many other discoveries—so many, in fact, that they face the same problem as the macroquantifiers: how to put it all together? The disparity of the documentation—auction catalogues, notarial records, subscription lists, library registers—does not make the task easier.

So far only one book historian has been hardy enough to propose a general model. Rolf Engelsing has argued that a "reading revolution" (*Leserevolution*) took place at the end of the 18th century. From the Middle Ages until sometime after 1750, according to Engelsing, men read "intensively." They had only a few books—the Bible, an almanac, a devotional work or two—and they read them over and over again, usually aloud and in groups, so that a narrow range of traditional literature became deeply impressed on their consciousness. By 1800 people were reading "extensively." They read all kinds of material, especially periodicals and newspapers, and read things only once before racing on to the next item. Engelsing does not produce much evidence for his hypothesis: Most of his research concerns only a small sampling of burghers in Bremen. But it has an attractive before-and-after simplicity, and it provides a handy formula for contrasting modes of reading very early and very late in European history. Its main drawback, as I see it, is its unilinear character.

Reading did not evolve in one direction, toward extensiveness. It assumed many different forms among different social groups during different eras. Men and women have read in order to save their souls, to improve their manners, to repair their machinery, to seduce their sweethearts, to learn about current events, and simply to have fun. In many cases, especially among the publics of Richardson, Rousseau, and Goethe, the reading became more intensive, not less. But the late 18th century does seem to represent a turning point, a time when more reading matter became available to a wider readership that in the 19th century would grow to giant proportions with the development of machine-made paper, steam-powered presses, linotype, and, in the Western world, nearly universal literacy. All these changes opened up new possibilities, not by decreasing intensity but by increasing variety.

I must therefore confess to some skepticism about the "reading revolution." Yet an American historian of the book, David Hall, has described a transformation in the reading habits of New Englanders between 1600 and 1850 in almost exactly the same terms as those used by Engelsing. Before 1800, New Englanders read a small corpus of venerable "steady sellers"—the Bible, almanacs, the *New England Primer*, Philip Doddridge's *Rise and Progress of Religion*, Richard Baxter's *Call to the Unconverted*—and read them over and over again, aloud, in groups, and with exceptional intensity. After 1800 they were swamped with new kinds of books—novels, newspapers, fresh and sunny varieties of children's literature—and they read through them ravenously, discarding one thing as soon as they could find another. Although Hall and Engelsing had never heard of one another, they discovered a similar pattern in two quite different areas of the Western world. Perhaps a fundamental shift in reading took place at the end of the 18th century. It may not have been a revolution, but it marked the end of an Old Regime—the reign of Thomas a Kempis, Johann Arndt, and John Bunyan.

The "where" of reading is more important than one might think, because by placing the reader in his setting one might find hints about the nature of his experience. In the University of Leiden there hangs a print of the university library, dated 1610. It shows the books, heavy folio volumes, chained on high shelves jutting out from the walls in a sequence determined by the rubrics of classical bibliography: *Jurisconsulti, Merdici, Historici*, and so on. Students are scattered about the room, reading the books on counters built at shoulder level below the shelves. They read standing up, protected against the cold by thick cloaks and hats, one foot perched on a rail to ease the pressure on their bodies. Reading can not have been comfortable in the age of classical humanism.

In pictures done a century and a half later, "La Lecture" and "La Liseuse" by Fragonard, for example, readers recline in chaises lounges or well padded armchairs with their legs propped on footstools. They are often women, wearing loose-fitting gowns known at the time as *liseuses*. They usually hold a dainty duodecimo volume in their fingers and have a far-away look in their eyes. From Fragonard to Monet, who also painted a "Liseuse," reading moves from the boudoir to the outdoors. The reader backpacks books to fields and mountain tops, where, like Rousseau and Heine, he can commune with nature.

The human element in the setting must have affected the understanding of the texts. No doubt Jean-Baptiste Greuze (1725–1805) sentimentalized the collective character of reading in his painting of *A Father of the Family Reads the Bible to his Children*. Restif de la Bretonne (1734–1806) probably did the same in the family Bible readings described in *The Life of My Father* (1779): "I could only remember with emotion the interest with which this reading was heard; how it conveyed to everybody in our numerous family a tone of goodheartedness and brotherhood (in the family I include the servants). My father always started with these words: 'Let us gather my children; it is the Holy Spirit that is going to speak.'" But for all their sentimentality, such descriptions proceed from a common assumption: For the common people in early modern Europe, reading was a social activity. It took place in workshops, barns, and taverns. It was almost always oral but not necessarily edifying. Thus it was for the peasant in the country inn described, with some rose tinting around the edges, by Christian Schubart in 1786:

> And when the evening breaks in,
> I just drink my cup of wine;
> Then the Schoolmaster reads to me
> From the newspaper what news there is.

The most important institution of popular reading under the Old Regime was a fireside gathering known as the *veillee* in France and the *Spinnstube* in Germany. While children played, women sewed, and men repaired tools, one of the company who could decipher a text would regale them with the adventures of *Les quatre fils Aymon*, *Till Eulenspiegel*, or some other favorite from the standard repertory of the cheap, popular chapbooks. Some of these primitive paperbacks indicated that they were meant to be taken in through the ears by beginning with phrases such as, "What you are about to hear. . . ." During the 19th century groups of artisans, especially cigar makers and tailors, took turns reading or hired a reader to keep themselves entertained while they worked. Even today many people get their news by being read to by a telecaster. Television may be less of a break with the past than is generally assumed. In any case, for most people throughout most of history, books had audiences rather than readers. They were better heard than seen.

Reading was a more private experience for the minority of educated persons who could afford to buy books. But many joined reading clubs, *cabinets litteraires*, or *Lesegesellschaften*, where they could read almost anything they wanted, in a sociable atmosphere, for a small monthly payment. Francoise Parent-Lardeur has traced the proliferation of these clubs in Paris under the Restoration, but they went back well into the 18th century. Provincial booksellers often turned their stock into a library and charged dues for the right to frequent it. Good light, some comfortable chairs, a few pictures on the wall, and subscriptions to a half-dozen newspapers were enough to make a club out of almost any bookshop. Thus the *cabinet litteraire* advertised by P. J. Bernard, a minor bookseller in Luneville: "A commodious establishment, large, well illuminated and heated, which will be open every day, from nine o'clock in the morning until noon and from one until 10, will offer starting now to booklovers 2,000 volumes which will increase by 400 volumes annually." By November 1779, the club had 200 members, mostly officers from the local *gendarmerie*. For the modest sum of three livres a year, they had access to 5,000 books, 13 journals, and special rooms set aside for conversation and writing.

German reading clubs provided the social foundation for a distinct variety of bourgeois culture in the 18th century. They sprang up at an astounding rate, especially in the northern cities. Perhaps one of every 500 adult Germans belonged to a *Lesegesellschaft* by 1800. All of these reading clubs had a basic supply of periodicals supplemented by uneven runs of books, usually on fairly weighty subjects like history and politics. They seem to have been a more serious version of the coffee house, itself an important institution for reading, which spread through Germany from the late 17th century. By 1760, Vienna had at least 60 coffee houses. They provided newspapers, journals, and endless occasions for political discussions, just as they had done in London and Amsterdam for over a century.

III

Thus we already know a good deal about the institutional bases of reading. We have some answers to the "who," "what," "where," and "when" questions. But the "whys" and "hows" elude us. We have not yet devised a strategy for understanding the inner process by which readers made sense of words. We do not even understand the way we read ourselves, despite the efforts of psychologists and neurologists to trace eye movements and to map the hemispheres of the brain.

Is the cognitive process different for Chinese, who read pictographs, and for Westerners, who scan lines? For Israelis, who read words without vowels moving from right to left, and for blind people, who transmit stimuli through their fingers? For Southeast Asians, whose languages lack tenses and who order reality spatially, and for American Indians, whose languages have been put into writing only recently by alien scholars? For the holy man in the presence of the Word and for the consumer studying labels in a supermarket?

The differences seem endless, for reading is not simply a skill but a way of making meaning, which must vary from culture to culture. We could not expect to find a formula that could account for all those variations. But it should be possible to develop a way to study the changes in reading within our own culture. I would like to suggest five approaches to the problem.

First, I think it should be possible to learn more about the ideals and assumptions underlying reading in the past. We could study contemporary depictions of reading in fiction, autobiographies, polemical writings, letters, paintings, and prints in order to uncover some notions of what people thought took place when they read. Consider, for example, the great debate about the craze for reading in late 18th-century Germany. Those who deplored the reading mania did not simply condemn its effects on morals and politics. They feared it would damage public health. In a tract of 1795, J. G. Heinzmann listed the physical consequences of excessive reading: "susceptibility to colds, headaches, weakening of the eyes, heat rashes, gout, arthritis, hemorrhoids, asthma, apoplexy, pulmonary disease, indigestion, blocking of the bowels, nervous disorder, migraines, epilepsy, hypochondria, and melancholy."

On the positive side of the debate, Johann Adam Bergk, author of *The Art of Reading Books* (1799), accepted the premises of his opponents but disagreed with their conclusions. He took it as established that one should never read immediately after eating or while standing up. But by correct disposition of the body, one could make reading a force for good. The "art of reading" involved washing the face with cold water and taking walks in fresh air as well as concentration and meditation. No one challenged the notion that there was a physical element in reading, because no one drew a clear distinction between the physical and the moral world. Eighteenth-century readers attempted to "digest" books, to absorb them in their whole being, body and soul. The physicality of the process sometimes shows on the pages. The books in Samuel Johnson's library, now owned by Mrs. Donald F. Hyde, are bent and battered, as if Johnson had wrestled his way through them.

Throughout most of Western history, and especially in the 16th and 17th centuries, reading was seen above all as a spiritual exercise. But how was it performed? One could look for guidance in the manuals of Jesuits and the hermeneutical treatises of Protestants. Family Bible readings took place on both sides of the great religious divide. And as the example of Restif de la Bretonne indicates, the Bible was approached with awe, even among some Catholic peasants. Of course Boccaccio, Castiglione, Cervantes, and Rabelais had developed other uses of literacy for the elite. But for most people, reading remained a sacred activity. It put you in the presence of the Word and unlocked holy mysteries. As a working hypothesis, it seems valid to assert that the farther back in time you go the farther away you move from instrumental reading. Not only does the "how-to" book become rarer and the religious book more common, reading itself is different. In the age of Luther and Loyola, it provided access to absolute truth.

On a more mundane level, assumptions about reading could be traced through advertisements and prospectuses for books. Thus some typical remarks from an 18th-century prospectus taken at random from the rich collection in the Newberry Library in Chicago: A bookseller is offering a quarto edition of the *Commentary on the Customs of the Residents of Angoumois*, an excellent work, he insists, for its typography as much as its content—"The text of the *Commentary* is printed in *grosromain* type;

the summaries that precede the commentaries are printed in *cicero*; and the commentaries are printed in *Saint-Augustin*. The whole work is made from very beautiful paper manufactured in Angouleme."

No publisher would dream of mentioning paper and type in advertising a law book today. During the 18th century advertisers assumed that their clients cared about the physical quality of books. Buyers and sellers alike shared a typographical consciousness that is now nearly extinct.

The reports of censors also can be revealing, at least in the case of books from early modern France, where censorship was highly developed if not enormously effective. A typical travel book, *New Voyage to the American Islands* (Paris, 1722) by J. B. Labat, contains four "approbations" printed out in full next to the imprimatur. One censor explains that the manuscript piqued his curiosity: "It is difficult to begin reading it without feeling that mild but avid curiosity that impels us to read further." Another recommends it for its "simple and concise style" and also for its utility: "Nothing in my opinion is so useful to travellers, to the inhabitants of that country, to tradesmen, and to those who study natural history." And a third simply found it a good read: "I had great pleasure in reading it. It contains a multitude of curious things."

Censors did not simply hound out heretics and revolutionaries, as we tend to assume in looking back at the Inquisition and the Enlightenment. They gave the royal stamp of approval to a work, and in doing so they provided clues as to how it might be read. Their values constituted an official standard against which ordinary readings might be measured.

But how did ordinary readers read? My second suggestion for attacking that problem concerns the ways reading was learned. In 17th-century England, a great deal of learning took place outside the schoolroom, in workshops and fields where laborers taught themselves and one another. Inside the school, English children learned to read before they learned to write instead of acquiring the two skills together at the beginning of their education as they do today. They often joined the work force before the age of seven, when instruction in writing began. So literacy estimates based on the ability to write may be much too low, and the reading public may have included a great many people who could not sign their names.

But "reading" for such people probably meant something quite different from what it means today. In early modern France the three R's were learned in sequence—first reading, then writing, then arithmetic—just as in England and, it seems, all other countries in the West. The most common primers from the Old Regime—ABCs like the *Croix de Jesus* and the *Croix de par Dieu*—began as modern manuals do, with the alphabet. But the letters had different sounds. The pupil pronounced a flat vowel before each consonant, so that *p* came out as "ehp" rather than "pe" as it is today. When said aloud, the letters did not link together phonetically in combinations that could be recognized by the ear as syllables of a word. Thus *p-a-t* in *pater* sounded like "ehp-ah-eht." But the phonetic fuzziness did not really matter, because the letters were meant as a visual stimulus to trigger the memory of a text that had already been learned by heart —and the text was always in Latin. The whole system was built on the premise that French children should not begin to read in French. They passed directly from the alphabet to simple syllables and then to the *Pater Noster, Ave Maria, Credo,* and *Benedicite*. Having learned to recognize these common prayers, they worked through liturgical responses printed in standard chapbooks. At this point many of them left school. They had acquired enough mastery of the printed word to fulfill the functions expected of them by the Church—that is, to participate in its rituals. But they had never read a text in a language they could understand.

Some children—we don't know how many; perhaps a minority in the 17th century and a majority in the 18th—remained in school long enough to learn to read in French. Even then, however, reading was often a matter of recognizing something already known rather than a process of acquiring new knowledge. Nearly all of the schools were run by the Church, and nearly all of the schoolbooks were religious, usually catechisms and pious textbooks like *The Parish School* by Jacques de Batencour. In the early 18th century the Brothers of Christian Schools began to provide the same text to several pupils and to teach them as a group—a first step toward standardized instruction, which was to become the rule a hundred years later. At the same time, a few tutors in aristocratic households began to teach reading directly in French. They developed phonetic techniques and audio-visual aids like the pictorial flash cards of the abbe Berthaud and *bureau typographique* of Louis Dumas. By 1789 their example had spread to some progressive primary schools.

But most children still learned to read by standing before the master and reciting passages from whatever text they could get their hands on while their classmates struggled with a motley collection of booklets on the back benches. Some of these "schoolbooks" would reappear in the evening at the *veillee*, because they were popular "bestsellers" retelling old tales of chivalry. So reading around the fireside had something in common with reading in the classroom: It was a recital of a text that everyone already knew. Instead of opening up limitless vistas of new ideas, it probably remained within a closed circuit, exactly where the post-Tridentine Church wanted to keep it. "Probably," however, is the governing word in that proposition. We can only guess at the nature of early modern pedagogy by reading the few primers and the still fewer memoirs that have survived from that era. We don't know what really happened in the classroom. The peasant reader-listeners may have construed their catechism as well as their adventure stories in ways that escape us.

If the experience of the great mass of readers lies beyond the range of historical research, historians should be able to capture something of what reading meant for the few persons who left a record of it. A third approach could begin with the best known autobiographical accounts—those of Saint Augustine, Saint Theresa of Avila, Montaigne, Rousseau, and Stendhal, for example—and move on to less familiar sources.

J.-M. Goulemot has used the autobiography of Jamerey-Duval to show how a peasant could read and write his way up through the ranks of the Old Regime, and Daniel Roche discovered an 18th-century glazier, Jacques-Louis Menetra, who read his way around a typical tour de France. Although he did not carry many books in the sack slung over his back, Menetra constantly exchanged letters with fellow travelers and sweethearts. He squandered a few sous on broadsides at public executions and even composed doggerel verse for the ceremonies and farces that he staged with the other workers. When he told the story of his life, he organized his narrative in picaresque fashion, combining oral tradition (folk tales and the stylized braggadocio of male bull sessions) with genres of popular literature (such as the novelettes of chivalry). Unlike other plebeian authors—Restif, Mercier, Rousseau, Diderot, and Marmontel—Menetra never won a place in the Republic of Letters. But he showed that letters had a place in the culture of the common man.

That place may have been marginal, but margins themselves provide clues to the experience of ordinary readers. During the 16th century marginal notes appeared in print in the form of glosses, which steered the reader through humanist texts. In the 18th century the gloss gave way to the footnote. How did the reader follow the play between text and paratext at the bottom or side of the page? The historian Edward Gibbon created ironic distance by masterful deployment of footnotes. A careful study of annotated 18th-century copies of *The Decline and Fall of the Roman Empire* might reveal the way such distance was perceived by Gibbon's contemporaries. John Adams covered his books with scribbling. By following him through his copy of Rousseau's *Discourse on the Origin of Inequality,* one can see how radical Enlightenment philosophy looked to a retired revolutionary in the sober climate of Quincy, Massachusetts. Thus Rousseau, in the first English edition:

> There was no kind of moral relation between men in this state [the state of nature]; they could not be either good or bad, and had neither vices nor virtues. It is proper, therefore, to suspend judgment about their situation . . . until we have examined whether there are more virtues or vices among civilized men. . . .

And Adams, in the margin:

> Wonders upon wonders. Paradox upon paradox. What astonishing sagacity had Mr. Rousseau! Yet this eloquent coxcomb has with his affectation of singularity made men discontented with superstition and tyranny.

Scholars have charted the currents of literary history by trying to reread great books as great writers have read them, using the annotations in collectors' items such as Diderot's copy of the *Encyclopedie* and Melville's copy of Emerson's essays.

But the inquiry needn't be limited to great books or to books at all. Peter Burke is currently studying the graffiti of Renaissance Italy. When scribbled on the door of an enemy, they often functioned as ritual insults, which defined the lines of social conflict dividing neighborhoods and clans. When attached to the famous statue of Pasquino in Rome, this public scribbling set the tone of a rich and intensely political street culture. A history of reading might be able to advance by great leaps from the Pasquinade and the commedia dell'arte to Moliere, from Moliere to Rousseau, and from Rousseau to Robespierre.

My fourth suggestion concerns literary theory. It can, I agree, look daunting, especially to the outsider. It comes wrapped in imposing labels—structuralism, deconstruction, hermeneutics, semiotics, phenomenology—and it goes as rapidly as it comes, for the trends displace one another with bewildering speed. Through them all, however, runs a concern that could lead to some collaboration between literary critics and historians of the book—the concern for reading. Whether they unearth deep structures or tear down systems of signs, critics have increasingly treated literature as an activity rather than an established body of texts. They insist that a book's meaning is not fixed on its pages; it is construed by its readers. So reader response has become the key point around which literary analysis turns.

In Germany, this approach has led to a revival of literary history as "reader response aesthetics" under the leadership of Hans Robert Jauss and Wolfgang Iser. In France, it has taken a philosophical turn in the work of Roland Barthes, Paul Ricoeur, Tzvetan Todorov, and Georges Poulet. In the United States, it is still in the melting-pot stage. Wayne Booth, Paul de Man, Jonathan Culler, Geoffrey Hartman, J. Hillis Miller, and Stanley Fish have supplied ingredients for a general theory, but no consensus has emerged from their debates. Nonetheless, all this critical activity points toward a new textology, and all the critics share a way of working when they interpret specific texts.

Consider, for example, Walter Ong's analysis of the first sentences in *A Farewell to Arms*:

> In the late summer of that year we lived in a house in a village that looked across the river and the plain to the mountains. In the bed of the river there were pebbles and boulders, dry and white in the sun, and the water was clear and swiftly moving and blue in the channels.

What year? What river? Ong asks. Hemingway does not say. But unorthodox use of the definite article—the river instead of "a river"—and sparse deployment of adjectives, he implies that the reader does not need a detailed description of the scene. A reminder will be enough, because the reader is deemed to have been there already. He is addressed as if he were a confidant and fellow traveler, who merely needs to be reminded in order to recollect the hard glint of the sun, the coarse taste of the wine, and the stench of the dead in World War I Italy. Should the reader object —and one can imagine many responses such as, "I am a sixty-year-old grandmother and I don't know anything about rivers in Italy"—he won't be able to "get" the book. But if he accepts the role imposed on him by the rhetoric, his fictionalized self can swell to the dimensions of the Hemingway hero; and he can go through the narrative as the author's companion in arms.

Earlier rhetoric usually operated in the opposite manner. It assumed that the reader knew nothing about the story and needed to be oriented by rich descriptive passages or introductory observations. Thus the opening of *Pride and Prejudice*:

> It is a truth universally acknowledged, that a single man in possession of a good fortune must be in want of a wife.
>
> However little known the feelings or views of such a man may be on his first entering a neighborhood, this truth is so well fixed in the minds of the surrounding families that he is considered as the rightful property of some one or other of their daughters.
>
> "My dear Mr. Bennet," said his lady to him one day, "have you heard that Netherfield Park is let at last?"

This kind of narrative moves from the general to the particular. It places the indefinite article first, and helps the reader get his bearing by degrees. But it always keeps him at a distance, because he is presumed to enter the story as an outsider and to be reading for instruction, amusement, or some high moral purpose. As in the case of the Hemingway novel, he must play his role for the rhetoric to work; but the role is completely different.

Writers have devised many other ways to initiate readers into stories. A vast distance separates Melville's "Call me Ishmael" from Milton's prayer for help to "justify the ways of God to men." But every narrative presupposes a reader, and every reading begins from a protocol inscribed within the text. The text may undercut itself, and the reader may work against the grain or wring new meaning from familiar words: hence the endless possibilities of interpretation proposed by the deconstructionists and the original readings that have shaped cultural history—Rousseau's reading of Moliere's *Le Misanthrope*, for example, or Kierkegaard's reading of Genesis 22. But whatever one makes of it, reading has re-emerged as the central fact of literature.

If so, the time is ripe for making a juncture between literary theory and the history of books. The theory can reveal the range in potential responses to a text—that is, to the rhetorical constraints that direct reading without determining it. The history can show what readings actually took place—that is, within the limits of an imperfect body of evidence. By paying heed to history, the literary critics may avoid the danger of anachronism.

By taking account of rhetoric, the historians may find clues to behavior that would otherwise be baffling, such as the passions aroused from *Clarissa* to *The New Eloise* and from *Werther* to *Rene*. I would therefore argue for a dual strategy, which would combine textual analysis with empirical research. In this way it should be possible to compare the implicit readers of the texts with the actual readers of the past and thus to develop a history as well as a theory of reader response.

Such a history could be reinforced by a fifth mode of analysis, one based on analytical bibliography. By studying books as physical objects, bibliographers have demonstrated that the typographical disposition of a text can to a considerable extent determine its meaning and the way it was read. In a remarkable study of Congreve, D. F. McKenzie has shown that the bawdy, neo-Elizabethan playwright known to us from the quarto editions of the late 17th century underwent a typographical rebirth in his old age and emerged as the stately, neo-classical author of the three-volume octavo *Works* published in 1710. Individual words rarely changed from one edition to another, but a transformation in the design of the books gave the plays a new flavor. By adding scene divisions, grouping characters, relocating lines, and bringing out *liaisons des scenes*, Congreve fit his old texts into the new classical model derived form the French stage. To go from the quarto to the octavo volumes is to move from Elizabethan to Georgian England.

Roger Chartier has found similar but more sociological implications in the metamorphoses of a Spanish classic, *Study of the Life of Buscon* by Francisco de Queavedo. The novel was originally intended for a sophisticated public, both in Spain where it was first published in 1626 and in France where it came out in an elegant translation in 1633. But in the mid-17th century the Oudot and Garnier houses of Troyes began to publish a series of cheap paperback editions, which made *Buscon* a staple of a variety of popular literature known as the *bibliotheque bleue* for 200 years. The popular publishers did not hesitate to tinker with the text, but they concentrated primarily on book design, what Chartier calls the "mise en livre." They broke the story into simple units, shortening sentences, subdividing paragraphs, and multiplying the number of chapters.

The new typographical structure implied a new kind of reading and a new public: humble people, who lacked the facility and the time to take in lengthy stretches of narrative. The short episodes were autonomous. They did not need to be linked by complex sub-themes and character development, because they provided just enough material to fill a *veillee*. So the book itself became a collection of fragments rather than a continuous story, and it could be put together by each reader-listener in his own way. Just how this "appropriation" took place is a mystery, because Chartier limits his analysis to the book as a physical object. But he shows how typography opens onto sociology, how the implicit reader of the author became the implicit reader of the publisher, moving down the social ladder of the Old Regime and into the world that would be recognized in the 19th century as "le grand public."

A few adventuresome bibliographers and book historians have begun to speculate about long-term trends in the evolution of the book. They argue that readers respond more directly to the physical organization of texts than to their surrounding social environment. So it may be possible to learn something about the remote history of reading by practicing a kind of textual archeology. If we cannot know precisely how the Romans read Ovid, we can assume that like most Roman inscriptions, the verse contained no punctuation, paragraphing, or spaces between words. The units of sound and meaning probably were closer to the rhythms of speech than to the typographical units—the letters, words, and lines—of the printed page.

The page as a book unit dates only from the third or fourth century A.D. Before then, one unrolled a book to read it. When gathered pages (the *codex*) replaced the scroll (*volumen*), readers could move backwards and forwards through books. Texts became divided into segments that could be marked off and indexed. Yet long after books acquired their modern form, reading continued to be an oral experience, performed in public. At some point, perhaps in monasteries in the seventh century and certainly in the universities of the 13th century, men began to read silently and alone. The shift to silent reading might have involved a greater adjustment than the shift to the printed text, for it made reading an individual, interior experience.

Printing made a difference, of course, but it probably was less revolutionary than is commonly believed. Some books had title pages, tables of contents, indexes, pagination, and publishers who produced multiple copies from scriptoria for a large reading public before the invention of movable type. For the first half century of its existence, the printed book continued to be an imitation of the manuscript book. No doubt it was read by the same public in the same way. But after 1500 the printed book, pamphlet, broadside, map, and poster reached new kinds of readers and stimulated new kinds of reading. Increasingly standardized in its design, cheaper in its price, and widespread in its distribution, the new book transformed the world. It did not simply supply more information. It provided a mode of understanding, a basic metaphor of making sense of life.

So it was that during the 16th century men took possession of the Word. During the 17th century they began to decode the "book of nature." And in the 18th century they learned to read themselves. With the help of books, Locke and Condillac studied the mind as a tabula rasa, and Franklin formulated an epitaph for himself:

> The Body of
> B. Franklin, Printer,
> Like the cover of an old Book,
> Its Contents torn out,
> And stript of its Lettering & Gilding
> Lies here, Food for Worms.
> But the Work shall not be lost;
> For it will, as he believ'd,
> Appear once more
> In a new and more elegant Edition
> Corrected and improved
> By the Author.

I don't want to make too much of the metaphor, since Franklin has already flogged it to death, but rather to return to a point so simple that it may escape our notice. Reading has a history. It was not always and everywhere the same. We may think of it as a straightforward process of lifting information from a page; but if we considered it further, we would agree that information must be sifted, sorted, and interpreted. Interpretive schemes belong to cultural configurations, which have varied enormously over time. As our ancestors lived in different mental worlds, they must have read differently, and the history of reading could be as complex as the history of thinking. Although readers and text have varied according to social and technological circumstances, the history of reading should not be reduced to a chronology of those variations. It should go beyond them to confront the relational element at the heart of the matter: How did changing readerships construe shifting texts?

The question sounds abstruse, but a great deal hangs on it. Think how often reading has changed the course of history—Luther's reading of Paul, Marx's reading of Hegel, Mao's reading of Marx. Those points stand out in a deeper process—man's unending effort to find meaning in the world around him and within himself. If we could understand how he has read, we could come closer to understanding how he made sense of life; and in that way, the historical way, we might even satisfy some of our own craving for meaning.

STRIKING A BALANCE: PRINT VS. NONPRINT IN THE LIBRARY

Bill Katz

Is reading really necessary? Apparently not, at least for a part of the public which is illiterate, or for those who depend primarily on visual and oral messages to get through the day. Blaring stereo, blood and gore movies, radio and television news between advertisements, and tombstones with recordings make the point that books are obsolete.

What has happened is that the AV (audiovisual) intelligentsia has won the skirmish, if not the battle. Some may remember a decade or so ago when the library press rang with the insistent battle cry of the AV warriors. They challenged the necessity of the library harboring only books and magazines. Communication, they argued, required film, recordings, pictures, and any group of images that denied Gutenberg. The harassed book mavens gave in bit by bit until today the innovation of media in libraries is standard.

Although still adamant about the imperfections of the book, AV champions, reinforced by computer hackers, seem more aware of the need for plural library services. Having managed the idiosyncratic miracle of removing the word library from the front door, they are content to admit that books and other reading materials help the symmetry of service. Fortunately, the average library user seems terribly unaware of the name changes and insists on asking about the "library" when it is now an information center, AV or a media and electronic nest.

It is suggested that this sad state of affairs is due in no small part to the capitulation of librarians to the audiovisual snobs. Furthermore, it may be the time to call a halt to library innovations that go along with the key assumption that visual and oral media are in and print is out. It is not right to welcome videotape and other replicas into the library, particularly when they impinge on the book budget. Also, the AV process encourages illiteracy. The library is simply accelerating the situation.

Depending on how you define illiteracy, about one-fifth to over one-third of our adult population has trouble even with the headlines in *The National Enquirer*. Some consider this a national disgrace; others consider it an explanation of why in nearly every poll at least one-fifth to as many as one-third of the people interviewed are "undecided" or "have no opinion." It shows up, too, in the audience ratings for Barbara Walters, the game shows, and the evening soaps. Mind you, there is nothing wrong with any of these escapes from the anxieties of getting through a day, but it's all a trifle mealy and meager. That may be the worst part about illiteracy. It locks one into the bland mass media.

Even Americans who can read the print on a cereal box, or feel confident with an IRS form, seem to favor AV over print and usually avoid public libraries. They'd rather listen and view than read. Since the 1930s, and for that matter many decades before, the percentage of library users hovers between 20 and 30 percent of the literate adult population. The numbers go down in communities with low educational and economic levels, rise in the upper-middle class areas. Except for the "informaniacs," who at best are no more than one percent of the adult population, use of all types of libraries seems to be diminishing, not increasing.

What's Happening in the Schools

Even when one turns to university and college libraries, the television screen has won. The library is a fifty-fifty proposition for most students. True, at least 60 percent tend to find the building, but almost all of these students are going there for purposes of study, or to listen to records or check out videotapes. Another 40 to 50 percent never use the library at all. The correlation between grades, success and library use is not high, so the pragmatists who are career-bound find better uses for library study time.

According to the Carnegie Foundation for the Advancement of Teaching report (*The New York Times*, November 2, 1986, p. 38), over half the students "never use the library to consult specialized bibliographies or to read a basic document referred to by an author." While there is no particular reason given for this sad state, the inference is that students prefer television. "To exhort students to use the library," the report goes on, "is useless if they do not prize a book, and many undergraduates, even when they come to college, have never been introduced to the joy of reading."

The situation is not any better in the elementary and secondary grades. "High school seniors actually spend less time reading books than fourth graders." And even further removed from the reading habit are parents who, for the most part, no longer read to their children.

One can hardly blame the state of affairs solely on the victory of the AV proponents, yet they have done their part, often with the best of intentions, to push the rising tide of mediocrity. There is an indication that turning from books to oral/visual stimulation accounts for the shift away from knowledge to the love of a high salary. For example, careers in investment banking or computers are enticing many students. In all fairness, some bankers do require literacy and even a command of the humanities for small talk at a dinner with business associates. At the same time, many people in these professions are more interested in developing strategic verbal skills than in literacy *per se*.

A New Kind of Oral Tradition?

Illiteracy is a disgrace, although one suspects it may be an acceptable disgrace. It is acceptable because we are gradually leaving the written tradition and slipping back to the oral tradition. After 5,000 years of laboriously mastering cuneiform and then computer printouts, we are giving up written language. The Shakespeare of the twentieth, going on twenty-first century, is not a noble bard, but a cassette.

As *Time* so succinctly explains: "Tell me a story used to be the plea of childhood. It is rapidly becoming the demand of adults. In bookstores across the country literature is assuming a different shape. In addition to traditional clothbound editions and paperbacks, books now lie coiled in little boxes, ready to unspool and speak to anyone with $7.95 and a tape player." (See the July 21, 1986 issue, p. 71–72, for more "lie coiled" and "unspool").

For another example of this trend, *The New York Times* reported that a Chicago book salesperson at an American Booksellers Association meeting stated, "For awhile, audio didn't look like it was going anywhere, but it has really started to take off." (*The New York Times*, May 26, 1986, p. C15). Ingram Book Company and Baker and Taylor now offer audiocassettes, as do jobbers who are equally at home with videocassettes.

According to some studies 90 percent of the families in America own a cassette player. Tapes are rapidly rivaling television and toilets in popularity. They cover the whole spectrum from how-to-do-it to popular novels.

Tapes eliminate the necessity for reading, and they do something else—they save time. If *Moby Dick* runs over 700 pages why not cut it back to a few minutes? That's precisely what Workman offers. Not only that, but the publisher suggests the avid listener can become an expert with an audiocassette tape that offers listeners "Ten Classics in Ten Minutes."

Given this extra time the listener can turn to TV shopping—still another advance, which eliminates even the necessity of reading a price tag on a fur coat or a ceramic toy dog vase. No-stop shopping eliminates the necessity to ease out to the local mall. True, one cannot purchase food through TV shopping, but that's coming. All it takes is a shopping channel that is willing to venture into the food business and buyers with the ability to use telephones to order what is seen, and, usually, some knowledge about credit cards.

In his *Talking Tombstones* (Oxford University Press, 1987), Gary Bumpert makes a systematic analysis of how the media and technology alter our perceptions and attitudes. He points out that people have grown more and more dependent on communication technology, less and less on reading and thought. While videotapes and cassettes are obvious, there are other contemporary examples of creeping illiteracy. Consider the ubiquitous Acoustiguide that tells you what to see in a piece of art at a museum. Then there is a version of Muzak, which pumps sound into the dentist's office when you'd rather concentrate on your agony or last year's *National Geographic*. There are numerous inanities, including the tombstone that has a recording of the dead person's voice. Push the right button and talk to the dead.

The computer also confounds the definitions of literary, reality, and drama. Many operate under the impression that a computer is synonymous with wisdom and knowledge. Actually, it's simply an information vacuum with a capacity to vomit up data on command. There's no built-in assurance that the information will be valid or that the person who accesses the data will use it wisely. The blurring of information and knowledge continues to confuse us, as does the odd notion that the machine eliminates reading. Up to now even the most sophisticated technology requires one to print out or display on a screen the same alphabet and combination of letters familiar to Gutenberg when he first began to print with movable type.

Be that as it may, there is a strong movement to have the computer speak, to join the other genuine AV group. The idea of the computer accepting voice commands is coupled to the notion that it will be able to reply in its own peculiar tones and not have to depend on a screen or a printout. This may not be in the immediate future, e.g., the computers reviewer for *The New York Times* (February 22, 1987, p. 16) says, "I cannot visualize a functional general speech recognition system coming on the market before the year 2000, if then." Still, he's in the minority, and 2001 is not very far off.

One may accept computers and their undifferentiated memory systems as an aid to everything in a library from cataloging and keeping track of staff to gathering bibliographies and full-text online. At the same time, the modern librarian is constantly in danger of giving up traditional values (i.e., books) for an interdependent technological system that has a place, but not at the expense of the book.

The Library Response

This is not the time to elaborate on the unique qualities of reading. Books need no defense, and, for the most part, librarians remain committed to reading. Some are deeply involved in literary education; Debra Johnson presents an excellent overview of this commitment in "Library and Adult Literacy Education" (*RQ*, Fall 1986, pp. 5–7). One must continue to wage the war against the AV crowd, if only to protect the ground still held for the book. In too many libraries the ground is subject to tremors.

The American Council of Learned Societies says that nearly half of the leading scholars in the humanities and social sciences rate the book collections in their libraries only fair to poor in meeting their research needs. One-third make similar evaluations about the journal collections, and about one-fourth think the same about the newspapers and other reference sources. In every field, more academic scholars said materials in their personal libraries had greater importance in keeping up with their fields than did materials in their institution's libraries. (*Chronicle of Higher Education*, August 6, 1986, p. 1+).

Studies such as this indicate the ambivalence many librarians feel about their collections. They appear uncertain, despite countless user surveys, as to the ultimate purpose, goal, and philosophy of service. If, as indicated, fewer rather than more people use libraries, if even researchers are unhappy with the contents of libraries, something is quite wrong. One may blame low budgets, but it is not only a lack of money.

Often the response, lacking any firm commitment to the public, is geared to the new technology. A dependence on the oral/visual communication patterns undermines traditional library service. It is a case of the significant falling victim to the fashionable and, not incidentally, the constant need to prove worth by counting circulation figures rather than obligation to the community.

There is a need to strike a more realistic balance between the new (AV and all its outgrowths) and the old (just plain reading matter). One should cease identifying the library with the computer advertisements and the pleas for progress made on television. No one will argue that there is not a place for some technology in the modern library. But does this mean we have to abandon our established audiences, our standards, our very reason for existence? Less confusion, more conviction in books and all they imply are needed.

Reading is necessary. And it is up to dedicated librarians to insure that everyone recognizes and acknowledges the role of the book in our society.

SAYING IT LOUDER

Dorothy Butler

Several months ago I started to think about what I might say to you today, and found myself in something of a quandary. Your brief was generously wide, inviting me to "feel free to be anecdotal"—a clear sign that the writer of the letter had read my books and knew about my tendency to gossip. Of course, the letter also drew my attention to the fact that the concern of this conference was to find more and better ways of "making the connection between books, babies, and libraries."

"What can I possibly say that hasn't been said already?" I asked my daughter, Chris, who I was visiting at the time. "Nothing, probably," she answered with brutal economy. "You just have to say it *louder*." She was, of course, quite right. We are not short of *theory* in this field; it is the tools with which the theory might be implemented that we seem to lack. I spared Chris my depressing suspicion that the outlook is less than rosy—that those of us who have been saying for years that children must make early contact with books if the glue is to stick are hardly even holding our own, let alone making headway. She needs all the strength and good cheer she can conjure up in her busy life as teacher, counselor, wife and mother of three school-age children, not gloomy prognostications from her own mother.

Let me pause for a moment, though, in case you feel that this address could turn into a lugubrious lament. Let me offer my first anecdote, gleaned in this same daughter's home a few minutes after the above conversation.

Some of you may recall my reference to a two-year-old called Anthony in the early chapters of *Babies Need Books*. This once chubby little chap, now a skinny, near-thirteen-year-old, is in his first year at high school. He

---

"Saying It Louder," by Dorothy Butler in *School Library Journal* Vol. 35, no. 13 (September 1989), pp. 155–160; reprinted with permission from Reed Publishing, USA, copyright © 1989 by Reed Publishing, USA.

is the eldest of Chris's three children, and, because he is one of my favorite people, I care very much that his new school, which he entered only a few weeks ago, should prove to serve his needs as well as his first school did. So I asked him how things were going.

Quite unself-consciously, he showed me an exercise book in which he is obliged to record his impressions of life in general, and school in particular, as part of his English language course. I read his first entries with interest. With the fluency I might have expected from this particular child, Anthony had touched on his personal concerns about making friends and getting used to new routines. What took my attention and touched my heart immediately, however, was his early complaint that the school library was not, in the first week, open at lunchtime; in the second, his satisfaction that it *was*; in the third week his exasperation that it was never, apparently, to be open during mid-morning break; and in his latest entry, the hope that it might be possible to organize a petition for the reversal of this outrageous injustice!

Now, this is a boy who loves camping and tramping, makes energetic use of his bike and skateboard, builds and repairs things with skill, swims and plays cricket and soccer with style. That *books* owned and borrowed are part of Anthony's very being is his own good fortune. One can see how they both support and extend his experience of people, and the world. Surely, this is what we want for all children.

Before I settle down to consider the ways and means by which libraries —and schools too, I believe—must address themselves to the recruitment of the babies and toddlers in their neighborhoods to books, I should like to look a little more closely at the benefits of a book-based life.

On all fronts we hear of the advantages to children of electronic equipment, the purchase of which, by schools and libraries, inevitably reduces the funds available for buying books. The unique capacity of the book for transmitting nourishment to the mind and spirit is increasingly unrecognized.

Facts are seen as all-important—and the easiest way to produce a fact is to press a button. I am moved to join T. S. Eliot in his plea: "Where is the wisdom we have lost in knowledge? Where is the knowledge we have lost in information?"

There is strong justification for the fear that most of the population is not aware of any loss. How can one experience loss if one has not experienced possession? And herein lies our greatest problem. How to tell such people that electronic contraptions cannot perform miracles, that the state of children's minds and imaginations is more important than the equipment in their schools or homes—and that language is the magic component? Language—the raw material of thought, the tool used by that incomparable computer, the human brain, to reflect, deduce and innovate —has been, in my lifetime, swept aside, subordinated, as an instrument of education, to inert machinery which, we are supposed to believe, will solve all our problems. Resourceful, expansive, living language, adequate for the purposes of Shakespeare and Galileo, Dickens and Einstein, is judged inadequate for the purposes of the modern world.

The ironical truth is, of course, that the highly literate child is likely to be the one who performs best on the computer keyboard anyway, not to mention his other greater exercise of discrimination in television and video-viewing. The child whose access to books is assured and accepted sees things in perspective, and is unlikely to be seduced into dull dependence on a flickering TV screen. This child is likely to recognize the shoddy—to employ a developing faculty of judgment, to want to tap the diverse resources of the *real world*. That there is an inherent unfairness in this must be admitted. Deprived of the literature of their culture—their birthright, that unique source of information and pleasure—many millions of the world's children are exposed to the crippling effects of the all-too-readily-available television screen. For these children, ours is a crime of both omission and commission.

At the State University of New York in 1984, Robert McNeil said of this influence: "I think this society is being force-fed with trivial fare, and I fear that the effects on our habits of mind, our language, our tolerance for effort and our appetite for complexity, are only dimly perceived." I could not help but smile nostalgically at McNeil's use of that old phrase *habit of mind*. Does anyone know what it means any longer? My parents' generation used it to describe the flavor or bent of an individual's habitual thought processes. Not only has the expression disappeared, nothing has taken its place. I.Q. is quite different.

Kathleen Jamieson, communications professor at the University of Texas, might have been speaking of my country, as well as of yours, when she said recently that "the nation's cultural education now is commercial advertisements and prime-time sitcoms and dramas; there isn't the kind of depth and richness that a study of history, the Bible, Shakespeare brought into cultural literacy in the past. And so, the grounds on which we are building argument [and here she was referring to the making of political and social decisions], is in some way substantially impoverished."

The truth is that many millions of children will be condemned to the new so-called "visual literacy" (which does not include books as we have known them in the past); their sentence has been determined by those features of the world we have created which will coarsen their tastes with banal images and strident sound in the earliest and most impressionable days.

Babies and small children need precision, beauty, lilt and rhythm, and the opportunity to look and to listen, both at will and at length, as well as to touch and feel and smell. Words are finely tuned instruments which must be encountered early if their shades of meaning are to serve the developing intellect and emotions. There must be a two-way flow. There is no substitute for the loving exchange between adult and baby, each determined to communicate by whatever method springs to mind and hand. Lifelong habits are entrenched in this apparently simple exchange.

In *Babies Need Books*, I said that "books can be bridges between children and parents, and children and the world." That simple statement, made nearly ten years ago, has been said and resaid countless times in the years between. I was certainly not the first to say it, in one way or another; my early parenthood, beginning over forty years ago, was enriched and informed by the work of my countrywoman, Dorothy Neal White, and by notable Americans such as Paul Hazard, May Hill Arbuthnot and Ruth Hill Viguers, with the English writers and critics Margery Fisher, Roger Lancelyn Greene and others on hand when I needed them for reference. What they all gave me, more importantly, was the priceless gift of stimulation, reaffirming my own conviction that children's very beings would be nurtured and sustained through story, and that the adults in their lives had a central role to play in the process.

In those halcyon days, through the fifties and sixties (which saw such a burgeoning of children's literature on both sides of the Atlantic), I imagined that we needed only time, hard work and faith. Within another decade or two, the children of the world, deluged as they were with books of irresistible attraction and quality, would all be *reading*—voluntarily, joyfully, responsively. That this sort of reading pre-supposed fluency did not strike me as a problem. I believed that motivation—determination to be numbered among the "real" readers—was the vital accelerant into the perfection of necessary skills. (I still believe this.) And these were heady days! We seemed to have solved the problem of book provision. Paperbacks appeared in the thousands; picture books in all their magnificence were suddenly within reach of ordinary families. The more idealistic of us envisaged a time soon to come, when every ten-year-old would have a paperback novel protruding from the hip pocket of his or her jeans.

Somehow, it didn't happen. Surprisingly, the provision of books was not the cure-all my generation expected it to be. I am haunted by a vision of a million bored children, their backs turned to a mountain of books—glorious books which would set their eyes sparkling, their hands grabbing, if only they could be encouraged to wade in.

We must face the fact that we have somehow failed to forge a link between these children and reading. For whatever reason, the connection is not there. What has gone wrong?

If we (and, of course, teachers) consider school-age children, we must admit that our efforts will be successful only part of the time. Producing children who perform to their own age level on a reading test is not the same thing at all as producing "real" readers. The real reader knows no barrier between page and mind; the book ceases to be a thing of wood pulp and printer's ink and assumes a nature of its own. To quote Aidan Chambers:

> . . . Literature in print transcends time and place and person. A book is a time-space machine; a three-dimensional object that has shape, weight, texture and smell, and even taste. And compressed into those abstract marks made on paper, it carries, by a mystery we still do not understand, a cargo of the deepest knowledge of one person delivered directly to the most secret life of another, who may be many hundreds of miles away and many years of time distant.

A thought occurs which is laughably obvious if we come to consider it, but is commonly overlooked: the book as we know it has not changed in form or function since its invention. The first person all those centuries ago who abandoned the awkward rolled scroll, apportioned work to pages, and finally bound them on one side so that they could be read in smooth succession, must have been a genius. Only the invention of the wheel compares. And like the wheel, which has never changed in shape, the book has never altered in basic form. As a vehicle for that mysterious "cargo of the deepest knowledge of one person" (to use Chambers's expression), it performs impeccably.

Why, then, do we find it so hard, in our modern setting, to ensure that books are received by children—seen by them—as conveyors of wonder, delight and excitement? This is not the place to examine this question in depth. Suffice to say that modern children, seduced from birth by a society which dazes while it entertains, ignores the omnipotence of language as a force of life, and scorns old-fashioned notions like the deferment of gratification and the gathering of wisdom—these children are receiving shabby treatment from those they trust. We are to blame. We find it hard—impossible in some cases—to weld child and book together because we don't do it soon enough. We allow other pernicious influences to gain sway in children's preferences and then, panicking, cast around for someone or some institution to blame.

Our commonest object of censure in this connection is the school. Yet we know from our own experience, from the findings of research and the conclusions of commissions, that children who come to school with active minds, well-developed capacities for self-expression, and burgeoning vocabularies seem to slide into reading effortlessly, naturally.

The process should be natural. In learning to read, being "at home" with books, knowing how they work to convey information and to tell stories, is the fundamental first step. Learning to read, in Marie Clay's phrase, is "getting the message." Children will extract "the message" from written prose with the same determination they use to glean meaning from spoken language—if the game can be shown to be worth the candle. And it can be—as it is for the lucky children who fall into the category described above, those for whom books are playfellows and bedfellows from babyhood. We must find ways to reach the babies and toddlers of our world if we hope seriously to increase the ranks of the real readers.

Our only direct route to children that don't read is probably through parents—and for "parents" one can usually read "mothers." Of course there is reason for satisfaction—for joy—if daycare centers and nursery schools include books in their programs. But, like schools, they are institutions that children go to. Real and lasting impressions come from the home. Certainly there are those children who will seize the first book they ever encounter in nursery or primary school, hurl themselves into the reading game, and astonish everyone by embarking on book-centered lives.

They are the exceptions. For every such child—and the phenomenon occurs in the art and music fields, too—there are thousands of children who could have been recruited, and were not. These children are exposed to books at school, may be involved in lively reading programs run by dedicated teachers, but they still bypass books and settle for the uncertain, often mindless gratification of the television screen.

Evidence abounds that lasting changes must be generated in children's homes if they are to occur at all. Short-term effects certainly flow from school programs energetically pursued at every level—and we can be surprised, on occasion.

Let us never become so disillusioned that we abandon any avenue. But until we can reach into homes, and actually change the nature of their influence on children's developing tastes, it is unlikely that we will markedly change the proportion of readers in our community. In fact, in the face of the growing influence of factors already mentioned which combine to convince children that reading is a dull and difficult pastime—certainly not an attractive occupation for out-of-school leisure time—it is likely that the situation will worsen.

I believe that public libraries constitute a unique bastion in this dismal scene. Their one overriding advantage is that they actually exist for the purpose of meeting the assumed reading needs of every member of the community they serve, regardless of age, sex, race, social class or intellectual level. This is not to say that libraries have in the past accomplished this, or that they are all doing so now. But the capacity to serve, however under-realized, still constitutes a powerful potential tool for the reversal of trends in people's lives.

But, still, *potential*. Why not *actual*? What would we need to do to empower libraries to play their real, intended role in people's lives? Particularly in children's lives?

Let's look at public libraries—of course, my conversance is with those in my own country. We have made enormous strides in the physical attributes of the libraries themselves. The high-ceilinged, cold, awesome buildings of my childhood have been replaced with warm, light, welcoming complexes in which the children's department, even if small, has cushions on the mats, books in low bins for easy access, and puzzles, puppets and stuffed toys to make small borrowers feel at home. The children who do come—remembering that babies and toddlers must be brought by parents—exploit these benefits to the fullest. Little can be said in criticism of the system from the point of view of these privileged children.

Librarians then? In my day they tended to be austere, unsmiling people dedicated to preserving books, rather than to serving people—and children must have posed problems in rooms ostensibly devoted to scholarship, rooms in which notices on the wall said, starkly, SILENCE.

My own children had much better luck, encountering that priceless blessing, a kind and friendly librarian who remained in place from the days of their babyhood until their passage into adulthood. Indeed, the garden around the Birkenhead Library was later named the "Nell Fisher Reserve"; I never drive past without remembering her. My grown children acknowledge her as a strong influence on their lives.

Miss Fisher had her own way of reserving a special book for a special child; she would rummage under her desk, and then slip it almost furtively into a child's hands: a secret treat, no less. Once, one of my children came in from school with the news that he had to walk back to the shopping center to buy some India ink for the map he was drawing. He had passed the shop, but had had no money with him. He was ten years old and the winter evening was already drawing in—but off he went. An hour later when I was starting to feel a little worried, he came in and his face was shining. "Miss Fisher had *Pigeon Post* for me!" he said jubilantly. "Good," said I. "Did you get your ink?" His expression changed to one of ludicrous dismay. "Heck! I forgot!" The lure of the library had been his undoing—but the influence of Arthur Ransome on his life more than compensated, we both believed, though we did not discuss the matter. (A friend down the road lent him some India ink and I ultimately took *Pigeon Post* into custody against an all-night stand, which might not have included map drawing.)

We all have our favorite tales to tell; but we are the favored ones—"on the side of the angels," as Forster would describe us. For each of us there are many thousands who do not see their local library as an extension of their living rooms, who do not pass on the comfortable habit of library visiting to their children. And it is from parents that children will learn, whatever the lesson.

We can safely say, then, that in your country and mine we have excellent children's libraries, suitably furnished and well-stocked (though no library ever has enough books, and provision is seldom high on the list of governmental priority). In the main, we have well-trained librarians who understand children's needs and are increasingly accepting of children as they are: noisy, sometimes insubordinate, setting no great store by order or timetable, but also honest, friendly, and full of such willing good cheer that the heart sometimes aches for them, given the state of the world we sentence them to live in.

The problem, then, does not lie predominantly with personnel or institutions. It is one of connection. There seems to be an invisible wall between a huge section of the populace and the libraries which hope to serve it. The seduction of apparently easier, all-too-available entertainment is not merely a deterrent to library enrollment, either. It is a cause of a crippling complaint which will keep its sufferers from books for life: the inability to read fluently enough to make the exercise worthwhile.

One is not *reading* in any rewarding sense until meaning pours, without apparent effort on the reader's part, from page to mind. I like J. B. Kerfoot's analogy of responsive readers taking the text for their scenario and producing it on the stage of their own imaginations, with resources furnished by their own experience of life. This sort of reading is like listening, another skill which—alas!—is being eroded by the day in our society. Further, the reader must "reach out," in Martin Buber's phrase, to meet the author, if maximum satisfaction and understanding is to be achieved.

The active use of mind and imagination required for this sort of reading demands an investment of self, an assumption that the rewards will be positive. How hard this is to implant if those other lures are given full rein in the early years, without competition from the experience of story between covers! How easy, if print and picture have been shared, with delight, from birth!

Last year, when she was two, my granddaughter Bridget asked me for "Humpty Dumpty" from her *Mother Goose* book. "You find it," I said, busy with something else. Quite soon, "Here's Humpy Dumpy," said Bridget, having found the right page. But she was pointing to the text, not the picture! "You read it," I said then—and she did, her finger moving indiscriminately over the words, without a glance at the picture. By heart, of course, but with total, untaught understanding of the way written language works to produce meaning.

And so we go round in circles. Children must expect to become readers—*want* to become readers. Observe the example of adults who read with enjoyment, and who have time and space in their lives to read, before they are likely to embark on the long hours of "practice" which will ensure the sort of fluency which this state demands. We know what the requirements are; we know that children exposed to written language from birth are unconsciously noting the patterns, the conventions of the text. They have a head start, but it is an advantage which only a close adult can confer.

Even once school days begin, children spend more than three times as long awake, in their parents' care, as they spend at school. It is parents who are powerful. They must be reached, convinced, and helped to exercise this power. And, in this connection, enlightened public libraries which have no "age of entry" have a clear advantage over schools to reach and influence. Achieving this access must be the concern of every public library which hopes to continue to exist. Bluntly, if the readers dry up, the libraries close down!

No prescription will suit all situations; methods and programs will be as various as the people and institutions involved. High on the list must be the raising of public awareness that "reading matters," that books are unlikely to become part of a person's entrenched way of life unless encountered early, and that school entry as a time to meet books is too late by five or six years.

Most importantly, those authorities who are seen by the public (however mistakenly) as oracular, must be persuaded to utter convincing exhortations on the subject of books and reading to the community at large. Campaigns run by local governments, backed by business interests, supported in principle by schools and in practical ways by libraries, to reach the parents of newborn babies in maternity hospitals—with vigorous follow-up—might be expected to bear fruit. And indeed, have done so already. I know of several energetic programs; the Orlando Public Library's "Catch 'em in the Cradle" venture first alerted me to their possibilities.

We still need, in all societies, the conversion of governmental authorities to the view that the funding of such schemes is a matter of national importance. We know that children are the citizens of tomorrow; that the horrifying problems we have created on social and environmental fronts will be theirs, not ours, to cope with. Why then, do we still treat children as second-class citizens, whatever lip service we give to our concern for them? As a society, we undervalue children; worse, we work very hard to divest them of their inexhaustible energy, their fresh creativity, their astonishing faith in us.

Empowerment of parents must be central to any scheme for change in children's lives, and this must mean more than access to financial help. Somehow, parents must be persuaded, not only of their responsibility to their children from birth, but of their own incomparable power in their children's lives. Parents must be brought to believe further that this power to influence has nothing to do with the wish to influence. They will influence their children, whether they intend to or not. They must be convinced that their love for their children will be their children's greatest strength, that unconditional human love is the most priceless of all human gifts, and that the capacity to give it has nothing to do with wealth, position, or education. They must come to know that their children will learn from them the capacity to love and relate to other people and that no other lesson will ever be as important as this one.

Frustratingly, one of the greatest stumbling blocks to success in this project is *simplicity*. Great changes are thought to require complex technology and huge sums of money. The simple triangle of parent, child, and book is not easily accepted as the passport it actually is to the essential qualities of life: the human capacities to love, laugh, and to learn. This is not likely to begin to change until support for a "Books from Birth" campaign is given, with appropriate fanfare by the "powers that be." This, while only a start, would be an important one.

Our lobby, therefore, must be to these "powers" as well as to parents. Ways must be found—and will be found—if our resolution is strong enough, our case conclusive enough, our voices heard often enough.

Children are our greatest resource. They must be helped to grow strong in spirit if our world—their world—is to become a better place. Their own survival may well depend on it. You and I know that this strength can flow from books, that language is the key to our humanity, that narrative language is the vehicle by which we order our thoughts, and that these are the things we must give our children. Our cause is not peripheral to the urgent causes of the world; it is central.

C. S. Lewis said that "through literature we become a thousand people and yet remain ourselves"; and I think my grandson, an ordinary kid in baggy beach shorts and yellow tee-shirt in Auckland, New Zealand, is simultaneously Jason among the Argonauts in search of the Golden Fleece; Chas McGill in wartime England, desperately concealing a Nazi gunner from parents and authorities, imperceptibly growing up amid the anguish, thrill and futility of it all; Beric, Rosemary Sutcliff's "outcast" in Roman Britain, knowing rejection, starting to understand prejudice—but courage, and love, too—and Sam, on his side of the mountain, determined to make his own, solitary way. Then three-year-old Bridget, his cousin, astride the verandah rail, chanting "Rumpeta, rumpeta, rumpeta," clearly inside the skin of one of that assorted band which accompanied the Bad Baby on his rollicking adventure on the elephant's back . . .

A boy and a girl, ten years apart in age, looking at the world through other people's eyes, yet seeing clearly with their own.

Once again Aidan Chambers says for me what I want to say: "While we can tell each other what is going on inside us and be told what is going on inside other people, we remain human, sane, hopeful, creative. In short, we remain alive."

LATCHING ON TO LITERATURE: READING INITIATIVES TAKE HOLD

Bernice E. Cullinan

"A love of reading and books," Bill Honig said in May of 1986, "is one of the most important gifts that we can give our young people. I want to encourage students to read and I want them to enjoy reading." With that statement the California State Superintendent of Schools captured the attention of librarians and teachers across the nation. Honig, with the help of his teaching staff and librarians, then launched a statewide reading initiative to encourage teachers to get actively involved in using literature with children, especially in the teaching of reading. This initiative quickly spread across the nation, eventually changing the face of library programs and reading instruction in school curricula.

To find out what is happening in literature-based reading programs, I surveyed state department reading and language arts directors. In this article I will give a brief history of the movement toward such reading programs and the current status of the movement.

The whole-language movement, which includes the heavy use of literature in reading programs, is a grassroots effort led by the already convinced: teachers and librarians who observe children learning to love to read through literature. The movement is grounded in three basic beliefs: that children learn to read by actually reading, that reading is a part of language learning, and that learning in any one area of language helps learning in other areas. To advance these beliefs, we must provide many books at all levels and provide unlimited opportunities for children to read suitable materials that support their desire to read.

A number of key events mark the movement's growth nationally. In

---

"Latching on to Literature: Reading Initiatives Take Hold," by Bernice E. Cullinan in *School Library Journal* Vol. 35, no. 8 (April 1989), pp. 27–31; reprinted with permission from Reed Publishing, USA, copyright © 1989 by Reed Publishing, USA.

the early 1960s, as a beginning teacher at the Ohio State University, I learned that the best way to teach was to use an integrated literature-based language and reading program. Since then, I've never learned a better way to teach. The philosophical stance was formulated from research on how children learn language. Linguists Michael Halliday and Noam Chomsky, and reading researcher Marie Clay, among others, showed that when children are surrounded with the meaningful use of language—in all its forms—they learn it readily and make it work for them. Professional leaders engaged in an international exchange of ideas through travels to Canada, England, Australia, and New Zealand brought ideas by innovative educators from here and abroad.

During the next decade, basic research was conducted in such areas as reading comprehension, the need for story, and the role of narrative in how children learn to read. The work of the Center for the Study of Reading, the National Assessment of Educational Progress, as well as the Wolf, Huck & King study on critical reading, convinced us that children need well-constructed stories in order to make sense of print. Much of this research underscored the fact that children who read a lot not only read well but become avid readers.

A parallel line of research on the effects of reading aloud built upon the work of Dolores Durkin, Robert Thorndike, Margaret Clark, Dorothy Cohen, and Carol Chomsky. Recently Gordon Wells in *The Meaning Makers* (Heinemann, 1986) presented even more convincing evidence from his longitudinal study showing the long-term effects of reading aloud to children. For example, one child, Rosie, was not read any stories before her entrance to school. Another, Jonathan, had more than 5,000 stories read to him before he began school. A sad but predictable fact emerged—all through his elementary school years, Jonathan remained at the top of his grade level in school achievement, while Rosie remained at the bottom. Six years of schooling could not erase the differences shaped during those early formative years.

Others who helped spread these ideas were Jim Trelease, in *The Read-Aloud Handbook* (Penguin, 1985), and coauthors Margaret Mary Kimmel and Elizabeth Segel, in *For Reading Out Loud!* (Delacorte, 1988). In fact, their ideas were so convincing that, in the New York City schools, Anthony Alvarado, the Superintendent of District #2, launched a read-aloud program asking teachers at all grade levels to read aloud to their students every day. He now begins every faculty meeting with a read-aloud session, and district librarians and teachers are currently developing a read-aloud curriculum.

There were others who helped spread the movement across the country. (I cite these here because for research to have an impact, the results must be publicized.) A major thrust in dissemination came through the cooperative efforts of two professional organizations—the National Council of Teachers of English (NCTE) and the International Reading Association (IRA). Yetta Goodman, as President of the NCTE, and Dorothy Strickland, as President of IRA, organized a group to plan Impact Conferences. Their goal was to spread the impact of research on child language learning to teachers, to librarians, and to reading specialists. These conferences featured internationally recognized researchers as speakers. At the end of their terms in office, Goodman and Strickland turned the leadership of the Impact Conferences over to incoming presidents Sheila Fitzgerald (NCTE) and me (IRA). After another three years, Julie Jensen (NCTE) and Phylliss Adams (IRA) took over and continued the cooperative effort until the work was fully institutionalized in both organizations. These organizations extended the work of the conferences through several publications, namely *Oral and Written Language Research: Impact on Schools* (edited by Goodman, Strickland & Haussler), *Observing the Language Learner* (edited by Jaggar & Smith Burke), and more recently *Children's Literature in the Reading Program* (edited by Cullinan). As a public service, Mott Apple Juice Company purchased 22,000 copies of *Children's Literature in the Reading Program*, and sent them gratis to elementary schools across the nation.

This brings us to the significance of Bill Honig's statement: "We want students to read good books." A group of California teachers and librarians took the lead in drawing up a list of recommended books for the California Reading Initiative. A year later, in May of 1987, as a direct result of the CRI, the National Reading Initiative (NRI) was formed and its Coordinating Council held its first meeting at the IRA's Annual Convention in Anaheim. The primary goal of the NRI is to create an awareness of the need for literature and to call attention to outstanding programs that are leading people to literature.

The NRI's first project was to find out what was happening in literature-based reading efforts; people were invited to tell us about successful programs. At the May, 1988, IRA meeting in Toronto, a draft of *Celebrating the National Reading Initiative*, a publication describing more than 60 successful programs, was presented along with eight of the outstanding programs noted in the book. It was decided that six more notable programs will be featured at the IRA meeting in New Orleans this May.

The grassroots movement in the use of literature continued to grow. Teachers formed support groups, often called Teachers Applying Whole Language (TAWL). These groups developed networks, created more than a dozen newsletters, and formed an international TAWL Federation.

I have learned a great deal from observation in my travels around the country speaking to groups of reading teachers. Everywhere I find a tremendous enthusiasm for literature. If I were to draw upon my direct experience alone, my report would be: "It's snowballing—there is tremendous growth in the use of literature." I have begun to wonder if I am reporting on a biased sample: I'm only invited to places where people are already convinced that using literature works. However, when I conducted a national survey last December, I received responses from 50 State Directors of Reading/Language Arts—an 100% response! This is a tribute to their professionalism as well as an indication that things are really happening (See Figure 1).

All those surveyed indicated that a lot of literature is central to a successful program. Michigan, Minnesota, and New York, for example, have integrated programs that are based on literature. Leaders in these states suggest illustrative titles, but are not ready to recommend a list of specific books. In Minnesota, for example, the schools use literature as a model for writing, as a way to understand cultural legends, and the basis for listening, reading, writing, and speaking (See Figure 2).

In New York, literature is the heart of the integrated program in which students are encouraged to choose books independently and use them as a source of pleasure. Activities for the Listening and Speaking strand, for example, may include: Discuss a story, express feelings about a story. Students explore the ways language works by reading books such as *The King Who Rained* and *Amelia Bedelia*. They engage in writing activities by composing stories and creating their own books. They respond to

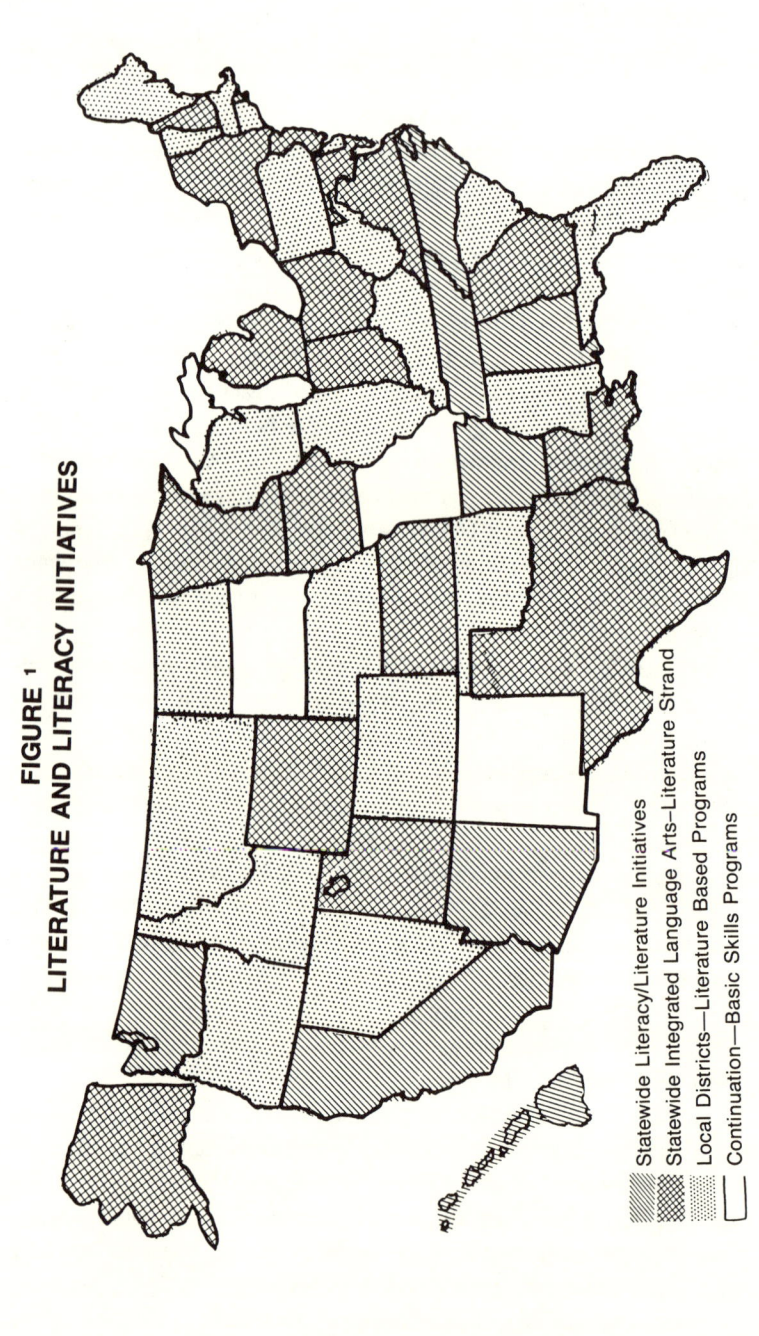

**FIGURE 1
LITERATURE AND LITERACY INITIATIVES**

Statewide Literacy/Literature Initiatives
Statewide Integrated Language Arts—Literature Strand
Local Districts—Literature Based Programs
Continuation—Basic Skills Programs

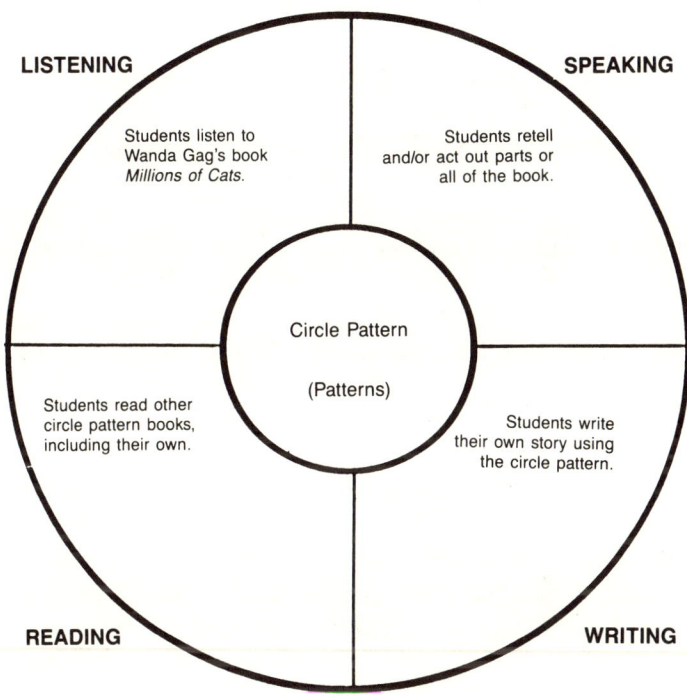

**FIGURE 2
COMMUNICATION INTEGRATION MODEL LESSON PLAN
(Primary)**

literature, a complete strand throughout, by comparing books by the same author or illustrator and by having a "story lunch" after reading *Chicken Soup with Rice*.

I won't say that literature-based programs are taking the country by storm. There are, however, statewide literature/literacy initiatives in nine states and, in 17 others, programs in school curriculums that hinge upon the use of literature. Survey results show that literature-based programs seem to be spreading. Most states have instituted an integrated reading/writing/listening/speaking language arts program with a strong literature strand.

Some of the statewide initiatives have a specific focus. For example, Alabama has a "Reading Incentive Program," Arkansas has a "Multicultural Literature Reading and Thinking Project," North Carolina has "Literature Pilot Programs" in all eight regions, and Rhode Island has a "Literacy Dropout Prevention Program." Hawaii has had a literature-based reading program since 1968.

The most comprehensive Literacy Initiative for Children is underway in Arizona, with three major components: Literacy Forum, Identification of Literacy Sites, and BOOKSTARTS. The Literacy Forum, comprised of university professors, district superintendents, curriculum coordinators, principals, librarians, teachers, consultants, and Department of Education specialists, met during the spring and fall of 1988 to identify issues that impact on literacy in grades K–3. The participants addressed the issues, proposed possible solutions, and developed position papers uniting research and practice that will inform others about the work on the Literacy Initiative.

To determine Literacy Sites, Arizona's Department of Education sent applications to every superintendent in the state: over 65 sites applied and more than 30 qualified. A Literacy Site is a place where children learn to love to read and learn to do it well. The site may be an entire school, a library media center, or a classroom. Plans call for selected people from the literacy sites to form a literacy cadre who will guide the continuing work of the initiative, including the development of model curricula, sample teaching units, alternative means of assessment, a handbook of effective practices, Learning to Read with Literature program specifics, and staff development programs.

The BOOKSTARTS component of the Arizona initiative is an ongoing sequence of annotated lists of book titles that are appropriate for children age five to nine. Each month, individual bookmarks are published and added to a packet featuring different types of books. Teachers and librarians can recommend the books that work for them by returning postcards of titles they have enjoyed reading to the state education department. Librarians, who have been involved from the beginning, are an integral part of the initiative, which is fully supported by State Superintendent of Public Instruction, C. Diane Bishop.

As might be expected in any major educational movement, there are a number of problems arising. Six that I see are inadequate program evaluation, the basalization of literature, cumbersome literature guides, difficulties in getting books, inadequate involvement of librarians, and control of the program.

- Program evaluation. We need convincing documentation that literature-based programs work. Administrators, school boards and parents trust our professional judgment but they need evidence to see that our children are reading more and reading and writing better than they did with other programs. Some schools use Literacy Folders that contain selected writing samples from every grade, holistically scored essays, and written responses to literature that indicate the comprehension of higher level reading skills. Writing portfolios include current student work and they are used by teachers to make instructional decisions about enrichment and remediation. Learner Profiles are one-page documents that include selected data that are reported to parents regularly during a child's school years. These data include scores on reading achievement tests, holistic assessment scores for reading and writing, and comments by teachers and librarians that highlight any special talents not measured by traditional testing procedures. One second grade teacher developed a simple record-keeping system by which children recorded the titles of books they read. During one year in second grade, the group as a whole read over 4,000 books. Another year, a lower-ability group of children read more than 2,000 books. The evidence exists, but we must gather it and present it in ways that laymen can understand.

- Basalization of literature. During a recent visit to a school in California, a principal proudly showed me eight to ten file drawers filled with worksheets for practically every title in the library. Questions about *The Snowy Day* were: What time of year did this story happen? Why didn't Peter join the big boys in their snowball fight? Where did Peter put his big firm snowball for the next day? and Why was his snowball gone? When I asked to speak to the librarian, thinking that I could explain my concern to her, I learned that there was *no certified librarian in the school.*

- Massive literature guides. Literature packets, literature guides, and curriculum materials based on literature are being developed at an amazing rate. I saw a 106-page guide for Arnold Lobel's *Frog and Toad Together.* A letter I just received from a California teacher shows that others share my worry: "I'm concerned about the claims made of '25 skills from one storybook.' These claims make me nervous because they perpetuate the myth that reading *is* skills. Work needs to be done to empower teachers and librarians to help them regain confidence in their ability to judge what helps students learn to read."

- A lack of materials and weak support. There is a lack of faith in teachers and, in many cases, a lack of books in classrooms. This fall I walked into a classroom in a New York City school and discovered that I had given away all of the books I always carry with me to read aloud. I asked the teacher if she had something I could read to the students. She walked over to a closet, unlocked the padlock on its door, and reached in to take out a handful of books. The books she handed to me were dingy, dirty, and old. I looked through them and could find nothing suitable that I could read aloud. I asked if she had anything else and she pulled another handful of dreary books from the closet. Desperately I searched again and settled for *The Five Chinese Brothers*—a book that celebrated its 50th year of publication. There were no books on shelves in the classroom for the students to read. Unfortunately, in this same school, the library was nearly as dismal. Broken glass covered many shelves and because of New York City's financial crisis of 1975, no new books had been purchased since that date. The librarian was tired and angry. She had to cover 26 "prep" periods for teachers each week when the teachers bring the students to the library door, leave them, and head for the teachers' room.
- Inadequate involvement of librarians and staffing with certified librarians. It seems only logical that a program based on literature require intense involvement from school librarians and that those librarians should be fully trained. Sadly this is not the case in many areas. Despite guidelines and standards stated in *Information Power,* many schools do not have trained librarians to guide the selection and use of literature. Librarians justifiably ask, "Why didn't they come to us if they wanted to know about good books?" This is a telling question that deserves to be answered. In states in which programs are working well, librarians are involved and were involved from the very beginning. Enlightened state leaders turn to librarians as a natural source of up-to-date information about quality literature. Keeping up with new books is a part of a librarian's job and learning how to use them with children is part of their training.

- Control of the program. In the survey, some state directors surveyed indicated a high level of interest in literature-based programs, but because local control is the practice, they have no state mandate. Some comments:

New York: "I would not presume to tell anyone *what* to read."

Idaho: "We're opposed to a prescribed list. Some might even regard it as a communist plot."

Iowa: "Iowa does not mandate textbooks or curriculum."

Massachusetts: "We have no state curriculum."

South Dakota: "South Dakota has local control; districts determine curriculum."

The situation is different in other states which are making progress. California, for example, has updated the list for grades 9–12, and has annotated the K–8 list. Arizona uses the more flexible lists on bookmarks. Texas is preparing lists that are easier to update. In each of these states, librarians are involved in the selection of books and preparation of book lists.

A literature-based program requires that children have access to quantities of good books. A literacy environment is one that has invitations to read all over the place. Many of the classrooms I visit are barren. Teachers tell me that they have difficulty getting books. Some have good school libraries where the librarian will prepare a collection for a month-long loan to a classroom; others visit public libraries to carry shopping bags filled with books back to their rooms. Even those who have money to spend and know which books they want have trouble ordering from book distributors. They assure me that it takes up to two years to get a new book into their hands. Somehow, their enthusiasm has waned by the time they get the book.

Despite this dismal condition in some areas, literature-based programs hold much promise for stimulating readers of the future, but such programs require intelligent use. Harold Rosen said it best:

> It is as though there is a deep lack of confidence in the power of literature to do its work . . . and a profound conviction that unless literature can be converted into the hard currency of familiar school learning it has not earned its keep. What will take children more deeply into the experience of the book? This is the question we should be asking

rather than, by what means can I use this book as a launching-pad into any one of a dozen endeavours which leave the book further and further behind, at best a distant sound, at worst forgotten entirely?[1]

In Mem Fox's book, *Wilfrid Gordon McDonald Partridge*, when Wilfred asked the many residents at the retirement home "What's a memory?" because he heard that Miss Nancy had lost hers, he received different answers:

Mrs. Jordan: "Something warm, my child, something warm."

Mr. Hosking: "Something from long ago, me lad, something from long ago."

Mr. Tippett: "Something that makes you cry, my boy, something that makes you cry."

Miss Mitchell: "Something that makes you laugh, my darling, something that makes you laugh."

Mr. Drysdale: "Something as precious as gold, young man, something as precious as gold."[2]

These characters could have been describing literature. Stories can be warm and reassuring, can come from long ago; some can make you cry, my child, and some can make you laugh. Literature is as precious as gold, as precious as gold.

We, too, will receive different answers about the future of literature-based programs. My own answer is that the mixture of children and books with enthusiastic guides will work. We *are* getting books into children's hands, and I trust literature to work its magic. Librarians, teachers, and parents need to cooperate in carrying out new and exciting literature-based programs. However, if the enthusiasm that I have seen is any indication, we have nothing to fear. Increasingly, librarians and teachers are finding ways to work together to ensure that children get the best literature published, and that the integrity of this literature is respected.

References

1. Rosen, Harold. *The Language of Primary School Children*. Penguin, Education for the Schools Council, 1973. p. 195.
2. Fox, Mem. *Wilfrid Gordon McDonald Partridge*. Illus. by Julie Vivas. Kane/Miller, 1985.

REINVENTING THE MEDICAL LIBRARIAN

By Rachael K. Anderson, M.S.

As many previous Doe lecturers have so eloquently noted, being selected for this honor provokes a host of reactions and emotions, including the realization that this is not an unmitigated blessing. This is an opportunity to remember and honor the great librarian of the New York Academy of Medicine, Janet Doe. One has been awarded a distinguished platform, a large block of uninterrupted time, and a captive audience of colleagues to whom one can speak on virtually whatever one wants, as long as the topic fits under the very broad thematic umbrella of the history or philosophy of medical librarianship. Despite an open agenda, some Doe lecturers, no doubt, clearly knew from the start what they would speak about, but my invitation unleashed a convoluted search for a topic.

Preparing a Doe lecture provides the opportunity, in fact impels the speaker, to look inward and backward—to explore and analyze—and for me, this spurred an enjoyable interlude in which I attempted to abandon my characteristic posture of attention to results and practical outcomes as I delved into our professional history and early records. But I must confess that my choice of subject is not divorced from pragmatic concerns. While I flirted at length with topics emanating from work on Columbia's IAIMS project—such as policy issues for accessing information resources or involvement of the library in nontraditional pursuits—I kept returning to what I regard to be the library resource most critical to achievement, in IAIMS as well as other endeavors, the caliber and qualities of the people, the librarians. Although this has been true in the past, there is

---

"Reinventing the Medical Librarian," by Rachael K. Anderson in *The Bulletin of the Medical Library Association* Vol. 77, no. 4 (October 1989), pp. 323–331; reprinted with permission from Medical Library Association, copyright © 1989 Medical Library Association.

reason to expect it to be even more important in the future. John Scully contends that

> organizations designed to thrive in the nineteenth and early twentieth centuries can learn to contribute to the twenty-first . . . only by reinventing themselves through refocusing on the individuals. The key strength of twenty-first century organizations will not be their size or structure, but their ability to simultaneously unleash and coordinate the creative contributions of many individuals.[1]

According to conventional wisdom, one who talks to you about others is a gossip, one who talks to you about oneself is a bore, and one who talks to you about yourself is a brilliant conversationalist. So, in my desire to dodge criticism for speaking too long, and in an ardent effort to abstain from the sin of inflicting boredom, I will talk to you today about yourselves.

Historians acknowledge that, despite scholarly efforts, writing history is not an objective recounting of facts, but invariably reflects contemporary concerns. As the product of an amateur historian, my presentation today is unabashedly influenced by the problems of recruiting staff that many of us have been experiencing in recent years.

Preoccupation with recruitment is not a diversion of recent vintage but a persistent and recurring refrain. Librarians became concerned about this issue after World War I ended, but the shortage of qualified library staff began to attract major attention after World War II began.[2] A 1942 editorial in the *Bulletin* (BMLA) deplored not the number but the quality of those graduating from library schools, and called on the schools to be more rigorous in selecting students.[3] In subsequent years, association leaders continued to call attention to the paucity in both the quantity and caliber of recruits to medical librarianship. Marshall noted the "dearth of properly qualified personnel" in 1946;[4] a 1947 BMLA editorial lamented the "numbers of medical library positions going begging";[5] Darling called "the personnel situation . . . still very acute" in 1956;[6] Brodman contended in 1965 that despite increasing budgetary affluence, medical libraries "have not attracted as many recruits as are needed";[7] and Kronick concluded from the data in MLA's 1969 manpower study that although a high attrition rate due to age could be projected in the following ten years, there did not then appear to be "a quantitative crisis in terms of manpower . . .

[but] a qualitative crisis [was] more of a reality."[8] In 1980–1981, the Study Group on MLA's Role in the Educational Process for Health Sciences Librarians, the Mirsky Study Group, deliberated under the sense of a growing, critical, unmet need for qualified health sciences librarians. Their concerns are confirmed by current recruitment difficulties and in NLM's plan to convene a panel this fall to recommend educational and training initiatives for librarians.

Our profession has repeatedly studied and recommended what is needed in medical librarians. While much of this activity dealt with the relatively objective qualifications acquired through education or experience, attention has also been called to those subjective and innate qualities which not only contribute to, but may actually be prerequisites of, effective medical librarianship. Today I will explore several factors influencing who has or has not entered this field, and I'll note a few characteristics esteemed in health sciences librarians. I think these are relevant to an understanding of who we are now—our makeup, our strengths, and shortcomings—and they may also assist in developing strategies for the future. Who and what we medical librarians are constitute powerful determinants of whether we can successfully address current and future staffing issues. My focus today is selective, and I will discuss only some attributes that appear critical for restructuring the concept of what a medical librarian should be in the future.

A familiar theme running through our literature is the relative importance of being trained in library science and being educated in the subject domain which one's library supports. For health sciences librarians, a background in the study of medicine and related sciences has always been prized and repeatedly pronounced a basic requirement.

Physicians initiated many of the early medical libraries. Garrison notes that in the eighteenth century, when medical practitioners became wealthy and could pursue leisure interests, some "became virtuosi in the collection of books and curios."[9] As medical libraries developed in the nineteenth century, they were generally small working collections tended by interested physicians. By the 1870s and '80s, physician-librarians were often the libraries' titular heads, while the actual work was carried out by clerical staff enlisted from ancillary medical services. After the turn of the century, some staff for medical libraries were recruited from among those trained in general librarianship, but this did not become common practice till the 1920s and '30s.[10] James Ballard, then director of the Boston Medical Library, stated it was "not necessary for a medical librarian to be a physician; at times it is a serious handicap. The average physician is not an executive or an administrator." But Ballard thought it might be advantageous for reference and research departments to be headed by physicians providing they had "all the other necessary qualifications."[11] By the 1940s training in librarianship was generally regarded as essential to avert problems such as the "subject specialist without professional library training [who] is likely to rely too much on memory . . . [and] become the so-called librarian in whose absence no one can find anything."[12] Janet Doe described the opportunities available in medical librarianship in an article encouraging women physicians to enter the field.[13]

In recent years, relatively few practicing health sciences librarians have been trained in biomedical subjects. The membership profile presented to MLA's Board of Directors in 1981 reported that over 40% of librarians in all types of medical libraries had humanities backgrounds, and about 20% in hospital and academic libraries had social sciences degrees.[14] Analyses of advertisements published in MLA's newsletter show that in both 1977–1978[15] and in 1986,[16] subject background was required or preferred for almost a quarter of these positions. According to data from a 1985 survey by Newcomer and Pisciotta, fewer than 19% of the responding medical school library directors had degrees in health-related subjects.[17]

A recent examination of the demographics of academic and research librarians highlights the poor representation of the sciences in their undergraduate background and points out the potentially serious consequences this poses for the profession as a whole in that "we have a fairly narrow educational perspective from which to examine issues or approach problems . . . [The] data . . . imply that we have little formal training or on-the-job experience in quantitative and technical disciplines, even though our jobs and our times require that training."[18] Prospects are dim for any near-term infusion of librarians with differing educational backgrounds since only 6% of students in library school last year held degrees in the sciences.[19]

A component of professional acculturation, which we acquire early and proudly in library education, is an orientation to service—though we have come a long way from the notion of librarian as devoted handmaiden to the physician, as exemplified by a 1919 librarian waxing rhapsodic that "to minister to and assist this wonderful wizard is . . . the privilege of the medical librarian."[20] The service imperative remains strong, but when applied as the overriding value in practice, it also has some deleterious side effects.

The traditional role of the librarian has been described as "hidden," such as that of a nursing school librarian in the mid-1950s who "develops a course . . . which turns out to be successful . . . in improving the level of education." The author asserts that "her contentment must not depend upon seeing her name on the credit line but in the knowledge that something she has done . . . is paying dividends".[21] While encouraging librarians to assume stronger educational and research functions, a physician speaking at our 1967 annual meeting pointed out that librarians "tend to spend their professional lives . . . on a job which . . . brings credit and frequently renown to the people that they are assisting with little recognition to themselves."[22] According to a recent report from a Special Libraries Association task force, the "invisibility" of the work of the information professional "adds to its general lack of appreciation and low valuation." Furthermore, "more aggressive players often 'take over' research results which information librarians derive. . . . They deprive the library of due credit."[23]

The medical librarian has been lauded as among "the most important of medical educators,"[24] and the profession regarded as "important to society" in that it grapples with problems "worthy of profound thought."[25] Yet, as Herbert White noted recently, "libraries, in the common perception, are defined by clerical functions," and they are "clerical traps" with librarians performing those duties which "take precedence in day-to-day . . . operations."[26] At least as early as 1941, concern had been voiced that librarians were dissipating their abilities in performing technical and routine procedures for which clerical staff should assume full responsibility.[27] Nevertheless, data from MLA's manpower study almost thirty years later indicated that "a significant part of the work performed . . . by professional librarians may be of a nonprofessional nature."[28] Although this behavior has been historically tolerated and, at times, sanctioned[29] as necessary in order to achieve a perceived higher goal of service, it is worth considering its possible ramifications for recruitment to the profession as a whole, as well as to our own specialty.

The characteristics and performance of practicing librarians exert a major influence on library career choice. Typically, many library school students come from the ranks of student and clerical assistants. Almost 53% of those enrolled in M.L.S. programs in 1988 had previous library experience.[30] However, the perils for the profession of reliance on this entry route stem from discrepancies between qualities needed for effective librarianship and those valued in the predominantly routine work of assistants. C. C. Williamson, who was concurrently director of libraries and dean of the library school at Columbia University, pointed out that while some of the ablest librarians may have discovered the profession through this type of employment, many others had easy entry because they stuck to student assistant jobs on which their superiors put "a premium on patience, regularity, and a certain kind of dependability, rather than on imagination, initiative, and the higher levels of ability."[31] Louise Darling has noted the significance of "experience at nonprofessional levels or appreciation gained from using libraries" in career decisions and the consequent importance of the individual librarian's personality as a "weapon in the recruiting arsenal." She concluded this has too often "proved a regular boomerang!"[32]

Over the last fifty years, leaders in medical libraries, as well as in general academic libraries, have pointed out the unlikelihood that people of outstanding ability will enter a field which is "bogged down by the minutiae of . . . work"[33] and in which "existing forms of organization have left few positions below the top . . . which appeal to those whose interest and training equip them to do something besides routine work."[34] In her MLA presidential address, Estelle Brodman exhorted us to "understand the place of the routine through a realization of the larger questions involved" and to provide "for the growth and flowering of the intellect of those who come to work with us." She noted that "if we wish to attract and keep more and better people in our profession, we must allow them the space to grow. By their very stature later, such librarians will be our best recruiting device."[35]

We cannot ignore the strong influence that societal attitudes toward gender and race have exerted on library staffing patterns. While these have also affected other professions, I think libraries have not recovered from their profound effects, and we continue to experience their negative consequences.

As recently as the mid-1960s, advertisements published in the MLA's newsletter candidly noted preferences for male or female applicants. Dorothy Hill and I documented the disproportionately small number of women in the administration of biomedical libraries in 1972 when they comprised over three fourths of the librarian work force.[36] In 1977, thirteen years after Title 7 of the Civil Rights Act had become law, the glaring disparity between the number of female biomedical librarians in the work force and the number of women holding top administrative jobs in the very same libraries was continuing. Men were then being appointed to head these libraries at a rate three times their representation in the libraries' work force.[37]

More recently, however, women are becoming directors of academic medical libraries at rates nearly proportional to their overall representation in the field. Newcomer and Pisciotta found that in 1986 women still constituted over three fourths of the librarian work force in these libraries and that since 1977, over 72% of the directors hired were female.[38] However, salaries for women in the field do not yet equal those of men. The *1986 MLA Salary Survey* showed that men earn higher median salaries at every level of experience and at every level of staff supervised.[39] Likewise, data from the most recent ARL survey of medical librarians in sixty universities indicate that women's salaries remain more than 13% below those of men. Salaries for women in the ARL medical libraries in 1989 lag at every level of experience, except for those with thirty-two to thirty-five years of experience.[40] These findings are significant as we look to the future of the profession, since over 80% of library school students today are women.[41]

Librarianship has also not been immune from the effects of racial prejudice. MLA did not admit the libraries of Meharry Medical College and Howard University to membership till 1939, and then only after nine years of heated Executive Committee discussions and pressure from outside foundations from whom the association hoped to solicit funds to support the Exchange. Strong concerns were expressed in MLA that the attendance of blacks at annual meetings would create social problems and diminish the pleasure and value of these meeting for the rest of the membership.[42] The deeply-felt, negative, personal convictions of several individuals who were among the association's most active members and leaders for another generation betoken a continuing inhospitable climate for recruiting minorities to the field for many years thereafter.

MLA began awarding scholarships to minority students in 1976, by which time other professions, with reputations for being both more prestigious and lucrative, were aggressively recruiting minorities. There are no data on the number of minority professionals working in all health sciences libraries today, but data from the 1988 ARL survey, which show that minorities—black, Hispanic, and Asian—comprise 9% of the professionals in the U.S. medical libraries, included a somewhat smaller proportion than the 11% in all the U.S. ARL libraries.[43] Data on students enrolled in library schools in 1988 show that "minority students continue to comprise an abysmally small number of future librarians."[44]

We can ask ourselves with regard to both major societal issues—gender and race—to what extent we are now reaping the consequences of our profession's past inhospitality to women and minorities. Now that prejudicial practices and attitudes are less inhibiting to the promotion of women and the admission of minorities, librarianship is in a rather uneven contest with other fields which have been recruiting aggressively to attract bright and ambitious women and minorities.

Librarianship developed in this country in the late nineteenth century, concurrent with a major shift in women's labor patterns when changes in household technology resulted in a "reservoir of underemployed, reasonably well-educated, young, unmarried women," whose services were no longer needed at home and who turned to outside work.[45] Alice Kessler-Harris, in her book *Out to Work*, points out how the fields they entered and the roles they undertook generally conformed to the prevalent and well-ingrained socialization that women belonged in the home and were responsible for family and household. In the work force, "they landed in its lowest places, without coercion, with their full consent and understanding. . . . Women's assigned role fit neatly into a set of societal expectations of the home."[46] By 1920, "women had carved out a series of professional areas, many of which were loosely construed as nurturing . . . and found themselves in job categories that were heavily female." These included nonsupervisory positions in libraries.[47]

According to Kessler-Harris, the "tacit understanding about the primacy of home roles" was a very forceful influence in inducing women to satisfy the growing demand for them to take jobs while "simultaneously restraining their ambition to rise in them." For the proliferating businesses and offices of that period, women constituted "a transient, yet educated, labor force . . . [which] found . . . rewards not in high pay and promotion but in glamor, paternalistic amenities, and the opportunity to serve." The qualities valued in secretaries and wives were complementary—"tact, an even disposition, quick work, endurance, and a winning personality." However, this occupational stereotype of women was not confined to businesses, and its "broad shadow" extended to other

> administrative and professional occupations equally consistent with home roles. Careers in nursing, libraries, teaching, and social work drew on years of socialization and a consciousness bred to serve. They fitted the demand for personal satisfaction, yet met the criteria for women's work. They were careers in the sense that they paid relatively steady salaries, . . . but they explicitly limited possibilities for advancement. . . . Because it was thought executive positions in all these areas ought to be filled by men, the search for male talent was intense, and the monetary rewards disproportionately high compared to those offered to women."[48]

Modern librarianship was forged in this environment, and some of the attitudes Kessler-Harris describes are evident in our own literature and other professional records. Here are some examples culled from the *Bulletin of the Medical Library Association* from 1912 to 1956:

> A library is always a place where the spirit of rest and refreshment seems to dwell, and to him who has helped bring about this atmosphere there is a sense of satisfaction in the well-doing of a good work.[49]

> Unfailing courtesy should be the watchword of the librarian. No matter how much of a crank or nuisance a person may be, he should be handled with gloves.[50]

> Above all, she [the librarian] must be gracious and tireless from morning to night.[51]

> A library that is as comfortably attractive as home sweet home, and that has librarians as warmly understanding as favorite aunties, will do

much . . . to insure traffic jams at the loan desk. . . . A competent librarian, who knows her stuff, is good, but a friendly librarian who knows names and faces is even better. Even if you can't find old Dr. Fussbudget's hazy reference . . . you will probably be able to seduce him by remembering . . . his name . . . and by calling him that with subtle charm and sympathy.[52]

> The librarian . . . knows much better how she can help and often direct the efforts of the 'family' she is thrown with during the working day. . . . [I]t is the contact with the teacher and the student, making sure both have just what they need to teach and learn that gives the librarian her best opportunity to help develop the *esprit de corps* that makes it possible for us to take the dark days that happen in school and on the job just as they do at home.[53]

This may sound quaint to us, but as Virginia Woolf remarked in *A Room of One's Own*, "What is amusing now . . . had to be taken in desperate earnest once."[54]

I have dwelt at some length on Kessler-Harris' thesis because its insights into pervasive societal influences during the period coinciding with the critical formative stage of librarianship's ethos can help us comprehend how these external forces may have informed and infused our fundamental professional values. I raise the issue here not to account for the historic disproportion in administrative opportunities which until very recently have prevailed for women in librarianship, although I have long been deeply concerned about this, but as a tactic for opening an avenue of research leading to a general redefinition of professional expectations and practice in light of current and future requirements. Some of our sacred cows may prove of dubious legitimacy when examined within the historical context of their conception. These enduring values may, however, be a continuing deterrent to attracting people whose choice of profession, in today's environment, is no longer driven by similar socialization.

A 1988 issue of *Working Woman* magazine listed "library-sciences expert" among the twenty-five hottest careers—careers the editors viewed as being stimulated by a demand for creative professionals in institutions that are managing their assets, including information, with new aggressiveness.[55] The hospitals, universities, and health-related corporations in which medical librarians work are motivated by comparable economic and competitive pressures for greater productivity, and information management is a recognized critical component of their institutional infrastructure. As the Matheson report points out, "Few organizations are as information-dependent as the AHSC (academic health sciences center), and few professions are as information-intensive as medicine."[56] And one of the basic premises underlying the guidelines in *Challenge to Action* is that "the free and open availability and exchange of information . . . is integral to the nature of . . . institutions [in the academic and health care communities]."[57]

Expressions such as "electronic library" and "library without walls" are already commonplace in the literature. Technology is extending human capabilities, and one does not need a library *per se* to access information electronically. The changing library has even been likened to the Cheshire Cat as it becomes "disembodied, disappearing . . . slowly but relentlessly."[58] While it is no more likely that we will witness the total demise of the physical library in the next few decades than we have fulfilled predictions made thirty years ago that microfilm would obviate the need for space for large research libraries, it would be foolhardy for us to assume that "past is prologue"[59] for librarians.

The emerging view of the medical librarian is similar to that of other academic, research, and special librarians as they all generally emanate from concepts exemplified by IAIMS development. Projections of what strengths and skills librarians will need are based on three assumptions: continuing advancements in information technology, growing recognition of the importance of information as a resource, and proliferating applications of information science in health-related disciplines, or medical informatics as it is commonly called.

A literature survey prepared as background for MLA's recent strategic planning noted a consensus that "technical work in libraries and information centers [is being] off-loaded to support staff . . . leaving librarians the dual responsibility of managing the development and use of information systems and the management of staff who assume the routine, but technology-based, work of the library."[60]

This changing technical environment has already led to substantial deprofessionalization of technical services departments even in the largest research libraries. While fewer librarians will be needed for these operations, their work will not be oriented to files and procedures as they assume more complex responsibilities that require better preparation and broader skills. Trends in collection development, cataloging, and acquisitions presage a demand for librarians with strong management skills, in-depth technical expertise, and a firm understanding of the principles, not just the practices, underlying the organization and retrieval of information.[61-63] IAIMS implementation points up the need for librarians to apply proficiencies in thesaurus building and authorities work to the construction and management of databases, and to collaborative research on natural-language processing and knowledge representation.

Additional expanded roles for hospital librarians have also been reported, including director of research administration[64] and clinical information coordinator, which expands the concept of clinical librarianship to encompass management of all departmental information.[65]

Public services librarians already encounter stronger demands, but further new roles are envisioned, roles which may challenge some long-held tenets of library service. These roles are variously referred to as "knowledge counselor,"[66] "information counselor,"[67] "database manager"[68] or "information manager."[69] What is being advocated, though, is renunciation of the neutral reference posture in which the librarian gathers, or points the user to, bibliographic citations or sources but does not evaluate, analyze, and synthesize them to deliver the information the user actually seeks. In lieu of the present "bibliographic open-mindedness," one author urges librarians to perform an information services role analogous to that already standard in collection development—extending to the dispensing of information the evaluation expertise we have not been loathe to exercise when selecting materials.[70] Matheson's report envisions the future librarian who delivers "repackaged and synthesized information."[71]

Success in such new roles hinges on quality of outcome and is not assessed by the traditional quantitative measures—numbers of volumes, of circulation transactions, of bibliographic searches. The shifting focus of library activities from what is referred to as "marking and parking"[72] of publications can be conceptualized as a professional maturation from *collection* service to genuine *information* service. Emily Fayen has noted that "librarians' reluctance to provide real answers and to vouch for their correctness contributes to the low value that is placed on libraries. . . .

Users discount the experience and knowledge the librarian draws upon in identifying appropriate sources . . . [and] perceive that they must do the real work . . . extracting the information." She contends "professionalism means more than requiring a librarian to hold a degree from an ALA-accredited school . . . it means being responsible for the services we provide and staking our professional reputations on their excellence."[73]

Those discussing future developments repeatedly identify several key attributes librarians will need to carry out their responsibilities in virtually all these areas, both in the newer roles and in those considered more traditional. These attributes are:

- Technical literacy—being conversant with information technology and knowledgeable about database design and function.
- Research competence—entailing, at minimum, familiarity with research methods. But it is increasingly important for many to have themselves developed research skills to determine user information behavior and needs, and to devise better ways of addressing them.
- Service orientation—leading to assertive, client-centered programs driven by acknowledged technical expertise and subject background.
- Management abilities—including proficiencies in interpersonal relations and communication.
- Leadership qualities—exerting leadership not only among other librarians but within the broader organizational context, thus positioning the library as an effective player in the overall institutional framework for administration and planning.
- Organizational knowledge—understanding one's environmental context and the functional role of information within it. As libraries emerge from the safety of their traditional isolation in institutions and become intricately intertwined with other units outside familiar domains, political savvy is critical for negotiating and building coalitions.

In other words, we still need those "achievers" Lois Ann Colaianni spoke of in her 1980 MLA presidential address, people who "take risks, cultivate contacts and alliances . . . and enhance their institution."[74]

Among the outcomes of the technological transformation of information access have been the career opportunities opened for specialists from other fields.[75] Information practitioners now enter the field through "training programs outside the bounds of library and information science education and [are] firmly based in one or another of several disciplines."[76] There is also evidence that skills and experience are becoming more significant to employers than formal qualifications.[77]

Pat Battin maintains the abilities most needed are "problem-solving skills, a high degree of flexibility, an ease with ambiguity, managerial and supervisory skills, and the capacity to operate continuously and creatively within a web of tensions." She believes that when an employer's "choice lies between credentials and talent . . . we must opt for the talent."[78] Others also emphasize the importance of personal traits which "cannot be taught . . . in school or on the job"—characteristics such as "a logical and orderly mind . . . expertise in problem solving . . . ambition . . . and be[ing] able to grow in the job."[79]

Maurice Line has contested the view that skills constitute "the 'heart' of librarianship," arguing "that qualities are fundamental, that knowledge can be fairly easily learnt, and that skills not only can but must be picked up in practice." He notes that "the qualities which are the most fundamental and important, might be considered largely inborn . . . imagination, capacity for conceptual thinking, analytical ability," thus pointing up the critical importance of "good recruitment" to the profession.[80]

If we are now genuinely serious about attracting more individuals from among the proverbial "best and brightest" and about improving our standing in what is, in effect, a recruitment competition with other fields, forthright analysis of our profession's human resources is in order. Have we been recruiting those with the abilities and qualities we say we want? And are the qualifications we have been seeking those which are truly needed? To what extent do we, the current practitioners, represent the prototype and model for potential recruits and for the medical librarian of the future?

In a period of burgeoning recognition for the value of information and of dynamic advances in related technology, librarianship has much to offer as a career. But not if our work and image are shaped by ideals and attitudes to which this generation has not been socialized and to which they do not subscribe. When I describe to outsiders what I do and the issues and policies with which we are grappling, I am frequently met with perplexed expressions as they say, but I thought you were a librarian! They are intrigued by the complexities of information delivery and access, and by the problems inherent in incorporating sophisticated technologies into tradition-bound organizations. Information issues that we have customarily treated as esoterica inhabiting the librarian's exclusive bailiwick have moved into the mainstream and are recognized as underpinning not only academia, but industry and society at large. But while people may express fascination with what I say we do for a living, they do not associate it with librarianship; the activities I depict do not correspond to their perceptions or memories of libraries and librarians.

If we are concerned about the future, let's not hastily categorize this as an image or marketing problem but, instead, honestly confront the current reality that underlies the perceptions. Over the long term, have the outcomes of recruitment efforts matched the professed goals? And do these actual outcomes now subvert plans and objectives for addressing true library personnel needs?

I appreciate the opportunity you and the association have provided me today to contribute to such a self-analysis by identifying some qualities, attributes, and values of librarians which I propose we scrutinize and, in some cases, challenge, as we recast not merely the image of the medical librarian, but the very substance.

References

1. Scully, J. The relationship between business and higher education: a perspective on the twenty-first century. *EDUCOM Bull.* 1988 Spring. 23(1): 20-4.
2. Darling, L. A decade of recruiting for medical libraries. *Bull. Med. Libr. Assoc.* 1956 Jan. 44(1): 45-56.
3. Editorials. *Bull. Med. Libr. Assoc.* 1942 Apr. 30(3): 183-4.
4. Marshall, M. L. Training for medical librarianship. *Bull. Med. Libr. Assoc.* 1946 Oct. 34(4): 247-52.
5. Editorials. The supply of medical librarians. *Bull. Med. Libr. Assoc.* 1947 Oct. 35(4): 382-3.
6. Darling, op. cit., 47.
7. Brodman, E. Money Talks, but people count. *Bull. Med. Libr. Assoc.* 1965 Oct. 53(4): 567-72.
8. Kronick, D.A., Rees, A.M., Rothenberg, L. An investigation of the educational needs of health sciences library manpower. Part VII: summary and conclusions. *Bull. Med. Libr. Assoc.* 1972 Apr. 60(2): 292-9.

9. Garrison, F.H. Libraries, Medical. In: Stedman, T.L., ed. *A Reference Handbook of the Medical Sciences*. 3d ed. New York: William Wood, 1915: 901-10.
10. Doe, J. The development of education for medical librarianship. *Bull. Med. Libr. Assoc.* 1949 Jul. 37(3): 213-20.
11. Ballard, J.F. Training for medical librarianship. *Bull. Med. Libr. Assoc.* 1925 Oct. 15(2): 30-1.
12. Hunt, J.W. Science librarianship. *Science* 1946 Aug 23. 104(2695): 171-3.
13. Doe, J. Opportunities for women in medicine: medical librarianship. *J. Am. Med. Wom. Assoc.* 1953 Dec. 8(12): 414-6.
14. Final report of the *Ad Hoc* Committee to Develop a Statement of Goals of the Medical Library Association. *Bull. Med. Libr. Assoc.* 1982 Apr. 70(2): 248-66.
15. Schmidt, D., Swanton, J. Qualifications sought by employers of health sciences librarians, 1977-1978. *Bull. Med. Libr. Assoc.* 1980 Jan. 68(1): 58-63.
16. Stroyan, S. Qualifications sought by employers of health sciences librarians, 1986. *Bull. Med. Libr. Assoc.* 1987 Jul. 75(3): 209-13.
17. Audrey Powderly Newcomer. Letter to the author. January 24, 1989.
18. Cain, M. Academic and research librarians: who are we? *J. Acad Libr.* 1988 Nov. 14(5): 292-6.
19. Moen, W.E., Heim, K.M. The class of 1988: librarians for the new millenium [sic]. *Am. Libr.* 1988 Nov. 19(10): 858-60, 885.
20. Smith, L.E. A suggestion to the medical librarians. *Bull. Med. Libr. Assoc.* 1919 Oct. 9(2): 30-3.
21. Morrissey, M. Relation of librarian to nursing school staff. *Bull. Med. Libr. Assoc.* 1956 Oct. 44(4): 452-4.
22. Watkins, C. Role of the librarian. *Bull. Med. Libr. Assoc.* 1968 Jan. 56(1): 36-40.
23. Special Libraries Association. President's task force on the value of the information professional: final report. Washington, DC: The Association, 1987.
24. Watkins, op. cit., 36.
25. Brodman, op. cit., 570.
26. White, HS. Basic competencies and the pursuit of equal opportunity: part 1. *Libr. J.* 1988 Jul. 113(12): 56-7.
27. Babcock, H. The subject specialist. *Bull. Med. Libr. Assoc.* 1941 Oct. 30(1): 67-71.
28. Kronick, op. cit., 294.
29. Greenbaum, J.R. Work analysis of functions and duties of the medical library staff. *Bull. Med. Libr. Assoc.* 1943 Oct. 31(4): 339-43.
30. Moen, op. cit., 859.
31. Williamson, C.C. Essentials in the training of university librarians—III. *Coll Res Libr.* 1939 Dec. 1(1): 30-2.
32. Darling, op. cit., 47.
33. Brodman, op. cit., 569.
34. White, C.M. Essentials in the training of university librarians: discussion. *Coll. Res. Libr.* 1939 Dec. 1(1): 35-8.
35. Brodman, op. cit., 569-71.
36. Goldstein, R.K., Hill, D.R. The status of women in the administration of health sciences libraries. *Bull. Med. Libr. Assoc.* 1975 Oct. 63(4): 386-95.
37. Goldstein, R.K., Hill DR. The status of women in the administration of health sciences

libraries: a five-year follow-up study, 1972-1977. *Bull. Med. Libr. Assoc.* 1980 Jan. 68(1): 6-15.
38. Newcomer, A.P., Pisciotta RA. Career progression of academic medical library directors. *Bull. Med. Libr. Assoc.* 1989 Apr. 77(2): 185-95.
39. Medical Library Association. *MLA 1986 salary survey.* Chicago: The Association, 1986: 4.
40. Association of Research Libraries. *ARL annual salary survey,* 1988. Washington, DC: The Association, 1988.
41. Moen, op. cit., 858.
42. Medical Library Association Archives. *Executive Committee papers. 1939 Mar.#Nov.* History of Medicine Division, National Library of Medicine.
43. Association of Research Libraries, op. cit., 7. (Unpublished data provided by Gordon Fretwell, E-mail to the author, April 5, 1989.)
44. Moen, op. cit., 885.
45. Kessler-Harris, A. *Out to work: a history of wage-earning women in the United States.* Oxford, England: Oxford University Press, 1982: 113.
46. Ibid., viii.
47. Ibid., 116-7.
48. Ibid., 230-5.
49. Myers, G.W. Hospital records in relation to the hospital library. *Bull. Med. Libr. Assoc.* 1911 Oct. 1(2): 55-7.
50. Ballard, J.F. Some problems in the administration of a medical library. *Bull. Med. Libr. Assoc.* 1914 Oct. 4(2): 36-49.
51. Naylor, M.V. The medical librarian. *Bull. Med. Libr. Assoc.* 1942 Jan. 30(2): 124-5.
52. Vincent, E.H. Your library and your public. *Bull. Med. Libr. Assoc.* 1950 Jan. 38(1): 27-30.
53. Morrissey, op. cit., 452.
54. Woolf, V. *A room of one's own.* New York: Harcourt Brace Jovanovich, 1957: 57.
55. Morris, M. Twenty-five hottest careers in 1988. *Working Woman* 1988 Jul. 55-64, 92-3.
56. Matheson, N.W., Cooper JAD. Academic information in the academic health sciences center: roles for the library in information management. *J. Med. Educ.* 1982 Oct. (pt. 2). 57(10): 13.
57. Association of Academic Health Sciences Library Directors and Medical Library Association. *Challenge to action: planning and evaluation guidelines for academic health sciences libraries.* Chicago: Medical Library Association, 1987: 3.
58. Molholt, P. Libraries and the new technologies: courting the Cheshire Cat. *Libr. J.* 1988 Nov. 15. 113(19): 37-41.
59. Shakespeare, W. *The tempest,* act 2, sc. 1, line 242.
60. Medical Library Association. *Changing roles of librarians: unpublished working papers for strategic planning environmental scan.* Chicago: The Association, 1987.
61. Hill, J.S. Staffing technical services in 1995. *J. Libr. Admin.* 1988. 9(1): 87-103.
62. Webb, G.M. Educating librarians and support staff for technical services. *J. Libr. Admin.* 1988. 9(1): 111-20.
63. Barker, J.W. Acquisitions and collection development: 2001. *Libr. Acq. Pract. Theory* 1988. 12(2): 243-8.
64. Thibodeau, P.L. Director of research administration. *Bull. Med. Libr. Assoc.* 1983 Apr. 71(2): 217-9.
65. White, A. A., Savit M.E.K, McBride M. E. Clinical information coordinator: a new spe-

cialist role for medical librarians. *Bull. Med. Libr. Assoc.* 1980 Oct. 68(4): 367-9.
66. Spaulding, F.H. Special librarian to knowledge counselor in the year 2006. *Spec. Libr.* 1988 Spring. 79(2): 83-91.
67. Horton, F.W. The emerging information counselor. *ASIS Bull.* 1982 Jun. 8(5): 16-9.
68. Fayen, E.G. Beyond technology: rethinking "librarian." *Am. Libr.* 1986 Apr. 17(4): 240-2.
69. Drake, M.A. Information management and special librarianship. *Spec. Libr.* 1982 Oct. 73(4): 225-37.
70. Rice, J. The hidden role of librarians. *Libr. J.* 1989 Jan. 114(1): 57-9.
71. Matheson, op. cit., 35.
72. Spigai, F. The librarian's role in providing information for management. In: Boehm, E.H., Buckland, M.K., eds. *Education for information management: directions for the future.* Santa Barbara, CA: International Academy at Santa Barbara, 1983. 49-54.
73. Fayen, op. cit., 241.
74. Colaianni, L.A. Where there is no vision the people perish. *Bull. Med. Libr. Assoc.* 1980 Oct. 68(4): 321-6.
75. Cronin, B. Post-industrial society: some manpower issues for the library/information profession. *J. Inf. Sci.* 1983 Aug. 7(1): 1-14.
76. Garrison, G. Challenges to information science education. *J. Am. Soc. Inf. Sci.* 1988 Sep. 39(5): 362-6.
77. Moore, N. *The emerging markets for librarians and information workers.* Boston Spa: British Library Board, 1987: 142. (Library and information research report.)
78. Battin, P. Developing university and research library professionals: a director's perspective. *Am. Libr.* 1983 Jan. 14(1): 22-5.
79. Preschel, B.M. Education of the information professional: what employers want. *J. Am. Soc. Inf. Sci.* 1983 Sep. 39(5): 358-61.
80. Line, M.B. Requirements for library and information work and the role of library education. *Educ. Inf.* 1983 Mar. 1(1): 25-37.

THE "QUIET REVOLUTION": A PROFESSION AT THE CROSSROADS

Herbert S. White

Teaching special librarianship to largely inexperienced students for 12 years, and offering countless continuing education seminars to special library practitioners for almost as long, has allowed me to develop and strengthen my convictions, and probably also my biases. I believe that special librarianship cannot be defined by type of library, but rather by the value system that is brought to the information interaction we have with our clients. Special librarianship, I am quite certain, is a state of mind and an attitude, and it is most directly defined by that marvelous motto that has served us so well for more than 60 years: "Putting Knowledge to Work." Putting it to work is not a passive process; it does not consist of developing huge collections without measuring or caring whether or not they are used or whether or not the information being searched for can be found, a practice too prevalent in many academic libraries in which ownership and not availability is all that counts. It is a process of giving users what they need, and what they need is not necessarily what they want or what they ask for.

Because of our emphasis on information service, special librarians are not likely to fall into the "type of materials" trap that bedevils other libraries. We know that World War II spawned the technical report as a mechanism for rapid communication, and it soon moved from sci-tech to the business community. For many special libraries it is these reports, and certainly not books, that form the lifeblood of the collection. For others, it might be engineering drawings, patents, laboratory notebooks,

---

"The 'Quiet Revolution': A Profession at the Crossroads," by Herbert S. White in *Special Libraries* Vol. 80, no. 1 (Winter 1989), pp. 24–30; reprinted with permission from *Special Libraries* © 1989 by Special Libraries Association.

or newspaper clippings. The rest of the profession has yet to make this adjustment. It catalogs books in great detail on a descriptive, but not subject, basis, it depends on professional societies to analyze periodicals, and it files everything else in cabinets with only perfunctory control. Our willingness to forego an emphasis on type of material for an emphasis on information need stands us in good stead, because it avoids quite neatly the question of what belongs in libraries. We are best primed, if we see and seize this opportunity, to become the supermarket for organizational one-stop information shopping.

One of the tremendous advantages that special librarians have over their colleagues in public, school, and, particularly, academic libraries is that they have more freedom to do what they feel needs to be done. They are, of course, constrained by budgets and headcounts ceilings, but these are minor constraints if they can demonstrate that what they want to do makes sense in the overall organization, as well as provides better information for decisions and saves money.

Nevertheless, there are pitfalls and traps we must recognize and deal with. For the remainder of this paper, I will try to identify these, and outline what we must do about them.

The Special Library "Versus" the Information Center. To a considerable extent, this has become, or should by now have become, the great non-issue of the 1980s. The initial development of information centers, and most particularly technical information centers, was based on the premise that libraries only operated in the passive environment of ordering material as requested, circulating it on demand, and borrowing it where necessary. Information centers, staffed by subject specialists, would interact with the information needs of the client, and then refer the specific document request to the library. Information centers and special libraries cannot coexist in the same organization without trivializing the library into a supply room or purchasing department. For several years my facetious, and yet serious response, to questions about the difference between managers of special libraries and managers of technical information centers has been "about $5,000 a year in starting salary."

The Special Library and the Information Analysis Center. This also must be listed although it should no longer be an issue. The implementation of information analysis centers (IAC) was first urged by Alvin Weinberg, who argued that scientific and technical information analysis was one of the greatest responsibilities of senior scientists.[1] IACs, as envisaged by Weinberg, analyzed documents, determined those with and without value, made recommendations to ultimate users, and prepared briefings and digests that dealt with content analysis and evaluation. The idea may have been good, but it never came to fruition. A few such centers were started (Weinberg's recommendations, then as now, must be taken seriously), but they foundered and disappeared when the suggestion of cost recovery began to be raised. Moreover, Weinberg's belief that the best and the brightest of the cadre of technical and scientific professionals should concentrate on information work never took hold. These individuals perceive, and continue to perceive (probably correctly), that their rapid path to advancement lies not there but in the laboratory, in marketing, or in administration. The reverse phenomenon occurred, and individuals with technical, but without library, backgrounds who have gravitated to our arena of work must be looked at with suspicion.

The Special Librarian and the Computer Center Manager. Increasingly, corporate organizations have placed the library under the management control of the group that selects, manages, maintains, and programs computer hardware. The decision to place special libraries into this organization probably follows most directly from the fact that nobody really knows where libraries do fit. They can be placed in Research and Development, but librarians are not laboratory scientists. They can be placed into an Administrative Services group, but they have little in common with the supervisors of cafeterias, mail services, and duplication centers. The truth is, of course, that libraries don't really fit well into any larger group any more than the corporate legal staff does. However, of all the possible reporting relationships for the special library, reporting to the computer services organization is perhaps the worst. Years on the board of directors of the American Federation of Information Processing Societies have convinced me that there is almost an unavoidable conflict between those who promulgate computers and their use as inherent and obvious good things, and those whose search for solutions to information problems inevitably brings them to a consideration of technology. Special librarians do, indeed, need computer professionals, but they need them as service experts contracted to implement needed protocols, to acquire the hardware and software appropriate to what the special librarian wants to do, and to fix what is broken.

The Special Librarian and the MBA-trained MIS People. Special librarians rarely report to these individuals, in large part because they rarely care to be weighted down by operational management responsibilities, perhaps least of all by librarians. The difficulty here is that these individuals, well versed in writing concept papers, making impact presentations, and presenting three-color graphics, don't know how to run information systems that deliver information in a form in which people can use it. The greatest danger, then, is two-fold. The first is that because they are pretending to run the information system, there really won't be any at all. The other is that the special librarian will end up doing all of their work, while they get the credit.

The Special Librarian and the Organizational Philosophy Toward Decentralization. The tendency toward decentralization of organizational decision making into so-called profit centers is both the result of an attempt to bring responsibility to the lowest possible organizational level and to implement the "small is beautiful" philosophy so prevalent in the last decade. In principle, and probably in practice, the premise makes sense for a lot of operations. After all, individuals at the most operational level should know best of all what they need and what they are willing to pay for. This does not work for special libraries, precisely because users can't really tell a good library from a bad one unless they've previously had access to a really good one. They can, of course, tell a cheap library from an expensive one, at least in terms of immediate and visible cost. We know that cheap libraries can lead to very expensive problems. Decentralization of decision making and library service tends to lead to very unequal levels of library service within the same parent organization. To the extent to which information ignorance develops that may seem acceptable (more likely unknown) to the local management, but the subordinates, whose development is thus stunted, frequently end up working for someone else, who then becomes the victim of the first manager's avarice. Decentralization of library service also leads to overlap and duplication, gaps, and confusion. Library service points do need to be decentralized and brought close to the work area of the specific patrons, although telephones, terminals, and electronic messaging can go a long way toward overcoming this problem. The development of special library policy for the organization and its management, however, needs to be a centralized process to ensure consistency and effectiveness. There is precedent in maintaining centralized services in an otherwise decentralized environment. It occurs most frequently, and quite correctly, in the approach to Legal Departments. Corporations can't afford inconsistent and contradictory legal advice, and the level of legal service is taken out of the hands of local managers. The same scenario should apply to special libraries, but we haven't made it as obvious.

The Special Library and the Overhead Budget Process. Special libraries are overhead organizations. It is probably better to recognize rather than hide this fact, because attempts to find allocation mechanisms for library costs to direct groups, by asking them to buy what they perceive as needed library services, usually lead to expensive record keeping and to the perception of libraries as nickel and dime operations concerned primarily with detail. There are many parts of corporate organizations for which the premise of a centrally budgeted overhead operation is accepted and recognized. These include accounting, personnel, and, of course, the chief executive officer and his staff. Their costs are allocated to user groups but not negotiated with user groups. The only difference is that they protect themselves better than we do.

The Special Library and User Expectations. Many professional users come from academic institutions to posts in which they will be served by special librarians. As students, they were prepared to expect little except harassment by rules. Through experience in numerous special library posts and consulting assignments, it has been my observation the users of special libraries, like the users of other libraries, accept what is offered to them and consider it adequate, even good. They accept our limitations of service in part because they like us and don't want to make trouble for us,[2] and in part because they have at least two alternatives to getting things from the library—getting it themselves or pretending they didn't need it in the first place.[3]

The development of adequate user expectations requires that we create, quite consciously and despite the probable reluctance of our own managers, an imbalance between what we can give people and what we tell them they ought to have. Creating that imbalance is marketing, and one very simple definition involves convincing individuals that they need what they do not now have. For special librarians this is not any sort of self-serving process, because our users frequently do not know what they could have until we tell them. Special librarians and, for that matter, managers in any other field, who never offer a service until they know how they are going to budget for it during the following year, are not likely to offer many new services.

The Special Library and the Failure to Control Organizational Information Cost or Turf. In other writings, I have commented on the failure of librarians to control their "turf," and probably nowhere does that issue become more crucial to success and survival than in corporate libraries.[4] It is the uniqueness of a skill or capability, or the unique authority to perform a certain function, that provides us with the primary source of authority. We already know from many management writings that most authority is not acquired through the legitimate process of formal assignment. It is seized as necessary to complete whatever it is we have to do. Purchasing agents understand issues of turf very well. After all, anyone can purchase. One finds a vendor, arranges a deal, and pays the invoice. The turf of the purchasing department comes from the fact that the rest of us aren't allowed to do what it does.

What is the special library's turf, and its exclusively? Here we run into two potential problems. The first is that we have no automatic exclusive hold on the information-gathering process. Others can do it, as long as they have money and higher-level management lets them. They can acquire books and journals; they can contract for online searching and document delivery. This leads to the second problem. They usually *do* have more money than the library does, because it is the formal library budget and not the dozens of pseudo-library budgets that receive scrutiny. Some special librarians even hasten this dilution of their own authority by urging user groups to spend their own money for library materials in the absence of adequate library funding, and of course library funds are always inadequate. The role for the special librarian here must be to claim and insist on his or her exclusivity, as purchasing agents have always done.

It is easy to demonstrate that such centralization is economically efficient, both because we can inevitably do information work better, faster, and cheaper; and because centralization of information costs provides far better organizational monitoring and mechanisms. The application of "turf" here is really quite simple. Either we get to do it or nobody gets to do it. If there really is no money, then make the others stop. Direct/indirect differentiations are irrelevant in the framework of corporate profitability. Money is money, no matter how spent.

Special Libraries and Organizational Propaganda. Management pressures for greater economy never end. In part, this is because there really may be financial problems, but primarily it is because corporate executives don't know what to spend in support of subsidiary activities, and because they know that assertive and ambitious managers will acquire more resources if there is ever any letup. Pressures to save money usually couched in hysterical terms are incessant, and individuals must learn to sift the reality from the verbiage.

Special librarians appear particularly vulnerable to the suggestion that they be "good soldiers" and absorb into their units misfits whom the personnel department would rather not fire, but for whom no other willing supervisor can be found. This phenomenon has become so common that special libraries can become known as a personnel dumping ground. Personnel administrators do this quite dispassionately, in part because they (along with others) don't understand the importance of high-quality staff in the library, and in part because librarians appear to be tractable victims. Special librarians also become easy targets for the suggestion that they somehow do more with less or at least as much with less, despite the warning by Hedberg a decade ago that such absorption only serves as a self-indictment for having squandered money in the past.[5] Management has the right to change budgets and, specifically, to decrease them. However, budget changes lead to a reformulation of programs and plans, which must, in turn, be approved by the very management that cut the budget. Declines in service, therefore, become their decision and their responsibility.

Special Libraries and the Need to Justify. Tons of management literature tell us that higher-level management requires exception reporting. That is, it is assumed that subordinates will claim credit for everything that went well, but they are likely to hide their problems from their bosses, and it is precisely that information that managers most need. Special libraries tend to be measured not by what they do, but by how much they spend. Since they spend very little, but are usually suspected of spending too much, any management discussion limited to the budget is a disaster from the outset.

Special librarians, in their formal and informal communication devices, need to do exception reporting. They need to communicate what went wrong or, more likely, what didn't happen when it should have. Some special libraries do attempt to do this, in documents that describe the size of backlogs and lists of unpurchased materials. However, such justifications that focus inwardly on the library and its value system are doomed from the start. The parent organization is not in the business of having a strong library, but it may want a strong library if it can be demonstrated that other things of more direct consequence will happen if there is a good library, or won't happen if there is a poor one. Library shortcomings need to be expressed in terms of impact on users and, most specifically, the key user groups whose success is so crucial that nobody will risk short-changing the library if, as a result, he or she might be blamed for a larger failure.

The Special Library and the Clerical Trap. We have all known for some time that all libraries are clerical traps; that is the work needed to keep the library functioning and the work most closely perceived by our patrons is clerical in nature (ordering, filing, photocopying, circulation, overdue notices). The professional work (literature searches, information dissemination, advanced reference) is not necessarily expected of libraries; although, when provided, it is always welcome. The clerical trap is sprung on us when there are not enough clerks, and, of course, there are never enough clerks. In corporate situations, where hiring freezes and head-count ceilings are a way of life, this problem is considerably worse than in academic libraries, which have an endless supply of cheap student labor. In companies, by contrast, clerks are expensive, and clerks in overhead organizations bear the double burden of being considered expensive and not visibly contributory to overall organizational goals. Special library managers are not likely to change this mind-set, but they must be careful to make their plans and programs fit the resources provided, particularly in the clerical area. Otherwise, all the professionals become clerks, and this is perhaps strangely acceptable to our management because its own history tends to consider libraries as a series of clerical routines. It is a necessarily strong special librarian who then insists that clerical functions be staffed or left undone, and this must be justified not in terms of personal pique or pride but of organizational effectiveness and economy. It makes no economic sense for professionals to do clerical work, and accountants can understand this. Precisely because clerical staffing in corporations is in such short supply, the clerical tasks available to libraries without competitive challenge are almost limitless. The clerical trap for special libraries is that professionals perform clerical *instead* of professional work. That cannot be tolerated, precisely because it is wasteful for the parent organization.

Special Libraries and the "Morality" of User Self-service. It has already been noted that libraries, as they are visualized by users who have run the university gauntlet, are educational adjuncts designed to promote user self-sufficiency. Some of these individuals become corporate officials, for whom the issue of self-sufficiency becomes a self-evident moral good. The issue never arises with regard to clerical tasks, which are willingly shunted to the library, but it comes to view most frequently in discussions of such activities as online literature searching, because, with decentralized terminal access, ultimate users *can* do their own literature searching. The question is whether or not they should. Here the special library's stake is crucial, and it is bewildering and depressing to find special librarians who seek to rid themselves of the task of bibliographic searching because "they are too busy." Can users do this better and at a lower cost? Generally not, although there are exceptions. There is no moral issue here. Users who want to do their own online searches should certainly be taught to do them. However, most will quickly tire of the novelty, and, if they find they can delegate this process to a special librarian who will do it quickly, effectively, and without economic hassle, they will.

The real crime comes when libraries vigorously espouse end-user searching, not as some perceived increase in service quality or effectiveness, but rather because this becomes the most "convenient" way to accommodate a cut in library budget or in library staffing. When this happens, the organization does not save money; it spends more money, but forces the cost underground. Such a scenario might be acceptable to the librarian's immediate supervisor, but it cannot be acceptable to top management if top management can be made to see what shell games are being played. It then becomes the librarian's clear responsibility, as the organization's cognizant information professional, to make sure that top management does know, even if this involves some risk.

Conclusion

Despite all of these dangers and pitfalls, the future for special librarians is bright if we seize our opportunities. This is because information needs are great and growing, and they are recognized as growing and deserving of financial investment. Our risk is that others may take this work away from us, and relegate us to the clerical tasks. We can always continue to count circulation and interlibrary loan statistics if that will satisfy us. If we lose this battle, it will be strictly a political loss, and not based on evidence, because there is no question in my mind that we are best prepared and best qualified, and that we can handle professional information needs in the special library's parent organizations more cost effectively than anyone else.

To do this, we must remain incessantly professional. Professionals, according to some definitions, are individuals who control the interaction between themselves and their clients. Doctors, of course, do this, and so do lawyers. For special librarians, this means that we frequently give our patrons what they want, but it is more important that we give them what they need, and it is most important that we understand and make them understand that at times they don't know what they need, and that there is nothing wrong with that admission.

Special librarians can, and must, lead the way into this new professional area of interaction, as they led their librarian colleagues into the integration of non-traditional materials, automation, selective dissemination of information, and the recognition that, in delivering materials to patrons, speed is more important than cost. Special libraries are better equipped to ward off trivialization—the greatest of all enemies. Our users are not fascinated by what we do, and are willing to judge us by results rather than by methods. The next step is to make them care more about what we do than how we do it, and that can be accomplished. Being cheap will not save a special library. Only being valuable enough will. Good libraries are not necessarily cheap, because cheapness is the ultimate irrelevancy in a billion dollar corporation. But they are effective, and they are worth what they cost. We do indeed put knowledge to work, because no organization can afford to have knowledge ignored or wasted.

References

1. U.S. President's Science Advisory Committee. *Science, Government and Information: The Responsibilities of the Technical Community and the Government in the Transfer of Information.* (The Weinberg Report.) Washington, D.C.: U.S. Government Printing Office, January 10, 1963.
2. White, Herbert S. "The Use and Misuse of Library User Studies." *Library Journal 110* (no. 20): 70–71, December 1985.
3. Mooers, Calvin N. "Mooers' Law: Or, Why Some Retrieval Systems are Used and Others are Not." *American Documentation 11* (no. 3): 204, July 1960.
4. White, Herbert S. "Library Turf." *Library Journal 110* (no. 7), April 15, 1985.
5. Hedberg, Bo et al. "Camping on See-Saws. Prescriptions for a Self-Designing Organization." *Administrative Sciences Quarterly 21* (no. 1): 41–65, 1976.